Compound Democracies

Compound Democracies

*Why the United States and Europe
Are Becoming Similar*

Sergio Fabbrini

OXFORD
UNIVERSITY PRESS

Great Clarendon Street, Oxford OX2 6DP

Oxford University Press is a department of the University of Oxford.
It furthers the University's objective of excellence in research, scholarship,
and education by publishing worldwide in

Oxford New York

Auckland Cape Town Dar es Salaam Hong Kong Karachi
Kuala Lumpur Madrid Melbourne Mexico City Nairobi
New Delhi Shanghai Taipei Toronto

With offices in

Argentina Austria Brazil Chile Czech Republic France Greece
Guatemala Hungary Italy Japan Poland Portugal Singapore
South Korea Switzerland Thailand Turkey Ukraine Vietnam

Oxford is a registered trademark of Oxford University Press
in the UK and in certain other countries

Published in the United States
by Oxford University Press Inc., New York

© Sergio Fabbrini 2007

The moral rights of the author have been asserted
Database right Oxford University Press (maker)

First published 2007

British Library Cataloguing in Publication Data

Data available

Library of Congress Cataloging in Publication Data

Fabbrini, Sergio.
   Compound democracies : why the United States and Europe are becoming
similiar / Sergio Fabbrini.
      p. cm.
   Includes bibliographical references and index.
   ISBN 978–0–19–923561–2 (alk. paper)
   1. United States—Politics and government—2001- 2. European—Politics
and government—1989- 3. Representative government and representation—
United States. 4. Representative government and representation—European
Union countries. 5. Comparative government. I. Title.
   JK275.F33 2007
   320.3—dc22   2007020655

Typeset by SPI Publisher Services, Pondicherry, India
Printed in Great Britain
on acid-free paper by
Biddles Ltd., King's Lynn, Norfolk

ISBN 978–0–19–923561–2

1 3 5 7 9 10 8 6 4 2

a Manuela, Federico e Sebastiano, con amore

Preface

This book is the outcome of a long journey, initiated in 1981 when I arrived for the first time in California. I had a NATO fellowship for investigating the transformation of American democracy after the social, political, and institutional crisis of the 1960s and 1970s. After UC, Riverside I went to UC Berkeley and then, in the second half of the 1980s, I spent a long period at Harvard as a Fulbright scholar. Since 1991, finally, I found in the Institute of Governmental Studies (IGS), at UC Berkeley, an extraordinary intellectual environment for thinking and discussing about America, thanks to the scholars who directed it, such as the late Nelson W. Polsby, who was my passionate mentor, or Bruce Cain, a friend who patiently helped me to understand the intricacies of American politics, and Jack Citrin, who always supported my research projects. Moreover, the Political Science Department of that university gave me a formidable opportunity for discussing with colleagues who enlarged my comparative prespective. Indeed, the first draft of the book was concluded when I was visiting professor of Comparative Politics at UC Berkeley in the Fall semester of 2005. Since the 1980s, I have continued to study American politics, going back and forth between the two shores of the Atlantic. However, I never forgot to be a European and, moreover, a scholar convinced that knowledge passes through comparison. I kept publishing articles and essays on America and Europe that I have finally used and re-elaborated in this book. My scientific research has been a permanent workshop, a constant exercise in thinking and writing on the same argument, the transformation of democracy in both America and Europe. The comparison between America and Europe has represented a sort of happy obsession of my intellectual life of the last twenty-five years. This obsession, sometimes, has made me a stranger in both America and Europe. I had to learn early on that bridging is a difficult job, especially when one deals with entrenched (and, sometimes, biased) views. I do not know if I was able to proceed in my comparison with the necessary fairness required of a scholar who, as I, tries to be loyal to the principle of *sine ira et studio*. If I was not, the responsibility is only mine. If, however, this book should have something novel to say on the oldest democracies of the world, then this is the merit of the many friends, on both shores of the Atlantic, with whom I had the fortune to discuss the topic over the years. Indeed, with my friend Larry Rosenthal that discussion has continued to go on for a quarter of a century. For having read and commented on previous versions of the book, I gratefully acknowledge my debt to Vincent Della Sala, Beppe Di Palma, Bruce Cain, Maurizio Ferrera, Gianfranco Poggi, Alberta M. Sbragia, and Alan Ware. Ton Notermans and Daniela Sicurelli gave me their competent editorial support. This book is dedicated to my family (my wife Manuela and my sons Federico and Sebastiano) who never left me alone in my (dangerous, indeed, for family life) transatlantic obsession.

SF

School of International Studies
Trento University
January 27, 2007

Contents

List of Figures

List of Tables

1

Introduction: Democratic transformations in Europe and America

I did not study America just to satisfy curiosity, however legitimate. I sought there lessons from which we might profit. Anyone who supposes that I intend to write a panegyric is strangely mistaken (. . .) for I am one of those who think that there is hardly ever absolute right in any laws.

—Alexis de Tocqueville (1835)

1.1. The Argument

Although there are many important scholarly studies on the political development and institutional transformation of Europe and America,[1] few attempts have been made to conduct systemic comparison of democratic experiences on the two sides of the Atlantic. European nation-states and America had such a different political development that comparison became constrained by the idea of reciprocal uniqueness or exceptionalism. Certainly, the difference in size between America and the single European nation-states was traditionally considered a further reason for their incomparability. For instance, at the beginning of the twentieth century, the great American historian Frederick Jackson Turner (1932: 289) stressed: 'in size, the United States is comparable not with a single nation of Europe, but with all of Europe, exclusive of Russia. It is also comparable with Europe in the fact that it is made up of separate geographic provinces, each capable, in size, resources, and peculiarities of physical conditions, to be the abode of a European nation, or of several nations.'

1

However, since World War II, the profound transformation of European and American politics has significantly reduced the institutional divergence in the organization and functioning of democratic systems which divided America and Europe for a century and a half. In fact, as Europe has changed from a collection of nation-states to an integrated polity (the European Union (EU)),[2] it has organized itself on an institutional and functional model more similar to the traditional American fragmented or polycentric sovereignty (i.e. a sovereignty shared by the federated states and the federal state, and thus by the different institutions of the latter) than to the unified or mono-centric sovereignty of the European nation-states (i.e. a sovereignty monopolized by their parliaments). Thus, the EU that has arisen from that transformation differs more from the institutional and political organization of its member-states than it does from that of America. At the same time, America, under pressure from domestic transformations and especially external responsibilities and powers since World War II, has made significant steps in the direction of reducing the effects of institutional fragmentation, especially in the foreign-policymaking process. The terrorist attacks on New York and Washington, DC of September 11, 2001 heightened the need to operate in a more centralized manner in order to counter the new global threats. However, the institutional structure of American democracy cannot accommodate centralizing tendencies for long.

After a long period of *institutional divergence* between the USA and the EU member-states, a process of *institutional convergence* is taking place between the EU and the USA. This process of institutional convergence has finally opened the possibility of a direct comparison between new-integrated Europe and the old-integrated America. Indeed, as early as the 1980s, Cappelletti, Seccombe, and Weiler (1986: 10) wrote: 'the comparison of convergence and divergence [between the US and the then European Economic Community or EEC] give us a unique perspective in which to analyse, understand and ... to *evaluate* one's own legal [but also political] institutions and even to foresee the probable future evolution within the trend of which they are a reflection'. They then pointed out (Cappelletti, Seccombe, and Weiler 1986: 10): 'seeing alternative approaches often stimulates us to ask questions about ourselves, questions which otherwise might not have been perceived'. Since then, several comparative studies have been done. However, all of them have tended to focus on the *federal* nature of the two polities (McKay 2001; Nicolaidis and Howse 2001; Ansell and Di Palma 2004; Fabbrini 2005*a*; Menon and Schain 2006), rather than on the logic of functioning of their democratic model, where, by democratic model, is meant the specific institutional organization of the political process finalized to take *accountable decisions*. Accountable decisions are, first, those applicable to individuals as well as collectivities and, second, decisions taken by decision-makers who have to account for them. Political systems which do not respect these two conditions cannot be properly defined as democratic (Dahl 2005).

It is my argument that the EU and the USA are similar because they are two different species of the same political genus: the *compound democracy model*. The compound model is proper of polities that have the features of both an interstate (confederal, intergovernmental) and a supra-state (federal, supranational) organization. A compound polity is a union of states and *their citizens*. At the founding moment, states are the basic units of the polity, in the sense that citizens belong to the union because they belong to one of its constituent units. Through such union, the states agree to pool their sovereignty within a larger integrated supra-state or supranational framework. They do so because such unions, to use the formidable expression elaborated by Hendrickson (2003), are primarily *peace pacts*. In their own way, both the USA and the EU are an attempt to go beyond a balance of power system for promoting peace and cooperation between independent states sharing a common territory. In fact, at the origins of European integration stood the idea that economic integration was functional for promoting political integration (Haas 1958). And a politically integrated Europe was considered to be the only viable answer to the twin dangers of anarchy or empire, as the integration of America more than a century and a half before was the answer to similar dangers. One might add that the USA was the explicit answer to an implicit threat of war, whereas the EU was the implicit answer to explicit experiences of war. In any case, both the EU and the USA are polities constructed for forestalling the possibility of war through the formation of a complex institutional structure able to induce cooperation between potential rivals, without however imposing any hierarchy on them.

If it is unquestionable that the USA and the EU started as a union of states, it is also unquestionable that the states which made those unions were and continue to be asymmetrically correlated. That is, they are significantly different in terms of demographic size, economic capacity, subregional resources, and degree of modernization. It is this *structural asymmetry* which precluded any endeavor to create a unified polity—that is a political system in which the decision-making power could be monopolized by only one institution (as in parliamentary European nation-states). Indeed, the USA and the EU are based on a multiple diffusion of powers in order to guarantee that any interest (any state, first of all) will have a voice in the decision-making process. In this way, both the USA and the EU try to disincentivize the formation of a majority able to control all the institutional levels of the polity. This is why compound polities are multiple separation of power systems, that is systems where the governmental powers are separated not only vertically (as in federal systems), but also horizontally (between the center's governmental institutions, as is not the case for any other democratic federal systems, except Switzerland). And this is why federalism cannot capture, by itself, the entire nature of the USA and the EU.

Compound democracies thus are democracies in which the political process generates authoritative decisions without the support of a government. Herein resides a crucial distinction with the other established democracies, which have adopted either a *majoritarian* (or *competitive*, Fabbrini 1998) or a *consensus* model (Lijphart 1999). In fact, competitive and consensus democracies differ in the modality of governmental formation, but both function on the basis of government decisions. In competitive democracies (such as Britain), the government is the direct outcome of the electoral process, whereas in consensus democracies (such as Belgium) it is the effect of a drawn-out process of negotiations taking place after the election between the main party leaders (see chapter 3). However, at the end of the day, both types of democracy need a government (or better a cabinet expression of a parliamentary majority) in order to function. In the EU and the USA, there is not a government per se. They are *governance* more than *government* systems, although the federal or Community institutions steer the decision-making process toward specific ends.

In sum, the decision-making process takes place through the interaction of separated institutions all of which share some quota of governmental power. In systems of multiple separations of powers the government is constituted by a collection of institutions located at different levels of the system, all of them structuring the decision-making process. Multiple separation of power systems make it possible for an interstate organization to operate as a supra-state polity. However, this possibility extorts a significant price, in terms of low decision-making capacity and uncertain accountability. Herein lies *the puzzle of compound democracies*. In order to maintain their compoundness, these systems need to diffuse power, but such diffusion of power, at this turn, hinders decisions and confounds responsibilities. A significant price, when it is paid by polities (such as the USA) playing a global role or (such as the EU) in the condition to play, sooner or later, a similar role.

1.2. Europe toward Compoundness

The growth of the EU in the second half of the twentieth century represents a radical transformation of European politics (Judt 2005). The EU is the most advanced experiment in the construction of a supranational or supra-states system in existence worldwide today. (Although supra-states rather than supranational might better reflect the nature of the EU, I will follow the predominant predisposition of EU studies to talk of supranationalism because of the negative reaction the term 'supra-states' seems to generate in certain countries or intellectual circles.) It is supranational because it has neither the exclusive characteristics of an international organization nor those of a domestic system that aggregates differentiated states (Slomp 2000), but *it has both*. The EU is a combination of intergovernmental (confederal) institutional elements and supranational (federal) structures (Fabbrini 2002; Hix 2005). It is a mixed institutional system, with a variable geometry or balance, overlapping jurisdictions, and with an uncertain territorial identity. In fact, it is the answer to the need to create a new inter-states system on the European continent, able to prevent and neutralize any plausible return to a warring condition. It is an inter-states, and not just a balance of power, system, exactly because it contains supra-states (or supranational) features which institutionalize, and thus constrain, the cooperation among previously rival states.

Though formally still sovereign, the European nation-states have witnessed the migration of a considerable amount of their sovereignty both to the supranational EU and also to subnational regional and local governments (Keating 1999). Gradually, the European nation-states have become EU member-states (Sbragia 1994) with few exceptions such as Norway and Switzerland. A silent divorce between sovereignty and authority has occurred (Caporaso 2000). Decision-making power over a growing number of traditionally domestic policy issues has been transferred from the nation-states to the network of Community institutions. Of course, the nation-states are part of those institutions, but their individual representatives participate in a collective decision-making process that dilutes their influence and power. Authority over the decisions that they must implement at home is shared with other member-state representatives and Community officials. Moreover, those decisions are the outcome of a political process with a fragmentation, porosity, and indeterminacy historically unknown to domestic political processes. As Ansell (2004: 9) writes, in Europe it is evident that 'the mutually reinforcing relations between territory, authority, and societal interests and identities can no longer be taken for granted'.

The EU has the characteristics of a system of *governance* which encompasses the institutional structures pertaining to *government* (Sbragia 2002). Informal decision-making processes combine with formal ones, public actors with private ones. It is a supranational democracy in the sense that it lacks the traditional attributes of a sovereign state (Greven and Pauly 2000), and in particular control over the legitimate use of force both internally and externally. The EU possesses neither a police force nor an army in the strict sense. Furthermore, it has fairly limited fiscal resources with which it could finance either one of such bodies, for its budget cannot exceed 1.3 percent of the gross national product (GNP) of its member-states. Clearly, a system of governance without state attributes can only develop in particular conditions, namely the absence of external (i.e. international and particularly military) challenges. In fact, the EU benefited from international isolation during the long Cold War period, gradually becoming institutionalized within NATO's system of military protection (Fabbrini 2004*a*). If it is true that the EU started as a peace pact, it is also true that the pact among its member-states was militarily guaranteed by a 'third' power, acceptable to all also because it was (geographically) a non-European power (Ikenberry 2000). With a financial budget unconstrained by military or security spending, the EU member-states were thus able to foster economic and social development which ensured the overall institutional success of the integration process.

As it has become institutionalized, the EU has gradually acquired the features of a compound polity—by which is meant a polity structured around a *multiple separation of powers*, both vertical (between Brussels and the member-states) and horizontal (among the European Council, the Council of Ministers, the Commission, and the European Parliament [EP]); a separation of powers rigorously safeguarded by the European Court of Justice (ECJ). Of course, there are other democratic polities in Europe with a vertical separation of powers (the federal countries of Germany, Austria, and Belgium; the quasi-federal Spain; or federal Australia and Canada among the Western established democracies), but none of them has a horizontal separation of powers as well (they are parliamentary democracies, even Austria, whose President of the Republic is popularly elected). The only other exception, apart from the USA, is Switzerland, which has both levels of separation; but 'size matters' (Dahl and Tufte 1973) in the sense that Switzerland, however similar in internal complexity to the EU, has no international role to play. Thus, comparing the EU with this country does not help in investigating the puzzle of compound democracies.

Within the EU, the member-states' interests are promoted and guaranteed by the European Council and the Council of Ministers, while supranational institutional interests are guaranteed and promoted by the European Commission, the EP, and the ECJ (Hix 2005). Since the Maastricht Treaty of 1992, the EU has developed into a veritable public policy regime (Fabbrini and Morata 2002; Wallace and Wallace 2003), strengthening its supranational side without detriment to its intergovernmental one. Such a balance is characteristic of political systems in which separated institutions have distinct bases of legitimacy: the strengthening of one institutional power does not necessarily imply the reduction of another. Indeed, in systems of multiple separations of powers, the relation between political institutions is rarely a zero-sum game. Interestingly enough, the EU has progressively absorbed, on a supranational level, a growing number of responsibilities for public policymaking which, within federations, are controlled by the federated states; while the traditional responsibilities of the federal level in federations (such as foreign policy) are controlled by member-state governments in the EU. This is why Sbragia (2005a) has defined the EU as a 'reversed federal state'.

It has been said that the EU represents the crisis of the Westphalian state (Caporaso 1996), because the individual European nation-states are no longer able to exercise exclusive authority within their territory. It used to be generally assumed in Europe that only specific organizational arrangements (those based on centralization of power) could enable exercise of that exclusive authority. Accordingly, the evolution of the polycentric and fragmented EU has been viewed as a substantive challenge to both the *external* and *internal* facets of the sovereignty of its member-states. Although actual sovereignty never corresponded to its theoretical model (Krasner 1999), it is nevertheless beyond question that the individual EU member-states have experienced a dramatic decrease in their capacity both to exclude *outside* authorities from their own decision-making process and to centralize the *internal* resources necessary for performing that process. The EU member-states are enmeshed in an institutional web with features of a compound polity unknown to domestic institutional arrangements. EU politics has become the domestic politics of its member-states (Cowles, Caporaso, and Risse 1999), while the domestic politics of the EU member-states has grown increasingly Europeanized (Featherstone and Radaelli 2003; Schmidt 2006). In sum, although the EU has a growing authority, it does not possess sovereignty in the traditional sense, and its authority is not supported by centralized institutions and procedures.

It is the first time in European history that established nation-states have decided to peacefully and voluntarily pool growing portions of their sovereignty in a larger institutional 'container' (Hoffmann 1995). If one considers that the USA started from a similar experience, then it is not surprising that the institutional structure and functional logic of the EU appear much less exceptional when compared with those of the USA.

1.3. American Compoundness and its Challenges

Since the Constitutional Convention of Philadelphia in 1787, the USA has been explicitly designed as a 'compound republic' (Ostrom 1987): that is, a democracy organized around multiple separations of power. Sovereignty was fragmented between the federated states and the federal state, and thus between separated institutions within the latter (Senate, House of Representatives, and President). Once defined the few competences of exclusive control by the federal center, all the remaining ones were recognized as proper to the federated states. At the federal center, the separation among governmental institutions was further secured by giving them different institutional interests to protect. Or better, connecting each of them to a different electoral constituency and staggering the time frame of their institutional mandate. This created incentives for the formation of multiple and concurrent majorities in the separated institutions at the various levels of the system, in such a way that an 'institutional ambition' could check another 'institutional ambition'. The jurisdictional powers of these various institutional entities thus had to overlap, although such overlapping generated inter-states and interinstitutional conflicts (the most dramatic instance being the Civil War of 1861–5). The American compound republic, too, was able to institutionalize itself thanks to particular conditions, namely a low involvement in international affairs (i.e. European affairs in the nineteenth century). For a long time, the USA was a security-consumer (and not a security-producer, as it has become since the second half of the twentieth-century), benefiting from British marine protection, thus dedicating its own resources and energies to continental enlargement and the building of a common trans-states market. Indeed, the new republic was able to legitimize itself by virtue of the economic success that ensued from the ever-expanding nature of its continental market, an expansion favored and sustained by Supreme Court rulings (Goldstein 2001). Isolation from European affairs and economic growth thus contributed to America's ability to put down roots and acquire legitimacy as a compound republic.

American compoundness was challenged, between the end of the nineteenth century and World War II, by dramatic internal economic transformations and by the country's new international role. A new institutional equilibrium could take shape, thanks to the fact that the constitution was already sufficiently consolidated. Under the pressure first of tumultuous domestic industrialization and then of growing international exposure, America started to alter its traditional institutional patterns and to create a real and proper federal center (Higgs 1987; Skowroneck 1987). It needed a viable federal state, both to regulate the economy and, above all, to promote and preserve its geopolitical interests. Politics became nationalized as never before, thus upsetting the equilibrium which favored the states in the nineteenth century. If the nationalization of American democracy entailed redefinition of the matrix which connected states and federal powers, its subsequent internationalization required a radical restructuring of the decision-making practices, and therefore of the relations between Congress and the President (Orren and Skowroneck 2004). This twofold institutional redefinition implied the transfer of competences and resources from the federated states to the federal state and, within the latter, from the Congress to the President. The growing influence of the federal institutions engendered popular discussion on their democratic deficit, with public opinion and social and political movements pressing for their democratization. Such democratization, already anticipated in many states by the popular election of the members of the presidential Electoral College, finally came about at the beginning of the twentieth century, with the Seventeenth Constitutional Amendment of 1913 which introduced the direct election of the senators, and with the utilization in many states of the direct primary for the selection of the presidential candidates. Nevertheless, these important reforms did not alter the separation of powers structure of the governmental system.

Thus, in America, the challenges of economic transformation and the country's international involvement of the twentieth century induced the central (federal) rulers to look for more centralized institutional practices. The federal government met the challenge of capitalist transformation by introducing a growing number of new policies. The states became the terminals of federal activism: if they wanted federal money for their policies they were obliged to comply with very detailed federal guidelines or regulations (Posner 1998). The challenge of the post–World War II international involvement was met by centralizing decision-making power on foreign and military policies in the presidency. The Cold War imperatives of the second part of the twentieth century played a crucial role in increasing the capacity of the executive branch to coordinate national politics. Those imperatives not only accelerated the centralization of foreign and military powers in the presidency (and to the offices of the 'personal President', to use Lowi's 1985 definition, namely the White House Office and the Executive Office of the President), they also created a public opinion in favor of such centralization. Thus internal complexity and density and external exposure pressured America into increasing its decision-making effectiveness. However, it was mainly the country's international involvement triggered by World War II and subsequently the Cold War which provided the federal government with the ideological justification it had never had before to grow more than the states, and to the President the justification to become more influential than the Congress (Schlesinger Jr 2004). In terms of authority relations, the territorial sovereignty of the country became much less fragmented than it had been in the past.

However, the defeat in Vietnam (in the late 1960s, de facto) and the resignation of President Nixon (in 1974) following the Watergate scandal[3] triggered a mobilization of interests and institutions opposed to presidential centralization. Congress regained significant influence in the field of foreign and military policy, while the credibility of the presidency collapsed to an equal extent (Polsby 2004). From the 1970s to the 1990s, presidential leadership has constantly weakened, regardless of the President's party (Calleo 2000). And also federal centralization has been successfully halted. Reaction against federal taxes and ideological change in the 1970s delivered important political resources to those rulers within the states who questioned the expansion of federal power (Conlan 1998). Thus, a swing occurred from the centralization of the 1950s and 1960s to the decentralization of the following three decades (Nagel 2001). Compound democracy continued to be so alive that its constraints, regardless of growing pressure for more coherent and effective federal action, produced a 'new political disorder' (Dahl 1994) by the end of the twentieth century.

The tendency for a separated system to foster political disaggregation and to confuse governmental responsibility was heightened in the late twentieth century also because America experienced the institutionalization, between 1968 and 2000, of a divided government regime, with each of the two parties in control of one of the separated institutions of government (Ware 2002). Yet, the terrorist attacks of September 11, 2001 restored large margins of maneuver to the President and the presidency, also because between 2003 and 2006 America returned to a unified party government, with the Republicans in firm control of both chambers of Congress and of the presidency (Hacker and Pierson 2005). In the aftermath of the terrorist attacks, the presidential leadership of the separated government has become unquestioned. Indeed, some scholars (Rudalevige 2005) have spoken of the return (after the experience of the 1960s) of a 'new' imperial presidency, while others (Lieven 2004) have compared the America of the twenty-first century to the centralized European nation-states of the first half of the twentieth century. However, the mid-term congressional elections of 2006, with the formation of a political majority in both the House of Representatives and Senate different from the presidential one, have again introduced powerful constraints on the imperial aspirations of the incumbent President. In fact, Congress still retains its formidable powers of check and balance, although it decided not to use them in the previous period of unified party government (Mann and Ornstein 2006).

Indeed, the institutional basis of the American compound democracy cannot easily be questioned. It is entrenched in the country's constitutional structure, and also in its constitutional culture. As Di Palma (2004) has argued, the efficient secret of American politics has been its liberal constitutionalism. American political development can be interpreted as a permanent dialogue, although frequently riddled with conflicts and contradictions, on the constitutional frame within which to carry on social and political interactions. 'Conceptions of authority and of purpose have been interconnected in American thinking about government from our early days. (...) The concern with the institutions of authority has continued to characterize American constitutionalism' (Beer 1993: 379 and 383). In the twentieth century, this *constitutionalism* has hampered the search for more centralized responses to external challenges, preserving the institutional conditions that have made the development of American compoundness possible until the twenty-first century. The constitutional system has adapted to new contexts without altering its compound nature. The American experience suggests that internal and (especially) external pressures may seriously challenge the compound democracy, but also that those challenges meet formidable resistance if they are countered by a firmly rooted constitutional structure and culture.

1.4. Comparing American and European Compoundness

The EU, by contrast, is not the outcome of a constitutional design, although it has gradually become a constitutionalized regime (Stone Sweet, Sandholtz, and Fligstein 2001). Through inter-states treaties being interpreted as quasi-constitutional documents by the ECJ, the EU has gradually institutionalized a de facto system of separation of powers which has significant similarities with the American one, regarding both the institutional structure and logic of the political process. As regards the institutional structure, the USA and the EU are based on subsystems endowed with their own bases of authority (the federated states vs. the member-states); both have a diffusion of decision-making powers among the central institutions (President–Senate–House vs. Commission–Council of Ministers–Parliament); both institutionalize (or try to institutionalize) a double representation within their legislative bodies (the Senate representing the states through their electors and the House representing individual voters vs. the Council of Ministers representing member-state interests through their executives and the Parliament elected by individual voters), although those legislative bodies have different resources of influence; both have a powerful and independent judicial body (the Supreme Court vs. the ECJ) and both have regulatory agencies independent of electoral institutions (the Federal Reserve and the IRCs vs. the European Central Bank and the European agencies) (Majone 2005a). This horizontal separation is further strengthened by a vertical separation of powers between the central institutions and the institutions of the constituting units (federated states or member-states). The USA is a federalized system, while the EU has gradually acquired the features of a multilevel polity. In both cases, the institutions of self-government and shared government are combined, although in different ways and on the basis of different organizing principles of territorial democracy (Elazar 2001).

As regards the political process, in both polities the function of elections is to choose personnel for political offices, not a federal or supranational government (Coultrap 1999). Voters elect officials to occupy specific offices and to perform specific duties, not to form a government. Political parties do not dominate the political process, because other actors (in the EU, member-state executives, regional governments, national parliaments; in the USA various states' constituencies and institutional actors; in both, corporate associations, lobbies, epistemic communities, and social movements) contribute to the decision-making process. Because both polities have porous structures with multiple access points, interest groups mobilize at different levels on a pluralist rather than neocorporatist model of interest intermediation (Schmitter 2000). In both the USA and the EU, the political process is based on sectional or geographic cleavages, more than on the traditional social or ideological cleavages of the European nation-states (Bartolini 2005). The level of political responsibility is subsystemic and the scope of political issues is specific. Polities without a government—that is, polities without a centralized institution legitimized to monopolize ultimate decisions—have inevitably an open and incoherent political process. The outcome of this political process is not only decided on the basis of power relations among political actors; it is also and frequently the product of a deliberative process in which ideas, information, expertise, and knowledge play a crucial role. Hence, the structure of multiple separations of power and the open nature of the political process are necessary to support and protect the compound logic of the political system.

Although American institutional structures and political processes differ from those of individual European nation-states, this is no longer the case if they are compared with the institutional structures and political processes emerging within the EU. The institutional structure and political process of both the EU and the USA have more similarities than differences. In any case, the EU shares more institutional and functional features with the USA than it does with its own member-states. This convergence is unprecedented in the history of the American and European political systems. Certainly the EU, contrary to the USA, is not based on a formal constitution. However, the cyclical enlargement of the EU (which is now constituted by twenty-seven countries)[4] has opened an inevitable and contested discussion on transforming the EU in a formally constitutional regime. Throughout the 1990s, the perception that the EU's decision-making structure and procedure was unable to deal with growing internal and external complexity significantly increased (Weiler 1999; Stone Sweet and Caporaso 1998). Indeed, the ink of the Nice Treaty of 2001 was not yet dry when discussion began on the need to elaborate a constitutional treaty for the EU. A constitution-making process was consequently set in train by the European Council meeting of Laeken in December 2001, leading to the creation of a constitutional convention which worked in Brussels from 2002 to 2003 and approved a Constitutional Treaty (CT). After long negotiations and some revisions, this CT was finally signed by the heads of state and governments of the EU member-states at the European Council held in Rome in October 2004. It seemed that the EU finally had its own Magna Carta, a 'Magna Carta (that) could have a formidable symbolic and practical meaning', as Mény (2000: 151) wrote some time ago. However, this CT was then rejected by French and Dutch voters in referenda held, respectively, in May and June 2005, although (at the end of 2006) two-thirds of the member-states (18 of 27) have already approved it. Certainly, the rejection by the French and Dutch voters of the CT has dealt a dramatic blow to the process of ratification, notwithstanding the mainly domestic motivations of that vote.

If it seems plausible to assert that '(t)he massive shift in scale, the greater heterogeneity of identities and interests, the wider range of development levels and, most of all, the unprecedented process of gradual and voluntary polity formation all conspire to make the contemporary outcome of a constitutionalized Euro-polity much less predictable than the earlier national efforts' (Schmitter 2000: 120), it is also plausible to argue that a polity as compound as the EU cannot consolidate without a basic and shared constitutional justification. It is the American experience which supports such an argument. In fact, America has been successful in pursuing the strategy of *e pluribus unum* because, since its inception, it has been constructed as an explicitly *compound democracy* constituted through and protected by the constitution. Or better, the American constitution has made possible the institutionalization of a compound democracy because it gave a common language to the competing and rival interests of the polity. The glue which kept together American compoundness was and continues to be the constitution, or better *the struggle for interpreting it.* Only once that glue did not work (during the crisis of the 1860s), but even then the Civil War had to be justified, on both sides, by reference to the constitution. If the US experience is of some validity, then the EU cannot fully institutionalize as *compound democracy* without the glue of a basic constitution. A document able to give, to the competing and rival interests of the compound polity, a common language for expressing their own differences. Thus, while America started from formal recognition of its compoundness and through the constitution transformed it into a specific model of democracy, the EU has become a compound polity without the support of any constitutional theory appropriate for a compound democracy. However, if the American experience offers useful insights for addressing some of the problems that the EU will have to resolve to become a constitutional compound democracy, the experience of the European nation-states may offer insights useful for addressing the challenges to internal compoundness that the USA is already facing in its action as a global hyperpower.

Of course, comparing similar cases does not mean equating them. Quite the contrary. As Skowroneck (1987: 10) rightly pointed out regarding the experience of the turn of the nineteenth century, '(t)he development of the national government did not portend a "Europeanization" of America, nor, for that matter, did the democratization of Europe portend its "Americanization"'; the same can be said apropos the experience of the turn of the twentieth century. The evolution of the EU toward a compound polity does not mean its Americanization, nor does the constant endeavor of America to neutralize the constraints of her compound nature portend her Europeanization. If it is true that the evolution of European politics from a national to a continental scale has brought with it an institutional organization of public authority with many features similar to the institutional organization of territorial sovereignty operating in America (Fabbrini 2004*b*), then it is possible to assert that the EU has something to learn from political experience on the other side of the Atlantic (Fabbrini 1999*a*). In particular that compound polities are intrinsically fragile institutional and conceptual constructs.

1.5. About the Book

The book is an exercise in historical-institutional analysis, although it uses, when necessary, concepts and categories from other analytical traditions (i.e. rationalism and constructivism). Its method is comparative and its scope is macro-systemic. It looks at the larger picture, sacrificing detail in order to emphasize general features and trends. Its intention is to provide the reader with a better understanding of the American and European democracies, on the assumption that such understanding is a necessary (though not sufficient) condition for achieving a more stable and fairer world. Moreover, its aim is to contribute to the debate on the democratic model best able to protect and promote the compound nature of the EU and the US polities.

The book is divided into two parts. The *first* deals with the period I characterize as *institutional divergence* between America and Europe. After the introductory chapter which sets out my argument on the comparability of the USA and the EU, Chapter 2 reconstructs the political developments which led to the institutionalization of different authority structures in European nation-states and America (political order). Chapter 3 analyzes the institutionalization of different governmental patterns in America and the European nation-states, the former based on separation, the latter on the fusion of powers (institutional order). Chapter 4 investigates the alternative routes which have led to the structuring of different relations between market and welfare in America and European nation-states (social order). Chapter 5 discusses the implications of these different orders for the structuring of partisan politics in America and the European nation-states (partisan order). Part II of the book examines the period I characterize as *institutional convergence*. Chapters 6 and 7 reconstruct the post–World War II political and structural changes characterized by the affirmation of America's international power and by the growth of the EU, arguing that those changes have made America and Europe more similar, notwithstanding the challenges they raised. Chapter 8 conducts a direct comparison between the institutional structures and the political processes of the USA and the EU, highlighting the features of their compound nature. Chapter 9 shifts the comparison to the level of the constitutionalization of the USA and the EU, investigating the differences but also the important similarities between them, and delineating the conceptual framework for interpreting the nature of the constitutionalization process in compound polities. Chapter 10 concludes by discussing the structural problems a compound democracy has to face: that is, the nature of its puzzle.

To conclude: Part I of the book deals with what divides (or better divided) America and Europe, Part II considers what makes them comparable (indeed, in this latter part, to make the comparison more stringent, I had to use the same argument from different angles). America and Europe have been divided for many reasons, but mainly because none of the European nation-states ever experienced the American project of creating a political union, out of separated independent and sovereign states, through peaceful and constitutional means. America and Europe started to be comparable as soon as the European separated, independent, and sovereign nation-states moved into the direction of peaceful and constitutionalized supranational integration. What interests me is to investigate the *logic of functioning* of the USA and the EU, inasmuch as it is an expression of a common project, that is to create a *political union among states and their citizens*. A union among states may be considered political (and not merely economic) when it creates, de facto or *de jure*, a political system which at the same time combines international and domestic features, or better conjugates interstate with supra-state features. Certainly, the combination between interstate (confederal, intergovernmental) and supra-state (federal, supranational) features may reach different *equilibria* in different periods, but no equilibrium might be possible without including elements of both of them. This variable combination constitutes not only the structural nature of polities like the USA and the EU, but also the reason why they have come to adopt (*de jure* in the case of the USA, de facto in the case of the EU) a specific democratic model that I define as *compound democracy.* The EU and the USA may thus be interpreted as (different types of) compound democracies, because they offer different specific institutional solutions to the same problem, how to take binding decisions in a polity structurally based, first, on both states and individuals and, second, on asymmetrical relations between those states. It is obvious that the USA and the EU reflect different stages of political development, the former being much more institutionalized than the latter. If this is the case, then especially Europeans may derive useful analytical insights from the experience on the other side of the Atlantic. Alexis de Tocqueville (1969: 18) wrote in 1835 in the first Introduction to his *Democracie en Amerique*: 'I did not study America just to satisfy curiosity, however legitimate; I sought there lessons from which we might profit. Anyone who supposes that I intend to write a panegyric is strangely mistaken (...) for I am one of those who think that there is hardly ever absolute right in any laws'. I would add that Americans, too, have many lessons to learn from the European experience. In sum, both Europeans and Americans may profit from the other's experience if they seek to do so *sine ira et studio.*

Part I

Transatlantic democracies: the era of institutional divergence

2

Differentiation in authority structures: state, nation, and democracy in Europe and America

2.1. Introduction

Although the state is generally considered to be a homogeneous product of Western experience, in reality both its institutional features and its relations with society have, throughout history, displayed marked differences among countries (Hall and Ikenberry 1989; Poggi 1991; Schulze 1994). If one considers the state as the institutional organization of public authority on a given territory, it is possible to discern a variety of patterns of state formation in Western countries. These diversities are due to a complex array of factors which have to do with both material conditions and subjective actions. The state is an organization, but it also is a cultural construct which represents the outcome of myriad acts of institution building and connected social justifications. The rules and the procedures of the state first became institutionalized through a long and arduous political process which involved the mobilization of a multiplicity of actors and ideas. The analysis here will focus on the diversified historical sequence which led, first, to the territorial organization of public authority and the intellectual spread and social internalization of a shared feeling of nationhood and then to the democratization of that public authority.

The Western nation-state is the outcome of two distinct historical processes: the construction of public institutions through which to exercise public authority on a given territory (or state-building), and the formation of a popular identity through which to create a sense of belonging among that territory's inhabitants (or nation-building). In the former case, we have, to use Finer's definition(1969–70: 7), the construction of

an 'institutionalized politics', and in the latter, to use Deutsch's definition (1953: 147), the promotion of 'a sense of cohesion and distinctiveness'. However different individual experiences of state-building may be,
Western countries have undergone two main patterns of state formation:
one characteristic of Western Europe, the other characteristic of America.
In the nineteenth century, these different patterns gave rise to different
authority structures which, in their turn, conditioned the ensuing process
of democratization.

Those authority structures embodied the principle of sovereignty that
became institutionalized in Europe (by which I mean, throughout the
book, Western Europe mainly) and America. Sovereignty is an ambiguous
concept, because it has an *external* and *internal* nature. International relations theory, which has dealt with the former aspect, has identified four
main types of sovereignty in the development of the international system: 'international legal sovereignty, Westphalian sovereignty, domestic
sovereignty and interdependence sovereignty' (Krasner 1999: 3), where
by 'sovereignty' is meant the 'institutional arrangement associated with
a particular bundle of characteristics—recognition, territory, exclusive
authority, and effective internal and transborder regulation or control'
(Krasner 1999: 227). Thus, territorial sovereignty, especially Westphalian
sovereignty, 'refers to (a) political organization based on the exclusion of
external actors from authority structures within a given territory" (Krasner
1999: 4). Externally, sovereignty is that property of a state which has
enabled the building of a Westphalian system: that is, a constellation of
autonomous and independent territorial units whose internal autonomy
is reciprocally recognized.

However, the Westphalian state can also be investigated from a Comparative Politics perspective, which means to investigate sovereignty more
from within than from without. My interest is in territorial sovereignty,
or a form of sovereignty whose authority structures are the outcome
of a political process developed within territorially bounded social and
cultural structures. Historically, America and the main nation-states of
Europe gave very different organizational forms to the *authority structures* through which rulers exercised power over the ruled in a given
territory, because—it is important to stress—'rulers, not states (...) make
choices about policies, rules, and institutions' (Krasner 1999: 7). Whereas
European rulers chose to operate within a *unified (or monocentric) organization of sovereignty*, their American counterparts did so within a *fragmented
(or polycentric) organization of sovereignty*. In this chapter I shall reconstruct
(on the basis of Stein Rokkan's approach, see especially Rokkan 1999)

the European and American patterns of state, nation, and democracy building, my purpose being to show the different authority structures that emerged in the nineteenth century—and thus the institutionalization of different modalities of partisan politics in the twentieth—on the two sides of the Atlantic.

2.2. State and Nation in Europe: The Rokkanian Approach

2.2.1. *European Political Development*

There are many influential theories of European political development (i.e. of state- and nation-building) (see the very important analysis of Bartolini 2005). The two more significant ones (and, for my purposes, the most useful) in comparative political analysis are Tilly's *exogenous* approach and Rokkan's *endogenous* approach (Fabbrini 2004*b*). Although Tilly's later approach (Tilly 1990*a*) 'places a very heavy emphasis upon class and class conflict as the motor force propelling state development' (Page 1995: 13), his general theory (Tilly 1975, 1985) is nevertheless based on interstate conflicts and wars as the driving forces behind state organization. As Spruyt (1994: 30) notes: 'Tilly explains the variation between types of organization by differential responses to the functional demand of waging war'. Tilly's approach, thus, stresses the role played by the international system in forging the European states from the seventeenth to the nineteenth century. By contrast, Rokkan is more interested in the internal sources of political development, which may vary from case to case but have nevertheless to do with the need of rulers to consolidate and extend their power in a given territory. Both approaches are concerned with European political development, and it is noteworthy that neither of them considers the American experience, not even as a *reference case*. Indeed, both approaches would have been enriched by a comparison with the American experience of political development, strongly influenced by both international constraints and domestic pressures.

In order to bring America back into the comparison, let me first deal with Rokkan's approach (Rokkan 1968, 1970, 1973*a*, 1973*b*, 1999; Rokkan and Meritt 1966) which envisages different paths in European nation- and state-building. While the state coincides with the territorial bounding of sovereignty, this process has followed different patterns of development. In general, the modern nation-states of Europe are the outcome of the long-drawn-out transformation of the feudal structures inherited from the disintegration of the Roman Empire. The state-building process came about in different ways because it was influenced by the differential impacts of four variables combining cultural and economic factors. Rokkan used these variables to build his conceptual map of Europe based on two axes of differentiation: the East–West axis, which differentiates between the highly monetized economy of the West and the agricultural economy of the East; and the North–South axis, which differentiates between the local (national) oriented Protestant cultures of the North and the supranational orientation of the Catholic culture in the South. '(For Rokkan) the North–South axis is central to the process of nation building, that is to say in defining processes of allegiance to or identification with national political organization. The East–West axis is crucial to the understanding of state formation—the creation of institutions of political authority' (Page 1995: 12).

The question that Rokkan addresses is why the European nation-states developed first on the peripheries of the western Roman Empire, and then in the latter's heartland, with its vast network of cities and local units and differentiated secular and religious authorities. Reporting on a paper that he had written for the UNESCO program on 'Comparative Cross-National Research' in 1973, Rokkan explained that 'his model' is based on 'four sources of variations in the structuring of territorially defined political organizations: (1) the distinctiveness, the consolidation and the economic, political, and cultural strength of the *territorial centre*; (2) the cultural distances of the *peripheries* from the centre and their economic and political resources for resistance against integration and standardization; (3) the internal strength and the external resource links of *cross-locally organized subcultures* such as churches, sects, castes; (4) the internal strength and the external resource links of *cross-locally organized economic units*, such as merchant leagues, credit networks, international corporations' (Rokkan 1973*a*: 18, emphasis in the original).

Although Rokkan's approach is still the subject of intense debate (Flora 1999), it seems plausible that Rokkan regarded these variables as crucial because they produced different incentive structures for central elites which wanted to maximize their power. In other words, the various types of variables implied different cost–benefit calculations for the central elites in pursuit of territorial bounding because they offered them different coalitional strategies. If state-building is a process which concerns (also) the neutralization of (individual, groups, or area) free-riding and defection options, then the four variables may explain a great deal about the chances of success of territorial bounding strategies. Where the spread of the Protestant Reformation in northern Europe made it possible to fuse the secular and religious realms and to create a local language of social communication (in place of Latin), an important barrier was raised against individual, group, or territorial exits from that given polity. At the same time, the exit options were much more difficult to circumscribe when the territory was organized around a network of economically independent trading cities, connected to their surroundings with land ownership divided into small estates.

It was not by chance that the sovereign territorial state developed in the peripheral areas (like France, Britain, and Spain) of the old Roman Empire, whereas at the core of the Empire, with its dense network of independent cities, alternative institutional organizations of power arrangements arose, for instance the city-leagues (in the German and Dutch areas) or the city-states (in the Italian center-north). Accordingly, state-building followed different routes because there were different power relations between the central and peripheral elites. In the heartlands of the Roman Empire, the richness of city networks and the differentiation of secular and religious authorities strengthened the resistance of groups and individuals opposed to integration with, and standardization by, the center. This was in contrast to the territories on the peripheries, where city networks were weak and where the differentiation between secular and religious authorities gave way to the formation of a national (Protestant) church. The establishment of a national church fostered vernacularization and thus stimulated the linguistic unification (or homogeneity) of a given territorial area. Rokkan (1973b: 90) writes: '(t)he great paradox of Western Europe was that it developed a number of strong centres of territorial control at the edge of the old empire: the decisive thrusts of state formation and nation-building took place on the peripheries of the territory left without effective control by the disruption of the Western Roman Empire'.

Thus, 'for Rokkan, centre-periphery structures are the essential features of the *territorial* structure of political systems, evolving in the processes of territorial expansion, political centralization, and population concentration' (Flora 1999: 6, emphasis in the original). Hence, structures are configurations of variables which furnish political actors with different resources; and they do so at different political times, because Rokkan's analysis is not only synchronic but also diachronic. The concept of *timing* is crucial in this regard, because different strategies may be pursued by political actors in the different sequences of the territorial organization of sovereignty (Orren and Skowroneck 1996). As Flora (1999: 14, emphasis in the original) again stresses: 'the concept of *timing* is systematically bound

25

up with Rokkan's model building through his distinction between four fundamental developmental processes of territorial political systems: state formation in the narrower sense, nation-building, democratization, and the establishment of the welfare states. Taken together, the features of these individual processes and the way they combine over time make up nation- or type-specific *developmental paths* or *trajectories'*.

For Rokkan, territorial centralization in Europe depended on structural conditions of the power relations between the center and both cross-locally organized subcultures and cross-locally organized economic units. The sovereign, territorial state developed where the center enjoyed clear supremacy over the periphery, also because there was no cultural distance between them; and where, of course, cross-organized subcultures and economic units could neither mobilize resources against the center nor acquire an internal cohesive authority structure. In these conditions, central elites were able to create systems of alliances with peripheral elites in order to extend their jurisdiction to a given territory—or better, their power within that jurisdiction. Moreover, the original pressure for territorial centralization *in the form of a state* arose from within the territory itself, although its consolidation was helped by the subsequent external development of a competitive inter-states system.

Other forms of territorial organization, like the city-state and the city-league, were available *when* the state started to develop. But the territorial state predominated owing to its greater capacity to mobilize the societal resources necessary to deal with internal challenges, over and above external ones. As Spruyt (1994: 185) stresses: '[s]overeign authority proved to be more effective in reducing economic particularism, which raised transaction and information costs, and it created a more unified economic climate. Central administration provided for gradual standardization of weights and measures, coinage and jurisprudence. Undoubtedly this was a lengthy process. (. . .) But (. . .) the dominant political actor, the king in France, the king-in-parliament in England, had vested interests in limiting defection and free-riding and in furthering the overall economy. The greater autonomy of urban centers in the Hansa [league] and the Italian city-states made such objectives more difficult to achieve'. The increased resources acquired through the state organization assisted the rulers in their strategy to consolidate and expand their territorial power, soliciting imitation by the neighbor rulers threatened by that power. Success thus bred emulation.

Once they had started along the road of state formation in the second half of the nineteenth century, the latecomer countries also adopted the then dominant model of state organization (the French one of administrative centralization, mitigated in the course of that century by representative features taken from the English model). After all, the system of states that consolidated between the Peace of Westphalia of 1648 and the Congress of Vienna in 1815 entailed adoption of the territorial state model (eschewing the alternative forms of rule). With the nineteenth century, the distinctive feature of the system of rule was, to quote Ruggie (1998: 180), 'that it has differentiated its subject collectivity into territorially defined, fixed and mutually exclusive enclaves of legitimate domination'. Thus (Ruggie 1998: 188), not only did the principle of 'reciprocal sovereignty become the new principled basis of the new international order', but the promotion of that principle was assumed to be the task of the unitary and centralized state.

In sum, whilst the dominant elites in England and France were able to buttress their claim to power through state formation, this institutional strategy was long neutralized by adverse conditions in the German- and Italian-speaking areas. As again Spruyt (1994: 130) writes: 'unlike the situation in France, no aspiring central actor managed to form a social alliance with the burghers in Italy. And, unlike the situation with the German towns, the divergent interests and variation between the Italian towns prevented them from forming city-leagues'. The result was that the Italian city-states and the German city-leagues for long competed against the territorial state in order to establish an alternative form of political rule. This is why, on assuming the French and the German story as ideal-types, Spruyt (1994: 112) points out that the former story 'is one of centralization and gradual establishment of sovereign authority in a juridical and factual sense [whereas the latter story] is one of dissipation'.

2.2.2. *Variants of European Nationalism*

Once the territorial state had prevailed, the new rulers had to justify their power by creating a new cultural (or ideological) myth. The *nation*, as a community of groups and individuals connected by a stock of shared experiences and predispositions, was the outcome of a process of social and intellectual construction: through the idea of a *nation* the experiences of separate groups and individuals were translated into a common experience (Smith 1991). However, that same idea was interpreted or elaborated differently by earlier and later European state-builders. The earlier ones, as in France, set about creating a state well before the definition of a nation became necessary. Indeed, it was the successful building of the state which created the strategic conditions for the gradual construction of a nationality *within* that state. By contrast, later state-builders, like those of Italy and Germany, operated exactly in reverse: the state was claimed, pursued, and finally created in order to give representation to an already culturally defined nationality: a nationality which never fully fit with the state that eventually came to be built.

In the latter countries, territorial bounding came about more under the pressure of an already established state-system than as an endogenous process of public authority centralization. And in fact, owing to the difficulty of building a territorial state, state-builders initially reacted to the pressures exerted by the established state system by constructing cultural boundaries with which to block those pressures. They created a cultural territory rather than a political one: a cultural territory protected by Romantic myths about the linguistic and biological community living within it. Inevitably, however, this cultural territory corresponded to a space (that of the Holy Roman Empire in the German case) which was politically indeterminate. And it was for this reason that nation and state never fully overlapped in Germany. Between the experiences of the earlier and later state-builders, moreover, there stood that of states (like the Netherlands and Belgium), which evaded the superimposition of state and nation regardless of the timing of that superimposition. These states consisted of compacts among different nationalities; or better, they consisted of states without a (single) nation but with many (single) nations. After all, these states developed in the broad buffer zone in Europe between northern Protestantism and the southern Counter-Reformation: that is, in the area most exposed to the religious conflicts of the seventeenth and eighteenth centuries (Daalder 1995). (These states came to be organized by the consensual model of democracy in the second half of the twentieth century, see chapter 3.)

Although one can plausibly argue that the experience of the oldest European states 'suggests the temporal as well as logical priority, of the state and the system of states to the formation of European nations and the rise of nationalism' (Smith 1995: 49), the argument requires at least two qualifications. First, it 'appl[ies] historically more in the western and northern parts of the continent than in the south and the east'; and second, 'even in the west and north of Europe, a dominant or core ethnic population formed the basis of both state and nation' (Smith 1995). The end result of these different processes was a differentiated concept and practice of nationalism; a differentiation that dramatically influenced the subsequent history of the main European nation-states.

Consider the historical experiences of England and France, on the one hand, and Germany and Italy on the other. One can single out sixteenth-century England and seventeenth-century France as the first two European countries to set off along the road of state formation, albeit in the absence of a widespread sense of nationhood. Of course, the state assumed different institutional features in the two countries, owing to their diverse histories and the differing nature of the social forces that sustained the growth of the state. In England, the state assumed the features of a representative organization (Rhodes 1994), although it had bureaucratic underpinnings (Ertman 1997) in that public authority was personified by the 'king in parliament'. In France, by contrast, the state assumed the features of an administrative organization, although it had some representative inputs (Ertman 1997) because public authority was personified in royal absolutism. These different institutional forms of public authority obviously reflected different social coalitions in the two countries in favor of the formation of a state. However, the relevant fact is that, because in both England and France, the state preceded the nation (Smith 1991), the advent of the latter (or better its construction) had to be adapted to the social practices which came to be associated with that territorial organization.

This historical sequence inevitably influenced the concept of *nation* constructed in each country, for the concept had to adapt to a polity which was already territorially defined and had an array of political norms and legal rules to delimit the space and terms of its elaboration. To be sure, the two nationalisms differed from each other: in England it had a pure individualistic-societal connotation, while in France it acquired a more collectivistic-cultural one. As Greenfeld (1992: 14) writes, England developed '(an) individualistic civic nationalism, (whereas) in France...its nationalism was collectivistic and yet civic'. However, in both cases, nationalism was elaborated as a sentiment of belonging more to a territorial state than to a pre-identified cultural community. It was civic because it did not imply the prepolitical sharing of biological traits, although that civicness presupposed the assimilation of defined cultural norms. Consequently, even at the level of the nation, one must speak in the plural, given that these different conceptions of the nation still today exert their influence in the West (Haas 1997).

The different historical sequence followed by the countries that came later to the experience of statehood, such as Italy and (especially) Germany in the second half of the nineteenth century, generated a qualitatively different concept of nationhood. Because the organization of public authority on a territorial basis encountered formidable obstacles in those countries, the elites then engaged in the project of state formation had to pursue a different strategy. They had to foster the cultural (rather than territorial) identification of the ruled, asserting the existence of a linguistic and ethnic *pre-political community*, also because of the lack of territorial boundaries delimiting and defining it. They thus created a sentiment of national identity which largely anticipated the subsequent process of state-building and which was also largely *independent* from it. National identity was not a choice but a destiny; not a matter of belonging to a given political territory but a prepolitical (quasi-biological) condition. This sentiment of cultural belonging eventually gave impetus to the building of the territorial state, although its cultural boundaries never fully coincided with the territorial boundaries of the state that finally came to be built. The existence of a cultural nation was thus perceived by the elites of the latecomer countries as a prior (if not logical) condition for the existence itself of the state.

This was evidently the logical rationalization of a specific structural context: that is, of the fact that the state-building process encountered formidable obstacles at the center of the former Roman Empire (contrary to what happened in its border Western territories). Especially in the geographical belt stretching from the center-north of Italy to the German Hanseatic area, these obstacles consisted of a tight network of cities, economically thriving and politically independent, which obstructed any institutional centralization of public authority. This was a feature entirely absent from the Western border areas, which comprised only a few urban centers able to exercise influence over very broad geographical areas. However, this different historical construction of the idea of nationalism generated different views of political life, views which largely influenced the subsequent political development of the countries concerned. In Germany, the construction of a national identity based on biological features (such as the sharing of 'German blood') opened the way to the subsequent degenerative re-elaboration of that concept in racial terms after World War I (Brubaker 1992), but it also continued to influence the elaboration of the new German democratic nationalism after the totalitarian period.

In fact, in Germany, unlike in France and England, the social practices associated with the concept of nationalism induced both the elites and the public to consider it natural for a democratic regime to entail the existence of a pre-identified *demos*. It was on the basis of this conceptual framework, for example, that the German Constitutional Court questioned the legality of the Maastricht Treaty of 1992, which established the supremacy of EU norms over domestic ones. The EU, it was established by the *Manfred Brunner and Others* v. *The European Union Treaty* decision of 1994, can claim superior legitimacy over its member states only if its decisions are the democratic expression of the will of a European *demos*, a condition that 'does not yet exist'. Indeed, the German Constitutional Court stated that the EU 'is not a State based on the people of one European nation'. In short, as a German legal scholar (Grimm 1997: 254) observed, 'The European level of politics lacks a matching public'. The criticism of the Court did not alter the course of European integration, however. The Court and its supporters in the country were forced gradually to acknowledge that their argument had a plausibility rooted in the historical experience of the German state, but not in that of other democratic nation-states.

The different timing of state-building at the center and the periphery of Europe thus made it inevitable that the rulers of the two regions would construct different notions of nationhood in order to legitimize their claims to power and influence: biological in Germany and civic in England and France. However, despite these differences, one may plausibly argue that there has been one predominant European model of nation-state formation: a model based (first) on the imposition of central public authority on a given territory, and (then) on the subsequent fostering (by the members of that public authority) of a notion of 'the people' (i.e. the sharing of a set of practices and experiences) among the individuals and groups resident in that territory. This European model of political development, including its variants, is significantly different from the model that has developed in the other half of the West, to wit, the USA.

2.3. Rokkan in Washington, DC: State and Nation in America

2.3.1. *The American Road to Sovereignty*

It is generally dismissed that America started as a constitutional pact among different and sovereign territorial states. The Articles of Confederation of 1781 and the Philadelphia constitution of 1787 represent two phases of the same process: to create a political union out of distinct sovereignties. Those two constitutions, in their own ways, tried to create a new international order on the American continent and at the same time make it the premise of a new domestic polity (Onuf 1983; Deudney 1995; Hendrickson 2003). Indeed, the disintegration of British rule left a territory which could have acquired features not dissimilar from those of the European system of states. Exactly to avoid this possibility (and thus to reduce the high probability of war between potentially rival states interested in expanding their own influence and in acquiring new resources within a common territory), the states' elites decided to go beyond the European project of 'balance of power' (whose capacity to guarantee peace was evidently low) (Onuf and Onuf 1994). For this reason, those states' elites devised an institutional system which, although based on an inter-states agreement, was nevertheless endowed with a supra-states authority. The American project, contrary to the European project, was finalized to create a new territorial sovereignty, based on the recognition of the distinct territorial sovereignty of the previously separated states and, at the same time, on their rearrangement in a larger institutional framework. The project was to create 'a republic of many republics' (as it was called during the founding period, see Hendrickson 2003: 240), that is, to compound within a new republic the distinct territorial communities of interest of the thirteen already-established republics. Once the new *unionist* project came finally to replace the previous one of the Articles of Confederation (with the approval of the Philadelphia constitution by nine of the thirteen states and thus its entrance into effect on March 4, 1789), then the elites pursuing it had to operate on the basis of specific cultural and economic premises.

Culturally, in America there was neither an overlap between the secular and religious realms (which greatly helped the process of state-building in Protestant Europe) nor competition between the secular and religious authorities (which greatly hampered the process of state-building in Catholic Europe). America came to define itself as a polity of Protestants rather than as a Protestant polity. The plurality of Protestant sects, and fierce theological competition among them, induced the central elites to distance the two realms, so that religious pressures developed at the civil level, not at the political one. And if America had only one language of communication, contrary to the several languages that connoted Europe, that language never achieved the mythical status of the national language, given that it was the language of the colonial power. It is too frequently taken for granted that America started as a culturally homogeneous society. Indeed, since the late eighteenth century, the crucial factor in America was

the territorial dispersion of the immigrant 'tribes'—national and ethnic groups, races and religious communities. With the exception of black slaves, immigrants to the United States came one by one, or family by family, and though they sought out (and were sometimes locked into) segregated neighborhoods, they avoided any larger segregation, moving freely around the country and creating radically mixed cities and states. Hence no one group was able to determine for long the character of local governments. In some general way, the political culture of the country as a whole was English and Protestant, but this culture was never firmly established either in the symbols or the substance of law and policy. Nor did the immigrant groups assimilate entirely in the dominant culture. (Walzer 1996: 9)

Economically, America was much closer to the European trading belt than to the areas that fostered the earlier process of state-building. The colonization process bred differentiated networks of trading cities, with ever larger areas of land distributed to a free peasantry which proved highly resistant to any attempt at centralization. In the same way, the creation of the American polity was never able to produce a condition of no-exit. The exit options, for individuals and groups, were always there, even after the end of the Civil War in 1865 (although the Civil War eliminated the exit options for states or territorial units). Neither religious or language barriers nor economic or territorial constraints operated. The enlargement of the polity (which went ahead interruptedly during the first century of the new republic) challenged any attempt to constrain the exit options.

The *rural-land frontier*...lasted from the beginning of settlement in the seventeenth century to the end of the nineteenth century on the eve of World War I. Based on the conquest of the land (the American share of the North American continent), it was oriented toward the direct exploitation of the products of the land, even in its cities. It was characterized by the westward movement of an essentially rural population interested in settling and exploiting the land and by the development of a socioeconomic system based on agricultural and extractive pursuits in both its urban and rural components. (Elazar 1994: 55–6, emphasis in the original)

Nor has America been a simple compact among distinct territorial communities like the European states divided along religious, linguistic, or national lines, because it has implied a degree of vertical (or supra-states) integration among its constituent states unknown to the latter. Certainly, the United States began as a compact of states not properly integrating them. The Articles of Confederation (of 1781–7) were an attempt to celebrate constitutionally a principle of territorial aggregation that resembled the consociational compact of Switzerland before 1848. That *first* American constitution reflected a strong corporate idea of territorial organization, in the sense that the new polity was intended to be the outcome of a pact exclusively between distinct and separated territorial communities or states. '[I]n the Articles of Confederation . . . the Congress had no authority over individuals: Congress could act only through the states themselves' (Dahl 1976: 87). The Continental Congress was regarded as a diplomatic arena by the thirteen states and no permanent executive power was introduced. Sovereignty continued to be monopolized by each of the thirteen states. However, because that constitution was expected to go beyond inter-states relations, its failure in dealing with domestic and international challenges created a context favorable for its reform. Indeed, the document drawn up at the Philadelphia Constitutional Convention of the summer of 1787 was more than a simple reform of the Articles of Confederation. It was a new constitution.

However, the corporate idea of territorial organization also influenced the institutional design of the *second* constitution. This influence was exerted by those who opposed it (the Anti-Federalists) on the principle that each state had individuality (Beer 1993: 384), but it was accepted as legitimate (and inevitable) also by those (the Federalists) who pursued a more supra-states project (Hendrickson 2003: 243). The individuality of the states was, first, reflected in the design of the new Senate, where all the states had two representatives regardless of their demographic size, representatives selected, moreover, by state legislatures. Second, it was reflected in the design of the Electoral College for the election of the President, where each state was assigned an Electoral College constituted by a number of Great Electors equivalent to the number of Senators and members of the House of Representatives pertaining to it (thus favoring the small states because of the clause of the two senators which institutionalized their overrepresentation). In sum, regarding the election of the chief executive, the corporate idea was reflected: (*a*) by the indirect election of the President, (*b*) by his election through the vote of Great Electors chosen by states' legislatures, and (*c*) by the fact that the number of Great Electors constituting the state Electoral College was not proportional to the population of each state (because of the clause of the two senators). Thus, it is true that the federal Senate 'could be considered a victory for the principle of corporate representation' (Beer 1993: 384), a victory further entrenched by the powers assigned to the Senate concerning the approval (through its advice and consent) of presidential nominees for the judiciary and the various executive offices, and of the country's international treaties. But it also true that the principle of corporate representation has continued to affect the selection of the chief executive officer of the country. In sum, 'the Federalists borrowed significantly from the

Articles of Confederation' (Ackerman 1991: 93), even when they decided, for example, not to adopt the principle of a legislative veto by the federal legislature on laws approved by the states' legislatures.

Thus, between 1776 and 1789, America moved in the direction of a new territorial state whose institutional features were nonetheless connoted by a combination of federal (or supra-states) and confederal (or inter-states) elements. Unlike the *Hanse* league, which prospered for centuries in Continental northern Europe, the league of American states came to adopt, with the second constitution, more centralized features. As Riker (1964) argued some time ago, this was due to the pressure applied by the main European powers (Britain, France, but also Spain), which were still involved (at the end of the nineteenth century) in the American continent and wanted to curtail the ambitions of the new American republic. Or, as other scholars have more precisely remarked recently (see in particular Deudney 1995), the centralizing (or supra-states) devices were considered necessary for avoiding that the European powers could play the interests of one state against those of others, thus transforming the American continent into a theater for their power games. In this insecure environment, the new republic could only prosper under a more centralized public authority. Certainly, the failure of the Articles of Con-federation (the 'American league') was also due to its difficulty in facing the challenges raised by an increasingly differentiated internal society which was beginning to display a crude socioeconomic contraposition of interests. However, even these challenges could have been an opportunity for external interference. Indeed, the Shay's Rebellion[1] in 1787, an exam-ple of a dramatic conflict which the Continental Congress was unable to handle, was considered to have been supported by British agents. Be that as it may, in less than a decade, America moved from a confederal to a federal definition of national public authority, with the latter, however, including important aspects of the former. A move that took the European culturally divided states centuries to accomplish.

In sum, even the new federal model did not definitively resolve the question of the double representation (of states and individuals) in a large republic. It would be misleading to assume that the question of national authority was definitively resolved with the compromises celebrated in Philadelphia. De facto, the two options (confederal and federal) continued to coexist, notwithstanding the Civil War, with their alternative strategies for organizing the relationship between public authority and the national territory. They were two options that in America assumed the form of a permanent confrontation between two coherent and widely embraced theories of republican government: the compact (confederal) theory and the national (federal) theory. This confrontation gave rise to a sort of reciprocal influence whose institutional outcome was a *compound republic* (Ostrom 1987). That is an institutional system of multiple and overlapping jurisdictions, with a variable combination of self-government (by the states) and shared government (between the federated states and the federal state), finalized to prevent the formation of a permanent majority (of states and individuals) able to affect the republic as a whole. It was a variable combination because the constitution, albeit within limits, allowed the representatives of the federal state and the federated states constantly to negotiate the allocation or distribution of public authority on the republican territory.

2.3.2. *The American Structure of Authority*

For several reasons, it is plausible to suggest that in America the pressure on the confederation, and then on the federation, was fueled by the same needs that induced state territorial bounding in Europe (Kratochwil 1986): to guarantee peace, to keep out external powers, to counter defection and free-riding, and to further the overall economy. But, here, territorial bounding concerned the bottom-up aggregation of independent states, and not just the top-down acquisition of a given territory. Given the polycentric nature of development in the previous colonial period, America did not have a territorial center in the European sense of the expression, but as many centers as it had states. There was certainly a prominent (Virginian) elite, but it never gave up its local roots to advance its national role. At the same time, while the cultural distance between the elites of the various states was relatively narrow, the economic and ideological distance among them was on the contrary wide. There were entrenched cross-locally organized subcultures and economic units in each state, or better, many states were entrenched organized subcultures and economic units. Indeed, since its inception in 1789, the federal constitution had been constrained by sectional conflict, certainly over slavery but also over antagonistic socioeconomic state systems (trade vs. plantation).

The second constitution necessarily had to acknowledge this sectional divide if it was to gain recognition from the main political actors. Hence, the constitution sought to conjugate two different (and hitherto considered to be antithetical) principles of sovereignty: one based on state interests and the other based on individual preferences. A separated system of organization of the public authority was the outcome: it was separated vertically (between the federated states and the federal state) and horizontally (within the Congress, between the House of Representatives and the Senate, representing individual electors and territorial units respectively; and between the Congress and the President). Moreover, since 1803, all the main political and institutional actors had recognized the ultimate role of the judiciary in establishing the boundaries of the vertical and horizontal separation of powers wielded by rulers operating within the authority structure of the republic. The power of judicial review made the judiciary into a policymaking actor in its own right. Hence, although the second constitution strengthened the capacity of the central rulers to guarantee the republic's external sovereignty, it still constrained the internal exercise of sovereignty to an extent unthinkable in Europe. It did so through the institutionalization of a *fragmented sovereignty* based on the diffusion of law-making authority among different rulers, located in the federated states as well as in the federal center, some endowed with electoral, and others with nonelectoral, legitimacy.

It was the constitutionalization of this fragmented sovereignty that made the Great Compromise in Philadelphia possible. The second American constitution was the first attempt in history to resolve the concomitant problem of avoiding the despotic tendency of the centralized universal empire and the anarchic tendency of a decentralized system of states. Although federal in form, the constitution preserved a mixed regime. A protected equilibrium was institutionalized between the two principles represented by the strong bicameral nature of the new public authority: the Congress. For a large part of the nineteenth century, the separation of powers was taken to be separation *within* the main institution of the separated powers, that is, the legislature. Internally to the latter, the separation of powers was intended to make the country's sectional divide or territorial conflict governable. The political role of the President was severely constrained: he acted more as a head of state than as a head of government. After all, as we have seen, the Electoral College that elected him had been designed to keep his election within the states' boundaries, rather than let the election promote a national constituency. It was not until the democratization of the Electoral College in the second half of the nineteenth century, with the election of the President's selectors or Great Electors in a competitive race between party lists, that the first steps were taken toward the nationalization of presidential elections (although some states already introduced the popular election of Great Electors in the 1830s). In sum, the America of the nineteenth century was federal in form but had strong confederal features. *Congressional government* was federal government through the states' representatives, the power of Congress deriving from its capacity to be the *patron* of the states' interests.

Though the new constitution extended federal jurisdiction across the entire American territory, such jurisdiction overlapped with the states' jurisdictions, which were protected at the federal level by a Senate representing the state legislatures (in fact, until 1913 the federal senators were selected by the latter). However, the same federal jurisdiction promoted by the House of Representatives continued to be largely defined by the states' interests. Sectional conflict, in fact, was the main source of congressional politics (and policy). 'Sectional conflict was revealed most regularly and consistently in the halls of Congress. There . . . sectionalism pervaded the less public and more informal political processes of the committee chambers, cloakrooms, and the Committee on the Whole' (Bensel 1987: 9). Thus, the overlapping of jurisdictions was necessary to guarantee the corporate compact along with individual preferences. Inevitably, it had two correlated outcomes. First, it forestalled the verticalization and centralization of public authority at the federal level; second, it left open the exit option at the level of individual states.

It is thus likely that the same constitutional design invented to deal with the problem of a compound republic made America unable (for a long period of the nineteenth century) to counter the threat of territorial defection. While 'regional strife has a weapon not available to other groups—secession' (Schwartz 1974: 107), it is also true that, in America, use of that 'weapon' was ambiguously guaranteed by the constitution. In fact, until the Civil War the (Southern) states continued to entertain the idea of secession, and it took a dramatically bloody war to remove the ambiguity. Nevertheless, ambiguity has continued to characterize the American constitutional experiment (Forsyth 1981; McDonald 2000). Although the outcome of the war made secession impossible, it deepened the already profound sectional divide in the country. The American post–Civil War republic continued to be largely defined by a geographical cleavage, initially between those favoring and those opposing a stronger national union, and then between different territorial-economic interests. Consequently, in the twentieth century, 'the comparative lack of religious or ethnic rivalry between the American regions has meant that the sectional stress in the United States has usually been grounded in economic competition. . . . sectional stress is political conflict over significant public decisions in which a nation is divided into two or more regions, each of which is internally cohesive and externally opposed to the other(s)' (Bensel 1987: 4).

The political development of America was thus constantly constrained by a territorial cleavage due to both an institutional conflict between different interpretations of the republic (confederal vs. federal, compact theory vs. national theory) and a sectional divide between different socio-economic structures (land-based economy vs. commercial economy), and their correlated cultural differences, with the two sides of the cleavages generally overlapping. It was territorial cleavage that could be governed through permanent negotiation among the institutional and policy interests of the actors representing it: a difficult undertaking, although 'only once did the American politicians fail in this endeavor' (Key 1964: 233). Consequently, whereas in Europe state authority was imposed on the basis of a fusion of powers which made it unquestionable (either in parliament, as in liberal England, or in the administration, as in absolutist France, or in the administration plus parliament of the nineteenth-century liberal France of the Third Republic), in America, federal state authority labored to impose itself because it was permanently constrained by the separation of powers (vertically between the federal state and the federated states and horizontally among the institutions of the federal center).

2.3.3. *Variants of American Nationalism: Constitutional Nationalism*

America is a case of a nation that developed without the support of a state (Boorstin 1965; Nettle 1968). Greenfeld (1992: 402, emphasis in the original) argued that '*nationality* identity in America...preceded the formation...of the institutional framework of the American nation, and even of the national territory'. This argument relies on what John Jay (now Beard 1964: 39) wrote emphatically in the *Federalist no. 2*, that is, that the Americans were (at the beginning) 'one united people; a people descended from the same ancestors, speaking the same language, professing the same religion, attached to the same principles of government (and) very similar in their manners and customs'. However, such representation of a pre-existing American cultural community (Morgenthau 1948) was called into question (Goldwin 1961; Davis 1978; Elazar 1987a; Ball and Pocock 1988; Konig and Matson 1990) for being more the ideological justification of the 'nationalist' interpretation of American history than the empirical description of the republic in the founding period. Indeed, the citizens of the various states maintained highly differentiated 'manners and customs', in particular between the Northern and Southern states, but also not insignificant differentiated 'principles of government', in particular regarding the proper scope of the union. The deep division on the legitimacy of slavery does not lend support to the representation of Americans as a culturally homogeneous people. Thus people became gradually aware that it had been united by a sequence of political acts, from the Declaration of Independence in 1776 to the Articles of Confederation of 1781 and subsequently the Federal Constitution of 1787 to the first ten constitutional amendments (or Bill of Rights) of 1789 (Wills 1978). In America, 'the making of the constitution is the act of founding the nation' (Preuss 1996: 21), where by constitution one has to mean the process of interpreting it through a continuous and conflictual debate. As a result of the federal constitution, the American nation began to be constructed as distinctly different from other nations. Different because the constitution allowed it to be interpreted as a nation constituted by a multiplicity of 'national identities'. Thus, the federal constitution has created a 'nation of nationalities', an integrated political order based on the mutual recognition of the cultural differences dividing the states (and thus dividing each of them internally, with the constant arrival of a plurality of ethnic and religious groups of immigrants in the post-Philadelphia period).

In the nineteenth century, this multiple America was held together by a democratic process which developed conterminously with the cultural construction of the American nation. Again, the American nation continued to be constructed through political means and procedures.

(Electoral) democracy was essential to America's complex 19th century process of nation-building...By the mid-nineteenth century, popular understanding made America and democracy synonymous. What visitors mistook for a hopeless vanity was really a matter of identity. Americans boasted about precisely those democratic characteristics that made them feel American, including a sovereign People who incorporated the very mix of nationalities *that most European commentators cited to prove no American nation could exist.* (Wiebe 1995: 82–3, emphasis added)

Through representative and judicial institutions, America was able to create a national legal order without activating a centralizing state structure. Indeed, throughout the nineteenth century, '(a) unified legal order was effectively maintained, but the distinction between state and society was blurred. The official realm of government, so clearly demarcated in Europe, seemed to blend inconspicuously with American society' (Skowronek 1987: 6). The fact that nation and democracy developed together contributed to reinforce a peculiar American concept of nationalism (i.e. *constitutional nationalism*). This concept powerfully helped, in course of the nineteenth century, the cultural construction of a nation without the support of a federal state. For Walzer (1997), this nationalism is intrinsically tolerant.

America therefore stands in contrast to the experiences of all the European nations: to the earlier state-builders, like France, whose nation-building process was supported by a previously institutionalized state authority; and to later state-builders, like Germany and Italy, whose national identity, before the creation of the territorial state, was an ideological construct without precise territorial references. America is a case of national sovereignty neither made possible by a central state nor hindered by separated national entities. Although its identity had a common linguistic basis, its commonality was politically constructed, not naturally inherited. According to some scholars (Lipset 1979), this overlap between nation- and democracy-building contributed to the creation of a liberal society in America (contrary to what happened in Europe). The *political* conception of nationality has been able to hold together states and individuals, that is to integrate territories and groups with different manners and opposed customs. After all, since its very inception, America has become an immigrant society, that is a structurally heterogeneous social, cultural, religious, linguistic, and ethnic world. Necessarily, America had to recognize its deep internal differences and recompose them within the political framework of the constitution (with its universal principles).

However, the political interpretation of American nationality should not be confused with the twentieth-century 'melting pot' interpretation of American nation-building (King 2005). The latter is based on the idea that the social and cultural interaction of different peoples has produced an outcome which comprises something of each of them, whereas the former implies recognition of those differences at the private level and their overcoming exclusively at the public one. Indeed, the concept of 'melting pot' was soon converted into a functional equivalent of Americanization, meaning forced assimilation into the prevailing Anglo-Protestant culture. In any event, the political interpretation of nationality views America as a 'hyphenated' society. As Michael Walzer (1996: 26, emphasis added) puts it, 'the adjective "American" ... points to the citizenship, not the nativity or nationality, of the men and women it designates. It is *a political adjective*, and its politics is liberal in the strict sense: generous, tolerant, ample, accommodating— it allows for the survival, even the enhancement and flourishing of manyness'.

Nor should this political interpretation of American nationality be confused with the civic nationality of Britain and France. In these latter cases, civicness refers to a set of values and attitudes enshrined in cultural practices and not in constitutional rules. One has to assimilate a culture, but one only has to accept a constitution. 'Americans are allowed to remember who they were and insist, also, on what else they are (because) if the manyness of America is cultural, its oneness is political' (Walzer 1996: 26). In a sense, this interpretation has a *post-national* feature consistent with the fragmented sovereignty of the American states. And it is an interpretation that traverses American history in its entirety, from the foundation to the later development (Glazer 1997). For example, the 1997 Commission on Immigration Reform stated: 'the foundation of national unity (consists in) uniting persons from all over the world in a common civic culture'. Here, past and future, description and prescription, all combine. America developed as a nation devoid of cultural, ethnic, racial, or religious content. At the same time, it could only prosper by being a political nation, for as it coalesced around the common rules of a written constitution, it was able to tame (or conceal) the potentially devastating effects of its territorial, cultural, ethnic, racial, and religious divisions.

2.3.4. *Variants of American Nationalism: Cultural Nationalism*

This political interpretation of American nationality does not capture the American experience in its entirety (Renshon 2001). Indeed, this interpretation was, and continues to be, challenged by opposing interpretations and practices: in particular by the view that American nationality has to be considered the outcome of specific cultural circumstances. If it is true that American nationality is different from European nationalities for its liberal nature, that liberal nature embodies the values, traditions, and practices (especially linguistic practices) of the Anglo-Saxon Protestants who came first to the country as colonizers, and not as immigrants like the groups that arrived later (Huntington 2004). They were thus able to define its identity and to protect it through time (also thanks to the dominant social position the heirs of those colonizers retained throughout American history). This cultural (if not ethnic) nationalism has represented a powerful counterargument (Lieven 2004) to the liberal thesis first put forward by Hartz (1955) and his followers and which seemed to predominate between the end of World War II and the 1980s. Indeed, this interpretation has tended regularly to re-emerge, because of the cultural challenges represented by the periodical arrival of waves of immigrants coming from different backgrounds.

Whereas the liberal thesis assumes a *political conception* of American nationality, the conservative antithesis asserts the latter's *cultural basis*. According to the liberal thesis America has been, since its beginnings, a naturally *liberal* country because it has not been conditioned by the cultural and ethnic background that constrained the formation of European nationalities. Conversely, according to the cultural thesis, America is a liberal country because of the cultural predominance of the white, Anglo-Saxon, and Protestant stock that created it in the first place. Hence, whereas the former takes American liberal nationalism as a necessity, the latter considers American liberal nationalism to be the outcome of public policies and social relations which promoted and protected Anglo-Saxon values. Although some of those policies might be considered illiberal (as we will see with reference to immigration), nevertheless their illiberal nature was justified by the end they had to achieve, namely to guarantee the existence of a liberal society. America, thus, has a history of exclusion and not only of inclusion. Exclusion, first of all, of those groups and identities which the predominant culture considered incapable of being even 'Americanized' such as Native Americans and African-Americans. In the latter case, the exclusion was for a long time supported by a legal doctrine which legalized slavery: in fact, the *Dred Scott* v. *Sandford* (1857) decision affirmed that African-Americans, even if free, could not be considered citizens (thus legalizing their exclusion from the civil and political rights of citizenship).

The Civil War changed the formal status of African-Americans but not the reality of their social and political exclusion. For more than a century, the policies which followed the Civil War in all the Southern states promoted and protected an outright system of racial exclusion or *apartheid* (Foner 1997; King D. 1997). African-Americans had to wait until the Civil Rights Act of 1964 before they became considered full members of the American nation. Moreover, American nationality not only 'stopped at the color line' (Horton 2005), but was also long denied to other groups of immigrants as well. After the Chinese Exclusion Act of 1882 and the Supreme Court ruling in *Ozawa* v. *United States* (1922), Asians were long considered not only ineligible for citizenship but also unsuited even for assimilation in the American melting pot. The strict immigration policies introduced in the 1920s and organized around the principle of national immigrants quotas were in reality largely biased in favor of northern Europeans, and they unequivocally penalized both

Asian and southern European immigrants on the ground that the former, contrary to the latter, were more assimilable into the Anglo-Protestant stock (King 2000; Zolberg 2006). Women, too, were kept on the margins of the American nation (Shklar 1991). Interestingly, with the arrival of new waves of immigrants, the boundaries of exclusion tended to widen: the Irish (Ignatiev 1995) or the Jews (Brodkin 2002) eventually became 'white', and their place in the exclusionary universe was taken (for the time being at least) by other groups, for example the Mexicans. This cultural interpretation of the American nation continues to furnish the narrative for American conservatism.

The forces which supported the Aliens Act of the 1790s or the Jim Crow laws of the postbellum America, or the policies of the 1920s, certainly did not go unchallenged. Liberal nationalism checked conservative nationalism and neutralized some of its exclusionary impulses. The struggle between the two American nationalisms was frequently resolved by the judiciary, which supported conservative nationalism for a large part of the nineteenth century, and liberal nationalism in the second half of the twentieth. Under the pressure of the civil rights movement of the 1950s, and despite (Katznelson, Geiger, and Kryder 1993) both a Congress dominated by a conservative coalition protecting the racial privileges of Southern whites and a presidency enthralled by the ideological xenophobia of McCarthyism, the Warren Court (1953–69) became instrumental in broadening the interpretation of American nationality. For example (Baum 1992), *Brown* v. *Board of Education* (1954) desegregated the school system, *Heart of Atlanta Motel* v. *United States* (1964) affirmed the universality of civil rights, *Reynold* v. *Sims* (1964) imposed the principle of equal representation proportional to the population in state legislature elections, and *Gideon* v. *Warnwright* (1963) granted the rights of due process and legal defense to defendants regardless of their economic circumstances. Indeed, the impact of the Warren Court on the material constitution of the country was comparable only to that of the first Supreme Court of John Marshal (1801–35). The Burger Court (1969–85) continued along the path marked out by its predecessor by further extending the constitutional concept of rights and creating new ones out of those not enumerated in the Ninth Constitutional Amendment: for instance, the right to privacy (in *Griswold* v. *Connecticut* of 1965), which subsequently provided the basis for recognition (in *Roe* v. *Wade* of 1973) of the constitutional right to an abortion (in the first three months of pregnancy, thus abolishing the 50 state laws which prohibited it except to save the mother's life).

However, the righting of a historical wrong like the exclusion of African-Americans from effective citizenship (with the Civil Rights Act of 1964), followed by the repeal, in 1965, of the restrictive immigration laws of the 1920s (thus opening American citizenship to all immigrants without preferential quotas), provoked a cultural backlash, especially in the Southern states. The policies of affirmative action and the official recognition of the country's multicultural identity that ensued from those decisions, soon encountered the resistance of groups that interpreted America as a cultural (not political) country. This reaction triggered the growth of a highly influential conservative nationalism which, in the early years of the twenty-first century, was the predominant cultural and political force; so predominant, indeed, that it influenced the view of the President and the majority party in both chambers of Congress between 2003 and 2006 (Hacker and Pierson 2005). In sum, like the European nationalities, American nationality too has had its varieties, in the sense that multiple traditions (Smith 1997) have competed against each other to define its very nature (and continue to do so).

2.4. Democracy-Building in Europe and America

In his examination of European political development, Rokkan (1973*a*: 29) stressed the challenges faced by territorial leaders in their attempts to consolidate territorial sovereignty. They had four tasks to perform, writes Rokkan. First, to form a boundary-defining state and develop an administrative machinery to control transactions within the territory or across boundaries (*territorial incorporation*). Second, to build institutions of socialization in order to create—through linguistic standardization, religious unification, and educational penetration—a specific political identity within that given territory (*territorial legitimacy*). Third, to institutionalize channels of participation, representation, and opposition (*democratic incorporation*). Fourth, to create territorial economic solidarity through measures for the equalization of benefits and opportunities both across regions and across strata of the population (*democratic legitimacy*).

Each of these tasks corresponded to a specific phase of territorial development, and each implied a set of different partners or different opponents. Of course, transition from one phase to the next was never linear and gradual, given that it required the dismantling of previous coalitions and the construction of new ones. Old coalitions tended to persist so that new political alliances had to be created to undertake the new task. This complex process of coalition rebuilding inevitably slowed the transition from one phase to the next; or else (in some areas), it cumulated tasks belonging to one phase with those of a previous or following phase. In other words, in Europe, the process of territorial consolidation was anything but uniform. Central territorial elites were able to overcome the four thresholds of territorial consolidation through conflicts and compromises that generated different institutional outcomes. Each threshold represented a choice point for the central elites, but the institutional solution found for the previous threshold constrained the institutional solution defined for the following one.

Nevertheless, one can argue that apparent in the European experience (*ex post*, of course, because, as Di Palma 2004 argues, history appears efficient only centuries after specific events have occurred) is a chain reaction which starts with the state, passes through the nation, and ends with democracy. To persist with Rokkan's approach, the first two thresholds were overcome *before* the second two: or better, the thresholds related to state- and nation-building were consolidated before fulfillment of the thresholds related to the diffusion of democracy. In other words, the state arose not only before the nation but also before democracy. Thus, from a European point of view, it does not make sense to talk of democracy arising before the nation's identification and mobilization. It was the active definition of the nation, as a specific territorial community protected by state authority, which created opportunity structures for actors interested in the achievement of democracy. European nationalism was both the forerunner of democracy and its adversary. National identity tended to bypass individual and social differences, emphasizing the sense of belonging to a common 'set of preferences'. Accordingly, nationalism prepared for democracy by promoting shared values. But the preparation took time; and more often than not, it took blood as well. Democracy arrived after nationalism had demanded that people die for the nation. Equality in the grave often seemed to be the necessary prelude for equality in the polling booth.

This process of territorial consolidation was anything but uniform in Europe because the different coalitions that made achievement of one threshold possible constrained the subsequent coalitions created to overcome the next threshold. Nation-building was thus hampered by the nature of the previous process of state-building, and democracy-building by the nature of the previous processes of nation-state building. In Europe, democracy was obliged to grow under the conditions imposed by those who already controlled the state, and by those who presided over the concept of national identity. Its antihierarchical and egalitarian biases were thus largely tamed by the already-established power structures of the nation-state (Lipset 1996). And democracy notwithstanding, sovereignty maintained its unified organization. A new regime arose with the liberal and political revolutions of the second half of the nineteenth century; but that regime of *statist democracy* maintained institutional continuity with the previous regime of *statist nationalism* (Rose 1996).

The process of territorial consolidation followed a quite different path in America. It did so not only because the boundary of federal authority was an open question until after the Civil War, as we have seen, but especially because the timing of territorial consolidation was completely different in America than in Europe. Herein reside two crucial distinctions between America and Europe. First, in America the federal state arrived after the consolidation of a sense of common supra-ordinate nation; second, in America the processes of nation-building and democratization were synchronic, not diachronic as in Europe. This explains why in America nationalism developed within the space of democracy (Kazin 1995), whereas in Europe it frequently challenged it.

In America, the institutionalization of channels of participation, representation, and opposition was largely implemented in the 1830s. And alternation in power between different political options had taken place since the very beginnings of the new federal republic: that is, the presidential elections of 1800 and the success of the Jeffersonian democratic-republicans against the Hamiltonian federalists. These thresholds were overcome in the context of a polity that was still radically decentralized. A low level of taxation was the key factor in keeping the federal government small and the states' government active. 'America's 18th century political heritage encouraged pulls away from the centre: states resisting national power, assemblies serving constituent interests, locally rooted legislatures guarding the right to initiate—or, more likely, not to initiate—new tax laws. Unlike the Jacobin legacy for France, republican ideology in America merely deepened the distrust of a national mobilization' (Wiebe 1995: 70). The fragmented and decentralized structure of sovereignty helped foster a *civil society democracy* (Bell 1991) different from the *statist democracy* institutionalized in Europe half a century later.

As it happened in Europe, but this time with the reverse effect, the coalition of interests that favored the growth of democracy restricted the opportunities available to the subsequent coalition to develop a stronger union. Thus, the existence of a democracy intended to protect decentralized interests largely constrained the options of those national rulers who wanted to promote the interests connected with centralization. In America, the states could long entertain the idea of exit, whereas in Europe the exit option was soon neutralized by the central rulers, because the idea was properly protected by democracy in the former case, whereas in the latter the peripheries had no procedural protection. Moreover, the institutional achievements of the democratic process not only postponed the state-building process, but also conditioned its features when it began. In fact, the development of a federal administrative machinery able to control economic as well as civil transactions within the national territory only came at the end of the nineteenth century and the beginning of the twentieth. Even during and after the Civil War 'the national overlay remained exceedingly thin: states and localities still gave meaning to citizenship and still regulated their own economies. Even where national rules mattered a great deal, as in the case of the Civil War laws establishing a single United States Currency, there was a major difference between uniformity and mobilization. A national currency facilitated transactions without trying to direct them' (Wiebe 1995: 70).

It was in the Progressive Era at the end of the nineteenth century that a civil service based on merit and not on party spoils was eventually created, although administrative reforms were already experimented with since the 1880s (the Pendleton Act 1883). Moreover, the huge industrial and territorial transformations of the post–Civil War period required new techniques of economic and social regulation. 'The close of the frontier, the rise of the city, the accentuation of class divisions, the end of isolation— these changes raised demands for national governmental capacities that were foreign to the existing state structure and that presupposed a very different mode of governmental operation' (Skowroneck 1987: 8–9). Thus, only in the twentieth century has America (at the national level) fully overcome the two thresholds of territorial and democratic legitimacy. Indeed, the building of institutions of socialization was traditionally the task (and prerogative) of state (peripheral) elites, not of national (central) ones. Not only was the educational system organized at the state level, but the creation of territorial economic and social solidarity was long regarded as the responsibility of the states, although the federal state did play an important role with the veterans program introduced in the aftermath of the Civil War (Skocpol 1992*a*).

Thus, in general, the two crucial legitimacy thresholds were overcome long after the national consolidation of democracy and the state, whereas in Europe they enabled transition from the territorial to the democratic phase of development. In sum, '[d]emocracy was firmly established in

America before a concentration of national governmental controls was demanded.... In America a new kind of state organization had to be fashioned through a highly developed electoral democracy to meet the governing challenges of the industrial age' (Skowroneck 1987: 9–10). Thus, the differing time sequences of territorial consolidation of sovereignty generated different patterns of authority structure in Europe and America: that is, different ways to organize the state, nation, and democracy.

2.5. Conclusion

The different process of political development in Europe and America has brought into being two distinct political orders on the two shores of the Atlantic. In the European nation-states, the political order was constructed around the experience and the idea of the state. In both early state-builders and late state-builders, the state has become the natural container of the nation. In fact, for the former the state was a historical precondition for the construction of the nation, whereas for the latter the nation preceded the state inasmuch as it was finalized to build it. In both cases, state and nation needed to be correlated, if the rulers of a given territory aspired to transform it into a recognizable sovereignty. Moreover, it was the combination of state and nation, or of nation and state, which made thus possible the development of democracy. Because, in the European historical experience, democracy came after the nation, or better after the nation-state was fully recognized (internally, by its own 'subjects' and externally, by other nation-states), Europeans have tended to assume the historical correlation as a logical necessity. It is the *demos* theory, on the basis of which a democracy is plausible only if there already exists a preconstituted nation, or better a nation constituted either through institutional means (as in the early state-builders) or through cultural means (as in the late state-builders).

The American experience of political development has been radically different from the European nation-states. In America, nationality has been the product of the democratic process, not its precondition. Nation and democracy went together, the one defining the other. It was the democratic process which defined the boundaries of the nation. The interaction between nation and democracy took place for long (at least for more than one century) in the absence of a (federal) state. The (federal) state has arrived, in America, much later than nationhood and democracy.

49

It was basically a democratic procedure which kept together for more than one century a growing number of reciprocally distrustful (federated) states, and the various distinct communities of interest operating through (and within) them. After all, having been born as a compound of independent republics, the new republic could not develop a significant centralizing mechanism at the federal level. What kept together those different republics was the constitution, or better the struggle over its interpretation. Indeed, the American compound republic was able to institutionalize in the nineteenth century (notwithstanding the Civil War of 1861–5 which dramatically challenged the 'peace pact' among the states of the late eighteenth century), because of the constitution. Since the very beginning, the constitution has created the narrative of different peoples acting as a common nation, *e pluribus unum*. Thus, in the American experience, the *demos* is a political, or better, constitutional, construct, whose coming into existence was historically independent from either a central state or a culturally defined nation.

The distinction between the European nation-states and American roads to the building of a modern political order seem of great interest for a better understanding of the post–World War II experience of European integration. The onset and development of the process of European integration (represented by the EU) has drastically transformed European politics. For the first time in European history, a new political system combining inter-states and supra-states features emerged from the ashes of the twentieth-century wars. An integrated Europe was the answer to the bellicose implications of the European state system of the previous era. Indeed, the EU is a way of questioning the very concept of sovereignty (MacCormick 1999). Europeans recognized that balance of powers among their sovereign states was no longer a recipe for peace. Those European states, as the American states in the late eighteenth century, had to sign a more compelling pact for securing peace in the continent. Thus after World War II Europe started to deal with the same question America had to face at the end of the eighteenth century and for a substantial part of the following century. How to create a nation of nationalities without the support of a pre-existing central state or a pre-existing cultural community (Brubaker 1999). A system compounding different (and well-established) nation-states has to look for original strategies of institutionalization. The experience of the European nation-states cannot help in this regard, because none of them was historically a compact of separated and sovereign territorial units. Nevertheless, as soon as the process of European integration deepened in the 1980s and 1990s with the formation of the EU, several voices were raised against the possibility of interpreting (Majone 2005*b*) the latter as a democratic polity. Other scholars (Weiler 1999) questioned even the possibility of transforming the EU into a future democratic polity. All these criticisms are based on the premise that a *demos* (or nation) is a structural precondition of democracy. Indeed, the American experience, especially of the nineteenth century, shows that a *demos* can be constructed through a democratic process constitutionally legitimized. After all, nations do not exist in nature, but they are cultural constructions, the outcome of successful strategies of identity-building. America has built a common supra-states identity, notwithstanding the persistence of different inter-states identities. It was the practice of democracy which made possible the accommodation of the specific cultural identities of the states with a common supra-states constitutional identity.

3

Institutionalization of different governmental patterns: separation and fusion of powers in America and Europe

3.1. Introduction

Different patterns of political development have favored the institutionalization of different patterns of governmental organization in America and Europe (Torstendahl 1992). Once governmental patterns had become established, they inaugurated paths that were difficult to change: the fusion of powers in Europe, the separation of powers in America. Political development in the European nation-states was based on the centralization of public authority, first in the crown and then in the state. Hence, the democratization process that had developed within the centralized structure assigned power of control over the centralized state to the parliament, removing it from the crown or the bureaucracy. This process of sovereignty transfer took time (at least one century from 1848 to 1948), but in the end it consolidated a tendency that had originated in the formation itself of the nation-state. Although the European nation-states moved from a *personal* to an *impersonal* sovereignty, they never challenged the latter's unified nature. The parliamentary state today represents the coherent institutionalization of sovereignty transfer because it has kept governmental powers fused together. By *fusion of powers* is meant that, despite formal recognition of a division of powers between the legislature and the government, these are de facto fused together by the political party or parties that connect the majority of the members of the former with its members in the latter (Wilson 1994). By embodying the popular will, the parliament has become the repository of popular sovereignty (Rohr 1995). Sovereignty has been reversed, and not only made impersonal; it now arises from below and no longer descends from above. In this system, all the other public powers depend on the parliament, or in any case are subordinated to it. One might say that, in European parliamentary systems, the sovereignty market is still controlled by a monopolist.

American political development followed a different trajectory because unified sovereignty was never a viable option. As a state system (although of a new type), America could never entertain the idea of a single supra-states sovereignty. While the Articles of the Confederation (1781–7) restricted sovereignty to the single states, the Philadelphia constitution endeavored to split it (vertically) between the federal state (or supra-states level) and the federated states (or the inter-states level). Moreover, it further splits it horizontally, among the institutions of the federal center (and a similar separation was subsequently adopted for the states' governmental institutions). Only the people could claim to be sovereign, and then only when it engaged in defining the basic rules and principles of the commonwealth: that is, when they made or amended the constitution. In America, therefore, from 1787 onwards sovereignty was enshrined in the constitution by the preamble *We the People* which transferred sovereignty from the people to the constitution. However, the very definition of *which people* did the transfer continued to be, for long, uncertain and ambiguous, at least till the Civil War of 1861–5. 'Confronted with the accusation that the "We the People" of the Preamble meant the people of a consolidated nation, Federalists explained that the states could not be enumerated without unreasonably presuming they would join; the phrase meant "We the People of the Several States", each a body politic solely accountable for the act of ratification' (Hendrickson 2003: 13).

In the European nation-states, sovereignty was deliberately embodied in the most representative institution (the legislature) so that it might be sheltered against challenges raised by internal undemocratic powers, as well as by external rival nation-states. In America, sovereignty was located in a document, the constitution (Ackerman 1991), sufficiently ambiguous for allowing different interpretations of its popular sources, and was distributed by the constitution among several institutions (the states and the federal center, and the separated governmental institutions of the latter). Thus in America, at the federal center, an indirectly elected President and (for long) Senate, a directly elected House of Representatives and an appointed judiciary share the same sovereign legitimacy, regardless of how they have been formed. They are *horizontally* equal before the constitution, while in the European nation-states no power can be considered equal to the parliament (because the latter alone represents the popular will). In Europe, sovereignty has traditionally been *parliamentary* in nature, whereas in America it has been *constitutional*. Thus, whereas in Europe the institution of the governors (the legislature) has coincided with the will of the governed (the people)—to the point that Britain (among the first European countries to constitutionalize itself) did not even bother to draw up a formal document—in America the constitution drew a clear distinction between decision-making by the governed (expressed by the constitution) and decision-making by the governors (expressed by the ordinary law) and had the former predominate over the latter.

It is important not to confuse the American separation of powers with a presidential *system*, although it has evolved in the twentieth century into a presidential *primacy* in governmental decision-making (particularly in foreign and military policy). It has not been possible to transform America into a presidential system of government because Congress has retained considerable power in the policymaking process (Polsby 2004). In a truly modern presidential system of government, as Linz (1994) points out, the president is a *predominant* governmental actor, not just a *pre-eminent* one as he came to be in post–World War II America (again particularly in regard to foreign and military policies). The separation of powers system resembles a competitive market in which separated but equal branches (Jones 1997, 1999) cannot acquire monopoly, although in different historical periods one of them may have the edge over the other. In fact, America's is a system of separated government which has manifested diverse institutional *pre-eminences* during its more than two centuries of democratic history (Fabbrini 1999*a*). Between the foundation of the new republic and the 1920s, the legislature had primacy, but since the 1930s that primacy has progressively shifted to the executive. Yet, presidential primacy has been significantly curbed and especially so in the period between 1968 and 2000, when two opposed political-party majorities formed in the Congress and in the presidency (the so-called period of *divided government*, the only exceptions being 1977–80 and 1993–4, and to some extent 1981–6, when the Republicans controlled the presidency and the Senate). Presidential primacy was thus dramatically reimposed by the terrorist attacks of September 11, 2001, to the point that during the *unified government* period of 2003–6 many observers talked of a presidential domination (and not pre-eminence) of the federal institutions (Rudalevige 2005). However, the mid-term congressional elections of 2006, forming a legislative majority different from the presidential one in both chambers, have brought back the divided government of the previous period, with its plausible implications of curbing presidential ambitions to dominate.

Thus, while one may talk of a *government* in regard to the European fusion of powers, the term cannot be applied to the American separation of powers. In America, the 'government' is constituted by the institutional interaction among the House, the Senate (i.e. the two branches of Congress), and the President (and even the courts, as I will argue below), whereas in Europe it is represented by a specific institution at the summit of the parliamentary structure. For this reason, I shall use the concept of 'government' when dealing with European systems, and that of 'executive' when analyzing the role of the American president.

3.2. The Logic of Separation and Fusion of Governmental Powers

3.2.1. *Politics and the Judiciary*

In America, the Philadelphia constitution introduced a new concept of democracy: a *dualist democracy*, which 'distinguishes between two different decisions that may be made . . . The first is the decision (made) by the . . . people; the second by their government. Decisions by the people occur rarely . . . Decisions made by the government occur daily' (Ackerman 1991: 6). The first decision concerns definition of the constitutional rules; the second, definition of the courses of action within those rules. No ruler is above the constitution, because no ruler can be above the people. But nor can the people be above the constitution, because they can become a People only through the constitution. '(T)he supremacy of the constitution is . . . presupposed not only over all branches of government, but also over the people themselves' (Preuss 1996: 21). While a monist democracy 'requires the grant of plenary lawmaking authority to the winners of the last general elections—so long . . . as the election was conducted under free and fair ground rules and the winners don't try to prevent the next scheduled round of electoral challenges' (Ackerman 1991: 8), a dualist democracy not only constrains the law-making authority, giving judges the power to ascertain the constitutionality of laws (a power of *judicial review* jealously protected by the Supreme Court), but it also distributes that law-making authority among different rulers, some endowed with electoral, and others with nonelectoral, legitimacy. 'Rather than granting a power monopoly to a single, popularly elected House of Representatives,

Americans tolerate a great deal of insubordination from branches whose electoral connection is suspect or nonexistent.' (Ackerman 1991: 8).

In America, since the celebrated *Marbury* v. *Madison* decision of 1803, the Supreme Court has exercised its power to conduct *judicial review*: that is, to evaluate the constitutionality of all the acts of the legislatures at both the federal and state level. Through the power of judicial review, 'any judge of any court, in any case, at any time, at the behest of any litigant party, has the power to declare a law unconstitutional' (Shapiro and Stone Sweet 1994: 400). Judicial review empowers the judiciary, and the Supreme Court at its summit, 'to measure the acts of Congress, the action of the executive and the laws and practices of the states against the Constitution and to invalidate those that conflict with the requirements of that basic national character' (Biskupic and Witt 1997: 275). Of course, one may criticize such power, either because it gives an unelected body the possibility to strike down legislation enacted by elected representatives (Dahl 1957) or because 'whoever is assigned to interpret a text to some degree makes it' (Shapiro 2002: 178). Judicial review is a process of juridical construction of the constitution; it is a kind of interpretative activity which is no different from law-making. The courts, and the Supreme Court especially, are policymaking bodies which influence the activities of the legislature and the executive, either directly (by striking down their acts) or indirectly (by soliciting them to take prior consideration of their views before drafting legislation). Although it is uncertain whether the American constitutional founders would have accepted this evolution of judicial power, it is certain that 'the upshot of their work was that in the guise of reviewing the constitutionality of state and congressional actions or inactions, the federal judiciary would later engage in what ... could ... be called judicial policy-making—or, if you like, judicial legislation' (Dahl 2001: 19).

It is important not to confuse (American) *judicial review*, celebrated by the early-nineteenth-century Supreme Court ruling, with (European) *constitutional review*, which was introduced into most European constitutions in the second half of the twentieth century. In Europe, even when (after World War II) the need for constitutional review of the acts of the parliament was recognized, the power was assigned exclusively to a special court (the constitutional court) consisting of both judges and political appointees. Moreover, the jurisdiction of this court was restricted to deal with conflicts between public institutions, and it did not extend to encompass those between public institutions and citizens (as in America). In no European nation-state has the principle of the judiciary's subordination to the legislature ever been questioned. In short, in Europe, the 'judiciaries do not possess jurisdiction over the constitution' (Stone Sweet 2000: 33) because this jurisdiction has been allocated to a special constitutional court obliged to operate in a specific legal space which is neither judicial nor political. By giving equal legitimacy to the executive, legislative, and judicial branches of government vis-à-vis the constitution, the American system of the separation of powers makes judicial review possible. 'In contrast', writes Stone Sweet (2000: 32), 'the subordination of the work of the judiciary to that of the legislature is a foundational principle of civil law systems, and therefore of Continental constitutional law'. This is why

European judges may not invalidate or refuse to apply a statute (legislation) as unconstitutional. From 1780 in Germanic states and from 1791 in France, for example, the prohibition of judicial review has been proclaimed in written constitutions, and the penal codes established penalties for any transgression. The paradigmatic statement of this prohibition is the French law of 16 August 1790, which remains in force today, and which has never been violated. (Stone Sweet 2000: 32–3)

Moreover, whereas the American constitution stands at the apex of a hierarchy of legal norms which judges must protect, European constitutional laws are 'formally detached from the hierarchy of laws which European judges are otherwise responsible for applying and defending' (Stone Sweet 2000: 33).

Post–World War II Europe thus found a way to adapt the principle of judicial review to its tradition of parliamentary sovereignty. It did so firstly by assigning exclusive and final constitutional jurisdiction to constitutional courts, thereby *preventing the judiciary from engaging in review as in America*; secondly by restricting the powers of constitutional courts to the settlement of constitutional disputes, *not of judicial disputes as well, as is the case of the American Supreme Court*; and thirdly by formally detaching constitutional courts from both the judiciary and the legislature, *contrary to America, where the Supreme Court is the apex of the judicial system*. In sum, in Europe 'ordinary courts remain bound by the supremacy of the statute (legislation), while constitutional judges are charged with preserving the supremacy of the constitution' (Stone Sweet 2000: 34). This European model of constitutional review, which has been largely inspired by the works of the Austrian constitutional scholar Hans Kelsen (especially 1928), recognizes that *legislative authority* in postauthoritarian Europe must clearly conform with a constitutional law as well. Nevertheless, this recognition has stopped short of giving constitutional power to judges. The Kelsenian model of constitutional review, unlike the Madisonian model, 'could be easily attached to the parliamentary based architecture of the state' (Kelsen 1928: 37).

In Europe, the institutionalization of a horizontal structure of governmental power (i.e. a system of separate but equal branches) has always been inconceivable. The struggle against royal absolutism led—albeit at different times (in England at the end of the 1600s, in France at the end of the 1700s) to the supremacy of the legislature; or in other words, to the assertion that only the parliament has the ultimate power to decide (i.e. the decision-making primacy of parliament). After all, when it becomes necessary to combat a concentrated power it is difficult not to produce an alternative power that is equally concentrated. The parliament thus came to supplant the king but preserved the unitary character of public power. Although the main functions of that power were subsequently divided, the legislative function had necessarily to be regarded as pre-eminent with respect to both government and judicial powers—in the sense that the government has since then been unable to act without the support of parliament (or of the majority of its members), and also in the sense that judicial power has never been able to raise an overt challenge to the supremacy of the legislature, given that the latter could always claim a popular legitimacy entirely (and necessarily) absent from judicial activity (in no European country are judges elected by the citizens, and they constitute a corps of public functionaries with its internal career structure). Preuss (1995: 6) remarks that 'until our day the French concept of constitutionalism has not embraced the institution of judicial review, i.e., the control of the constitutionality of an enacted law through the judiciary'.

3.2.2. Checks and Balances and Parliamentary Supremacy

Whereas in the course of the nineteenth century (Vile 1967: 210), 'in England and France the theory of the balanced constitution was to be transformed into a theory of parliamentary government. [On the contrary]...in the United States...it had been transformed into something uniquely American', that is, into a system of separated government. While Europe has gradually shifted to a fusion of powers and a separation of functions, America has moved in the opposite direction. Since the beginnings of the federal system (inaugurated by the second constitution of 1787), America has endeavored to separate powers but to combine functions (Huntington 1968). Thus, the constitution has divided the legislature in two separated branches (Senate and House of Representatives), in their turn separated from the executive (the President), separated because each of them has been endowed with distinct electoral bases and their activity has been subjected to differing time constraints. However, for a large part of the nineteenth century, this institutional separation was bridged by the states' political parties' role. Through their political parties, the states continued to keep under control federal public authorities. The states' political parties organized the election for the House of Representatives (comprising representatives of the country's electoral districts and elected for two years); they influenced the selection of the senators (two senators from each state elected for six years, with one-third of the senators concluding their mandate every two years in coincidence with the House of Representatives' mandate, although until the mid-nineteenth century some were selected in off years) by the states' legislatures (and subsequently organized their direct election since 1913 on the basis of the Seventeenth Amendment); and they affected the selection of the Great Electors of the President, who remains in office for four years,[1] first through their control of many states' legislatures (which had initially to choose the Great Electors of the state) and then through the organization of the process for their direct election. Even the federal judiciary, represented by the Supreme Court (constituted since the Circuit Judges Act of 1869 by nine members whose tenure is lifelong) and lower federal courts, appointed by the President on confirmation by the Senate, was affected by states' political parties, whose leaders were able to mediate between presidential and senatorial (i.e. states' party leaders) preferences.

Notwithstanding the role of (nineteenth century states') political parties in connecting federal governmental institutions, the structural incentives have continued to favor their separation. The three powers (House of Representatives, Senate, and President) have been able to maintain substantial independence from each other primarily because of the constitutional guarantees which have protected them. The President does not require the confidence of Congress, or of its majority, in order to act. Nor does he have the power to dissolve the legislature, unlike many heads of state (presidents or monarchs) in the post–World War II parliamentary democracies,[2] because the mandate of each institution is constitutionally set. Free from the need to support the President, the Congress may pursue its own institutional interests, different from those of the President. Of course, in order to avert a permanent deadlock of governmental activity, this separation of powers has had to be moderated by a sharing of functions. By means of the principle of checks and balances, the framers of the federal constitution (and Madison in particular) introduced a mechanism which made the separation of powers workable (Polsby 1986). Thus the President has the power of veto over laws approved by the Congress, but his veto can be neutralized by the latter if there is a majority vote of two-thirds in favor of the same law in both chambers (Spitzer 1988). Although the President has the power to appoint members of his administration, or federal judges, these appointments must be approved by a Senate majority. At the same time, the President may conclude treaties with foreign countries, but they can only become the law of the land if approved by a qualified majority in the Senate (two-thirds of the senators present). In short, in America, the system of checks and balances induces the actors in control of the separated institutions to cooperate with each other (Polsby 1997*a*), lest the decision-making process lapse into paralysis (Dahl 1994). However, this constitutional separation has been strengthened by the formation of divergent institutional interests. The distinct electoral bases and the different time frame of the institutional mandate have made the governmental institutions expression of different 'communities of interest' (Ostrom 1987), local in the case of the House of Representatives, state in the case of the Senate and national (in the twentieth century) in the case of the President. Indeed, with the declining role of states' political parties in the twentieth century, one might argue that the American system of separated government has been fully institutionalized.

A system of this kind made and continues to make no sense in the Europe of the fusion of powers. In Europe, once the supremacy of the legislature had been affirmed, the system was able to function according to a mono-centric logic because the parliament was the exclusive locus of political power, in the sense that the parliamentary majority was able to exercise that power with no need for cooperation with other institutional actors. In the fusion of powers system, voters elect the legislature and the legislature *selects* from its members the government (or cabinet), which can operate only with the (direct or indirect) confidence of the legislature. No other institutional power, including the judiciary, may challenge parliamentary supremacy. Indeed, the judiciary cannot even be properly termed a 'power'; it is mainly a public body whose institutional role is to guarantee the faithful application of the laws approved in and by the parliament. Thus, while the institutional logic of a separation of powers system is generally *horizontal*, the institutional logic of a fusion of powers system is *vertical*. The former system is antihierarchical in nature, whereas the latter inevitably has a hierarchical structure. With the broader terms of the distinction between the two governmental patterns thus defined, it is now necessary to analyze their institutionalization, the purpose being to elucidate the complexity of their historical evolution. I shall start with the American case.

3.3. The Institutionalization of the American Separated System

3.3.1. *Separated Government: America's Congressional Era*

A system of government can be called 'separated' when its institutions are separated but nevertheless share the same governmental functions. As Neustadt, the most influential scholar of the American presidency of the past generation, put it, 'the Constitutional Convention of 1787 is supposed to have created a government of "separated powers". It did nothing of the sort. Rather it created a government of separated institutions *sharing* power' (Neustadt 1990: 29). Separation is possible because the principal institutions of government (in this case, the presidency and Congress) are endowed with both reciprocal independence and autonomous legitimacy (which were therefore the bases for their respective processes of institutionalization). Different institutional equilibria have arisen between the central (federal) governmental institutions so that it is now standard practice to call the long nineteenth-century phase of the legislature's pre-eminence 'congressional government', and the subsequent post-1930s phase of executive pre-eminence 'presidential government'.

However, despite the concern of the American founding fathers to prevent abuses of legislative power, and despite their decision to counter-balance the legislature with an executive independent of it, throughout the republic's first century Congress maintained its hold on governmental power (Dahl 1976). This congressional pre-eminence allowed the states to control federal power, through their crucial role in electing (in the case of the House of Representatives) and selecting (in the case of the Senate) their members. The contradiction between the two roles of the President (on the one hand, head of the executive and, on the other, head of the state) was resolved in favor of his ceremonial role as the head of state. This outcome was also made possible by a narrow, generally accepted, interpretation of the constitution which resolved that the Congress was the first branch of government. The President was thus prevented from transforming himself into an outright popular leader—to the extent, in fact, that both public and governmental actors regarded the President as invested with less power than the Speaker of the House of Representatives, less indeed than certain especially influential senators (Young 1966).

Thus the presidencies of Thomas Jefferson (1801–8), Andrew Jackson (1829–36), and Abraham Lincoln (1861–5)—which are generally considered to be examples of authoritative presidencies—were the exceptions rather than the rule during the first century of the republic. As well as being affirmations of particularly strong personalities, they were the outcome of extraordinary periods in the nation's political life: of partisan conflicts in the first case; of social conflicts in the second; and of state conflicts in the third. They are important because they demonstrate the decision-making vulnerability of Congress under extraordinary political conditions. Simultaneously, however, this importance was circumscribed by the inability of these presidencies to establish themselves as precedents for later ones in periods of more ordinary political conditions. Furthermore, the system for the election of the two bodies of the government had features such that Congress (and the House of Representatives in particular) was apparently the sole body of representation, in that its legitimacy resided in popular will, while the President was obliged to resort to the constitution in order to justify his institutional salience. This situation strengthened the institutional interest of the legislature at the expense of the institutional interest of the executive. Congress employed two main devices of internal organization in order to translate this representativeness into governmental capacity (Lowi and Ginsberg 1990): the committee system and the party caucus system.

With respect to the former, by 1825 both the House and Senate had established a system of standing committees which enabled Congress not only to give more rational organization to its representative activities, but also to reinforce its governmental activities. For this reason, congressional government, which started to consolidate from the 1820s onwards, should be more appropriately described (as Woodrow Wilson wrote in 1885, now 1956: 56) 'as a government by the Standing Committees of Congress'. The party caucus system evolved in parallel with the committee system, and each reinforced the other. Right from the first session of the first Congress, members began to form coalitions on the chief policy problems of the moment, doing so around two distinct groupings of preferences which then organized themselves into permanent caucuses. From this point of view, one may assert, like Lowi and Ginsberg (1990: 191), that 'for the first century or more of the Republic, America had literally a party government in Congress'. The point of linkage between committee government and party caucus government was, throughout the century, the Speaker of the House of Representatives; and it was the competition among the parliamentary caucuses for control of the Speakership that transformed the latter, especially between 1890 and 1910 (the period of the so-called partisan Speakerships of Thomas Brackett Reed and Joseph Cannon), into a substantial seat of institutional power (Davidson, Webb Hammond, and Smock 1998; Polsby 1986: 116–19). In sum, as Peters has written (1997: 89), 'the power of the partisan speakers... was set against the weakness of the presidency that they confronted'.

Between the 1900s and World War II, congressional primacy within the separated government was severely undermined by two basic, interrelated processes: the nationalization of American politics and the democratization of the federal institutions (see Chapter 5). These were processes, therefore, that were reinforced by the progressive delegation of legislative powers from Congress to the presidency. When they were complete, the nature of the institutional innovation that they had engendered became evident. The reflections of Woodrow Wilson are particularly significant in this regard. Twenty-three years after publication of his key work, *Congressional Government* (1885, now 1956), Wilson, now in his role as a political leader, published a series of lectures in which he conducted a detailed critique of the government by legislature which he had previously advocated (and which he had eulogized to the point that he proposed its full ripening into British parliamentary government). Thus, in *Constitutional Government in the United States* (1908), Wilson delineated the new tasks imposed by historical change on the executive and its leader. In this unprecedented context: (*a*) only the presidency could achieve the administrative cohesion which ensured efficient government intervention in the market; (*b*) only the president could put himself forward as the representational focus of national interests and thus as a symbol of national unity, because he was not beholden to any particular group or section. And it was Wilson again, but this time as President, who arrogated himself to the role of the country's highest political representative. As he said in his first inaugural address (1913): 'We know our task to be no mere task of politics but a task which shall search us through and through, whether we be able to understand our time and the need of our people, whether we be indeed their spokesmen and interpreters.' (Tulis 1987: 135–36).

World War I and the overwhelming crisis of 1929 accelerated—after the interlude of the traditionalist presidencies of Harding (1921–4), Coolidge (1925–8), and Hoover (1929–32)—the process of empowerment of the executive vis-à-vis the legislature (Toinet 1989). This increased role of

63

the President vis-à-vis the Congress also meant a reduction of the states' influence over federal policy. Of course, this process was neither linear nor devoid of contradictions: the first two presidencies of F. D. Roosevelt (1933–6 and 1937–40) were constantly marked (until one year before the outbreak of World War II) by conflicts with Congress but especially with the Supreme Court. Yet, as Shaw (1987: 1) remarked, '1933 is more than a convenient landmark. It is widely considered to mark a significant break with the past for the presidency and therefore for the American political system. It marks the beginning of the modern presidency.' In sum, at the end of the 1930s, the American government had established the pre-eminence of the President. The dominant role that the country came to perform in international relations during and after World War II consolidated new power relations which worked in favor of the executive within the institutions of the American system of separated government. Throughout the nineteenth century, the international dimension had exerted a limited (though not negligible, Katznelson and Shefter 2002) influence on America: geographical distance from Europe, the militarily weak challenge represented by the Native Americans, and the protection of the British Navy had prevented any pressure for the centralization of political power and its control by the executive. Thus, World War II was a veritable turning point in the country's history because of the legacy that it left behind: America established itself as a world military power which soon came into conflict with the rival Soviet Union. The outbreak of the Cold War between 1946 and 1948 further increased the country's external involvement and, institutionally, the presidency's decision-making pre-eminence over the Congress. The net result of this process was a deepening of the federal separated government.

In sum, at the end of fifty years of change, the functional relationship between the two institutions of government was the reverse of what it had been before. The decision-making primacy of the presidency and the decision-making retrenchment of Congress were unequivocal. Nonetheless, this functional reversal brought with it distinct institutional changes. Although the primacy of the presidency led to the rapid acceleration of its institutional development (in the form of unprecedented organizational expansion), the reduced power of Congress by no means slowed down its institutional evolution (indeed, Congress accelerated its institutionalization, Polsby 1968). Since Congress is prima facie a representative institution, the reduction of its decision-making role could not alter its relation with the electors (or *external nature*). The effect of Congress's retrenchment was that it was compelled to adjust its *internal nature* (i.e. to change the distribution of power and its functioning) but not to alter its identity as a representative body. The presidency, by contrast, underwent radical change in its identity (its *external nature*) as a result of its newly acquired political representativeness, a representativeness which was the foundation for its ascent to governmental primacy. This change, however, simultaneously induced the presidency to embark on enormous organizational development which altered its *internal nature*. Hence, we must refer to Congress in terms of *evolution* and to the presidency in terms of *transformation*. In short, in the two centuries of the republic, as Mezey (1989: 48) has aptly observed, the presidency has been transformed 'into an institution radically different from the one described in the Constitution, an institution that would be barely recognizable to those who designed it... the Congress, in contrast, although also a very different and more prominent institution today than it was two hundred years ago, remains in its essential aspects what it was then: a legislature, with the basic structure and format that have always characterized such institutions'.

3.3.2. *Institutionalizing Different Governmental Primacies in America*

Although the rise of the presidency was driven by processes of environmental change and institutional democratization of the system of government between the 1890s and World War II, these processes encountered no impediment in the constitution. It should be stressed that the indefiniteness of the constitutional formulation of presidential powers provided fertile terrain for that transformation. 'Indefiniteness', however, should not be taken to mean an absence of definition; it should instead be understood in the literal sense as the generic delineation of presidential powers and privileges. Not coincidentally, one of the twentieth century's foremost scholars of the presidency has called article II of the constitution, the one devoted to the definition and allocation of executive power, 'the most loosely drawn chapter of the Constitution' (Corwin 1957: 2). This constitutional feature of the executive proved crucial for the development of presidential government for two principal reasons. First, it did not obstruct the President's demands to endow his actions with greater governmental force. Second, it justified Congress's renunciation of its previously acquired governmental pre-eminence. Thus, the presidential government inaugurated in the 1930s should be seen as resulting from the interaction between presidential demands and congressional delegations.

The Philadelphia delegates certainly wanted an independent executive, but as evinced by the written record of their debates (Farrand 1966), none of them, not even Hamilton, wanted an institutionally dominant executive. A dominant executive, indeed, would have jeopardized the equilibrium among asymmetrical states. Although they agreed in principle on the need to defend the executive against the hegemonic purposes of the legislature (which is why they gave veto power to the former), they were, however, much less in agreement on how this defensive veto should be defined. At the Philadelphia Constitutional Convention of 1787, they settled for maintaining the British Tudorian experience (the only one they knew directly) by separating the executive from the legislature, although they replaced the hereditary king with an elected President. This is why Huntington (1968: 93–139) could argue some time ago that America perpetuated a fusion of functions and a separation of powers when Europe was beginning to move in exactly the opposite direction. Furthermore, considering that the first President was certain to be George Washington, the Philadelphia delegates decided, consciously or otherwise, to postpone definition of the terms of the presidential office, placing their trust in the guidance provided by the hero of the war against the English. As a consequence, the final draft of the constitution was not formally concerned with constraining the President to legally prescribed behavior (Dahl 1976: Ch. 10).

This explains the uncertainty of the text that engendered the extra-textual history of the American presidency. The presidency transformed itself into the pre-eminent institution precisely because its chief actors, the presidents, were able to exploit an internal default condition (Ostrom E. 1991) which was particularly advantageous to them. There was, therefore, nothing deterministic in this transformation. The form that it took resulted from the choices made by the chief players in the game of government, by the presidents first and foremost; but it did so within the system of constraints and opportunities as it was institutionalized through previous politico-historical development. The transformation came about without constitutional traumas—though with fierce political conflicts—precisely because of the nature of these constraints: presidential choices were constrained, not by positive legal prescriptions ('an individual action is permissible only if there exists a law which expressly authorizes it'), but by a general principle of legality ('an individual action is permitted unless there is a law which expressly and unequivocally forbids it').

The most important aspect of the constitution's indefiniteness was that it did not set rigid behavioral restraints on Congress and President. The latter consequently took advantage of favorable conditions for the promotion of both the extensive (i.e. the organizational enlargement) and the intensive (i.e. the deepening of jurisdiction) institutionalization of the executive—and hence also to promote his personal fortunes. More precisely, the presidents took advantage of emergency conditions in both domestic and foreign affairs to show, in Rossiter's words (1948: 218), that 'if the Constitution is rigid, the executive power therein stated...is not', and that 'although much of the President's power to act decisively in emergencies has proceeded from Congress, strong Presidents have grounded most of their unusual actions in the broad terms of Article II'. Thus, since the 1930s, the growing decision-making role of the President has implied the inevitable development of the Presidency. It is for this reason that one can appropriately use the term 'presidency' only with reference to the twentieth century: not by chance, the constitution makes no mention of 'presidency' and invariably uses the term 'President'. Nevertheless, the increased representative capacity of the latter could never have been converted into increased governmental capacity without the institutional development of the former. Hence it was the increased influence of the President that led to the development of the presidency; and consequently, it was the development of the presidency that led to presidential pre-eminence. In other words, without the institutionalization of the presidency *qua* office the affirmation of the President *qua* personification of that office could never have come about.

In sum, the indefiniteness of executive power gave rise to constitutional flexibility, enabling the shift from congressional to presidential pre-eminence without a formal constitutional amendment (with all its potential for conflict) being necessary. In fact, the very same actors that supported the strengthening of the President, the New Dealers, 'rejected the traditional form of an amendment' (Ackerman 1991: 51), given the difficulty of successfully completing the amending process especially in the federal Senate (where several Southern senators enjoyed positions of great power as chairmen of important committees). After all, the crucial Thirteenth (1865) and Fourteenth (1868) amendments (crucial because they increased federal authority vis-à-vis the authority of the states) were accepted and thus approved by the Southern states only because of Congress's threat (i.e. Northern states' senators and representatives) to suspend indefinitely the election of their (Southern) senators and representatives to the federal legislature (House of Representatives and Senate); a threat difficult to use more than once. Consequently, the new institutional equilibrium came to be formalized by judicial rulings rather than by a formal constitutional change. As Ackerman (1991: 51–2) pointed out, the supporters of presidential government 'relied on the New Deal Court to elaborate their new activist vision through a series of transformative opinions'.

3.3.3. *Separated Government: America's Presidential Era*

The constitutional area which best illustrates the indefiniteness of the constraints on presidential behavior is that of the executive's so-called 'inherent powers'. This issue has generated cyclical conflicts between governmental institutions: indeed, the ink was not yet dry on the constitution when the theory of the executive's inherent powers began to divide the political elite who had written it. The heated debate between Hamilton and Jefferson (especially during the last year of the first Washington presidency) centered precisely on the definition of the default condition on presidential behavior. Whereas Hamilton claimed that if the constitution did not prohibit the President from doing something, then he could do it, Jefferson was convinced that this contention reflected a monarchical vision of the presidency.

The singular aspect of the affair, however, was the behavior of Jefferson (Banning 1983: ch. 5). As Secretary of State, he had strongly opposed Hamilton's (then Secretary of the Treasury) economic and financial policies intended to increase the role of the federal government in promoting industrial development because he considered them monarchical (as Jefferson wrote to James Madison on March 15, 1789, he was convinced that 'there are some among us who would now establish a monarchy', now in Koch and Peden 1944: 464). But then as President (1801–8), he had no qualms about resorting to the same theory of inherent powers to justify his decisions in foreign policy in particular (Tucker and Hendrickson 1990). Although Jefferson's practice confirmed Hamilton's theory, and although particularly tenacious presidents were able to expand their power on other matters, throughout the nineteenth century conditions were anything but favorable for such expansion. Not until the twentieth century did it become clear that although (the federal) Hamilton had been defeated on the doctrinal front, he took full revenge on (the republican) Jefferson (and Madison) along the historical dimension. All presidents after Theodore Roosevelt and Woodrow Wilson, and especially F. D. Roosevelt, exploited the new domestic and international conditions to justify an exercise of powers which, although unwritten, 'came with the territory'.

Hamilton's revenge owed a great deal to judicial power. Two rulings by the Supreme Court were of special importance in creating the legal premises for this recourse (Fisher 1997). With the first, *In re Neagle* (1890), the Court gave broad interpretation to the executive duties of the President in domestic policy, while with the second, *United States* v. *Curtiss-Wright Corporation* (1936), it ruled that the President was the only federal organ of foreign policy. The implications of the theory of inherent powers were not only external, although it is in the area of foreign policy that modern presidents have most forcefully asserted their freedom from the institutional constraints of separated government. And here one may cite their increasingly frequent recourse to two executive instruments par excellence: executive orders (in domestic policy) and executive agreements (in foreign policy).

A forceful challenge was raised against these presidential claims by the *Steel Seizure* case of 1952, when the Supreme Court acted to restrict the expansion of presidential prerogatives. On that occasion the Court quashed Truman's executive order bringing the steel industry under the control of the federal government—a measure that Truman sought to justify on the grounds that it was necessary for the country's war requirements in Korea. The repeal, however, was unable to halt presidential greed by forestalling use of the executive order. The same applied to executive agreements in foreign policy; here too, the Supreme Court handed down an important decision, although this one operated in reverse. In *United States* v. *Pink* (1942), the Court recognized as constitutional the government's decision to stipulate agreements, and not treaties, with foreign countries. This was a decision that the executive found much to its liking because it could now evade the control procedures that the Senate applied to treaties, and the President now had unprecedented opportunities for autonomous action in foreign policy.

Regarding domestic politics, the main institutional impetus to presidential government came when the Budget and Accounting Act was approved in 1921 (Wildavsky 1988: 60–3). This law symbolizes the process whereby powers were delegated from Congress to the presidency; a process, as we have seen, engendered by the constitution's indefiniteness regarding the executive's legislative responsibility. Indeed, section 3 of article II runs: 'He shall from time to time give to the Congress information of the state of the Union, and recommend to their consideration such measures as he shall judge necessary and expedient.' This formulation has been used to justify diametrically opposed forms of presidential behavior. Throughout the nineteenth century, it was used by Congress to restrict the President to a wholly secondary role in legislation. During that period, presidents did not even bother to go to Capitol Hill to inform the legislators about the 'state of the Union', they instead sent a written message, which was read out by the Speaker of the House of Representatives and the Vice President in his capacity as chairman of the Senate, or by their respective clerks. During the twentieth century, by contrast, it has been Congress that has urged the President to assume, on the basis of this formulation, powers of legislative initiative which include setting the parameters of the federal budget (Mervin 1987).

Congress certainly did not renounce its essential power—that is, the power that derived from 'holding the purse-strings'—when it passed this law. Moreover, congressional delegation of powers to the President was constrained by a sort of 'legislative veto' inserted in many congressional acts, thanks to which the Congress preserved the possibility of taking back those powers if abused by the President. Although the Supreme Court ruled the legislative veto unconstitutional, in *Equal Employment Opportunity Commission, Appellant* v. *Westinghouse Electric Corp* of 1983, the Congress has continued to approve laws with some functional equivalent to a legislative veto. Presidential budget proposals nevertheless defined the initial terms of the exercise of such power. And more generally, the law formalized a role for the President (one unprecedented in American history) as legislative leader in the absence of which it would be improper to talk of presidential government (Blond and Fleisher 1990: ch. 4). Furthermore, the affirmation of this new presidential role led to reinterpretation of the old instruments available to the President: in particular, his power of veto (Spitzer 1988). Use of the presidential veto (both the regular one and the so-called 'pocket veto')[3] increased dramatically (635 and 9 overridden by Congress) with F. D. Roosevelt. It continued with Truman (250 and 12 overridden) and Eisenhower (181 and 2 overridden); and then, with subsequent presidents, it became the executive's routine weapon of belligerence against the legislature (an average of 9 vetoes per year in the period 1960–99 and an average of 0.82 per year overridden in the period) (Office of the Clerk of the House: http://clerk.house.gov, 2005, my calculation). This situation has changed radically with President George W. Bush, who between 2001 and 2006 only had to veto one congressional act (the Stem Cell Research Enhancement Act 2006).

Under the impact of nationalization and democratization, presidential government signified 'President as head of government' as opposed to the 'President as head of state' of the congressional government period. With the advent of presidential government the President used his prerogatives (military, judicial, and diplomatic) as head of state to justify the redefinition, to his advantage, of his prerogatives (executive, military, and legislative) as head of government. In short, the dual constitutional connotation of the President was resolved in favor of his role as head of the executive in presidential government, and in favor of his role as head of the state in congressional government. The shift from congressional to presidential pre-eminence did not challenge the stability of the constitutional system also because, when it did happen, that system was already fully legitimate. But certainly it deepened the institutionalization of the American system of separated government. In fact, the strengthening of the presidency without the institutional weakening of the Congress brought the separation of powers system to full maturity. This system has shown that the executive and the legislature stand in a positive-sum relation, not a zero-sum one as in a fusion of powers system, owing to the independent electoral basis and different time frame of their institutional role.

3.4. The Institutionalization of European Fusion of Powers Systems

3.4.1. *Fusion of Powers Systems in Europe: The Semi-Presidential Variant*

The European experience of the institutionalization of governmental patterns has been radically different from America's: not only because none of the European nation-states (with the exception of Switzerland) has ever adopted a separation of powers system, but also because the European nation-states have undergone a different institutional evolution. The liberal experience of some European nation-states in the second half of the nineteenth century was severely hampered by restrained popular participation in the affairs of state, to the point that none of those states (not even Britain) can be properly defined as democratic. The democratization of the post–World War I period was thus accompanied by the instability of the democratic regime—an instability which degenerated into collapse in many Continental European nation-states during the second half of the 1920s and 1930s (Rose 1996). Certainly, in much of Europe the rule of law was the norm throughout the nineteenth century, but popular participation was prevented by a variety of legal instruments. Also the liberal European nation-states retained paternalistic (or even authoritarian) features which protected the decision-making process against popular scrutiny. It was not until the end of World War II that Western Europe saw the general adoption of the principle of universal suffrage and the formation of a modern party system (with the significant exception of Portugal and Spain, which remained authoritarian until 1974 in the former case, and 1976 in the latter, and of Greece, which experienced an authoritarian resurgence between 1967 and 1974).

However, the newly reconstituted political regimes of Continental Europe, as well as those never interrupted by authoritarian coups, such as Britain, continued their own traditions of the fusion of powers. Germany, occupied by the Allied forces, designed a new democratic regime consistent with its parliamentary past, although it was rationalized and given a federal framework. The dramatic failure in 1933 of the Weimar Republic, established after World War I, had warned the German as well as other European political elites that both a stable government and ordered party competition must be guaranteed. The former was achieved through institutional devices such as the constructive vote of no-confidence (which entails that a government can be dismissed only if there is an immediate alternative), the latter through various electoral devices such as the imposition of a threshold for representation in parliament. Thus, after World War II, the Western European nation-states (with the exceptions already mentioned) institutionalized democratic governmental patterns coherent with their unified concept of sovereignty.

However, important variances can be discerned in the way that the fusion of powers system became institutionalized in Europe. Whilst the majority of the Western European nation-states came to adopt a parliamentary system of government, some of them (most significantly France of the Fifth Republic inaugurated in 1958, Elgie 2003) have adopted the governmental system of 'semi-presidentialism',[4] which represents the most significant institutional innovation introduced (Elgie 2004) in the European fusion of powers model. As said, Fifth Republic France is the most representative example of the semi-presidential system. A system of this kind is also generally referred to as 'dual executive' (Poulard 1990) in that the government is headed by both a President of the Republic and a Prime Minister. The President of the Republic is directly elected by universal suffrage in a national college and with a majoritarian electoral system, on the basis of which, if none of the candidates obtains the absolute majority in the first ballot, a run-off is held between the two candidates receiving the most votes in the first round. The election of the President is held separately from the election of the legislature (and, until the reform of October 2, 2000, it was also temporally and not only institutionally distinct, in that the presidential mandate lasted seven years and the parliamentary mandate five years, whereas after the reform both mandates will last five years). The legislature, too, is elected by means of a majoritarian/uninominal electoral system on the basis of which, if no candidate in the various uninominal districts obtains an absolute majority of votes in the first ballot, a run-off election is held between the candidates obtaining more than 12.5 percent (initially 5%) of the votes in their district. The President of the Republic is responsible for appointing the Prime Minister, who, however, must be supported by the National Assembly. In short, the President of the Republic presides over a government which, given the mechanism of the legislature's potential vote of no-confidence in the Prime Minister, must nevertheless seek parliamentary approval (Duverger 1986).

The executive is dual in nature because both the President of the Republic and the Prime Minister are vested with management of the affairs of government. However, this dualism has not proved easy to manage in practice, because since the second half of the 1980s parliamentary elections have tended to produce a political majority different from the one that previously supported the President of the Republic.[5] Hence the functioning of the system has depended on the political consonance or dissonance between the presidential and parliamentary majority. In the former case, the semi-presidential system has given pre-eminence to the President of the Republic (by virtue of his direct popular investiture); in the latter, it has given pre-eminence to the Prime Minister, but not across all policy areas (foreign and military policies were long considered *reserved domains* of the President of the Republic). Thus, in a context of political consonance, executive dualism has been significantly neutralized, to the point that the Prime Minister has behaved more as chief of staff to the President than as an autonomous political actor. Checks on the government headed by the President have been guaranteed by the parliamentary opposition, although the popular legitimacy of the President has made the government much stronger than any opposition. By contrast, in a context of political dissonance, the dualism has been institutionalized within the executive as a form of 'cohabitation' between government and opposition (Elgie 2001). In this case, the Prime Minister, as the expression of the parliamentary majority, has had the legitimacy to assert with the force of constitutional law his or her prerogatives as head of the government, but these prerogatives have not been extended to the point that the President of the Republic has been confined to a ceremonial role. This system is therefore engineered by confrontation between government and opposition, although this confrontation may take different forms in different political contexts.

Because semi-presidentialism ultimately recognizes only the legislature as empowered to make laws, the double legitimacy of its executive should not be confused with the double legitimacy of executive and legislature in systems with separation of powers. Consider the power of veto: whereas in America the President exercises formal power of veto over legislation approved by Congress, nothing comparable is available to the President of the semi-presidential French Republic. His powers of veto are limited and are entirely administrative or procedural in nature (i.e. they cannot be exercised vis-à-vis legislation). In sum, the semi-presidential system is essentially characterized by a single sovereignty (Duverger 1986). In this system, the legislature is the sole repository of popular sovereignty, although it is not the sole source of legitimacy for the government because this it must share with the voters who elect the President of the Republic. Since its inception in 1958, this system of government has been loudly contested by important sectors of the French political elite and public opinion. In the 1960s and 1970s, the Socialists and Communists considered it as akin to a *coup d'état permanent* (Mitterrand 1964), because it was introduced against the will of the parliament of the Fourth Republic by its main architect and beneficiary, Charles de Gaulle, following his appointment as head of government in the critical summer of 1958 when France was paralyzed by a dramatic civil war in its Algerian colony. However, when a conservative President was replaced by a Socialist in the presidential election of 1981, those protests subsided. That election, in fact, demonstrated that the governmental system could work in the interests of the main political parties, so that its consolidation became irreversible. After being circumscribed to a few Western European nation-states, since the democratization of Eastern European nation-states this governmental system has become the most widely imitated and adopted (Elgie 1999).

3.4.2. *Fusion of Powers Systems in Europe: The Parliamentary Variants*

Significant variants were institutionalized after World War II in European parliamentary systems. These variants related institutionally to electoral and party systems, and socially to the nature of the most pronounced cleavages in each domestic society (Fabbrini 2001). These divisions sprang from the long historical process that had led to the formation of the nation-states and then to the growth of an industrial society. And they permanently conditioned the political allegiances and electoral choices of the citizens of the various domestic societies. Where the divisions within domestic society were primarily ethnic, religious, and linguistic (as in Belgium, Austria, and the Netherlands), or ideological because of the struggle between Communists and anti-Communists (as in pre-1993 Italy or in Fourth Republic France of the period 1946–58), the political elite adopted a proportional representation (PR) electoral system for the formation of the parliament which well reflected the multipolar logic of the party system. In these countries, electoral competition was not required to produce an electoral majority; on the contrary, such an outcome would have been feared by all the main groups. The institutional structure of political competition was designed so that the elites of the various parties could form a government through postelectoral negotiations. Indeed, this parliamentarianism came to be termed (Lijphart 1999) *consensual* because it fostered the consociation of the main parties at governmental level through the formation of oversized governmental coalitions. Because these societies were deeply divided in terms of group identities, the competition had to be institutionally structured so as to prevent the formation of majorities and minorities, because of distrust among the various groups, and to give all of them access to the decision-making process.

Alternation in government was and continued to be considered implausible in both ethnically and ideologically divided societies. However, their parliamentary systems organized this lack of alternation differently. Whereas the formation of grand coalition governments was feasible in ethnically divided societies, it was precluded in ideologically divided ones for geostrategic reasons. Although Communist parties were representative of large sections of electorates in the latter societies, they could not participate directly in the executive because of their strategic alliance with the Western bloc's rival superpower, the Soviet Union. Their electoral strength, however, could not be dismissed. Thus, in Italy of the 1948–93 period and in France of the Fourth Republic (1946–58), the solution found was to blur the dividing line between the parliamentary majority and the government in micro (or 'pork-barreling') legislation and frequently in the meso legislation (e.g. sectorial laws), although in the macro-legislation (foreign or economic policies) the two camps fiercely confronted each other. In sum, the Communists' amendments to the government's specific law proposals were generally accepted in parliament, so that Communists could vote with the parliamentary majority (or parts of it) on several issues, although they were not accepted into the executive (in Italy, even in the so-called 'national solidarity' period of 1976–8, the Communists were allowed to participate in the parliamentary majority but not in the government). Thus, whereas the other consensual parliamentary systems (and especially the Netherlands because of its constitutional tradition) made the government the final locus of the decision-making process, this did not happen in consensual Italy or Fourth Republic France, where parliament continued to play a role in decision-making.

The parliamentary system has functioned differently in those European societies in which domestic cleavages have been predominantly socio-economic in nature. Here, parliament has been formed by means of a political competition based on a two-party or bipolar logic. Indeed, the alternation in power (or the reasonable expectation thereof) between two alternative parties or coalitions has been the engine driving the system. A socioeconomic division does not signify cultural distrust among groups, although it may imply a radical class struggle. Parliamentarianism of this kind has been termed *majoritarian* because it produces a clear electoral majority through adoption of a strict majoritarian electoral system (as it is the case of Britain with its majoritarian, plurality, and uninominal electoral system). Yet, if this form of parliamentarianism is distinguished from the other by alternation in power of different majorities, it might be more accurately termed *competitive* (Fabbrini 1998), because governmental alternation is realized also in countries with nonmajoritarian electoral arrangements (i.e. PR electoral systems however constrained by a bipolar logic as in Germany, Sweden, Spain, and Greece) (Sartori 1996). Consensual and competitive parliamentary systems are therefore significantly distinct because they express or organize the political processes of two different kinds of societies. Indeed, their successful institutionalization in Europe after World War II was due to their capacity to organize different societies. Regular alternation in power in the competitive parliamentary systems, and the stability of the democratic regime achieved in the consensual parliamentary systems, led to the full institutionalization of each. Of course, neither of these parliamentary systems is normatively better than the other; they are merely suited to different societies.

Although the functional logic has been the same in the two parliamentary systems, it has been organized differently. If a parliamentary system is to work properly, there must be reasonable cohesion within the majority—cohesion promoted and guaranteed by a disciplined political party or a political coalition able to link the majority to its executive (Wilson 1994). In a parliamentary system, the executive depends on the confidence and support of the legislature (or better of its majority). However, the disciplined party or political coalition—which is the 'efficient secret' of parliamentarianism—has been much more effective in competitive parliamentary systems than it has in consensual ones. In the latter, the legislature's fusion with the executive has been induced by a bargaining network which comprises the leaders of the main political parties. Moreover, although the parliamentary systems of European (middle to large) nation-states were and are generally bicameral, competitive parliamentary systems have tended to stress the popular chamber's empowerment to give or remove confidence in the government, whereas consensual parliamentary systems have allocated balancing power to the second chamber or senate as well, for guaranteeing a plurality of institutional arenas in which to develop elites' negotiations. Of course, the second chamber has retained important powers also in those competitive parliamentary systems (like Germany) organized territorially along federal lines (Tsebelis and Money 1997). The differing degrees of party discipline in the two systems are thus an outcome of their differing electoral logics. In the competitive model, party discipline is the effect of an electoral process characterized by marked bipolarity. In this case, the parliamentary majority, which comprises a clearly identified electoral majority, has an interest in preserving its cohesion in order to remain in power. Moreover, voters going to the polls in the context of a two-party or bipolar party system are able to make a clear *retrospective* judgment on the government, which has not only strengthened the latter's cohesion further but also ensured its accountability to the voters.[6]

This is not the case with consensual parliamentary systems, where the government emerges after the elections as the result of a long process of negotiation among the party leaders, negotiation which is a permanent feature of the governmental game. In these systems, governments are usually reshuffled between elections because the leaders are not constrained in their choices by a clear electoral majority. The voters who go to the polls in the context of a multiparty system with a multidimensional cleavage structure tend to choose their own party on the basis of their *prospective* judgment of its capacity to represent a specific view. One may say, therefore, that while in competitive parliamentary systems voters choose the government and its opposition, this is not feasible in consensual parliamentary ones. Indeed, in the latter, the contraposition between majority and opposition may even threaten the stability of the democratic pact, in that the system can only work if all groups have guaranteed access to decision-making power (Lijphart 1999). Consequently, whereas in competitive parliamentarianism the executive has been counterbalanced by a clear opposition, this too legitimated by the bipolar logic of the electoral process, in consensual parliamentarianism the system has been guaranteed by reciprocal control among the party elites within the government itself.

3.5. Conclusion

America and Europe have institutionalized different governmental patterns. Since its constitutional beginnings, America has created a separation of powers system mitigated by a complex structure of checks and balances for inducing cooperation between the actors in control of the separated institutions (Polsby 1997*a*). This governmental system has allowed for different phases of institutional pre-eminences. The long era of congressional pre-eminence was followed by the era of presidential pre-eminence, with no formal alteration of the constitutional structure of the separated government. By contrast, the European nation-states, regardless of their internal variances, have built governmental systems based on the institutional predominance of the legislature (and thus of the government expressed by the latter's majority). However, in the French semi-presidential system, the role of the legislature in forming and supporting the government has been mitigated by the direct election of a President of the Republic empowered to codirect it with the Prime Minister representing the majority in the legislature.

These parliamentary systems are generally hierarchical, because the parliament and thus the government are the ultimate decision-making institutions, although the degree of hierarchy is higher in competitive than in consensual parliamentarianism (and it is even higher in the French semi-presidential system, especially in a context of political consonance between the parliamentary and the presidential majorities). In Europe, once the supremacy of the legislature had been affirmed, the system was able to function according to a monocentric logic: in the sense that the parliament was the exclusive center of political power, its parliamentary majority was able to exercise that power through its government, although it was constrained by the action of the opposition operating however within the parliament. In America, the horizontal structure of the governmental system has fostered a polycentric logic of functioning: in the sense that no institution is the exclusive center of political power (but decisions are taken through the interaction of concurrent majorities within each of the governmental institutions, the House of Representatives, the Senate, and the President). Consequently, whereas in the America of the separation of powers, democracy has been guaranteed by the reciprocal control exercised by separated institutions (in the congressional era by the Senate vis-à-vis the House and thus in the presidential era by Congress vis-à-vis the President), in parliamentary as well as in semi-presidential Europe, democracy has been guaranteed by the reciprocal control exercised by distinct political forces (parties or party elites). Indeed, because there is no government in America, neither is there an opposition (Ackerman 2000).

This historical difference in governmental patterns between America and Europe came to be gradually reduced in the second half of the twentieth century with the development of the European integration process and the formation of the EU. Especially after the Single European Act of 1986 and the Maastricht Treaty of 1992, the EU decision-making system came to be organized along the lines of a horizontal separation of powers among the European Council, the Council of Ministers, the Commission, and the Parliament (to which corresponded also a vertical separation of powers between Brussels and the EU member-states) much more comparable with the US governmental system of separation of powers than with the EU member-states' governmental system of fusion of powers. Certainly, pressured by the Cold War and then by the war on terrorism, America has sought to relax the constraints of the separation of powers in order to create broader margins of decision-making capacity for the President. But, although presidential power has increased dramatically in foreign and military policy, the separation of powers has continued to constrain the exercise of presidential prerogatives.

4

Alternative paths to a modern social order: territoriality, market, and welfare in America and Europe

4.1. Introduction

After having examined the formation and development of both a political and an institutional order in America and the single European nation-states, I will now analyze the building of a market economy and a welfare system (whose combination might be called a modern *social order*). Even the building of such social orders has followed different paths in America and in the European nation-states. Several factors explain why the formation of a national market was a *political* project in the European nation-states, whereas it was the outcome of a *judicial* action in America. Contrary to the European experience, America has shown that it is possible to build *a market without a state*, provided that a legal order is effectively promoted and guaranteed by the judiciary system. Throughout the nineteenth century, the institutional foundation of American federalism hindered any Hamiltonian attempt to pursue federal neomercantilist policies like those implemented by the single federated states. However, the differentiation of these policies and their constraining effects on trans-state trade soon conflicted with the need to promote and sustain economic growth. When America became a nationalized country in the course of the twentieth century, however, her federal structure continued to prevent stable centralization of economic authority at the national level. Moreover, the federal structure helped dilute the social and political pressure that in Europe was instrumental in justifying an active role by the state in the workings of the economic system. Federalism hampered the formation of a trans-state class movement pushing for the public control of the economy in order to protect the weaker interests operating within it. Instead, the territorially decentralized organization of state authority fostered the formation of sectional cleavages more than social or economic ones. This territorial diffusion of power also impeded the formation of a common interest of the business community, which in fact continued to be divided along regional lines.

Nothing of the sort happened in the economic histories of the main Western European nation-states. Here it was the state which created the conditions for the growth of the market, whose successful operation was considered necessary to generate the fiscal resources required for military ambitions. In fact, no single European nation-state had a territorial organization of power comparable with the one that emerged from the 'Great Compromise' reached at the American Constitutional Convention of 1787. Only after World War II did some European countries (such as Germany in 1949, Austria at the beginning of the 1950s, and finally Belgium in 1993) move in the direction of a federal organization of territorial power. Other European countries have since taken the decentralization route, such as Spain with its democratic constitution of 1978, Italy with the reforms of the 1970s and then of the 1990s, France with the reforms of the 1980s, and Britain with the devolution of the 1990s. However, for a large part of modern European history, democratic federalism has been unknown in practice, although it was very well-known in theory. Thus, in order to detect the formation of a modern social order on the two sides of the Atlantic it is necessary to start with the territorial organization of powers in America and in the single European nation-states. I contend that the difference in that territorial organization may help explain the divergent trajectory taken by America and European nation-states in building a market economy, which in turn constrained the setting up of a different welfare system on two shores of the Atlantic.

4.2. Territorial Organization of Power in America and Europe

4.2.1. The Features of American Federalism: From Dualism to Competition

As we have seen, since its constitutional foundation, the federal structure of the new American republic has had evident confederal features, features which largely contributed to keeping federal state authority within stringent bounds (Lowi 1978). Today, it is taken for granted that America invented and implemented modern democratic federalism. That is a system, as Riker argued some time ago (1964), of a constitutionally protected separation of powers between the center and the states, whereby each level of government has areas in which it takes the final or ultimate decisions. This presupposes a territorial distribution of powers with geographically defined component units. A (modern democratic) federal system necessarily requires a written constitution in order to guarantee both levels of government, the right of the component units to be involved in decisions to amend or change the federal constitution (although this they can do unilaterally in regard to their own constitutions), and a double principle of representation at the federal level expressed by a bicameral legislature and a decentralized government, in particular regarding taxing power.

Although American federalism has displayed all these characteristics since its foundation, the latter have to be interpreted as criteria rather than specific institutional arrangements. Indeed, in America, federalism retained important aspects of the previous confederal system (expressed by the Articles of Confederation of 1781). In particular, it retained a principle of territoriality which affirmed equal representation of the states in the federal Senate (and their selection through states' legislatures). It was the Great Compromise reached in Philadelphia between the small and slave states, on the one hand, and the large and nonslave states on the other, which granted equal representation to the states in the Senate (and, as we know, representation in the House proportionally to their populations). Indeed, those same criteria have been implemented through different institutional forms in Europe after World War II. After all, for the most prominent scholar of federalism (Elazar 1987a), the essence of federalism consists in the institutionalization of particular relations among territorial units which recognize their specific needs, more than in a particular set of institutions.

Since its constitutional foundation, American federalism has been a dual system of territorial government (Marbach, Katz, and Smith 2006); that is, a territorial organization of power where intergovernmental relations (between the federated states and thus between them and the federal state) are based on reciprocal institutional *independence*, on reciprocal functional *autonomy*, and on a clear distinction *of jurisdictions*. The American constitution defines the matters pertaining to the center (foreign affairs, defense, control of the currency), leaving all the others to the states. There are only two levels of government in this system; and they are based on general authorities which are reciprocally independent (especially in the appointment of their decision-makers). Each authority has all powers, or none at all, in each sphere; and each is organized like the other, in the sense that each has its own legislative, executive, administrative, and judicial institutions with which to realize its constitutional prerogatives (Blondel 1992). However, as Elazar (1994: 260–1) argued, beneath this duality there have always been 'congeries of local communities, cities, schools, special districts and, in some cases, townships and boroughs. [Most Americans lived and continue to live] within the jurisdiction of many local governments simultaneously'. Common to all these governments is their territorial base. American politics was and continues to be organized around units of territory, rather than around economic, ethnic, or social classes units. Although specific ethnic or religious groups have chosen to settle in specific territories in order to maintain their community identity and to secure the power to promote it, those territories have been open (with significant exceptions) to anyone wishing to settle within them. This combination of cultural specificity and multidiversity of the states and localities has traditionally woven together the threads of American territorial democracy (Sbragia 1996).

Thus, although dual, American federalism has always had the complexity of a territorial matrix. Of course, complex systems generate many conflicts, and America has been no exception. Conflict between the two levels of government on the allocation of powers has been decided *primarily* by the courts. In particular, the Supreme Court has come to play a strategic role in the American federal system. By means of the Judiciary Act of 1789 the Congress created the judiciary system and defined its jurisdiction. According to the provisions of this act, the federal judiciary is constituted by a Supreme Court and by a two-tier system of inferior courts. Although during its first decade this court system was insignificant, since the Supreme Court chaired by John Marshall (1801–35), the decisions of the judiciary, and of its apex in particular, constituted the American federal system and defined the relations between the federated states and the federal center. The entire history of American federalism has been largely constructed by Supreme Court decisions.

The ambiguities left unresolved by the Philadelphia constitution of 1787 meant that the federal structure was subject to constant redefinition, and struggle, among states and between the latter and the federal state. As Elazar (1987b: XVI) noted, '[t]he federalism of the Constitution was made crystal clear, just as the division and sharing of powers was left ambiguous'. It is not surprising, therefore, that American federalism has changed during its long history, not only because federal arrangements are never stable, but also because the interpretation of federalism that predominated at the beginning of the new republic was based on factors (such as a commercial economy, a limited mobilized society, a weak administrative apparatus, and the country's international isolation) which were called into question by the advance of the urban–industrial frontier (Elazar 1994). After all, America was a developing country when it adopted its federal form of territorial government. These changes have also been expressed in the syntactic structure of American public discourse. As Sbragia (1992) noted, until after the Civil War, when the power of the federated states still predominated, it was customary to say 'The United States are'; later, when the federal center finally asserted its power, the wording became 'The United States is'.

Crucial in this regard was the Fourteenth Constitutional Amendment of 1868, whereafter the Supreme Court ruled that the Bill of Rights applied also to the states, and not just to the federal government as previously. In fact, apart from the shame of the *Dred Scott* v. *Sandford* (1857) decision taken by the Taney Court (1836–64), which did not allow the status of citizens to an African-American (see Chapter 3), the decision was also intended to strike down the so-called 'Missouri Compromise' which denied slavery in the north-western states, thus recasting the social foundations of American federalism. The decision provoked a fierce reaction by the Northern abolitionists which gave the Southern states a pretext to move from nullification to secession. Although post–Civil War judicial decisions established the legal conditions for a normatively homogeneous federalism, America did not yet become the constitutional homogeneous country that it was supposed to be. The racial divide continued to hamper its political development because of the segregation policies that the Southern states were still allowed to pursue. However, with the nationalization of American politics, the dual organization of territorial power evolved towards a *competitive federalism* characterized by state and federal jurisdictions which frequently overlapped and competed for control of crucial public policies (Dye 1990). This was a competitive federalism which, between World War II and the late 1960s, became for some authors (Ostrom V. 1991) even *coercive,* with the legislative approval of federal programs compelling the states to accept federal guidelines and objectives in return for federal resources (the so called grants-in-aid programs). At the end of the 1970s, one-third of the federal domestic budget consisted of grants-in-aid programs (Chubb 1992).

4.2.2. *Federalism as Antimajoritarianism in America and Europe*

Federalism is mainly an antimajoritarian device for the organization of territorial power (Filippov, Ordeshook, and Shvetsova 2004), in the sense that a federal system prevents the formation of a national electoral majority able to control the entire governmental system inasmuch as it makes possible the formation of different majorities in its different territorial units. By means of the Philadelphia Great Compromise, America introduced a permanent antimajoritarian territorial constraint into the federal government (Ostrom V. 1991). A Senate constituted by two senators for each state, and endowed with formidable powers in legislation (the Senate's approval is necessary before any law can be sent to the President for signature), in judicial and executive policy (its advice and consent are constitutionally required, as we know, for approving the nominations of federal justices, members of the presidential cabinet, and top officials of the executive establishment), and in foreign policy (its advice and consent are constitutionally required for the approval of any international treaty involving the country), was an antimajoritarian bastion against any pro-majoritarian tendency to centralize power at the federal level. Recognizing those broad prerogatives to the Senate, the constitution gave the states *veto power* on national decision-making which they could use against undesired outcomes. The American Senate is not only antimajoritarian because anticentralistic, but also because its internal working came to be informed, since its very beginning, by a consensus-oriented ethos. One has only to think of the practice of *filibuster*, the rule permitting a senator, or a series of senators, to speak for as long as they wish and on any topic they choose, unless a supermajority group of sixty senators brings debate to a close by invoking cloture.[1]

However, at the turn of the nineteenth century not even the powerful Senate could raise effective resistance against the wind of nationalization and democratization that traversed the country. Nevertheless, even after the Seventeenth Constitutional Amendment of 1913 which changed the method of election of senators from indirect to direct, the now directly elected Senate preserved its antimajoritarian complexion—that is, its 'undemocratic features' (Dahl 2001: 17)—because its representative composition was still unrelated to demographic size. The effect of the Great Compromise reached in Philadelphia in 1787, which allowed 'strategically placed and highly privileged minorities—slaveholders, for example—(to gain) disproportionate power over government policies at the expense of less privileged minorities' (Dahl 2001: 18), was unchanged.

Indeed, as Sbragia (2005*b*: 100) notes, in 2004 'more than a quarter of the American population is represented by six senators while 7 percent of the population is represented by thirty-four senators'. Which is why one might rightly say that 'the Senate is the most malapportioned legislature in the world' (Sbragia 2005*b*). Thus, through the constitutional protection of the interests of the small states (and in the past of the slaves' states), American federalism absorbed the confederal bias against centralization, although it tried to offset it with a House correlated to the population (whose representatives are elected in districts of comparable population). However, because also the House of Representatives was largely controlled by state parties during the nineteenth century, it is evident that federal authority was effectively constrained by state interests in that crucial century of the rise of a modern market system.

In the nineteenth century, federalism proved to be an obstacle not only against the formation of a national economy but also against the reduction of social inequality among citizens. Policy diversity in the states was the norm, but such diversity gave rise to differing levels of social intervention by states. The situation changed in the following century, and especially in the 1930s, when the pressure for redistributive policies urged more active federal intervention in the economy and society, an intervention which would inevitably reduce the policy prerogatives of the states. Indeed, the more centralized federalism of the post-1930s was justified by the need to reduce the market's harmful side effects, which could not be tackled by the individual states with their different policy frames. In the 1930s, American federalism acknowledged that policy diversity among states might not only be an incentive to innovation but also a constraint on social equalization. After all, federalism comprises a constant tension between the center and the states: the former is necessary to promote uniformity across the nation, whereas the latter are the champions of economic, social, and cultural diversity. It is for this reason that American federalism has allowed phases of centralization to alternate with phases of decentralization. However, even when a stronger role by federal authority in the economy and society has enjoyed popular legitimacy, the constitutional structure of a fragmented sovereignty has continued to protect the fluidity of inter-states relations, granting ample margins for maneuver to rulers and territorial units with stakes in opposing centralization. After all, 'American federalism is at once a system of law and a structure of power. It has both a juristic and a behavioural aspect. [The point is that] our juristic federalism does not unambiguously determine our behavioural federalism' (Beer 1993: 23–4).

This institutional form of territorial government was long absent in the main European nation-states. Even during their liberal phase, none of the main European countries adopted a territorial solution which diffused power rather than centralized it. Throughout the nineteenth century, France and Britain continued to follow the *unitary* path taken during the formation of their states between the revolt of the Netherlands against Spain in 1567 and the Treaty of Utrecht in 1714. Inspired by the 'centralizing, hierarchical, statist principle of absolutism', both countries substituted the feudal concept of corporatism 'with a notion of a single-entity commanding universal loyalty on the part of all subjects or citizens' (Elazar 1987a: 128). Sovereignty was thus concentrated into a single center, as theorized at the time by Jean Bodin (1530–96). With the Jacobin success after the French Revolution of 1789, the centralist ideology became (either by necessity or choice) the European norm. Forms of federal or decentralized distribution of powers were preserved only in peripheral situations such as those of the small countries of Switzerland and the Netherlands. However, the Napoleonic Wars greatly reduced the margins for alternative decentralized experiments. The Netherlands finally adopted the new statism, whereas Switzerland (thanks to its territorial isolation) was able to preserve its decentralized government, although in 1848 it finally had to switch from a confederation to a federation. Nor can the German *Zollverein* which arose after the Congress of Vienna of 1815 be considered a proper confederal state, because territorial power was closely controlled by the strongest state in the confederation, the highly centralized Prussia (Ziblatt 2006).

The success of the centralized territorial state in Europe in the nineteenth century did not prevent the adoption of forms of decentralization in some formally centralized unitary states. Such decentralization came about in Britain, the Scandinavian countries, and then Belgium and the Netherlands (and even, in a very limited sense however, in multinational autocracies such as Russia and Austria). But, apart from Switzerland, none of these countries can be considered democratic. It was not until the development of democratic impulses after the two great European wars of the twentieth century that there was any substantial movement toward federal forms of territorial government. Until World War II (with the exception again of Switzerland), the European states were generally centralized states that granted no role (or legitimacy) to intermediary powers between citizens and state authorities. Whether their unified sovereignty was justified by war or by the need to modernize, it produced a territorial organization of public authority centered on a bureaucracy or parliament.

It was inevitable that this organization should function according to a top-down decision-making logic where the peripheries were treated as mere terminals of the center's will (or its territorial offshoots). Especially when the center became the expression of an electoral majority, the structuring of territorial relations in the main countries of Western Europe tended to reflect a majoritarian thrust.

Thus, from 1848 to 1949, with the exception of Switzerland, America was the only consolidated federal form of democratic government on either side of the Atlantic. However, after World War II, some European countries shifted toward the decentralized organization of territorial relations (Watts 1998). West Germany, with the Fundamental Law of 1949, introduced a novel form of federalism designed to thwart any attempt to rebuild a centralized state (as the Third Reich had been). This was a novel form of federalism because it arose from the disaggregation of a previously centralized state and not, as in the case of America, from the aggregation of previously independent units (Watts 1987). By institutional logic, a federal system arising from the disaggregation of a previously centralized state tends to be more centralizing than one arising from the aggregation of previously separated constituent units (Sbragia 1992). In fact (Gunlicks 2003), the German Fundamental Law of 1949 inaugurated a *cooperative* federalism model which granted a more substantial role to the center. Contrary to the American competitive model, intergovernmental relations in cooperative federalism are based on reciprocal interdependence (and not on reciprocal independence), and they operate within a framework of shared governance and overlapping jurisdictions (not one of separation and distinction). This system produces low policy diversity and high policy complexity among its constituent units. Powers are divided by function and not by policy area, and there is only one administrative structure for both levels of government, controlled by the component units (or *Länder*).

The German system requires joint decision-making between the component units and the center (Scharpf 1997), whereas American federalism continues to rest on distinct decision-making processes at the level of the states and the center. However (Jefferey and Savigner 1991), in Germany, the greater role played by the federal center has been offset by the strong influence of the *Länder* on its decision-making process. Not only does the chamber (*Bundesrat*) representing the *Länder* have exclusive power to legislate on all issues (especially financial) concerning the latter, but its representatives act on behalf of the *Länder*'s executives and not their electors. The *Bundesrat* is an 'ambassadorial chamber' (Ackerman

2000), in that its members vote as the *Land* (by *collective* vote), not as individuals (like American senators). The *Bundesrat* consequently exerts powerful influence on federal policies because of its direct connection with the *Länder* governments. Moreover, although the *Bundesrat* may not participate in the crucial parliamentary process of voting confidence in the Chancellor (only the popular chamber or *Bundestag* has this power), it is a powerful antimajoritarian restraint on the executive (especially when it expresses a territorial majority different from the popular majority in the *Bundestag*).

In sum, in the German *Bundesrat*, the *Länder* are represented by their governments, whereas in the American Senate the states are represented by their voters (and before 1913, by their legislatures). In the German *Bundesrat* the *Länder* vote is collective, whereas in the American Senate the senators vote individually. Although Germany has followed a different route from America in giving representation to its constitutive states, it too has introduced antimajoritarian features into its national decision-making process. In fact, it is true that the *Länder* are not represented equally, because their vote in the Bundesrat is somewhat related to population size, but the range of variation is contained within very strict limits. Moreover, the *Länder* and the center are constitutionally obliged to cooperate, and not to compete, in resolving policy problems (the Fundamental Law severely restricts the exclusionary powers pertaining to either the center or the *Länder*). The constitutional design of American federalism precludes any possible evolution toward cooperation among levels of government (Beer 1995); yet the complexity of America's policy problems has frequently called into question the institutional distinctiveness and separation of jurisdictions between the federal state and the federated states.

4.3. Territoriality and Market-Building in America and Europe

4.3.1. *Market-Building in America in the Nineteenth Century*

The different institutional structuring of territorial powers in America and Europe has largely conditioned the formation of the market on the two sides of the Atlantic (Fabbrini 2005*b*). Although markets are political constructs (Przeworski 2003), their construction may follow different patterns. The characteristics of a market not only reflect the period of its formation but also the institutional environment in which it finally takes shape. In America, a modern market economy developed in the absence of a central state; in fact, the market was already *developed* when the federal state came fully into being at the turn of the nineteenth century (Nettle 1968). In Europe, by contrast, the pre-existence of a central state was a condition for the creation of the market, but it was also its constraint. In fact, the creation of a market economy required the dismantling of many hierarchical relations structured in both state and society, and it was much more difficult to achieve in Europe than in America. This different building (in the nineteenth century) of the relationship between state and economy on the two sides of the Atlantic inevitably influenced the conception of democracy. In America (Lipset 1979), a contractual view of democracy arose, or was constructed, while in the European countries democracy, in that it resulted from a sequence of fierce conflicts between social classes and bureaucratic interests for control of the state (Daalder 1995), received a strong *statist* interpretation.

On comparing American and French experiences in the nineteenth century, Grimm (1985: 97) wrote:

in America, where class distinction, feudalism, state controlled economy had never been established, there was no need for a liberal reform of society . . . In France, on the contrary, political power first had to bring about the situation which, for the Americans, seemed to be the natural order. Hence, the French revolution destroyed the absolute monarchy, but not the sovereign state. It merely changed the subject of sovereignty.

Thus, whereas in America freedom of economic enterprise—though restricted since colonial times by communitarian–religious constraints— anticipated the birth, and thereafter guaranteed the growth, of political freedom itself (Dahl 1976), in Europe, and in France and Germany in particular, it was the conquest of political freedom that created the conditions for the development of economic freedom (Tilly 1990*b*). It is for this reason that the market has always enjoyed much more legitimacy in America than in Europe. Of course, as Karl Polanyi (1944) argued long ago, a market economy was built and protected through specific public intervention (which granted property rights and defined the boundary between private and public interests). However, 'although Polanyi is correct in recognizing that the legal order must support market activity, and understood the vital role of the state in constructing and maintaining the market, he did not specify the particular instruments that the state might use in pursuing that goal' (Egan 2001: 38). And here emerges an important difference between the American and European experiences of market-building. In nineteenth-century antebellum America, the market was promoted primarily at the local and state level. As McDonald wrote (1990: 218): 'state and local governments engineered a massive shift of resources from public to private uses through the distribution of public lands, the granting of legal privileges and immunities, direct capital investment in some projects—especially railroads—and the provision of a wide variety of police, education, and social welfare services'. Thus confirming what James Bryce had already noted in his celebrated *The American Commonwealth* (1888).

This decentralized support for the market was made possible by a crucial factor: the control exerted by the states over fiscal resources. Only with the Sixteenth Constitutional Amendment of 1913 did the federal Congress acquire the power to levy and collect taxes on incomes, from whatever source they derived, without apportionment among the states, and without regard to any census or enumeration. Thus, according to several accounts (Mann 1993*a*), throughout the nineteenth century, with the partial exception of the Civil War period (1861–5), the ratio of government expenditure to GNP was routinely one-fifth or one-sixth of the ratio recorded in the largest European nation-states. Thus, for more than the first century of its life, the new American republic was based on the power of the states rather than of the federal government. The federated states resisted any attempt to centralize power to Washington, DC: 'locally rooted legislature (safeguarded) the right to initiate—or, more likely, not to initiate—new tax laws. Unlike the Jacobin legacy for France, republican ideology in America merely deepened the distrust of national [that is, federal] mobilization' (Wiebe 1995: 70). In Europe, by contrast, the centralized state not only established the legal conditions for the birth of the market, but also intervened in its material structuring (Mann 1993*b*).

In sum, the American historical experience demonstrates the closeness of the connection between the political and the economic constitutions (Elkin 1996; Della Sala 2005). The dual polity of the nineteenth century allowed the states to set the national economic agenda, countering various attempts to strengthen the supra-states features of the polity, through the formation (for example) of a central bank. The states organized the material infrastructure of the economy (the communications system in particular), but they also defined the normative boundaries between the private and public realms (Lowi 1992). However, their resistance was eventually neutralized by a combination of economic pressures and judicial activism; in fact, it was mainly by means of Supreme Court decisions that the federal state was able to reduce the states' grip on the market. The conflict between the federal state and the federated states has highlighted the constant feature of American territorial democracy that consists in its combination of federal and confederal features (Elazar 1987a). A fragile combination which induced the judiciary to play a crucial role in the building of the American market.

4.3.2. *The Role of the Supreme Court and the Birth of the American Regulatory State*

The different structural, institutional, and political contexts of America and the individual European nation-states have thus generated two opposed trajectories of market-building. In federal America, the market's segmentation along state lines very soon proved to be a hindrance to its further development. 'Between 1875 and 1890 business organizations began to challenge state restrictions, and pressed courts for relief' (Egan 2001: 35). With the federal Congress largely controlled by state and local interests, and the President still not enjoying sufficient policymaking influence, the interests pressing for a national market appealed to the judiciary to challenge the legislation in force; a challenge that the judiciary was able to raise because of its power of *judicial review*, which gave it a policymaking role. Indeed, the power of judicial review is crucial for understanding the role performed by the courts in the building of the American market. However, because the state courts sided with the states' claims to preserve their tariffs and barriers, it fell to the Supreme Court to create a national free trade economy proportionate to the federal dimension of the polity.

In America, the power of judicial review has been applied in various domains: the relations between federal government and the federated states, or between the various federal governmental institutions, or again between the federal and state institutions and the citizens (Hodder-Williams 1992). It is for this reason that the judiciary has been of crucial importance in defining the terms of the changing distinction between private and public interests (Dubinsky 1994). It was the Marshall Court (1803–36) which made the most concrete contribution to the process of building a national market by laying down the legal conditions for its formation. *McCulloch* v. *Maryland* (1819) recognized the supremacy of the national law over state law in areas in which the Congress might claim 'implicit powers'. *Dartmouth College* (1819) granted constitutional protection to the contract rights of corporations, thus making the further development of these new economic actors possible. The landmark cases of *Gibbon* v. *Ogden* (1824) and *Brown* v. *Maryland* (1827) affirmed the supremacy of acts of the federal Congress over acts by states if taken in areas covered by the so-called Commerce Clause (article 1, section VII.3 of the constitution stipulates that 'Congress shall have power to regulate commerce with foreign nations, and among the several States, and with the Indian tribes'). With these decisions, the Court de facto favored the dismantling of state trade barriers—a sort of *negative integration* of the national market—thus setting a legislative agenda for its subsequent *positive integration* by congressional legislation. Furthermore, it was the Court which gave the federal government broad latitude in determining monetary policy, an area which was not technically within its remit (Bzdera 1993).

Certainly, the role of the Supreme Court did not go unchallenged. In fact, in its last years, the Marshall Court played a more limited federalizing role because it was pressured by the states. The Taney Court (1836–64) granted the states some of their crucial powers, especially in the field of domestic order, with two important decisions: *Biscoe* v. *Bank of Kentucky* (1837) and *New York* v. *Miln* (1837). It even introduced, in *Coley* v. *Board of Port Wardens* (1851), the singular theory that, on questions of commerce, the power to regulate should be assigned either to the federal government or to the states in relation to the issue or sector subject to regulation. Nevertheless, the pressure to build a continental market continued to be applied. *Ableman* v. *Booth* (1858) confirmed the supremacy of the federal laws in areas subject to the implicit powers of the Congress. Then, after the Civil War, the full development of a common American market was made possible by previous judicial decisions which had created the conditions for the advent of the new protagonists of economic development, namely the large trans-state corporations. Yet the institutional dispersion of national sovereignty inherent in the American political system, coupled with the legitimacy enjoyed throughout the nineteenth century and thereafter by the *idea* of an unrestrained market economy, prevented any direct intervention by the federal state, instead of private economic forces, to foster economic growth in strategic sectors. It is important to bear in mind that 'not until the creation of the Federal reserve in 1913 did the United States acquire a central banking system' (McKay 2001: 27).

In this context, postbellum industrial America came to establish a *regulatory pattern* for public intervention in the economy. At the end of the nineteenth century, in America strategic functions of market regulation were allocated to independent *regulatory agencies*. While the first American regulatory agency was the Steamboat Inspection Service created in 1837, it was in the last years of the century that the first wave of administrative regulation of the market took the form of antitrust and public utility control measures. The Interstate Commerce Commission instituted in 1887, and operating within the framework of the Sherman Anti-Trust Act finally approved in 1889, set the regulatory pattern. It was then followed by the other regulatory waves: that of the New Deal period (1930s), which regulated the stock market and collective bargaining in the industrial sector, and that of the Great Society period (1960s), which also involved social regulation.

Certainly, in their turn, these trends encountered significant judicial resistance. They were obstructed by the Fuller Court (1888–1910), which in *United States* v. *E.C Knight Co* (1895) severely restricted the applicability of the Sherman Act, and in *Pollock* v. *Farmers Loan & Trust Co* (1895) declared the Income Tax Act approved by Congress in 1894 to be unconstitutional. During the first decade of the twentieth century, the Supreme Court actively opposed the federal regulations approved by the Congress, doing so in the name of a laissez-faire economic ideology. For the White Court (1910–20), the Taft Court (1920–30), and finally the Hughes Court (1930–7), the federal government had no power to restrict the economic freedom of the firms by regulating the conditions for its exercise. In particular, the Court reiterated that freedom of contract could only be curtailed through legal due process, not by a congressional act. The Congress was also precluded from infringing the power of the states in areas such as health, child labor, and minimum wages by using the interstate Commerce Clause. However, the Supreme Court's resistance did not prevent the formation of an economic regulatory regime and the electoral success of the New Deal coalition in 1933 made that regime irreversible. This economic regulatory regime was then further strengthened by the social regulation of the 1960s.

4.3.3. *The American Regulatory Regime and the Post–World War II Experience*

In general, regulation consists in prolonged and focused control exercised by a public agency on economic activities deemed of social relevance (Selznick 1985). It is a way for public authorities to govern society by setting rules rather than by directly managing societal activities. It prefers recourse to administrative rather than political means. All regulation is the outcome of a political judgment which selects the activities considered of social importance and defines the rules for their control. By its nature, regulation concerns a sector or an industry, not economic activity in general. This sector approach is institutionalized by the establishment of an agency which intervenes only in a given field. An agency, therefore, is a specific answer to a circumscribed problem, and its legitimacy derives from the process of its creation and the quality of its expertise.

In America, the Congress creates an agency to which it delegates powers that may be legislative (such as the power to define binding rules), administrative (such as the power to interfere with the management of a firm), or judicial (such as the power to close down specific activities). The agency's officials are nominated by the President with congressional supervision and monitoring. However, the power of an agency is also dependent on its technical expertise and the independent use made thereof by the agency's officials. The regulatory state thus reflects the intricacies of the separation of powers. The agency is expected to act independently of the electoral cycle. The difficulty of identifying a governmental position is resolved through the depoliticization of a problem. Efficiency has become another check on the political institutions (Rose-Ackerman 1993).

Through the formation of ad hoc independent agencies, the federal state has laid down a very complex set of rules to regulate competition among the economic actors operating in a particular sector. Indeed, a regulatory state should be viewed as a normative framework (Cassese 2001) within which to evaluate the performance of a public administration. The regulatory approach has fostered the formation of a specific American administrative culture attentive to the efficiency outputs of an action, and not only (as has been the case in Europe) concerned to ensure compliance with a procedure. Indeed, also at the level of the logic of administration, America has followed a path different from Europe in the twentieth century.

The rules of regulatory activity have been different in nature and have had different impacts, and agencies have used different regulative techniques to accomplish their tasks (Eisner 2000): the definition of standards to be followed in the production process; the selective screening of products, processes, and producers; the obligation on producers to inform about the nature of goods or services offered; the prohibition of anticompetitive practices; the fixing of tariffs for access to a service; control over prices; the allocation of public interest quality to particular activities or products; the regulation of industrial relations within a specific sector; the establishing of rulemaking and rule-adjudicating procedures for the settlement of economic disputes; the public subsidizing of activities of special public importance. However complex and effective these measures may be, the aim of the regulatory state is to guarantee the public good in various economic activities without jeopardizing the private structure which supports them. Regulations are not only direct but also indirect (Majone 1992). Agencies not only use command-and-control techniques but they also rely on persuasion, the circulation of information, and alteration of the incentives structure of given economic activities in order to affect the functioning of economic sectors.

The number of these agencies has grown enormously in America since World War II (Majone and La Spina 1991; Majone 2005a), either in the form of regulatory agencies operating within the executive branch (such as the Environmental Protection Agency, the Occupational Health and Safety Administration, the National Highway Traffic Safety Administration) or in the form of agencies independent of both President and Congress (for instance the Federal Trade Commission, the Securities and Exchange Commission, the Interstate Commerce Commission). Of course, these latter agencies have displayed a higher degree of independence (from the governmental institutions) than have the former, and it is in reference particularly to them that America has been called a *regulatory state*. Indeed, the powers of the independent agencies have so increased in the time that they have come to be considered a 'fourth branch of government' (Mejer 1999). Certainly, their growing power has been periodically questioned, exactly because that power has been accompanied by political irresponsibility. Moreover, their multiplication has created enormous problems of coordination, with cases where the competences of certain independent agencies overlap, and their rules contradict each other.

In sum, since the end of the nineteenth century, and then after the New Deal period, there has arisen in America a specific form of state intervention—the regulatory state—distinct not only from the European mercantilist state but also from the nightwatchman state of the Jeffersonian tradition ('the best state is the least state', Wills 1999). This kind of public intervention has been justified by the separation of powers system and by a diffused pro-market political culture. The Supreme Court made it possible, but also conditioned its development.

4.3.4. *American Regulation and European Nationalization*

The American regulatory state has consisted in public intervention which has not substituted private economic actors with public ones (Prechel 2000). The purpose of economic regulation has been to prevent the formation and use of monopolistic powers in the market. It has consisted in policies intended to sanction restraints on trade or predatory pricing practices, and its aim has been to guarantee a competitive economy. In economic regulation, the public good has coincided more with the interests of consumers than with the interests of specific groups involved in the productive process (like workers or entrepreneurs in Europe). Its criteria have been based on calculations of economic efficiency. The regulatory state has been quite successful in promoting a competitive market in America, but it has also had significant drawbacks.

In many cases, private actors have utilized the regulatory activity of the independent agencies to promote their interests, rather than the other way around (Moe 1989): the agencies, that is, have become captive to particular interests. Indeed, the 'revolving door' system by which agency officials have moved from public to private roles has significantly diminished the independence of agencies. The independent agencies, moreover, have not always respected the criteria of economic efficiency so that their action has become bureaucratized. Finally, some independent agencies have used their independence from the separated institutions of government not only to protect specific constituencies but also to promote their specific administrative interests. Indeed, the lack of political control over the action of the agencies has been generally recognized as the main weakness of the regulatory state. It is probable that the Administrative Procedure Act (APA) of 1946, which was intended to set order on the regulatory agencies, ended by producing harmful effects. By requiring that agencies be accountable to the interests affected by their action, APA encouraged and justified interference by private interests in their decision-making processes.

Nothing comparable to American regulation has come about in the European nation-states. Whilst in nineteenth-century America the judiciary was crucial (though in contradictory fashion) for the building of a national market, in no European nation-state did the judiciary play an autonomous policymaking role for the same purpose and in the same period. The legal order of the market was established by legislative or administrative decision, in relation both to the predominant political ideologies and parties and to the stage reached by the country's economic development. This was therefore political rather than judicial intervention in the economic system. After the Colbertist experiment in absolutist France it was clear to all European states that their (military) fate 'was naturally much affected by their economies. [This is why] European states were generally much involved in [their] workings' (Calleo 2001: 48). While classical mercantilism served the absolute state's need to finance its wars against neighbors, Calleo writes, the liberal mercantilism of the nineteenth and early twentieth centuries enabled it to catch up with the colonial expansion of the capitalist economy, which, for the European nation-states, was another way to wage war against its neighbors. Not only has 'mercantilism encouraged imperialism—as the means to control more trade and thus gather more resources' (Calleo 2001: 42), but it has created a public attitude toward the market based on the idea that it should pursue national strategies defined *only* by the state (i.e. by its political and administrative personnel).

Hard pressed by the formidable challenges raised by war and economic competition in the first half of the twentieth century, the European nation-states did more than merely establish a reliable system of property rights, taxation, and commercial regulation. In Continental Europe especially, the state defined the sectors crucial for the country's growth (Tilly 1975). And in many cases it assumed direct responsibility for their development and promoted corporatist arrangements among the representatives of the main economic interests in order to exert political control over the main economic resources (investments, profits, and wages). Europe then responded to the dramatic economic crisis of the 1930s and the epochal transformation induced by World War II by extending public control or ownership to large sectors of the economy. Thus, while America pursued market-correcting strategies in dealing with industrialization and internationalization, thereby preserving the private nature of the economic system, Europe adopted market-substituting strategies, thereby reducing the private nature of the economic system. The European market-substituting strategies continued to be pursued after the defeat of the authoritarian and totalitarian regimes (Hall 1986; Pierson C. 1996).

Indeed, since World War II, the European nation-states have gradually replaced the state's mercantilism with the nationalization of strategic sectors, coupled with Keynesian policies for the public support of aggregate demand. Again the nationalization of industrial sectors has been justified by a national need to support the country's economic development: an understandable justification, and especially so if one considers that many European nation-states emerged economically destroyed from World War II and thus had to protect their reconstruction and maximize their economic resources. State planning of the economy thus became the approach generally adopted by the newly formed European democratic governments. Public control over macroeconomic variables was ensured by centralized fiscal policies. In some cases, nationalization was imposed by the need to accelerate both economic recovery after the war and technological development in order to reduce the gap with America. In other cases, it was required by the political endeavor to establish new industrial relations between workers and employers in the context of a corporatist or communitarian national ideology. Whatever the reason, the postwar European states became an economic actor per se, rather than the creator of the institutional conditions for a market economy (Fligstein 2001).

Not so in America. The market was supported by legal, rather than political, rules. When the federal state began to intervene conspicuously in the economy with the New Deal policies of the 1930s and 1940s, it made sure not to substitute market forces with public actors. Even during World War II, in America the mobilization of national industry to support the war effort was largely overseen by private businessmen operating in public agencies. In the post–World War II period, American Keynesianism served the purpose of supporting the strongest industrial interests more than to promote a national interest. Indeed, as President Dwight Eisenhower (1953–60) remarked in his farewell address, for fighting the Cold War, America ended up in promoting a national policy which nurtured the interests of an industrial–military complex. In any case, while in Europe the national interest has tended to coincide with the state (i.e. with the view of the most influential public officials), in America, by contrast, it has tended to coincide with the market (i.e. with the views of the most influential private interests).

In Europe, the free market economy has never achieved the degree of legitimacy that it enjoys in America (Suleiman 2003). In Europe, in order to gain legitimacy, the market economy has been obliged to become a *social economy* or an *economie controllée*. This explains why the European market economy has always comprised an interweaving of private and public ownership, and why the pursuit of private interests has been considered appropriate (by the post–World War II national constitutions) only if coherent with the public interest as defined by the state through its sovereign parliament (as stipulated by the French Fourth Republic constitution of 1946, the Italian constitution of 1948, or the German Fundamental Law of 1949). There have thus been two quite different paths to market-building: the American legal-regulatory one and the European mercantilist-statist one. The path taken by America has been congenial to a political system organized around a multiple *separation of powers* and thus with a very weak and rather incoherent central public authority. The path taken by European nation-states, by contrast, has been congenial to political systems characterized by a *fusion of powers*: that is, systems centered on the parliament and the central administrative apparatus, whose decision-making has been largely determined by the preferences and resources of the government and its parliamentary majority. Retrospectively, one may say that America's path has been appropriate to a compound polity, while the one followed by European nation-states has been appropriate to noncompound polities.

4.4. Different Welfare Systems in America and Europe

4.4.1. *Alternative Patterns of Welfare-Building in the Twentieth Century*

From the point of view of the relation between state and market, therefore, there is no single cross-Atlantic pattern of experience (Esping-Andersen 1992). Although, throughout the West, the state has been given the task of defining the public rules necessary for the economic game, those rules have taken different forms and have been used for different purposes. These different patterns opposed America and Europe in the nineteenth century, and they continued to do so in the early decades of the twentieth century, notwithstanding pressure to turn the democratic state into a *welfare state* (Wilson 1998). However, after the 1929 crisis (which demonstrated that any self-regulating market strategy was bound to fail) and the social mobilization induced by World War II, both sides of the Atlantic saw powerful pressures on the state to reduce the inequalities and injustices caused by the capitalist economy. In both America and Europe, the postwar state dramatically increased its social (and not only economic) responsibilities. As Marshall (1950) famously put it, on both sides of the Atlantic the state of civil and political rights expanded to the point that it became also the state of economic and social rights. Nevertheless, the different paths along which they developed continued to constrain the common tendency to promote welfare policies.

In America, the centralization required by the promotion of national social policies immediately encountered strong resistance by the states. Indeed, until 1937, the Supreme Court frequently ruled in favor of the latter, judging any social program promoted by the federal government as unconstitutional because it stripped the states of prerogatives. In *Schechter Poultry Corp.* v. *United States* (1935) and *United States* v. *Butler* (1936) the Court struck down as unconstitutional, respectively, the National

Industrial Recovery Act (NIRA) and the Agricultural Adjustment Act (AAA), which had been introduced by the New Dealers in Congress, following the lead of President F. D. Roosevelt, in order to dampen the dramatic consequences of the economic crisis of 1929. In *Morehead* v. *New York*, the Court even affirmed that neither the federal government nor the state governments were empowered to legislate on the minimum wage. Certainly, the threat to 'pack' the Court by President F. D. Roosevelt and the Democratic Congress after the elections of 1936[2] induced the Court to adopt a more restrained constitutional doctrine (the judicial restraint long defended, albeit in the minority, by the Supreme Court justice Holmes between 1902 and 1932).

Certainly, the change of legal approach was also the outcome of a different intellectual and political climate. From April 1937 onward, the Supreme Court refrained from obstructing the President and Congress in their social policy initiatives, thereby acknowledging that the dramatic social and economic problems triggered by the 1929 crisis could not be resolved by the market's invisible hand. Thus, with the crucial decisions of *West Coast Hotel Co.* v. *Parrish* and *National Labor Relations Board* v. *Jones & Laughlin Steel Corp*, both of 1937, the Court not only cleared the way for the federal regulation of industrial relations but also increased the interpretative span of the Commerce Clause. In fact, the Hughes Court established (with the above second decision) that the federal government was empowered to regulate interstate commerce not only for antitrust reasons, but also to create fairer relations between capital and labor. Through a judicial self-restraint, the Court became a copartner in the attempt of the President and Congress to redefine the terms of state and societal relations in the context of an industrial economy unable to regulate itself.

Nevertheless, the American system of vertical and horizontal separation of powers, coupled with the racial and ethnic fragmentation of the working class, set formidable restraints on any strategy to introduce universal social protection policies. Moreover, the easy access of interest groups to the courts not only hindered political national mobilization in favor of those policies, but further segmented social claims for protection. In Europe, by contrast, institutional and political conditions worked in favor of national welfare schemes. After World War II, the central administration maintained control over social policies even in those states (like Germany) which became federal; the central organizations of the trade unions applied pressure for national inclusive policies; and the political parties had an interest in representing a population which finally enjoyed universal suffrage. While in Europe the failures of the market were addressed by a few inclusive and hierarchical associations of workers pressing for classwide (not industrywide) public protection, in America the same failures were addressed by a policymaking process organized around a pluralism of functional interest groups and lobbies. Only with the War on Poverty programs of the 1960s did the American federal state begin to undertake larger-scale social protection schemes with redistributive implications, like Medicare or Medicaid. However, whereas the European public protection policies substantiated a state which assumed redistributive and stabilization functions, the federal intervention of the American state never altered its basically regulatory character.

Thus, the shift to the state's extended social responsibility did not erase the distinctive features of specifically American and specifically European political development (Wilenski 2002). European nation-states (from the British Labour government of 1945–50 onward) responded to the social crisis induced by the collapse of the market and wartime social mobilization with a redistributive and universal welfare state—that is, one designed to reduce social inequalities through redistributive policies and the delivery of social services to all citizens (regardless of their occupational status) (Ferrera and Rhodes 2000). America responded to the same crisis by creating an industrial and residual welfare state—that is, one not intended to control the workings of the market, and which therefore provided welfare only for groups excluded from it (Esping-Andersen 1990). Whereas European nation-states expanded their universalistic welfare states in the course of the post–World War II period, America gradually adapted the state's assumption of new social responsibilities to its traditional regulatory patterns.

4.4.2. *Social Regulation in America and Welfare Policy in Europe*

In America, whilst the purpose of the 1930s program (Social Security) was to protect the white middle and working classes, the 1960s programs (Medicare and Medicaid) were instead targeted on the poor and minorities. During the 1960s, America shifted from economic to social regulation. The latter was intended not only to remedy numerous negative externalities generated by the market (pollution, work-related injuries, unsafe products) but also to empower individuals belonging to underprivileged groups (such as minorities and women). In the 1960s, individual, minority, and gender rights gradually came to be considered constitutive parts of the social regulation promoted by the federal state. Antidiscriminatory measures, or ones guaranteeing equal treatment to underprivileged groups, were implemented. In particular, given that the new approach was inspired by the Civil Rights Act of 1964 which acknowledged the social humiliation inflicted on African-Americans despite the outcome of the Civil War of a century before, social regulation gave rise to new policies of affirmative action and social protection designed to right historical wrongs (Bardach and Kagan 1982).

These policies (centered on protecting noncommodity values) were important developments in the American regulatory state, although they did not go so far as to demarketize aspects of work and social life. It is for this reason that American social regulation should not be confused with European nation-states' social policies based, although in different degrees, on universalistic social services supported by fiscal policies with redistributive effects. While the postwar European welfare states have been based on the supply of *merit goods* (public housing, health services, public education, pensions), the American social regulatory state has been based on the production of *public goods* (equality of opportunity, gender fairness, protection of the environment, product safety, information for consumers) (Majone 2005a). Hence, the policies of the 1960s continued to be inspired by a promarket principle, given that their aim was to level the playing field by giving the underprivileged the same initial opportunities as the privileged (a goal only partly achieved, however). Accomplishment of this endeavor inevitably entailed the use of fiscal instruments (especially for relieving the most dramatic conditions of poverty), however, these policies did not alter the basic fact that 'the American government played a very limited role in redistribution and macroeconomic stabilization' (Zweifel 2002: 67)

America has thus taken a different approach to market failures. Both economic and social regulation expresses the American political culture's hostility to interference by the state in the market and in class relations. America has continued to pursue market-correcting, rather than market-substituting, strategies. Nevertheless, such strategies have encountered robust resistance by traditionally privileged groups, which indeed were able to reverse them in the 1980s and 1990s with the electoral success of the neoconservative movement.[3] The 'racial line', which in the 1930s prohibited promotion of a universalistic social security system (agricultural workers, mainly African-Americans, were excluded from the provisions of the Social Security Act, a price the New Dealers had to pay for the legislative support of the Southern Democratic congressmen, Katznelson, Geiger, and Kryder 1993), continued to constrain the action of the federal state. Indeed, in the 2000s, America is still unique among the transatlantic countries in not having a universal health protection system, with the result that more than 42 million of its inhabitants have no health insurance. Quite different has been the inspiring principle of social intervention by the European nation-states. In Europe, in particular since World War II, the state has pursued social policies to insulate certain properties of working life (safety, health, age) against market logic (Esping-Andersen 1992).

Thus, following the Great Crisis of 1929, on both sides of the Atlantic the state was called upon to remedy the failures of the market. On neither side was there any better means than the state to satisfy the social needs of millions of new voters integrated into national politics by the mass parties, and to ensure balanced economic growth. Both in America and in Europe, the state responded positively to these needs. In the post–World War II era, all the transatlantic countries began a historically unprecedented process of accelerated and general economic growth, and of increased social well-being sustained by the state through social welfare policies and Keynesian economic policies. This led to the further expansion of the state, a process also driven by the functional adjustment of nation-states to the twin requirements of promoting capitalist accumulation and guaranteeing democratic legitimacy. However, notwithstanding this common trend toward the assumption of greater social responsibility by the state, the divergence between the American and European approaches to welfare has persisted (Wilenski 2002). America has maintained its residual welfare state model based on a social regulation approach, while the European nation-states have continued to develop their universal model in both its social democratic and corporatist versions (Esping-Andersen 1990).

If we consider postwar government revenue as a percentage of GDP as indicative of the state's involvement in society we find that, regardless of the differences among the European states in social protection schemes, Europe has grown increasingly distinct from America. In the 2000s, American net social expenditure was less than 60 percent of the average net social expenditure of European nation-states (Alesina and Glaser 2005: 21; OECD 2005). One may even argue that the difference between the welfare states in Europe and America is not solely a matter of degree, with the European pattern connoted by a greater role of the state in society, and the American pattern by a state with a much more limited role; rather, it seems to be a difference in the concept itself of public authority. Unlike in Europe, in America (Offe and Preuss 1991: 145) 'the individuals (are allowed to) pursue their diverse interests and their particular notion of happiness (without) the danger of an omnipotent government imposing its notion of collective happiness upon the people'. But if the Americans are more free to pursue their notion of happiness, they are also less protected when they suffer social misfortune (Holmes 1995). America has created a market society which is more dynamic than the European ones but which is also more unfair than the latter. The GINI index of social inequality rose from 0.399 in 1967 to 0.464 in 2003 (US Census Bureau, http://www.census.gov/). Indeed, the American individualistic approach has generated greater social and economic inequality than in the European nation-states. At the beginning of the 2000s, the richest quintile of the American population earned 11 times more than the poorest quintile, while the same richest quintile earned 4.6 times more than the poorest quintile in Belgium, 5.8 times more than the poorest quintile in Germany, 7.1 times more than the poorest quintile in France, and 9.6 times more than the poorest quintile in the UK (Phillips 2002: 124). Of course, such inequality has inevitably biased the political process in favor of the more well-established groups in society (APSA 2004). At the same time, in the European nation-states, the more egalitarian structure of society, the outcome of the post–World War II welfare states, has significantly decelerated the growth of the economy, and thus undermined the viability of those welfare systems.

4.5. Conclusion

America and European nation-states have followed quite radically different paths of market-building. The institutionalizations of these different paths have constrained the strategies for dealing with the negative effects of the operation of the market. Since the turn of the nineteenth century, America has built a regulatory state, that is, an institutional apparatus finalized to pursue market-correcting strategies. At the same time, even after World War II, the single European nation-states have continued to pursue market-substituting strategies, that is, they created institutional apparatuses for implementing some form of public control of the economy. It was within this different structuring of the relations between the market and the state that different types of welfare systems have developed on the two shores of the Atlantic. Even at the level of the formation of a modern social order, America and the single European nation-states have followed different roads and have created different institutional structures and public policy regimes. However, in the second half of the twentieth century important changes took place, especially in Europe.

In fact, the process of European integration has incentivized a sort of supranational federalization process. The EU expression of that process has progressively acquired the features of a multilevel governance system organized around an indigenous principle of territorial democracy (known as 'subsidiarity'). Moreover, the lack of budgetary resources at the Community level, coupled with the separation of powers at the decision-making level, has progressively turned the EU into a regulatory regime. It is through regulation that the EU has promoted a single common market: regulation largely motivated by decisions of the ECJ which have systematically removed national barriers to the free circulation of capital, services, goods, and workers. At the same time, global competition has obliged individual EU member-states to dramatically reduce their political control over the national economy. At least since the beginning of the 1980s (after the failure of the nationalization policies pursued by the French Socialist governments of Mauroy I and II), each European nation-state has been forced to liberalize and privatize its economy, thereby squeezing the fiscal bases of their welfare systems and increasing the flexibility of their labor markets. Consequently, at the European nation-states level, too, public intervention has changed considerably: with regard to the market, the state has acquired the features of a regulatory regime; and with regard to social protection, it has shed many of its traditional welfare policies. In sum, the social order of twenty-first-century European nation-states is much less different from the American social order than it has been in the past.

5

Different structuring of partisan politics in America and Europe: the role of parties in the political process

5.1. Introduction

Partisan politics has come to be structured differently in America and the single European nation-states. This differential structuring has been the effect of a plurality of factors. However, the different nature of the political development which took place in America and in the European nation-states in the nineteenth century set the path which was subsequently followed. The different institutional context of America and the European nation-states has thus differently constrained the role of the parties in the political process. As regards the party system, America has come to experience, in its two-centuries-long democratic experience, different types of party systems because of the changing nature of the predominant cleavage. However, all of those party systems have been characterized by one or another form of sectional cleavage. American political parties have tended to represent the interests and culture of one or another section of the country, where by section one has to understand a geopolitical area with its correlated economic, social, and cultural traits. On the contrary, sectionalism has never played a crucial role in structuring European nation-states' party systems. It was rather the ideological or ethnic or religious or class cleavages that have organized the relations between European political parties. Even in the era of individualized politics, European nation-states' political parties have continued to preserve an identity related to the representation of specific ethnic, religious, class, or ideological groups, although such identity has not precluded them from pursuing 'catch-all voters' strategies.

As regards the parties' role in the political process (by which I mean the process connecting elections with government), in America, parties were strong organizations during the nineteenth-century congressional government—that is, when the legislature had the decision-making primacy, and the separation of powers was largely interpreted as separation within the legislature. However, with the full institutionalization of the separated government in the twentieth century, a quite unfavorable environment for parties has come to take root. In fact, in fully fragmented sovereignty systems, parties tend to disaggregate in electoral and institutional terms, because power is diffused among various arenas and institutions. Disaggregated parties are inevitably weak political actors, and their weakness favors the growth of alternative forms of representation through interest groups, lobbies, and social movements. After all, where power is disaggregated, the access points to the decision-making process are multiple, a multiplicity which precludes any 'gatekeeping' role by the parties. On the contrary, the European nation-states have continued to be characterized by strong and influential party organizations, both in electoral and in governmental processes. European parliamentary systems, despite the differences between competitive and consensual ones, continue to have one particular feature in common: as a rule, they are environments that encourage party (i.e. collegial) action, although they increasingly display the assertiveness of strong governmental leaders (Poguntke and Webb 2005a). The same applies to the European semi-presidential systems (like France of the Fifth Republic) that, although they stress the role of a directly elected President of the Republic, make the activity of the parties indispensable for ordering the political process and creating a governmental majority. Thus, in the monocentric sovereignty systems of the European nation-states, where the legislature is fused with the executive, the parties operate within a highly favorable institutional environment. Because power is concentrated, the parties are able to build and maintain cohesive organizations with which to acquire and manage it. Strong parties in control of centralized decision-making structures inevitably preclude other forms of representation. Interest groups, lobbies, and social movements play a role also in European nation-states' political process, but that role is generally subordinate to the parties. Hence, the differences between America and the European nation-states—in the nature of the political, institutional, and social order—have also favored the formation of different partisan orders on the two shores of the Atlantic.

5.2. The Structuring of Partisan Politics in America and Europe

5.2.1. *The Implications of National and Industrial Revolutions*

The different patterns of political and economic development in Europe and America and the different institutional modalities for organizing territorial sovereignty inevitably affected the early structuring of partisan politics in the two continents. Structurally, the formation of partisan politics was inevitably influenced not only by the nature of both national and industrial revolutions but also by the timing of the process of democracy-building (Orren and Skowroneck 2004). Certainly, in America there was no 'national revolution' in the European sense. The American Revolution was an anticolonial struggle, the first war of independence of the modern era. Thus, it did not involve conflict between competing moral authorities (such as state and church) or between competing elites at the center and the peripheries, but rather conflict between a coalition of colonies and their motherland. In this sense, America is the first new nation (Lipset 1979) of the modern era because it was born from a struggle against an external power rather than from a struggle to overcome an internal divide. America did not have a center–periphery cleavage to overcome because it was a union of peripheries, a voluntary aggregation of separated states which set up a very weak supra-states (or central) authority. America was not created by a center already established but by established peripheries agreeing to create a center. At the same time, nineteenth-century America gradually became a nation without having to tame a rival religious authority as happened in the European nation-states. Its sectarian origins encouraged a pluralism of faiths that placed America on a path different from the one pursued by both Protestant and Catholic Europe. America had no need to nationalize the church, because it had no church but several sects. Nor did America need to counter the influence of a previously established Catholic Church, because the foundation of America itself derived from the search for 'a city on the hill', that is, for a place located as far as possible from that influence. The solution was the separation of the civil and religious spheres (Feldman 2005). Although that separation was repeatedly challenged by religious revivalist movements and continues to be so as it happens in the early years of the twenty-first century, it nevertheless persisted, nurturing mutual accommodation among a plurality of faiths. Consequently, America never witnessed the rise of religious parties with their lay counterparts. In some states, religious groups were able to acquire powerful influence in political affairs, controlling legislatures, mobilizing citizen action groups, and conditioning newspaper and media networks. However, they never played a crucial or distinctive role at the federal level, because they were obliged to join larger coalitions if they wanted to gain recognition and acceptance.

Moreover, the industrial revolution of the second half of the nineteenth century pitted the commercial interests of the northeast against the landed interests of the Southern plantation elites, more than it did the economic interests of capital against those of labor. In America, the conflict between capital and labor, although particularly fierce at the turn of the twentieth century, took a form quite different from that in Europe. That is to say, it did not produce class or Socialist parties as happened in the European nation-states, because the conflict exploded in a material and institutional context different from that of the latter. This is not to imply that there was no class conflict in America; indeed, *there was* a class conflict, and it was violent even by European standards (Smith 1993). However, the conflict did not give rise to a party system structured around a class cleavage because exit options were available to individuals and groups. High internal migration and the possibility of westward expansion at the height of industrial transformation diluted the pressure for class confrontation. To use Hirschman's terminology (1970), the possibility of exit options reduced the potential impact of voice strategies; an impact that, on the contrary, European nation-states experienced all along the industrial revolution, because of the previous successful accomplishment of state bounding. Thus, nineteenth-century America was not driven by the religious and class conflicts that beset Europe in the same period and which gave rise to the cleavages that structured the European party systems in the following century. It seems likely that the possibility of individual and group exits helped prevent the formation of both class and religious parties, these being the traditional European voice parties. 'Going west' was the alternative to the voice strategies used by European workers to dampen (through their own unions and parties) the negative effects of the construction of a modern capitalist economy.

The structuring of partisan politics in America was also significantly affected by the process of democratization. In America, indeed, democracy not only arrived before the state but it also preceded the formation of a modern capitalistic system (Wilentz 2005). Before (white and male) workers could develop a collective consciousness as members of the same class, they were individually integrated in the political system by a set of political and civil rights to which they had been entitled since the first decades of the nineteenth century. This individualized integration neutralized what might have been enormous pressure for the formation of a militant working class. Because a worker became a citizen as an individual, she or he did not have to organize with others in order to conquer her or his citizenship. 'American parties, unlike many European parties, were not originally organized by and for an already large industrial working class seeking, in addition to the franchise, a radical transformation of capitalist society' (Epstein 1986: 136). In America, in fact, already by 1824, which was almost fifty years before mass male suffrage became established in most of Europe, all but three American states had extended the right to vote to almost all adult white males. 'Almost no group of white men was denied a place in the nineteenth century party system' (Wiebe 1995: 80). Moreover, the distribution of government jobs among faithful party workers, which began under Andrew Jackson and Martin Van Buren in the 1830s and 1840s, again in an institutional context of a radically decentralized polity, helped spread the democratic belief that government was open to all and not just to few.

In the European nation-states, national and industrial revolutions took place in a very different context. Moreover, the process of democratization was largely promoted by the new social and political actors emerging from both the national and industrial revolutions. It was the existence of a nation which justified its democratization. But democracy was built also for neutralizing the negative effects of the industrial (capitalistic) revolution. Being a self-recognized social class made it possible, for industrial workers, to organize for achieving political rights. Political rights were a basic condition for participating in the political process and thus for steering the state toward control of the private forces of the market. One might say that, in the European nation-states, democracy came after not only the nation but also capitalism. Such historical sequence generated a structure of partisan politics which was finally institutionalized at the turn of the nineteenth century. Indeed, as Lipset and Rokkan (1967) argued some time ago, in the twentieth century the European nation-states' party systems continued to replicate the cleavages that had emerged within them in the wake of the national and industrial revolutions. The former revolution triggered conflict between central and peripheral rulers, and hence between state and church. The latter revolution created a contraposition between landed and industrial interests, and hence between capital and labor. The main European political parties of the twentieth century inherited those conflicts, becoming the representatives of the coalitions forged by those historical transformations (Bartolini 2000).

5.2.2. *The Territorial Constraints on Partisan Politics*

In America, the structuring of partisan politics was also affected by institutional factors, in particular the federal nature of the compound republic. In America, the federal structure has restricted not only direct intervention by the (federal) state in market activities, but it has also curtailed the organizational development of political parties able to appeal to a national electorate (Lowi 1978). In America, federalism, even during the period of the country's full industrialization, contributed to further hampering the formation of the class cleavage. America has never had a trans-state class mobilization (Katznelson 1985). Because America's party systems, in their various formats, were not based on class conflict, they generally lacked a national working class party. Working class interests had to be represented within one or the other of the two main political parties, together with other social and economic interests, thus diluting their political impact (Lipset and Marks 2000). Indeed, the lack of a national working class party, between the late nineteenth century and early twentieth century, is considered (Katznelson and Zolberg 1986) a crucial factor for understanding why America did not promote a social economy through public control (state participation in ownership, nationalization, collectivization) of the crucial economic sectors or resources. Certainly, and especially in the 1930s, the federal state was induced to intervene in the economy by introducing redistributive policies that affected the workings of the market and its predominant interpretation. However, as we have seen, America pursued market-correcting strategies, contrary to the market-substituting ones of European nation-states. Thus, in the years of the industrialization process, federalism precluded the politicization of market-building, restricting political mobilization to the level of states, counties, and localities. Unlike European partisan politics, which soon acquired national features, American partisan politics for long continued to be decentralized. Inevitably, therefore, its institutionalization generated a party system organized around regional, state, and local issues. American national parties were (and they largely continue to be) confederations of state and local parties, vehicles for the promotion (or the defense) at federal level of sectional, state, county, and local interests (Epstein 1986).

Quite the contrary happened in European nation-states, where the predominant role of class cleavage, especially in the first half of the twentieth century, led to the formation of powerful national working class parties, parties which then pressured the state to exert political control over the economy in order to curb the harmful social effects of the market system (Esping-Andersen 1992). With the institutionalization of partisan politics, European nation-states' parties appealed primarily to national constituencies, socially or religiously defined. While decentralized politics allowed America to maintain relatively weak federal separated institutions, nationalized politics pressured European nation-states into strengthening their own centralized institutional structure. In America, the territorial distribution of power characteristic of a compound polity thus prevented the class cleavage from becoming predominant even at the height of the industrial revolution. 'Americans of the late nineteenth century were deeply attached to their party-labels... links with economic class divisions always existed, though less clearly than elsewhere. [But], each major-party label had strong embittered sectional associations and also considerable reinforcement from ethnic and religious divisions' (Epstein 1986: 249). Moreover, that territorial distribution of powers prevented not only workers but also capitalists from perceiving the (federal) state as their own state. Thus, if federalism and the ethnic heterogeneity of the working class helped foster a disjuncture between labor and ethnic identities, with the latter more important than the former in motivating political participation (Roediger 1999), at the same time the decentralized nature of the American federal state prevented its direct use by the business elites, which in fact came to distrust it (Vogel 1996). Without a Socialist party there was no need, in America, for a capitalist or religious party such as those created in Europe to counteract socialism. In sum, 'America's precociously democratized federal polity has always made it difficult for either capitalists or industrial workers to operate as a unified political force in pursuit of class projects on a national scale.... American workers learned to separate their political participation as citizens living in ethnically defined localities from their workplace struggles for better wages and employment conditions' (Skocpol 1992*b*: 574).

Lacking truly national political parties, the American way of integrating ethnic, cultural, and territorial diversities relied on the 'hurly burly' of pressure politics and congressional sectionalism at the federal center. Society, or better social classes, came to be fragmented in a plurality of specific interest groups, operating in an autonomous way, pursuing very specific aims. The working classes came to be organized in sector-based, if not factory-based, trade associations and unions. Without the pressure of a nationally homogenizing conflict such as the struggle between the classes, and with state-based social mobilization, America has been able to preserve its decentralized institutional nature. That is to say, it has been able to maintain a low level of federal taxation and very limited federal intervention in social and economic relations (notwithstanding the significant federal social policies for war veterans introduced in the aftermath of the Civil War, Skocpol 1992*a*). Till the 1930s, politics was mainly a local and state activity. After all, it was much easier to overcome the constraints of collective action at the state rather than federal level (Jacobs, Novak, and Zelizer 2003). Weakened from below by ethnic dishomogeneity (and especially by the racial divide) of the working class and the relative fluidity of religious cleavages, and constrained from above by the federal separation of powers, nineteenth-century and early-twentieth-century American parties were never able to develop the kind of organizational structures that could support permanent national mobilization. Neither the Republicans nor the Democrats had truly national extragovernmental organizations, and their national committees were structured as confederal coalitions of state, county, and local parties (Epstein 1986: 123). At the same time, the party congressional caucuses worked as arenas for coordinating or negotiating sectional divisions. A presidential party formed only on the occasion of the four-yearly national convention for selection of the party candidate. Thus, although nineteenth-century American politics was characterized by strong party organizations, states and localities were the main fields of action by the latter. 'As local agencies, political parties energized the community ... In a nation of mobile people, parties called out to the community's shifting population with a steady drumbeat of appeals ... bringing them out to the polls on election day' (Wiebe 1995: 78).

This radical decentralization of politics was unknown in nineteenth-century and early-twentieth-century European nation-states. Although some of them registered the formation of territorial cleavages, the political impact of the latter was gradually muted by the growing nationalization of electoral politics, induced by political parties interested in mobilizing a constituency expression of entrenched classes and religious communities (Bartolini and Mair 1990). And thus, after World War II, both the main European nation-states' political parties, the Christian Democrats and the Social Democrats, have been formidable vehicles for socializing the market (Sassoon 1996). Important aspects of working life (such as working conditions, health and safety, retirement benefits) were demarketized by both parties, albeit through different types of welfare system (Esping-Andersen 1990), once they had gained control of the governmental majority in the European nation-states. In sum, although America had several party systems from its foundation to the mid-twentieth century (Chambers and Burnham 1975), all of them were based on sectional divisions. This is the political cleavage between states and regional areas expressed in radically different conceptions of the balance of powers to be struck between the states and the center of the federation (and their correlated social and economic implications). And it should not be forgotten that this division provoked one of the most violent and bloody civil wars of the modern age. This cleavage has continued to accompany American political development, even when the federal state has become more prominent than the federated states. In European nation-states, on the contrary, the party systems have come to be based on various combinations of socioeconomic, ethnic, cultural, religious, and ideological divisions since the end of national and industrial revolutions.

5.3. Parties and Separated Government in America

5.3.1. *Parties and Government in Congressional America*

In America, if the federal (institutional) structure has affected the structuring of the party system, the governmental (institutional) structure has defined the role the parties came to play in the decision-making process. It is commonly accepted that the founding fathers of the American republic feared party politics, with its factional implications, and designed a governmental system intended to keep projects of partisan politics at bay (Ranney 1975). However, the ink was not yet dry on the new federal constitution before the Madisonian model of separated government revealed its weaknesses, and it did so precisely at the level of federal decision-making. The first Jefferson presidency of the early nineteenth century was already characterized by an unforeseen operationalization of the constitution, whereby the political parties were used to link the separated institutions. A Jeffersonian model thus arose within the Madisonian one: which amounts to saying that electoral politics entered the constitution. As Hudson (1996: 38) wrote:

the separation-of-powers structure erected formidable barriers in the way of forming a coherent governing majority in the United States, but it did not take long after the ratification of the Constitution for the ingenious politicians of the period to develop a way of uniting the branches of government behind a popular government. The key to uniting the branches was the political party, and the first practitioner of the method was the third US president, Thomas Jefferson.

Without a political party able to link, first, the majority in the House with the one in the Senate and, thus, the two majorities with the President, separated government was seemingly unable to function. After the 1830s, Jefferson's intuition was amply borne out by the birth and development of a mature electoral democracy. With the granting of male suffrage, indeed, only the political parties were able to integrate the new electors into the government without this causing the latter's paralysis.

Although the life of American political parties has not been easy, the long pre-eminence of the legislature in national politics did much to alleviate their lot. Moreover, since the national political parties were traditionally coalitions of state and local political parties, the pre-eminence of Congress helped safeguard their organized action, given the territorially representative nature of the latter. As we know, the separation of powers was not completely institutionalized in the nineteenth century. The presidency performed a role anything but central in that century (Pious 1996); indeed, it was a prime concern of the founding fathers to give the presidency an exclusively executive function, while simultaneously protecting it against pressures applied to it by the legislature (considered to be the more important institution as the one liable to impose a possible 'tyranny of the majority') and by public opinion. Although the candidate for the presidency came to be selected by different methods, all of these methods, however, guaranteed the pre-eminence of the congressional elites, first, and of states' party leaders, later. After the *self-nomination* procedure at the end of the eighteenth century, for the first two decades of the 1800s presidential candidates were selected by the congressional caucus, known as 'King Caucus', or better by the elite that had created the new constitutional republic (Sterling 1966). In a context of reciprocal fear and significant differences between the states constituting the new republic, this oligarchic method allowed for the building of relations of mutual trust among the representatives of those states, thus keeping under scrutiny the recurrent inter-states tensions. But the populist wind very soon began to erode the elitist equilibrium, and in the 1830s introduction of the *national convention* system assigned power of selection to the party leaders of the states and counties, removing it from the country's restricted federal oligarchy. Once the national party convention had been adopted in the 1830s, the congressional leaders were able to influence its outcome through their connections with the organizations and leaders of the local and state parties. And at the same time, they were able to control the President, once the presidential candidate had been elected by the states' electoral colleges, because the members of the states' electoral colleges were nominated by states' legislatures, whose members were connected to congressional party leaders.

The presidents thus elected were necessarily conditioned by the congressional parties. The presidential election was a congressional business, therefore, because its members were closely involved (via the state and local party organizations) in the activity of those legislatures. In short, because Congress had the resources with which to control the behavior and choices of the President, the parties performed a crucial role as the representatives of state and local interests, thus influencing or controlling the decision-making process within the legislature, for almost the whole of the nineteenth century (Polsby 1986, 2004). The leadership of the majority party in the Congress maintained the connection with the President; the party leaders of the various congressional committees controlled and ordered the process; the Speaker of the House, some individual senators, and the leaders of the party caucuses in both chambers were the main actors in the decision-making process. And all of them were connected to the party leaders of the states. However, as we know, this institutional equilibrium was radically challenged, and thus transformed, by the two processes of nationalization and democratization of American politics. The nationalization process had important consequences for congressional government because it challenged its inter-states basis. The great economic changes wrought by the crisis of the 1880s, the formation of industrial and financial conglomerates (the first great corporations) of such size that they were able to alter the workings of the market, the birth of powerful interest organizations which exerted quasi-monopolistic control over one or more resources of crucial importance to the economic system, the revolution in production techniques, and the introduction and development of standardized mass production—because of these and other processes the states' control of federal government through Congress showed its decision-making inefficacy.

Indeed, it was highly implausible to govern a country which was becoming a great industrial power through the legislature and its very elaborated consensus-oriented internal procedures. In this new structural context, Congress's governmental action rapidly revealed its shortcomings, both in terms of the local nature of its policy directions and the slowness of their formulation. Now that congressional action was constrained by its representation of sectional and state-consolidated interests, it showed itself unable to give prompt definition to new national policy directions. And the weak administrative apparatus, which had proved congenial to congressional government, also swiftly revealed its inability to sustain the expansive impetus of the federal government. These institutional limitations of Congress, as well as the growth of the administrative apparatus, favored the rise (in the first decades of the twentieth century) of the presidency as the pre-eminent institution of separated government. And it was the affirmation of new (national) economic and social interests that prompted presidents to give both a representative reinterpretation to their role and a governmental one to the prerogatives ascribed to them by the constitution (Lowi 1985). The net result of this transformation was a deepening of the separation of powers at the federal level through the formation of a properly presidential branch. This context of highly institutionalized separated governmental institutions has ended up making the life of the parties extremely difficult.

5.3.2. Democratization of American Governmental Institutions

The American founding fathers made no secret of their preoccupation with democracy. As Madison put it in *Federalist no. 51*, when framing a new system of government, 'you must first enable the government to control the governed; and in the next place oblige it to control itself' (now in Beard 1964: 225). Regarding the first target, they imposed close restrictions on the eligibility to vote (suffrage was initially granted only to white, property-owning males) (Wood 1969), whereas, regarding the second target, they devised a complicated electoral system for the formation of the government: a House of Representatives elected by district voters, a Senate chosen by state legislatures, and a President indirectly elected by an Electoral College, in turn composed of ad hoc electors chosen by the state legislatures.

However, from the outset, this system was challenged for its democratic deficit. The fear that the system might collapse into a congressional regime provoked strong mobilization among the (white and male) electorate. It was the election of 1824 which triggered that fear, but its seeds were in the congressional interpretation of the constitution. As Lowi (1997: 4) observed, in the first years of the new republic:

[T]he presidency was drawn further and further into congressional domination...[because Congress] literally controlled selection of the chief executive himself: first, it controlled the system of nominating candidates for president (King Caucus), [and second] it also controlled the system for electing the president, because virtually everyone had to expect that with three or more serious candidates for president, most actual elections would end up in the House of Representatives, given the great difficulty of producing the absolute majority of Electors required by the Constitution.

In fact, article II.3 of the constitution stated that 'if no person have a majority, then from the five highest on the list the...House shall in like manner chuse the President'. This proposition was subsequently changed by the Twelfth Amendment (1804) in the following way: 'if no person have such majority, then from the persons having the highest numbers not exceeding three on the list of those voted for as President, the House of Representatives shall choose immediately, by ballot, the President'. Thus, when no candidate obtained the absolute majority of electoral votes during the presidential campaign of 1824, the Congress decided to select the President. Its choice was unwise, however, because it preferred the insider John Quincy Adams (Vice-President during the previous Monroe presidency) to the outsider Andrew Jackson (despite his fame as a military hero), even though Adams had obtained only 30.5 percent of the popular vote (and 84 electoral votes) compared with Jackson's 43.1 percent (and 99 electoral votes). This decision inevitably provoked a violent reaction by the Jacksonians against Congress's choice (or rather, the choice by the Democratic-Republican party's King Caucus) which established the conditions for acceleration of the democratization process (Chambers and Burnham 1975).

The presidential elections of 1828 were run as fully popular elections. Almost all of the then twenty-four states had eliminated property ownership as a requisite for entitlement to vote (although women did not obtain the right to vote until 1920, and African-Americans were not fully integrated into the electorate until 1964), so that in 1828 voters were four times the total of 1824 (Wilentz 2005). Moreover, by 1828, numerous state constitutions had been altered to allow the electorate, and not the state legislatures, to select the members of the presidential Electoral College on the basis of competing 'slates' (or lists) of Great Electors. Thereafter, the election of the Electoral College was given, in many states, a partisan structure whereby votes were pledged to one or other of the presidential candidates. This shift explains the importance of the competing slates of Great Electors, each with its votes pledged to a particular candidate. The election of 1828 saw the creation of something akin to a dual voting system: the formal mechanism of the electoral vote and the informal one of the popular vote. The ability of the political parties to structure the vote made it possible to resolve the duality: when the Great Electors assembled in the capitals of their respective states to select their candidate for the presidency, they voted on the basis of pledges made to the ordinary voters who had chosen them. Finally, 'by 1836, all states except Maine, chose their Great Electors by a winner-takes-all system that was tied to the popular presidential vote in the state' (Cain 2002: 302). In sum, the practice began of allocating *all* the state's electoral votes to the candidate who obtained the *plurality* of popular votes in the state.

However, this practice was plainly not satisfactory. Its majoritarian character gave rise to cases of political incongruence between the popular vote and the electoral vote. Two such cases were particularly scandalous: in 1876 the Republican Rutherford B. Hayes was elected President (by the Great Electors) even though he had obtained only 48 percent of the popular vote compared with the 51 percent of his Democratic rival Samuel J. Tilden. In 1888, the Republican Benjamin Harrison was elected President (by the Great Electors), although he had received around 0.6 percent fewer popular votes than his rival Grover Cleveland. Other cases, although less significant because the outcome was not affected, can be cited; for instance, the elections of 1880 and 1884. And of course, in more recent times, the most striking case was the presidential election of 2000, when not only the losing candidate in the popular vote obtained a majority in the electoral vote, but the counting of the popular vote in the state of Florida (which decided the race) provoked fierce controversy between the two candidates and was then resolved by a majority decision (5 to 4) of the Supreme Court. Nevertheless, the institutional strengthening of the Electoral College by opening it up to popular participation was crucial in preventing the parliamentarization of the separated government (and thus in protecting the interests of the smaller states). Of course, with the consolidation of the two-party system in the presidential election, the majoritarian logic (represented by the winner-takes-all principle) introduced into the antimajoritarian Electoral College (which overrepresents the smaller states because of the two-senators clause) transformed de facto the presidential election into a popular election. But it was and it continues to be a majoritarian logic within states' constraints.

In addition to the Electoral College, other bastions were crumbling. Indeed, one of them, the Senate's constitutional right to be elected indirectly (or better to be selected by states' legislatures), collapsed outright. As early as the 1830s, the Jacksonian wind of electoral change was blowing through the state legislatures and the federal senators. In many states, candidates for the state legislatures (then all bicameral) were required to announce, in the event of their being elected, their choice of candidates for the federal Senate (since then, only Nebraska has become unicameral in 1937). Thus popular elections at the state level rapidly began to influence the nonpopular elections for the federal Senate, which still remained formally the province of the respective legislatures. However, it was not until the advent of the Progressive forces at the turn of the century that election of the federal senators became fully democratized. The year 1913 saw definitive approval of the Seventeenth Constitutional Amendment, which abolished the right of state legislatures to elect senators and assigned that right directly to the voters—although by that time more than half the states had already introduced some sort of functional equivalent to direct election. Certainly, even if these processes of democratization were not desired and encouraged by the parties, they were not necessarily opposed to them. After all, democratization of the Electoral College, of the selection of presidential candidates, and of the system of senatorial elections enabled the parties to consolidate their influence in electoral politics. However, other reforms of the Progressive period seriously compromised this influence. First, criticisms of the abuses committed by the party machines (in organizing the inclusion of new immigrants in the electoral process) led to legislation (especially at the states' level) which imposed strict legal restrictions on the exercise of the vote (the so-called 'system of 1896'). This system, which hampered the parties' ability to mobilize voters, weakened them in the electoral arena because it greatly reduced the size of the active electorate (McCormick 1986).

Second, the creation of a modern federal state based on a professional civil service connected to the presidency and no longer based on patronage, and which distributed public sector jobs from Congress, gradually diminished the role of the political parties. As Skowroneck (1987: 187) remarked: 'modern American state building...shattered an outmoded form of party government... [although] it failed to reconstruct a vital role for party in the new democracy.' This was bad news for the congressional parties, whose members had previously relied on patronage to build electoral support, but good news for the President, whose executive power was enhanced by an efficient bureaucracy under his control. Third, the democratization of internal congressional politics weakened the parties' capacity to control decision-making within that institution. Emblematic of this process was the seniority system adopted in 1910 by the House of Representatives following a revolt by the legislators (many of whom held progressive views and had been elected for the first time in 1908) against the centralist methods of the Speaker, who was dubbed 'Tsar Cannon'. This provision, which abolished the Speaker's authority to appoint the chairmen of the congressional committees (the longest-serving member could now automatically take over as chairman), further reduced the ability of the congressional party leaders to command the voting choices of members of the congressional caucus.

As the two processes of democratization and nationalization weakened congressional party government, and thus the capacity of states' party leaders to influence federal policy, at the same time they triggered the reverse process in the executive. The presidencies of F. D. Roosevelt, more so than the President's party, became the representational link with the political and social forces that had acquired increasing national influence in the previous fifty years but still did not have a decisive impact at the federal level. Hence, while the increased representative capacity of the presidency, strengthened by administrative growth, justified its governmental ascendancy, the diminished representative capacity of Congress, weakened by its inability to rely on patronage, conversely explains the diminishment of its governmental power. Thus, with the 'Roosevelt revolution', as Einaudi termed it (1950), there was a scaling down of the parties' governmental role. As Milkis (1993: 5) has argued: 'the Democratic party became during the late 1930s the party to end all parties. Under Roosevelt's leadership, it was dedicated to a program that eventually lessened the importance of the two-party system and established a modern executive as the principal focus of representative government in the United States'.

In sum, the institutional equilibrium of the nineteenth century changed radically at the turn of that century. The country's impetuous industrial development and its ponderous international expansion could not be governed by a weak federal authority. The need, first to regulate the internal industrial economy and society, and then to promote the country's geopolitical/geoeconomic interests internationally, started to strain the American compound republic. Both processes increased the role of the federal institutions vis-à-vis those of the states and the role of the President vis-à-vis Congress. In this new context, political parties inevitably had to look for a new role to play.

5.3.3. *The Parties in Search of a New Role in the Era of the Modern Presidency*

The growth of the modern presidency significantly challenged the decision-making role that the parties had performed in the congressional government period (Mezey 1989). The institutional and political innovations introduced by the presidencies of F. D. Roosevelt (1933–45) made the life of the parties (Richley 1992) much more difficult than it was in the past. Indeed, Roosevelt's first two presidencies were characterized by constant institutional conflict with Congress and the Supreme Court.

Such was the nature of that conflict that Roosevelt was forced to find different inspirational criteria for his political action, and hence for the exercise of his leadership. From this conflict sprang what has been called (Tulis 1987) the 'rhetorical Presidency': namely, an institution of government that founded its legitimacy on direct communication (rhetorical but not necessarily demagogic) between the President and citizens. Thereafter, presidents 'went public' (Kernell 1992), also because popular support was crucial if they were to gain the upper hand in conflicts with rival institutional actors (for instance the Congress or state legislatures). The parties were squeezed into the middle of this multiple institutional conflict (Rozzel and Pederson 1997). The President claimed a personal popular role which undermined the capacity of the parties to control the decision-making process (Skowroneck 1997).

The reinforcement of the executive's structure gave the President operational autonomy in addressing the new governmental tasks of the modern presidency. At the same time, the country's increasingly important role in international politics from the 1940s onward accelerated the strengthening of the President's popular role: he was now the sole representative of the country (and of its people) in the system of international relations and conflicts. The more the country was internationally exposed, the more its population needed a domestic leader and not a party with which to identify—all the more so if the country was engaged in what was perceived to be a life-or-death international struggle with an intrinsically antagonistic power like the Soviet Union. Not surprisingly, it was during the Cold War that America underwent the centralization of governmental authority around the presidency (in foreign and military policies in particular) that the European nation-states had already experienced. Again, external threats continued to exert formidable pressure for the rationalization and centralization of domestic authority structures, thus confirming Tilly's approach to state centralization.

The ascent of the President (and therefore of the presidency) during the 1930s and 1940s significantly reduced the political role of the parties in American democracy. Parties remained strong organizations as long as the Congress retained its central role in the federal decision-making process, but they had difficulty in continuing to do so with the growth of presidential government and the subsequent full institutionalization of the separation of powers between the Congress and the President. Indeed, a fully institutionalized separation of powers makes the institutional habitat in which the political parties operated much more inhospitable. After World War II, the party system, already horizontally splintered in individual states, now also fragmented vertically into the individual federal institutions of government. Nationally, bipartisanship survived, but it did so in the form of two-party subsystems at the levels of the presidency, the House of Representatives, and the Senate (Eldersveld and Walton 2000). Under these conditions, the national political party as such only came into being at the four-yearly conventions that selected the presidential candidate. However, its existence (i.e. its program and identity) was merely a reflection of the program and identity of the candidate finally chosen. Of course, on conclusion of the convention, each institutional subsegment of the party regained its autonomy.

Although their importance was reduced with the growth of presidential pre-eminence, the parties found a way to regain a role in the separated system. They specialized in connecting officeholders in the various governmental branches, and especially in organizing support for the President within the Congress (Schramm and Wilson 1993; Ranney, Wolfinger, and Polsby 1999). The parties continued to be important in attenuating the effects of governmental separation (Polsby 1983a), but this was a 'labor of Sisyphus' where they had constantly to bind together what the system of government had set asunder, also internally to the parties themselves. Nevertheless, by acting as 'para-constitutional factors' (Riggs 1988), they successfully dampened what was potentially devastating conflict between the institutions. In the second half of the twentieth century, therefore, the parties performed a more limited role in the decision-making process. Within the Congress, they became 'procedural coalitions' (Cox and McCubbins 1993), useful for favoring working relations between its members, and thus between the latter and the President. A role they could play effectively because their lack of an ideological identity made the formation of trans-party coalitions, reflecting the position taken up by the President, possible (Aldrich and Niemi 1996). However, the fluidity of party cleavages further increased the pluralism of the political process. In the American politics of the second half of the twentieth century, political parties had to compete with other actors (interest groups, lobbies, social movements, epistemic communities, territorial organizations, local constituency associations, political action committees) for representing interests in the electoral process (Salisbury 2000). Moreover, given the full separation of powers at the level of the federal institutions, they could not even attempt to be the main actors for the governmental aggregation of the interests that emerged through the electoral process. In sum, the nonparty actors not only intervened autonomously in the electoral arena, but they also did the same in the governmental arena through their contacts with single members of the Congress or officials of the presidency (Hernson, Shaiko, and Wilcox 2004).

5.4. Parties and Government in Post–World War II Europe

In Europe too, and especially since World War II, the executive branch has increased its role within the governmental system (Helms 2005). However, the ascendancy of the executive has not restricted decision-making by the parties; rather, it has strengthened the parties' ability to exert political influence (Ware 1995). Although the executive has increased its role in all parliamentary systems, this has been much more evident in competitive than in consensual democracies. In competitive democracies, in fact, parliament has been formed by elections, but it has been the governmental majority that came to be chosen by this means. During the course of the second half of the twentieth century, it was the electoral formation of the executive that gradually shifted the locus of power from the legislature to the executive (Powell 2000). This was a shift of no little significance, because it also strengthened the electoral competition between parties or political poles. By contrast, in consensus democracies, the parliamentary majority has been the outcome of long postelection negotiations, not of a clearly identified electoral majority. Inevitably, executive influence in these systems has been bounded by the party elites operating in or outside the legislature. Those not in the government (generally the leaders of the parties) have had no interest in granting decision-making autonomy to the executive. Thus, whilst the parliamentary systems have also displayed the increased influence of the executive throughout the post–World War II period, it is also true that the executive has predominated to different degrees at different times (Budge and Keman 1993).

These two types of parliamentarianism have introduced different institutional arrangements for the action of their executives (Sartori 1996; Lijphart 1999). Whereas in consensual parliamentarianism (such as Belgium's) the executive must undergo formal investiture as a collective body by parliament, this is not the case in competitive parliamentarianism. Indeed, the British Prime Minister is appointed by the monarch according to the outcome of the national elections, and the German Chancellor is voted in by the Bundestag on a personal basis and can only be voted out when an alternative Chancellor has received the parliament's support. This difference in forms of government investiture speaks volumes about executive power. Whereas in Germany and Britain parliamentary confidence is lodged wholly with the Chancellor or Prime Minister, these being the true leaders of the executive and thus of the parliamentary majority supporting it, in Belgium—where it is the government as a whole which receives the parliament's approval—the executive's leader is scrutinized by the parties in the parliamentary majority, to the point that his or her decision-making capacity has been frequently curtailed.

One might say (Le Duc, Niemi, and Norris 1996; King 2002) that differences in electoral systems and party competition have induced consensual and competitive parliamentarianisms to form different expectations concerning the leadership's role. Consensual parliamentary systems entail a collegial leadership that only in exceptional circumstances can be replaced by a strong personal leadership, while competitive parliamentary systems have long recognized the need for effective governmental leaders, albeit bounded by collegial constraints. Thus, although mass political communication has strengthened the role of individual leaders more than that of collective organization, in both parliamentary systems the parties have retained a decision-making role (Mény and Knapp 1998). In no parliamentary system, in fact, can the governmental leader operate without the support of the parties in the executive and the parliamentary majority. This is a necessity which has its costs for the Prime Minister. In these systems, because the members of the executive (ministers, vice ministers, junior ministers) are not at the disposal of the Prime Minister but represent the various party factions or groups in the parliamentary majority, they impose constraints on the Prime Minister, whose actions must take account of their preferences (if she or he wants to stay in office). It is for this reason that a parliamentary system tends to foster a collective logic of action by the executive.

Within single-sovereignty systems, there are distinct differences between parliamentary and semi-presidential systems. In the French semi-presidential system, the direct and separate (from the election of the legislature) election of the President of the Republic has progressively transformed the political parties (especially the potential governmental parties) into parties of the President. That is to say, they have become organizational structures that (although they have a certain program identity) are closely identified with their candidates for presidency of the Republic. However, the parties dominated by the leaders of semi-presidential France cannot be equated with the American presidential parties. In America, at the presidential level, the party program is the program of the candidate selected every four years to compete for the presidency, whereas in France parties have identities distinct from the candidate for the presidency, although they are adapted to his or her political priorities.

The semi-presidential system differs from its parliamentary counterparts also as regards the relationships among the executive, the parties, and the leader (Elgie 2003). Unlike the parliamentary systems in which the influence of the Prime Minister is bounded, albeit to varying degrees, by the collective (party) constraint of the cabinet over which she or he presides (James 1999), in semi-presidential government the pre-eminence of the President of the Republic is institutionally unequivocal *unless* there is a different parliamentary majority. In the latter case, the leader of the government tends to be the Prime Minister, although she or he is bounded by the views and influence of the President of the Republic. In the American separation of powers system, the President's authority over his executive is institutionally guaranteed, while in the French semi-presidential system it is, by contrast, only politically guaranteed. In both cases the electors elect a President, but whereas the American President has no need of legislative support when forming his executive (although his choices must receive the Senate's advice and consent), this is not the case of the French President; and should such support be politically lacking, his authority is substantially curtailed, although it is never entirely annulled. Thus, while the European parliamentary systems have encouraged governmental strategies of action based on the parties, and the French semi-presidential system has encouraged a stronger role of the President of the Republic but within party constraints, the American system of separation of powers has weakened party cohesion, opening spaces for strategies of action based on the agenda of an individual leader rather than a party.

The history of the European parties, especially in the twentieth century, has been quite different from that of the American parties (Katz and Crotty 2006). Whether parties originated outside or inside the parliamentary institutions, in Europe they soon began to create organizations that are able to control or influence the parliamentary process. After starting on the left side of the political system (Duverger 1951), the organizational thrust inevitably extended to the clubs and associations of both the right and the center. Between the two world wars, and especially after World War II, party-building became a feature shared by both left-wing and right-wing politics. Party models differed significantly across Europe (Panebianco 1988), and especially so in regard to the locus of decision-making power. While mass Socialist and Popular parties tended to locate decision-making power in the extraparliamentary organization of the party (Sassoon 1996), Conservative and Liberal parties instead tended to preserve the role of the parliamentary elite as the party's leading group. This difference in organization was due to several factors: the origin of parties (internal or external to the parliament), their social identity (class-based or appealing to a broader public), and their culture (mass or elitist). Nevertheless, the difference did not alter the crucial fact that parties came to play a central role in both the electoral process and governmental institutions of all the consolidated European democracies.

The European political parties of the left, right, and center have thus grown up as cohesive organizations identified with national programs and intent on gaining access to centralized governmental power (Katz and Mair 1992). The ascendancy of the executive over the legislature has further strengthened the decision-making role of the European parties (Gallagher, Mair, and Laver 2005), in contrast to what has happened in America. Certainly, also in European nation-states, since the 1970s, the identification of voters with parties has declined while the public distrust of parties has increased (Dalton and Wattenberg 2000; Pharr and Putnam 2000). Moreover, also in European nation-states, the parties have come to be challenged in the organization of electoral campaigns by other actors, especially by (televised) media actors (Hallin and Mancini 2004). Nevertheless, although electorally less relevant than in the past, European political parties are still much more influential in electioneering and decision-making than are and used to be the American ones. Indeed, in European nation-states, parties continue to control the key for accessing both the electoral and governmental processes. Nonparty actors (interest groups, lobbies, movements, associations) have come to play an important role in the political process; nevertheless, the parties continue to be the gatekeepers of the latter.

5.5. American Parties between Decline and Transformation

5.5.1. *The Personalization Process in America*

For Cain (2002: 310), 'one of the distinctive characteristics of US political reform is that it frequently seeks to limit the influence of political parties'. The tendency of the American system of government to reward individual rather than party action was dramatically accelerated by the electoral and institutional changes introduced during the turbulent decade of the

1960s. Since then, the electoral process in America has undergone a significant process of personalization. Candidates for the presidency have grown increasingly independent of the traditional party organizations. A highly personalized method of selecting the presidential candidate has arisen: so personalized, indeed, that it has produced outright candidate parties. This personalization has also been due to the increasing role of the media in the electoral process. However, the main reason for it has been the parties' changing role in the selection of presidential candidates, and it was the primaries system introduced by the Democrats in 1972, in particular, which radically changed American politics (Polsby 1983b).

In the second half of the 1960s, as the country divided over the military intervention in Vietnam, a deep-rooted tangle of contradictions and conflicts came to the surface. The violence that exploded at the 1968 Democratic National Convention in Chicago brought on to the public agenda— with an urgency unprecedented even by the Progressive upheavals at the beginning of the twentieth century—the issue of democratizing the political parties, given that these, as well as the country's other governing institutions, were now held in extremely low public esteem. When reform of the political parties got under way in the 1960s it was not oriented by a specific party model (Crotty 1982). In addition to tensions and contingent pressures, it stemmed from highly diverse political cultures. But one of its main components was indubitably the antiparty tradition that sprang from the more populist variant of Progressivism (Crotty 1980). In twentieth-century America, the democratization of political parties generally signifies reform of the process by which the presidential candidate is selected. In fact, the outcome of the 1960s' turmoil was adoption of a selection process based on *direct primaries*. Again, that democratization has been an effect of the need to reduce the democratic deficit of the federal (supra-states) governmental decisions. Because of the growing decision-making role exercised by the President, a formidable popular pressure for making him more accountable to the voters has come to develop.

Although the first direct primary had been held in Wisconsin in 1903 (Merriam 1908), it was only in the last three decades of the twentieth century that it became the predominant system for selecting the presidential candidate. Certainly, in the 1910s, experimentation with a *mixed system*, where selection was still centered on the national convention but was influenced by the results of selected direct primaries, was pursued. This system was scrapped at the end of the 1960s and replaced, in 1972, by a selection system *based mainly on (presidential) primaries*. Mainly, because some states have nevertheless continued to select the delegates for the party national convention through the so-called *caucus system* (i.e. in meetings of local party members). Thus, while the presidential primaries introduced at the beginning of the twentieth century performed a supplementary role in the selection of the presidential candidate—who was still chosen at the four-yearly party conventions held ever since the 1830s— the presidential primaries system introduced in 1972 led to the de facto superseding of the national convention. That is to say, today the presidential primaries no longer merely supplement the convention system; they have taken its place. It is true that primaries were extremely popular in the 1910s (suffice it to consider that in 1916, as regards the Democratic Party, and in 1916 and 1920 as regards the Republican Party, more than half of the delegates to the national convention were selected by means of primaries, 53.5% in the former case and 58.9% and 57.8% respectively in the latter). Thereafter, however, their use gradually declined (in 1968 only 15 states held presidential primaries, and the delegates elected through them represented 40.2% and 38.1% of the delegates at the national conventions of the Democrats and Republicans, respectively) (Stanley and Niemi 2003: 66).

This situation changed radically after the reforms of the late 1960s (Stanley and Niemi 2003). Since 1972, around two-thirds of convention delegates have been selected by presidential primaries on the basis of the support for a particular presidential candidate. Consider the 1990s: in 1992 the Democratic Party held 40 presidential primaries, with the delegates elected amounting to 66.9 percent of the convention total, and the Republicans held 39 presidential primaries with the elected delegates representing 83.9 percent of the convention total. These percentages were then repeated during the 1996 presidential elections, although on that occasion the Republicans held more primaries than the Democrats: 43 as opposed to 36. In 2000, 65.6 percent of Democratic and 82.7 percent of Republican delegates to the national convention were chosen by primaries (held in 39 states for the Democrats and 42 states for the Republicans). Then, in 2004, 81.4 percent of delegates at the Democratic Party national convention were chosen by 39 primaries (while, of course, the Republican Party, in that it had an incumbent President, organized only the national convention). It is for this reason that the convention now does no more than formalize a decision—the choice of candidate— already made during the presidential primaries. Not only its deliberative capacity but also the decision-making power of the party leaders, traditionally emphasized by the convention, has been significantly reduced.

Since the 1970s, America has been the first and (to date) only country to adopt the direct primary as its system for the selection of candidates (specifically presidential candidates, but also candidates for congressional and states' legislatures and various counties' offices). What Ranney (1990: 182) noted at the beginning of the 1990s was still valid at the beginning of the following decade: 'perhaps the sharpest contrast between nominating procedures in the United States and those in other democratic countries is provided by the U.S. use of direct primary'. Even in the European nation-states where primaries are used, they should be more properly termed *party primaries*, rather than direct primaries (Fabbrini 1998: 76–104), in that the candidate is selected by the members of the party (no longer solely by its leaders), not by ordinary voters. Indeed, it is important to stress (Ranney 1990: 182) that the direct primary is 'a procedure in which candidates are selected directly by the voters in government-supervised elections rather than indirectly by party leaders in caucuses or conventions'. Although they have been required to make their internal selection process transparent, the European (nation-states') political parties have to date been able to preserve the boundary between the members and the electors (of the party). Important changes are beginning to emerge, such as the adoption by the Italian center-left of the direct primary in 2005, but this was made possible by the unstructured nature of the Italian party system after the collapse of the post–World War II party system in the 1990s, and in any case it had mainly a symbolic purport. By contrast, where the parties have kept their role at the center of the political system (as in all European national democracies), the democratization of their procedure of selecting candidates for public office has not challenged their organizational and collective identity (Hopkin 2001).

5.5.2. *American Candidate-Oriented Politics*

The direct primary is thus a method with which to *select* candidates who then stand for election (although, in the presidential primary's case, it is a method to select delegates for the national convention, where they will support a particular presidential candidate), an election which is decided by the voters, not by the party officials or institutional representatives. There are differences within the direct primary system in regard to *who* is entitled to vote. Nevertheless, despite these differences, none of the primaries in question draws a distinction between the party member and the party voter; indeed, if possible, the direct primaries system has entirely eliminated the distinction. Consequently, because they are selected by those who then vote for them, candidates have been able to leapfrog the traditional party intermediation between candidates for public office and the voters.

Especially in the case of presidential primaries, the thrust of the reform was to *institutionalize* this superseding of the influence of party leaders and officeholders (Polsby 1983*b*). In fact, the reform process moved in two directions. The first concerned the composition and functioning of the national convention, which still undertook the candidate's formal investiture (Davis 1997). With the elections of 1972, restrictive criteria were imposed on the representation of the so-called *unpledged delegates*, those not directly chosen in the primaries (or caucuses). In 1972, no more than 10 percent of delegates could represent the party organization or its representatives in office (in the state and federal legislatures). The percentage was reduced to 8 percent in 1984 and it was then established at 11 percent during the 1990s. Finally, further criteria were introduced, not only to ensure a more open dialectic at the convention (abolition of the so-called 'unity rule' under which the local and state delegations were obliged to vote unitarily) but also to protect the decision-making autonomy of individual delegates (putting an end to the last-minute *bandwagoning* that had marked previous conventions). Although the constraints introduced in 1972 were subsequently relaxed, still today they characterize the organizational setup of the national conventions of the two national parties. The operational effect of this reform is evident: the candidate does not have (nor does he need to have) any form of dependence on the party in government (i.e. on the members of his party in Congress). But this also means that the latter feels no obligation to support a President chosen by others.

The second concern of the reform centered on the rules governing the financing of electoral campaigns (Sorauf 1992; Malbin 2003). Approved and subsequently amended between 1971 and 1976, it was the federal Election Campaign Act which imposed tight controls on private financial contributions to electoral campaigns and also regulated their public funding on radically new bases. As regards private funding, the law stipulated that individuals and interest groups could respectively contribute no more than a maximum of $1,000 and $5,000 to a candidate's election campaign. As regards public funding, it determined that federal contributions to election campaigns should be devolved directly to the candidates and no longer paid to the party's electoral committee. Both provisions were evidently intended to deprive the parties of control over resources of crucial importance for their action. It is now the candidates who personally receive funds and support, no longer the parties. Indeed, running for office has become an extremely expensive activity in a candidate-centered process (Donnelly, Fine, and Miller 2001). While in 1980, the total cost of the presidential election was $62,700,000, in 2004 it was more than doubled, jumping to $150,100,000. This dramatic rise in campaign costs obliged the candidates to increase their fund-raising activities: considering both Democratic and Republican candidates, total presidential campaign receipts soared from $125,200,000 in 1991–2 to $673,900,000 in 2003–4 (US Federal Election Commission, *Reports on Financial Activity, Final Report and Quadrennial Reports*, various years).

From the 1970s to the 1990s, the combined effect of these two reforms was a drastic cutback in the parties' electoral role. The electoral process registered a progressive change which clearly worked in favor of the candidate (Wattenberg 1991). The candidate became the crucial actor in the electoral process, although this did not signify that the electoral competition was a game based exclusively on personal qualities. In his conclusions to a study on the 2000 presidential elections, Bartels (2002: 69) pointed out that 'what is surprising is not that the electoral impact of candidate traits was modest... [but that] the modest effect of candidate traits was... large enough to be decisive'. Thus, as regards the presidential election in particular, the personalization of the competition was the most distinctive feature of the entire electoral process in that period. Candidates used primarily their own resources to fund their campaigns: their reputations, their networks of campaign contributors and supporters, their policy preferences, and their communication skills made the difference. Consequently, presidents elected on a personal basis increased the personalization of the presidency. Without the support of a party in keeping his relation with Congress, the President had to strengthen his popular (or rhetorical) leadership more than his governmental one.

5.5.3. *The Revolution of Air Conditioning and Party-Rebuilding*

Contrary to many expectations, America has not become a democracy without parties. Adapting to the new context of candidate-oriented politics, since the mid-1990s, American parties have registered a significant process of rebuilding, both as electoral and as governmental actors. Party-rebuilding was due to several factors. First, the financial factor. 'As the demand for political money increased and the contribution limits remained fixed, candidates needed to find alternative ways to raise the large sum of money to run campaigns that increasingly relied on paid consultants, computer-generated mail and television advertising' (Cain 2002: 312). In particular, the candidates recurred to the 'soft money' raised by the parties. Through that money, the parties have transformed themselves into superb support structures—equipped with formidable technologies—for the various candidates. Particularly at the *electoral level*, parties have turned into highly efficient support organizations for candidates. If between the 1960s and the 1980s, as Aldrich (1995: 288) remarked, 'an alternative means to office became a viable alternative to the older form of parties in-the-electorate. It became technologically feasible for a candidate—to be sure almost invariably a major party's affiliate—to substitute his or her own campaign organization for the party's. This became possible first at the presidential level', since the 1990s the parties have regained much of their organizational strength. The support of the parties has become a condition for electoral success. Certainly, the Bipartisan Campaign Reform Act approved by Congress in 2002 (better known as the McCain–Feingold reform of campaign finance) stopped the parties from spending unregulated and unlimited 'soft money', although the parties are allowed to raise regulated 'hard money' and spend it without limits if independently from candidates' campaigns.[1] However, the law has stemmed the flow of unregulated money to the parties, but it has not changed the fact that parties still control quite a lot of money for financing properly the candidates' campaigns. To be sure, there are good reasons for arguing that this reform will not change the money-driven politics of American elections (Samples 2006).

Second, party-rebuilding was due to a combination of ideological and technological factors (Sabato and Larson 2001; Maisel 2002). With the transformation of Southern politics as a reaction to the civil rights legislation of the 1960s, many if not all Southern conservatives have migrated from the Democrats to the Republicans, making the two parties much more internally homogeneous than ever in the past. Particularly since the 1990s, and then fully in the first half of the 2000s, the two parties have become much more distinct (ideologically) and much more cohesive (organizationally), deepening also their sectional character. This was also due to technological innovations, such as the 'air conditioning revolution' (to use the efficacious expression of Polsby 2004), that created the conditions for a significant reshuffling of the social structure of the Southern states. If a large number of African-Americans moved to the North as an effect of civil rights legislation in the mid-1960s, a large number of the white middle class moved in the opposite direction, southward, as technological advances made the Southern states climatically and economically desirable. By 2002, Southern whites represented four-fifths of the Southern states' population and African-Americans only 19 percent (while they were 41% in 1860). The South has thus become much more homogeneously white, well-off, elderly, and religious, thus giving life to an ethnic (and religious) America that the Republican Party has come to represent in its entirety. With the disappearance of its Southern conservative wing, the Democratic Party has also become a much more homogeneous organization. For the first time, in the post–World War II period, the parties have clearly distinct political identities (Lieven 2004; Fabbrini 2006). Indeed, they have attracted the support of militant (and ideological) constituencies, support they have thus transferred to candidates, making thus the difference especially in competitive races.

For this reason, probably it is no longer the complete picture, as Katz and Kolodny (1994) argued in the mid-1990s, that American parties are 'empty vessels' susceptible to be conquered by the most organized candidates and interest groups. Especially the Republican Party has become a clearly identified 'vessel' (Taylor 2005), the repository of mobilized ideological constituencies (mainly located in the Southern and central states). In short, if it is true that in America, since the reforms of the late 1960s, 'the party is in service to its candidates and office holders, it is structured to advance the need and interests of ambitious politicians. That is, this is a party designed around the ambitions of effectively autonomous politicians, responsible for their own electoral fates and therefore responsive to the concerns of their individual electoral constituencies' (Aldrich 1995: 289), then it is also true that the support of the parties has become necessary for winning the elections. Party-rebuilding was also due to a third factor, namely the institutionalization of the divided government between 1968 and 2000 (see Chapter 3). It was the politics by other means, started with the attempt to impeach the Republican president in 1973 and thus conducted until the attempt to impeach the Democratic president in 1999, which has created a polarization between the elites of two parties much deeper than the polarization between their voters (Fiorina 2005). Thus, a highly conflictual divided government has increased the *governmental* role of the parties. Indeed, if the data indicate a decline of the 'party in the electorate' (i.e. a decrease in the number of voters who identify with one or the other party, Abramson 2007), then the same cannot be said for both the 'party as organization' and the 'party in the government'. Regarding the latter, not only since the 1990s has the cohesion of the congressional parties significantly increased (as is shown by the unusual unity of party voting within the Congress, McCarthy,

Poole, and Rosenthal 2006), but the 'party in the government' was trans-formed (between 2002–6) into a proper and unusual 'party government' (Hacker and Pierson 2005), as America has never had (given the internal ideological cohesion of the majority party in control of the presidency, the House of Representatives, and the Senate). This experience of party government was interrupted by the mid-term elections of 2006, which have created a congressional majority different from the presidential one.

Will this process of party-rebuilding reverse the long trend toward a reduction of the electoral and governmental roles of the American parties? It seems implausible. A highly personalized political process, conjugated with a deep institutionalized separation of powers system, continues to represent a very unfavorable environment for political parties. American political parties effectively adapted to the new candidate-centered poli-tics, but their electoral and governmental role is continually challenged by other actors—and by the candidates and their organization first of all. While American partisan politics has undergone major institutional changes since the 1960s, the same cannot be said for partisan politics in the European nation-states. Certainly, in the latter too, partisan politics has been affected by the increasing role of the media in the political process and by the mobilization of a plurality of nonparty actors (Cain, Dalton, and Scarrow 2003). However, none of the European nation-states has witnessed a growth of candidate-centered politics of such magnitude as in America. Thus, while in European nation-states elections are still run by political parties and the parties control the selection and affect the choices of governmental leaders, in America, in both the electoral and governmental process, parties have to contend with a plurality of very influential nonparty actors.

5.6. Conclusion

Even at the level of partisan politics, America and the European nation-states thus have structured different patterns. Regarding the party sys-tems, American politics has been traditionally organized around different types of sectional cleavages. The inter-states features of the compound polity have influenced the politics at the supra-states level. Certainly, American politics was and continues to be influenced by other divisions, be they ideological, religious, economic, social, or cultural. However, the sectional fracture and its changing dynamics have constituted the peculiar property of the various American party systems (and a crucial indicator of the voting behavior of the members of Congress). On the contrary, in the European nation-states, sectional cleavages have never imposed themselves as the inspiring principle of party systems' logic. Of course, in certain European nation-states (such as Spain or Italy), territorial divisions emerged periodically. However, unless they were expressions of nationalistic claims to independence (as in the Basque country in Spain), those divisions were unable to alter the established structure of partisan politics. In general, they were reabsorbed by and within the predominant parties or they gave rise to new parties thus integrated in the domestic party system. At the same moment, the separation of powers system of the American government has constituted a very unfavorable institutional environment for political parties. In particular in the twentieth century, parties have come to play a secondary role in the electoral and governmental process. Other nonparty actors (such as interest groups, lobbies, or movements) in many cases played a more influential role in the political process. Although at the turn of the twentieth century, a process of party-rebuilding has started, especially within Congress, the American governmental process continues to be characterized by a plurality of actors (among which the parties). In the European nation-states, on the contrary, the parties are the gatekeepers of the electoral and governmental arena.

Nevertheless, even partisan politics has changed significantly, in Europe, since the growth of the integration process in the second half of the twentieth century. The outcome of that process, the EU, has highlighted a form of partisan politics at odds with the partisan politics of its member-states. The EU does not have a party system in the traditional European sense, but its partisan politics has become organized around different types of party system, in its member-states and within the supranational institutions (in particular, of course, within the EP). EU politics, moreover, has become constantly characterized by sectional rather than class or religious cleavages. Certainly, within the EP, traditional divisions are apparent, such as the division between the left (European Socialist party) and the right (European Popular party). However, the structural division in the EP, as well as within the European Council of Ministers, is not between left and right. It is a division between member-states which favor more integration and member-states which favor less integration, or between mobile alliances of member-states with highly developed and less developed economies, or between member-states with significant agricultural or significant industrial interests. Moreover, although the parties play an important role in the elections for the EP, they play such a role at the member-states level. The transnational party organizations are more rhetorical than effective organizations. The parties in the EP are coalitions (or confederations) of member-states and subnational parties. Finally, because in the EU the decision-making power is dispersed, the chance of having a party government is nil. Parties are not the gatekeepers of EU politics. They have to operate in a much more competitive environment. Lobbies, professional associations, regional governments, epistemic communities, movements, and a congeries of other micro-interests affect the supranational political process without passing through the mediation of the parties. The EU is not a postparty polity. It is a pluralistic polity as its member-states have never been.

Part II

Transatlantic democracies: the era of institutional convergence

6

American compound democracy and its challenges: the domestic implications of global power

6.1. Introduction

After World War II, a radical transformation of both American and European politics has taken place.[1] In America, the unprecedented role played by the country in the international arena ended up challenging its own compoundness. The requirements of managing a growing global power have led to the strengthening of the federal center and the presidential office within it. Although the end of the Cold War left America for a decade without a clear external challenge for disciplining its internal pluralistic domestic decision-making process, and although a long period (between 1969 and 2000) of divided government has favored a weakening of the presidency, the terrorist attacks of 9/11/2001 brought back the need to have a more centralized decision-making system in the federal center with which to run the new 'war on terrorism'. Indeed, between 2003 and 2006, the USA has had a presidential system more than a presidential government within a system of separation of powers (on the distinction between the two, see Chapter 3). Congress delegated full authority to the President, in particular in the crucial field of war powers. No presidential request has met congressional opposition, to the point that, in the period 2001–6, the President had to use his power of veto only once to block a congressional act (see Chapter 3).

Thus, while Europe, through the formation and development of the EU, has moved in the direction of the 'compound republic' model characteristic of the US experiment, America has tried to run in the opposite direction. While Europe, especially in the 1990s, has created a fragmented sovereignty system, which pools the sovereignty of its member-states in EU institutions, America, after 9/11/2001, has tried to reorganize the functioning of its internal decision-making structures by transferring power to the sole executive. In sum, as Hendrickson (2006: 1) pessimistically argued, after 9/11/2001 'the United States has undergone a movement very nearly the opposite of Europe's. If Europe ended up where America began, the "world's only superpower" has by contrast assumed the mantle of the now deceased European monarchies. . . . [making] an unmistakable advance in the long and bloody route from federal union to universal empire'. Indeed, both movements experienced considerable resistance of opposite natures. In Europe, the path toward supranational compoundness has met the opposition of states, sectors of public opinion, and political personnel linked to a national vision, while in the USA the attempt to neutralize the institutional constraints of compoundness had to come to terms with powerful counterforces. In this chapter, I discuss the challenge to the compound nature of American democracy raised by the global role the country has played since the end of World War II. But before doing so, it is necessary to define more precisely the theoretical justifications and analytical features of American compound democracy.

6.2. America as Compound Democracy: Justifications and Implications

6.2.1. *Compound Democracy as an Anti-Hegemonic Political Order*

Although started as a peace pact (Hendrickson 2003), the (new) 'republic of many republics' had to find a justification for its design not based merely on security considerations (Lind 2006). Indeed, it was not a purely inter-states agreement, but also a supra-states project. Undoubtedly, James Madison was the main promoter of the supra-states project, the politician and theoretician who more forcefully argued for giving a 'republican' (we would say, today, a 'democratic') justification to the new constitutional pact (Kernell 2003), finalized to compound different republics in a common institutional framework (Hendrickson 2003). Certainly, 'neither the Preamble, nor Madison's successful endeavor to provide the constitution with a deeper foundation than that of a normal treaty between the governments, prevented it from being considered from the start as a species of contract or compact. Ratification was unequivocally a matter for each state individually; none could be bound without their assent' (Forsyth 1981: 65). Nevertheless, the constitutional project of creating a 'republic of many republics' came to have a theoretical justification (especially in those newspaper articles collected in *The Federalist*, Wills 2001) which is worthy of consideration (especially for Europeans). That constitutional project was justified by the need to preclude the formation of permanent factional majorities.

On the basis of Madison's reflections, such a republic made of many republics was efficaciously defined as a *compound republic* (Ostrom 1987), in order to better distinguish it from the unified and centralized experiments later pursued in Europe. A compound 'republic' (or democracy)[2] is a polity which structurally obstructs the formation of a factional majority through the institutional fragmentation of its sovereignty. While in Europe indivisible sovereignty was considered a condition for the consolidation of public authority (indeed, that indivisibility came to coincide with political modernity as such, after the confused premodern experience of the feudal overlapping of distinct sovereignties), the representatives of the thirteen American states endeavored to create a system of public authority based on the conscious segmentation of sovereignty, first along territorial lines (i.e. between the federated states and the federal state) and subsequently between governmental lines (i.e. between the federal governmental institutions). For those representatives, the consolidation of public authority in a system combining inter-states and supra-states features implied, necessarily, the fragmentation of that authority. Consequently, on the basis of the American experience, one might assert that a compound democracy is a system of horizontal and vertical separation of powers (Fabbrini and Sicurelli 2004). Only such separation was considered necessary for promoting the basic imperative of the system: precluding the formation of a factional majority at the system level (Dahl 2006).[3]

James Madison (now Beard 1964: 69), writing in *Federalist no. 10*, stated:

> By a faction, I understand a number of citizens, whether amounting to a majority or minority of the whole, who are united and actuated by some common impulse of passion, or of interest, adverse to the rights of other citizens, or to the permanent and aggregate interests of the community. There are two methods of curing the mischief of faction: the one, by removing its causes, the other by controlling its effects.

The separated government in an extended polity represents the institutional tool for pursuing this second method. As again Madison argues in *Federalist no. 47*, the multiple separation of powers is the necessary device for preventing factionalism and the danger of the tyranny of the majority:

'the accumulation of all powers legislative, executive and judiciary in the same hands, whether of one, a few or many, and whether hereditary, self appointed, or elective, may justly be pronounced the very definition of tyranny' (Beard 1964: 211). Although in the course of the twentieth century, the founding fathers' fear of 'tyranny of majority' came to be interpreted (Beard 1913, now 1986) as the fear of a popular majority of dispossessed and poor people mobilized against the social privileges of those who elaborated and supported the constitution, at the end of the eighteen century and subsequently all along the nineteenth century that fear had a quite different object. It was mainly the fear that a majority of states could impose its own will on the other states (Onuf 1983).

After all, the possibility of regional coalitions engaged in advancing their own interests and cultures in the new republic was high in a context where 'the formation of three confederacies, one consisting of the four northern, another of the four middle and the third of the five southern States' (Hendrickson 2003: 9) was considered by many an alternative to both the unionist and balance of powers projects (see Chapter 2). After all, the fear of the formation of a factional territorial majority was well founded, if one considers not only the deep diversity among states and regions at the founding moment, but also and above all the asymmetrical relations (in terms of geographical and demographical sizes, economic resources, and potential development) between the states which eventually created the union. Indeed, for preventing such an outcome, the constitution, first, defined clearly the few prerogatives and powers of the federal center, leaving all the others (even those unspecified or unpredicted) to each of the federated states; second, it made each institution at the federal center independent from the others; and, third, it allocated to each federal institution a power of 'partial agency' in the action sphere of the others. In other words, 'where the *whole* power of one department is exercised by the same hands which possess the *whole* power of another department, the fundamental principles of a free constitution are subverted', as Madison wrote in *Federalist no. 47* (now in Beard 1964: 211, his emphasis).

Adopting modern terminology, one might say that the systemic logic of a compound democracy is to promote an *anti-hegemonic political order*. In a compound democracy, no single interest or ambition should be able to permanently control the whole. Madison writes in *Federalist no. 51*: 'In the extended republic of the United States, and among the great variety of interests, parties and sects which it embraces, a coalition of a majority of the whole society could seldom take place on any other principles than those of justice and general good' (now in Beard 1964: 228). In a compound democracy consisting of different and contrasting state interests, the institutional architecture must restrain the hegemonic tendencies of some units in order to guarantee that 'no one community of interest need deny or dominate the rest' (Ostrom 1987: 104). The large geographic size of the republic was considered a feature that would help to minimize the danger of the formation of a majority (Fabbrini 2003*a*).

Thus, in drafting the American constitution, a veritable Copernican revolution was wrought in democratic political theory and this revolution was mainly James Madison's work (Matthews 1995; Kernell 2003). Madison saw on a small scale exactly the opposite of what Rousseau and all other political thinkers saw before him (Fabbrini 2003*a*; Dahl 2006). Madison believed the small 'republics' had perished because they lacked effective treatments for the mortal disease that is factionalism. This, Madison argued, was a disease that only a large-scale republic could cure. As he explained in *Federalist Papers no. 10*, in large republics the factionalism that arises on one side or the other can be diluted across a broader area, or at least counterbalanced by an opposing factionalism arising from some other part of that broad area, if the powers are separated and independent. In brief, 'extend the sphere, and you take in a greater variety of parties and interests; you make it less probable that a majority of the whole will have a common motive to invade the rights of other citizens; or if such a common motive exists, it will be more difficult for all who feel it *to discover their strength*, and to act in unison with each other' (now in Beard 1964: 74, italics added). Thus, in contrast to the post-1789 Europe that established a monistic model of political organization stood a post-1787 America that established a pluralistic model of it. This Madisonian model also had an international underpinning. To preclude factionalism in the small republic was necessary also for precluding its aggressive projection onto bordering republics. The construction of a 'republic of republics' was a condition not only for internal but also for external peace.

6.2.2. *Compound Democracy as an Antihierarchical Institutional Order*

An anti-hegemonic political order implies horizontal relations between governmental institutions, or better it has to be supported by an *antihierarchical* institutional order. In a compound democracy all the federal or supra-states institutions, regardless of their direct and indirect relations with the popular will, have to enjoy equivalent degrees of power. This is why popular sovereignty was placed in the constitution (through the preamble, *We the People of the United States*) and not in any of its public institutions, such as parliament in the European nation-states (Ackerman 1991, see also Chapter 2). However, the people of the preamble are not an abstract entity. They are the aggregation of the people(s) of the different states. Indeed, the constitution is the symbolic pact among people belonging to separated states for pursuing a more perfect union. It is a peace pact between states through their citizens. Because they have been created by the people through their constitution, all the institutions of the republic enjoy the same legitimacy, whether they are directly elected (as is the House of Representatives), indirectly elected (as the Senate was until the Seventeenth Constitutional Amendment of 1913, and as the President still is through the device of the Electoral College), or cooperatively nominated by the President with the advice and consent of the Senate (as is the Supreme Court).

The participation of citizens in the electoral and political process should therefore take place via an institutional framework that has the task of cooling their immediate preferences in order to bring to maturity their mediated preferences, which are the only ones that can create the conditions for the subsequent deliberative process between the institutions (Sunstein 1993). From the carefully staggered elections of the various governing institutions to the equally carefully separated electoral constituencies to which each voter belongs (each one being the expression of a distinct community of interests), the constitution has devised a participatory trail that encourages the citizen-electors to rethink and redefine their individual preferences, thus hindering the formation of stable hegemonies (Cain and Jones 1989). The antihierarchical nature should be supported by the fact that each institution represents different electorates or communities of interests, operates along different time spans, and pursues distinct political or territorial interests: separated institutions which, however, are structured within a system of checks and balances which encourage them to cooperate *through competition* in order to generate collective goods in the form of public policy decisions. In this sense, the US compound polity is antimajoritarian but not consensual. Impeding the formation of a majority of the whole through the promotion of different majorities in different institutions which balance each other through reciprocal competition is not a recipe for consociation.

After more than two centuries and notwithstanding its various historical vicissitudes, the US compound democracy continues to be based on the same institutional features designed in the founding period. As

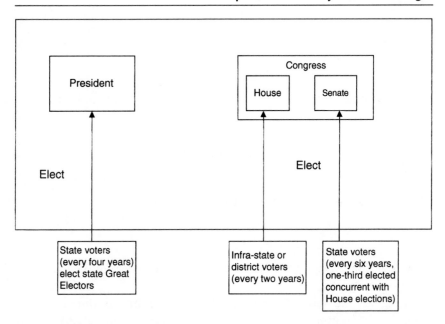

Figure 6.1 Election of the members of US governmental institutions

regards the horizontal dimension (Figure 6.1), the separation of powers concerns first the Congress, which is the main legislative body since it has the power of initiative, being divided into two chambers (House of Representatives and Senate). The Congress is thus separated from the President, who has the executive power, and each of them is separated from the Supreme Court which has federal judiciary power. Regarding the governmental institutions, their independence is guaranteed not only by the constitution, but also by two supplementary devices. First, by the fact that their members are elected by different electoral constituencies (a supra-states constituency although divided along state lines in the case of the President, a state constituency in the case of the senators and infra-state or district constituencies in the case of the House representatives). Through this device, those members have to account to different communities of interests, whereas these communities of interests are, however, defined by states' boundaries. Second, by the fact that their election takes place in fixed but differentiated time intervals[4] in order to preclude, *as much as possible*, the formation of a unified majority in all the three governmental institutions *at the same time*. Such separated sources of electoral legitimacy and staggered terms of representation should contribute to

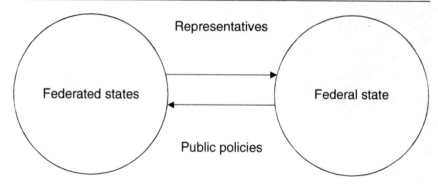

Figure 6.2 Relations between the center and the states

keep the Congress and the President mutually independent (Bednar 2003) (Figure 6.1).

As regards the vertical dimension (Figure 6.2), in the American compound polity power is distributed among multiple territorial levels. Constitutionally, however, only federal and state authorities are recognized as a source of public authority. Policy competences are divided among these two levels of authority but only the powers of the federal center are outlined in the constitution. The remaining competences are allocated to the states. The states can therefore exert any of the powers that are not explicitly allocated to the federal level. State and federal authorities can autonomously act in the policy areas of their competence (Dye 1990). They can also act with the support of autonomous and separated administrative, judicial, legislative, and executive institutions. Also here the federalizing process took place gradually, through different combinations of confederal and federal institutions. This process not only did not prevent the states from retaining relevant powers in many fields of public policy (Derthick 2001), but also did not alter the compound nature of the US territorial system, although clearly federal power has increased vis-à-vis states' power, especially since the 1930s. However, this system continues to be 'a system of government with multiple centers of authority reflecting opposite and rival interests... accountable to enforceable rules of constitutional law' (Ostrom 1987: 21). In sum, the neat separation between the federated states and the federal state does not imply the impossibility of reciprocal influence. Indeed, the federated states influence the center through the representatives of their various communities of interest (especially through their senators), while the federal center influences the states through the various policies it pursues (Figure 6.2).

The American compound republic is thus a pluralistic institutional order, which is the expression of the asymmetrical power of its constituent state units, of the cultural complexity of the polity, of its geographical and demographic size, and of the multiplicity of territorial and social interests the polity has to accommodate. The American compound republic reflects the first historical attempt to create a democratic political order out of a double and contradictory source of legitimacy, corporate bodies (states), and individuals (citizens). That contradictory source is institutionalized in the same constitution, which, from the outset, has inevitably entertained a structural ambiguity on the foundation of the new political regime. The structural ambiguity of the constitution has been kept under control (apart from the Civil War experience) by interpreting the citizens as members of the states (as it is confirmed by the states' constraints on the various electoral systems for the federal institutions). The constitution is thus the expression of a conscious constitutional choice which has created a panoply of multiple institutions to represent a variety of different territorial and social interests. The organization of public authority segments sovereignty along territorial and governmental lines because it recognizes the existence of multiple jurisdictions, alternative loyalties, and overlapping identities within the system. The constitution provides the (individual and corporate) incentives to promote strategies of action based on mutual independence within a shared framework of rules and values.

6.2.3. *A Compound Democracy as an Anti-Unilateralist Decision-Making System*

An antihierarchical order requires a supplementary reinforcement in order to be protected, namely a decision-making system organized around the *sharing of powers*. Madison himself recognizes that, in order to guarantee reciprocal control among institutions, the principle of separation cannot be applied without giving such institutions at least some capacity to act within the sphere of action of the others (Grofman and Wittman 1989). Thus, the existence of shared governmental spheres becomes consistent with the application of the principle of separation of powers. As Neustadt (1990: 29) stated: 'The limits on command suggest the structure of our [American] government'. This separation can function 'as long as one unit of government, or set of governments, cannot dominate other units of government' (Ostrom 1987: 137). This is possible inasmuch as the separation among institutions is protected, not only by the constitution or by the incentives of the institutional interests, but also by a supplementary device. That is the power of each institution to have a voice (or rather a veto) in the functioning of the others. In short, the separated institutions are structured within a system of checks and balances which requires them both to compete and to cooperate in order to generate collective goods, lest they run into a stalemate.

Because the President's signature of the legislative acts approved by Congress is required for transforming them into laws, it is appropriate to stress that the President de facto shares with Congress the legislative power. Through his veto (or the threat of using it), that is his refusal to sign a congressional act, the President has a powerful means of affecting the legislation, although he retains many other indirect means to influence the decision-making within the legislature. Because the Senate has the power of 'advice and consent' on many presidential decisions (concerning the nomination of his secretaries, or the nomination of the Supreme Court and other federal judicial courts' members, or the approval of treaties signed with foreign countries), it is appropriate to stress that it de facto has the power to affect presidential policy. Because the House of Representatives has the power of purse, it can influence de facto many presidential policies, both in the domestic and foreign realms, which require money to be carried out. Because the Supreme Court (as the top judicial institution of the country) has the power of judicial review of legislative acts, it de facto has the power of affecting the exercise of legislative power. The American compound system is thus based on the sharing of functions and the overlapping of competences (Figure 6.3).

American governmental institutions can therefore constitutionally protect their own decision-making autonomy also through a system of multiple checks and balances. A compound democracy, then, is a political system in which decision-making capacity is constrained and limited through the sharing of its resources by distinct and separated institutions. If this pluralistic order leads to slowing down the decision-making process or to a frequent postponement of its outcome, then it is plausible to infer that the system is fulfilling its own duty. *A nondecision might be a necessary price to pay to avoid a bad decision*; a bad decision being any decision of the majority which does not include (or take into consideration) at least part of the interests of the minorities. Or better, any decision taken unilaterally by one institution and thus imposed on the

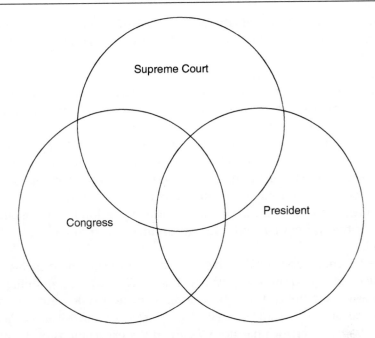

Figure 6.3 Power-sharing among American federal institutions.

other institutions. These minorities might represent territorial, but also cultural, religious, or economic interests. The complex structuring of the decision-making process is thus congenial to a self-contained democracy, that is, to a polity which has to preserve diversity without precluding its dynamic development. In sum, 'each department' (i.e. each governmental institution) must be able to exercise potential veto positions in relation to the other 'departments' (or governmental institutions) as a condition for promoting interinstitutional control. Thus, the existence of shared governmental spheres becomes consistent with the application of the principle of separation of powers.

Of course, corresponding to the horizontal structure of the governmental institutions is a vertical organization of the legal order, with the federal constitution as the supreme law of the land. However, this supreme law itself is not boundless. Indeed, the People who established it introduced specific constraints on its exercise, first of all that it should not infringe on the states' prerogatives and powers. Needless to say, a system of this kind is far from coherent. As Hamilton in *Federalist no. 85* stresses, 'the compacts which are to embrace thirteen distinct States in a common bond of amity and union, must necessarily be a compromise of as many dissimilar interests and inclinations. How can perfection spring from such materials?' (now in Beard 1964: 370). The institutional imperfection of the system is the price to be paid to reach its main political target: namely to aggregate diversified states and their citizens within a shared supra-states institutional framework. Such aggregation is possible only if that institutional framework disincentivizes any interest or faction (any state or coalition of states or any group or coalitions of groups) from controlling the whole. This is why that framework has to make possible a recurrent competition between units as a condition for promoting anti-hegemonic outcomes. Anti-hierarchy and anti-hegemony supposedly help each other. Indeed, a compound democracy is in danger when a permanent (territorial or social) majority is in a position to use the entire range of the system's territorial and governmental institutions to impose its will.

The US compound republic has thus been an experiment in institutional design (Ostrom 1997; Polsby 1997*a*) directed at promoting an anti-hegemonic polity through an antihierarchical order and an anti-unilateral decision-making system. However, as we have seen in Part I of the book, experience has not vindicated the expectations of its main architect, James Madison (Huntington 1981). In fact, the anti-hegemonic imperative has been challenged by the formation of both minority and majority coalitions. In the first case, coalitions of state interests have long influenced specific policy fields, such as the conservative coalition of the Southern states with regard to civil rights. Because those coalitions were frequently expressions of minority interests, one might say that in order to preclude the tyranny of the majority, the USA has ended up promoting the tyranny of minorities. In the second case, majority coalitions, such as the New Deal and neoconservative coalitions (respectively of the 1930s and 1940s and the 2000s), were able to gain control of all the separated institutions, thus imposing (especially in the latter case) their own views in the absence of effective institutional (and political) checks. Also the antihierarchical institutional design has been challenged by the growth of presidential government, with its centralizing and nationalizing implications, a growth mainly supported by the dominant role the country has come to play in the international arena after World War II. Indeed, the latter left two superpowers (the USA and USSR) engaged, from 1948 to 1991, in what came to be called a Cold War confrontation on a global scale. The institutional implications of the international role played by the USA need now to be more precisely discussed.

6.3. Political Transformation in America: The President in the Cold War Era

The Cold War speeded up a reordering of the relationship between the federal institutions of government, Congress and the President, in favor of the latter (Silverstein 1996). Moreover, the increasingly far-reaching role of the President has brought about the institutionalization of a truly executive branch. A strengthened President needed a modern presidency (Ackerman 2000). Thus, after World War II, each President found himself having to work with an executive of extreme and increasing complexity (Hart 1995)—indeed, with what was by now a veritable 'stratified presidency' (Fabbrini 1993) comprising diverse organizational levels: the *administrative presidency* represented by the Independent Establishments and Government Corporations, (in 2007) sixty-odd agencies formally controlled jointly by the President and Congress but in fact highly sensitive to the President's interests and programs; the *departmental presidency* consisting (in 2007) of the fifteen federal departments[5] headed by President's secretaries and comprising further administrative agencies responsible for managing specific policy problems; and the *personal presidency* consisting (in 2006) of the White House Office (WHO) and the Executive Office of the President (EOP), the latter comprising agencies of strategic importance to the President like the Office of Management and Budget (OMB) and the National Security Council (NSC), the former responsible for coordinating budget policy and the latter for monitoring security policy.

In particular, the Cold War stimulated (and justified) the formation within the presidency of a sort of 'informal regime of crisis management' (Gaddis 1991: 117) located within the personal presidency and standing at the head of an enormous military and intelligence apparatus (Preston 2001). It was the National Security Act of 1947 which created a close foreign policy establishment next to the President, weakly constrained by the separation of powers. As the President's responsibilities increased after World War II, so did his need to equip himself with the means to exert direct control over the activities of his presidency, both departmental and administrative. The more the presidential apparatus expanded, the more the President extended his personal presidency to control it, in an ever-increasing spiral, but with the outcome that he came to control it less and less (Warshaw 1996).

The personalization of the presidency has enabled the President to surround himself with personal supporters rather than traditional politicians of party provenance (Preston 2001). Presidents have brought with them the people who helped them to win the electoral campaign. If the total executive staff (inclusive of all the people working in the EOP) totaled 1,240 at the beginning of the Truman presidency (1949), that number increased to 4,116 at the beginning of the first Nixon presidency (1969), it was scaled down to 1,570 at the beginning of the first Clinton presidency (1993) only to rise back to 1,652 at the beginning of the first George W. Bush presidency (2001). The WHO (within the EOP) increased from 243 in 1949 to 341 in 1969, 392 in 1993, 398 in 2001 (Stanley and Niemi 2003: 254–5). In sum, the 'size, complexity, and organizational capacity of the modern presidency has grown dramatically' (Jacobs and Shapiro 2000: 492). During the Cold War, the personal presidency thus acquired a decision-making predominance in foreign policymaking, not only vis-à-vis the Congress, but also vis-à-vis departmental sectors of the executive branch (such as State and Defense departments). Although that predominance was questioned in the post-Watergate years (on Watergate, see Chapter 1) and was more limited in domestic policymaking, the paramount centrality of the Cold War order strongly supported the maintenance of those power hierarchies in the general structure of the national policymaking process.

However, the domestic implications of the long era of the Cold War were not devoid of contradictions. The increasing role of the President did not go unchallenged; it could not have been otherwise, given the features the Cold War came to assume. Indeed, a contrast between the open institutions of domestic politics and the closed institutions of foreign policy started to emerge as soon as US foreign policy did not enjoy the consent of the country. This happened, of course, with the Vietnam War, whose outcome triggered a deep institutional conflict. In fact, if the defensive requirements imposed by the threat of the rival superpower justified the progressive centralization of the decision-making processes within the same executive; if the strengthening of the President and his personal presidency over the departmental presidency came about because each was able to ensure the most rapid response to the threat in question, nevertheless this closed decision-making system was at odds with both the transparency of congressional debates and with the more public character of the departmental presidency (Jones 1999).

Moreover, in the aftermath of the Vietnam War, the governmental institutions came to represent opposing priorities or values, the republican values in the case of Congress and the national interest values in the President's case. This cultural contrast was nothing new in the history of the USA. Nor was it new that the President—each and every one—had an inevitable tendency to represent the latter, more than the former. Again (see Chapter 3) one need only think of the experience of Thomas Jefferson (Tucker and Hendrickson 1990). As a political thinker, Jefferson vehemently rejected the European theory of *raison d'état* with its double corollary that, first, the interests of state override those of civil society and, second, that the requirements of external conflict may justify the abandonment of domestic legality. Subsequently, however, when Jefferson became President (1801–8), he was equally vehement in his pursuit of a statist and expansionist foreign policy which had little in common with humanitarian principles (e.g. proceeding with the Louisiana Purchase of 1805 against congressional will). The Cold War exacerbated this conflict, to the point that it created, on the wave of the military intervention in Vietnam, unprecedented divisions in the country's national identity.

The Cold War, therefore, did not resolve the tension between the branches, although it allowed the President to have a leeway in foreign policy. However, the outcome of the Vietnam War did change the context of US foreign policy (Natham and Oliver 1994). First, the number of participants in US foreign policymaking increased significantly. Since the 1970s, the old and tight-knit foreign policy establishment, located chiefly on the East Coast, was replaced by a new and more diffuse elite of highly ideologized foreign policy professionals with links in the South-West. The number of economic and ideological groups interested in foreign policy grew enormously thanks, in part, to the globalization of the economy but also because of the proliferation of international issues, ranging from drug trafficking to ethnic conflicts, with backwash effects on domestic politics. As Mann observed at the end of the 1980s (cited in Hart 1995: 223), since Watergate 'foreign policy (has lost) its distinctiveness as a domain of presidential responsibility' ending in his optimistic assertion that 'the trend toward congressional involvement in foreign policy is irreversible'. Of course, the media also played an important role in defining the order of priorities on the foreign policy agenda. Second, congressional subcommittees became more influential in foreign policymaking. This process had its roots in the generation of Watergate congressmen and in the organizational and legislative reforms that they set in train. In fact, democratization/decentralization led to the formation of powerful subcommittees, supported by the aforementioned new groups, protected by specific regulative prerogatives, and able to draw on the services of huge specialist staffs and legislative offices able to deal with the principal areas or sectors of foreign policy. This jurisdictional specialization increased the effectiveness of individual subcommittees (these being real rivals to the executive's corresponding sector or area agencies), even though this increased effectiveness was rarely tied to a more comprehensive foreign policy strategy of Congress as a whole, the exceptions being the policies toward South Africa and Nicaragua in the 1980s.

The presidents sought to respond to the assertiveness of congressional committees and subcommittees in foreign policy (especially since the War Powers Resolution of 1973) through a further centralization of the decision-making process within the personal presidency. This intensified the rivalry between the NSC and the State Department for control of foreign policy, a rivalry which intertwined with the traditional rivalry between the State and Defense departments. In fact, while the appointment of the Secretary of the State Department must be approved by the Senate, the National Security Adviser is more of a personal appointment by the President. In matters of foreign policy, therefore, it is obvious that the former is sensitive to Congress's wishes, while the basic constraints on the latter are the President's wishes. The progressive shift in the 1970s and 1980s of the decision-making center of gravity to the NSC represented the presidential response to the post-Watergate foreign policy claims of Congress, namely, reducing the influence of the Secretary of State. The President also tried to reduce the influence of Congress on his choices. However, the struggle between the two governmental branches that the Constitution established for the privilege of controlling the country's foreign policy (Fisher 2004) did not cease. The President, as the nation's only organ in its foreign relations and Commander-in-Chief of the armed forces, claimed prerogatives that go beyond the powers enumerated by article II of the Constitution, asserting that his claim was ratified by the Supreme Court in its decision of 1936 (*US* v. *Curtiss-Wright*). The Congress, in turn, has continued to dispute this affirmation of presidential prerogatives, at least since the approval of the War Powers Resolution in 1973.

The increased power of the American President throughout the Cold War period is thus indicative of the effects exerted by the international conditions on the behavior of the executive power in a separated governmental system. Indeed, the Cold War context could hardly favor congressional ambitions. Nevertheless, Congress could not be easily marginalized, not in the least because it retained much of its formal powers. And also because a sort of *divided government regime* came to be institutionalized between 1969 and 2000.

6.4. Presidential Power in the Era of Divided Government

6.4.1. *Republican Presidents and Democratic Congresses*

The partisan division of the separated government has represented an important political transformation of the American system of government after World War II. One speaks of a divided government when each of the two opposing parties controls one or the other of the separated institutions of government (Fiorina 1992; Ware 2002). From 1948 to 2000, the USA had a divided government for 65.3 percent of the time, or 34 years of 52 (Conley 2002). Divided government has been fostered by the crisis of the traditional political parties. In fact, without effective parties in the electorate it was difficult to generate regular electoral realignments, that is coherent majorities in the various governmental institutions. However, as we have seen in Chapter 5, the very institutionalization of divided government has paradoxically led to a strengthening of the parties within the governmental institutions, and particularly within Congress. With the political transformations induced by the Civil Rights Act of 1964 which pushed the Southern states conservative wing of the Democratic Party toward the Republican Party, the two parties have become much more internally homogeneous than in the past and thus the conflict between the two parties has become more ideologically intense. Consequently, the fight between the institutions controlled by them has become more virulent than in any period of the past. Moreover, in the 1990s, the difficulty of governing with a divided government was exacerbated by the end of the Cold War, because it deprived the President of a crucial resource for asserting his preeminence over the other governmental institutions (Tushnet 2003).

Although the USA experienced brief periods of divided government between the end of World War II and 1968,[6] it was with the electoral success of the Republican candidate in the presidential election of that year that a sort of divided government regime came to be institutionalized in the country,[7] lasting till the elections of 2000. Indeed, the divided government era started in a very dramatic way with the resignation of the Republican President Richard Nixon in 1974 under the threat of impeachment.[8] After the House Judiciary Committee did approve articles of impeachment against him (by wide margins) and did report those articles to the full House, Nixon decided to resign prior to House consideration of the impeachment resolutions, because both his impeachment by the House of Representatives and his conviction by the Senate were near certainties (he was substituted by Vice-President Gerald Ford from 1974 to 1976). Although the (especially domestic) agenda of Richard Nixon was not at all at odds with the liberal agenda of the Democratic Congress, the presidential claim to exasperated secrecy in the management of foreign policy (and especially in relation to the war in Vietnam) soon created deep tensions between the Republican executive and the Democratic legislature. Thus, when the press made public the ruthless attempt by the President and his personal aides to use the resources of the executive for illegally controlling their political adversaries, a dramatic constitutional crisis exploded between the two branches of government. With the Watergate affairs and the 1974 resignation of President Nixon a new era started.

The Jimmy Carter presidency (1977–80) tried to create a new mood of cooperation with the friendly Congress. However, although the President and the majorities of the two chambers of Congress were Democratic, this cooperation did not proceed well. The effects of the direct primaries system in selecting presidential candidates appeared evident. The members of Congress, excluded from having a significant role in selecting the presidential candidate, perceived themselves to have no obligation in supporting him, once he was elected President. Indeed, the Democratic President was not able to convince the Democratic Congress to advance (or even to accept) his main policy agenda. The combination between a personalized President and a divided government regime re-emerged with Ronald Reagan's subsequent two terms of office (1981–8). When analyzing the Republican Reagan presidencies, one notes their twofold feature: on the one hand, they displayed a continuity with the previous history of the modern presidency, as Greenstein points out (2000: 147): 'Reagan took Roosevelt's use of the presidential pulpit as the prototype for his own political leadership'. On the other hand, they introduced a series of novel features into it. This was because Reagan, in exercising his leadership, had to deal with the decline of his political party, both as agency for the mobilization of electoral support and as political link between him and the Congress. Reagan's answer to this new context was the deeper personalization of presidential action: but this enormously increased public expectations of the President (Rockman 1988). The President made more and more promises while becoming increasingly unable to fulfill them, not least because he was prevented from doing so by politically hostile congresses. To cope with this incongruence, Reagan fueled a constant climate of tension, governing as if he were in the middle of a permanent election campaign (King A. 1997). After the initial policy success of the period 1981–2, Reagan relied increasingly on his popular leadership, to the detriment of the governmental one (Hinckley 1990).

The net result of Reagan's rhetorical presidency was to accentuate the separation of the institutional system, further fragmenting the political process. An unprecedented neofactional regime evolved as it was impossible to find effective ways of aggregating interests and opinions. In turn, in such a fragmented political process periodic gridlocks between the President and Congress in crucial areas of domestic and foreign policies were inevitable. However, devoid of solid institutional support, his popular leadership steadily declined. Beset by a series of scandals (such as the *Iran–Contra* affair)[9] he ended up, in his second mandate, as a congressional hostage. As Heclo (1989: 289) observed at the end of the 1980s, in that period America seemed to be governed by a regime of *establishments*, in which the various rulers of the separated institutions informally aggregated in close networks to deal with specific problems but with scarce or no relations among them. This regime (Heclo 1989: 320) was 'open...and fluid in its attachment'. In sum, even a presidency by plebiscite (Rimmerman 1993) was unable to escape the constraints of a divided government in a system of separation of powers.

The election of the Republican George H.W. Bush in 1988, after the two Reagan mandates, came about in singular circumstances. In fact, Bush's victory was offset by the defeat of his party: the Republicans lost further ground in the House (three fewer seats), in the Senate (one fewer), and also among governors and in state legislatures. In short, the election of 1988 greatly reinforced the divided government. Bush tried to avoid conflict with Congress, especially in domestic politics. Scholars almost unanimously agree that the Bush domestic presidency took largely the form of what Mullins and Wildavsky (1991) have called a procedural presidency. Bush rarely used press conferences to apply pressure on the rival institution. He preferred to resolve conflict by setting up ad hoc committees consisting of members from the two branches of government, holding informal meetings, sheltered from the media, with the leaders of Congress, and by making personal telephone calls to his political adversaries. Campbell and Rockman (1991) have called the domestic Bush the 'let's deal President', the President, that is, who when confronted with a problem prefers to negotiate, to find an agreement, to exchange favors with the opposite party congressional leaders.

However, in foreign policy, Bush pursued a quite different strategy. Here, he forcefully asserted his presidential role. Indeed, the Gulf War of 1991 represented a formidable opportunity for imposing a presidential preeminence in war powers vis-à-vis the Congress. Bush tried to make of the Gulf War a presidential war in a way that bears few precedents, even if one considers the Truman case of 1950, when the USA went to war against North Korea on the basis of a United Nations (UN) resolution and not a declaration by Congress. It is doubtful whether Truman could have said what Bush did on March 18, 1991: 'It was argued I can't go to war without Congress. And I was saying, I have the authority to do this' (*Weekly Compilation of Presidential Documents*, March 8, 1991, Washington DC, US Government Printing Office, p. 284). Indeed, as Gergen wrote (1991/1992: 7) 'Bush practically ignored Capitol Hill as he made his decisions [on the Gulf Crisis]. While the administration spoke positively of consultation with Congress, it engaged only in notification—and usually after the fact.... In the six months of the gulf crisis, Democratic leaders of the Senate and House of Representatives had less influence upon the Bush White House than Margaret Thatcher, who resigned as British prime minister in November 1990, or Prince Bansar bin Sultan, the Saudi Ambassador to Washington'. Of course, Congress reluctantly recognized this presidential pretension. Indeed, it gave its support to the presidential war only after long and fierce debate.

6.4.2. Democratic President and Republican Congresses

A new Democratic President, Bill Clinton, substituted the Republican George H.W. Bush after the 1992 election. However, the two Clinton presidencies (1993–2000) had much less opportunity to use the international context to impose presidential preeminence. The Cold War ended in 1991 leaving America as the only superpower on the globe. Moreover, no challenge to American global primacy appeared to be in sight at the beginning of the 1990s. Domestic policy became more salient than foreign policy, with the institutional implication of strengthening the role of Congress vis-à-vis the President. Certainly, in the first half of his first mandate (1993–4) Bill Clinton could act in the context of a government which enjoyed a party majority (because both chambers of Congress continued to be controlled by the Democrats), however the way of his selection as party presidential candidate also kept the Democratic congressional elite alienated from him. Moreover, the circumstances of his electoral victory certainly did not allow him to claim supremacy over the legislature. Clinton was able to beat George H.W. Bush more because of the presence of a third candidate (the Independent Ross Perot) in direct competition with the latter, than because of the electoral consensus he received. In fact, he emerged victorious even though he obtained only 43.3 percent of votes, compared to Bush's 37.7 percent and Perot's 19 percent. This can explain why Clinton found it extremely difficult to get the approval of his party-friendly Congress for many of his proposals; indeed, the most important of them (to set up a national health system) was sanded down by the congressional Democrats (Skocpol 1997). However, the situation changed drastically with the mid-term elections of 1994. For the first time in the post–World War II period, the Republicans gained the majority in both houses of Congress, doing so on the basis of a radical program ('Contract with America') supported by a revitalized party. Moreover, the promoter of the program, Newt Gingrich, was elected Speaker of the House of Representatives. This, therefore, was a return to divided government, but now interpreted as a Republican government arbitrarily conditioned by a Democratic President.

With the Republican conquest of the majority in both chambers in the mid-term elections of 1994, Congress, and the House in particular, reversed the previous decentralizing trend, creating the organizational conditions for a true party government *within* the legislature, in order to confront the Democratic President. The Republicans transformed the divided government into a formidable tool with which to weaken or even call into question the very legitimacy of the Clinton presidency (Campbell 1998). A tremendous assault on the presidency was launched from Republican quarters with the aim of impeaching the President. This assault grew even fiercer after Clinton's re-election in 1996. From 1994 to 2000, the new Republican majority of the Congress acted as the only legitimate governmental majority of the country. The Speaker of the House of Representatives, Newt Gingrich, portrayed 'himself as a Prime Minister with more influence over policy than President Clinton' (Schickler 2002: 99). The assault on Clinton was so constitutionally improper (Ackerman 1999) that it backfired. The Republicans performed very poorly in the mid-term elections of 1998: the partisan balance remained the same, but for the first time since 1934, the President's party gained five seats in the House in a mid-term election. This unexpected outcome created the political conditions for Newt Gingrich's resignation from his high congressional office once an internal congressional investigation disclosed his misbehavior regarding financial contributions to his campaign. Nevertheless, even with the more moderate Speaker Dennis Hastert, the impeachment strategy of the Republican Party continued, ending in a formal vote of the Senate in 1999 which failed to achieve the qualified majority of two-thirds necessary to dismiss the President.

The threat of impeachment, that dogged both Clinton presidencies dramatized a political practice which was inaugurated with Nixon's resignation of 1974. With the electoral representativeness of the two parties in constant decline (measured by extremely low electoral turnouts in the 1980s and 1990s if compared with other established democracies), the two parties ended up using the governmental institution controlled by each of them to defeat their rival (thereby also delegitimizing the institution controlled by the other). Thus the conflict between the parties came to assume the features of an outright battle between institutions. Certainly, as Mayhew (1991) showed, the institutional combat between the governmental institutions did not prevent the approval of important pieces of legislation, but it made the legislative process extremely conflictual. If divided government had its origins in the electors' will of putting one party in control of the other because either of the two parties seemed fully reliable (Jacobson 1990), nevertheless the outcome was quite unsatisfactory. The price for avoiding a bad decision was the creation of a new political '(dis)order'. Writing in the mid-1990s, Dahl (1994: 1–2, italics in the text) indicated the characterizing feature of the decade: 'government policies are made in response to a greater number and variety of conflicting and substantially independent interest groups.... Political institutions... are weaker than before.... The new order, then, is more *fragmentation* and less *integration.*'

What Ginsberg and Shefter (1991) called politics by other means at the beginning of the 1990s had grown even more blatant by the end of that decade. The Republican Congress used its institutional instruments of control and supervision over the President for partisan ends. Inquiries by various committees and subcommittees followed one after the other relentlessly, their purpose being to reveal the personal weaknesses of the President or of his closest aides, the covert conditioning exerted on them during the electoral campaign by real or presumed financial backers, or decision-making confusion in one or another of the presidential departments. The Democratic President, for his part, had no qualms about using the intelligence agencies under his control (the CIA especially, Draper 1997) to delve into the private lives of congressional leaders. It was a battle that (also) had judicial implications, for Congress deliberately used its hearings under oath of members of the presidency, or called for the intervention of the Department of Justice's special prosecutor,[10] to place the President and his policies in difficulty. In sum, a new constraint (in addition to those deriving from the conflicts between the governmental institutions and from the contrasts within the stratified presidency) was placed on presidential action (and leadership), that of the President's *personal reputation* (Roberts and Doss 1997).

Revelations, investigations, prosecutions (RIPs):[11] these were the new weapons of interparty competition in the divided government period. However, in this conflict the greatest price was paid by the presidency. David Calleo wrote in 2000 (Calleo 2000: 72): 'over the past three decades, the Congress, the courts and the states have frequently combined to cut the presidency down to size. Nothing illustrates this trend more than Clinton's ordeal. Despite the President's continuing popularity with the electorate and his impressive achievements in the economic field, his presidency has been subjected to the most savage constitutional attack since Nixon's time.' The weakening of the presidency in this period epitomized a more general trend of reduction of the role and resources of federal institutions vis-à-vis state governments. In fact, already in the 1980s with Reagan's New Federalism, the relationship between Washington DC and the states institutionalized since the New Deal of the 1930s and the Great Society of the 1960s came to be reversed in favor of the latter.

6.5. September 11: Rise and Fall of Presidential Power

6.5.1. *The USA toward Unilateralism in Foreign Policy*

In the 1990s, with the weakening of the presidency, the conservative leaders of Congress also forced on the federal government a political agenda largely at odds with the one of the President. The Republican electoral success in the mid-term elections of 1994 made public a view of unilateralism in foreign policy which challenged the entire multilateral system of international relations built up since the post–World War II period under the impulse and direction of the USA (Ikenberry 2000). Clearly, Clinton could not fail to react to this initiative. The result was a forceful unilateral Congress and a moderately multilateral President. The international changes of the 1990s, combined with the divided government regime, rendered it extremely difficult for the USA to benefit from a 'strategic consensus' (McCormick 2000: 76). The controversial success of the Republican candidate George W. Bush in the elections of 2000 over Clinton's Vice-President and Democratic candidate Albert Gore (Dershowitz 2001) was accompanied by a partial abatement of the divided government. The Republicans retained the majority in the

House (221 vs. 212 seats), whereas the Senate was evenly split (50 vs. 50 seats), with the Vice-President Dick Cheney breaking the tie. However, in May 2001, when Republican Senator James Jeffords of Vermont switched party, control of the Senate went to the Democrats.

Faced with the dissipation of presidential leadership and the disappearance of the Soviet menace, on his election George W. Bush chose to distance himself from any serious international engagement and sought to build more cooperative relations with the friendly Congress. Domestically, he endorsed the congressional agenda of the second half of the 1990s which focused essentially on tax reduction and the restructuring of social spending, in order to squeeze further the federal state and to increase the powers of the federated states. Internationally, he endorsed a moderate version of the unilateral perspective previously pursued by the Republican Congress. As *The Economist* (2001: 24) noticed at the time, Bush's international approach was based on 'a willingness to go along with international accords, but only so far as they suit America, which is prepared to conduct policy outside their constraints'. In any case, the presidential priority was domestic not international issues. In sum, after the presidential and congressional elections of 2000, US foreign policy moved progressively toward a more coherent unilateralist position. Krauthamer (2001) called this position a 'new unilateralism', because it consisted in accepting international accords when convenient and rejecting them when they were perceived as obstacles to a desired course of action.

With 9/11/2001 the ambiguities and uncertainties of the previous decade came to an end. 'To Americans, Islamism has effectively replaced Soviet communism as a mortal danger' while that was not the case for the Europeans. In fact, 'to Europeans, the threat of Islamic terrorists . . . is not simply comparable to that posed by the Red Army twenty years ago—not great enough, in other words, to require transatlantic solidarity under US leadership' (Ferguson 2005). There are numerous examples of the unilateralist approach which predate 9/11, including (Emmot 2002): a refusal to ratify the Comprehensive Test Ban Treaty and the Convention on the Rights of the Child; the withdrawal from the ABM Treaty; a refusal to adhere to the International Criminal Court and the Kyoto Protocol on the environment. This unilateralism unfolded within the context of continued American criticism of the UN (kept under constant pressure by the threat to withhold membership dues) along with pressure on the International Monetary Fund (IMF), the World Bank, and the World Trade Organization (WTO) to promote American interests. However, 9/11 allowed the George W. Bush Presidency to recompose those various unilateral acts of foreign policy in a proper political doctrine, already defined as 'the new sovereignty' (Spiro 2000).

This foreign policy doctrine was made public in September 2002 by the President, as the National Security Strategy (Daalder and Lindsay 2003). For this doctrine, the war on terrorism has taken the place of the previous Cold War. Terrorists might ally with rogue states that could provide them with access to weapons of mass destruction (WMD). In this scenario, the USA has a special responsibility. For meeting its responsibility, the USA has to build and maintain a military defense capability beyond any challenge. Indeed, already the *Pentagon Planning Guidance* of 1992 (Waltz 1999: 699) stressed that 'the advanced industrialized nations [were to be discouraged] from... even aspiring to a larger global or regional role'. And Bush (2002: iv, 29) reconfirmed that 'we must build and maintain our defenses beyond challenges'. American military superiority has thus been made 'the centerpiece of American security policy' (Ikenberry 2002: 49). This unipolar structure of military power frees the USA from the obligation to abide by international laws when its interests are at stake. Indeed, in response to the new threat of global terrorism, the USA claimed its right to engage in *preemptive* action in order to impede new acts of terrorism. As Bush (2002: 15) affirmed, in order 'to forestall or prevent... hostile acts by our adversaries, the United States will, if necessary, act pre-emptively... the United States cannot remain idle while danger gathers'. There are few examples of preventive action in the post–World War II context, such as the Yom Kippur War (1967) when Israel carried out a preventive strike against Arab forces amassing on its borders (Anderson 2002), but not of preemptive ones (on the difference between 'prevention' and 'preemption' see, among others, Mann 2003). And there are also many examples of preventive action in the bipolar struggle of the Cold War period, when the superpowers did not refrain from intervening in their respective spheres of influence (albeit with different strategies) when their leadership seemed challenged.

However, the principle of preemptive action was never formally celebrated in the Cold War era (Sands 2005). Even the Gulf War of 1991 itself, the first war of the post–Cold War period, was justified, by the USA and its allies, with the need to restore the international legality upset by the Iraqi invasion of Kuwait, rather than to alter it. In sum (Bush 2002: 31), 'in exercising our leadership... we will be prepared to act apart when our interests and unique responsibilities require'. This strategy found its utmost implementation in the 2003 invasion of Iraq (an invasion not supported by the UN Security Council).

6.5.2. Rise and Fall of Presidential Unilateralism in Domestic Politics

The unilateral strategy on foreign relations also played in favor of presidential unilateralism in relations with Congress. The new international strategy of 'American national sovereignty comes first' also implied a renewed domestic strategy definable as 'the President comes first'. Thus, a radical transformation of the international environment created the conditions for presidential leadership to re-emerge domestically. The midterm elections of 2002 were a formidable occasion for the President to work for the future of his governmental leadership by sponsoring and supporting candidates close to him and his team. In fact, the surprising success of Republican candidates in those elections (the Republicans increased their majority in the House and regained the majority in the Senate) was widely perceived as a personal success for the President.

After November 2002, the weakening of the American presidency (Neustadt 2001) was not only arrested but reversed. The terrorist attack reinvigorated the popular leadership of the President; the electoral success of the President's party in Congress created the conditions for the relaunching of his governmental leadership. 'As 2002 closed, observers suggested that Bush had created one of the most powerful White Houses in at least a generation as part of a strategy aimed at recovering executive powers ceded to—or seized by—Congress during the Watergate era' (Rudalevige 2005: 12). Crucial in this regard was the extensive interpretation, advanced by the President and accepted by the now fully Republican Congress, of the constitutional clause of the Commander-in-Chief (article II, section 2, clause 1, states that 'The President shall be Commander in Chief of the Army and Navy of the United States'). According to presidential interpretation, the President has the power to declare war, and not only to make it, as the Constitution, on the contrary, expressly negates (article I, section 8, clause 11, recites: it is the power of Congress 'to declare War, grant Letters of Marque and Reprisal, and make rules concerning Captures on Land and Water'). Indeed, three days after 9/11 and with only one dissenting vote in the House and none in the Senate, Congress approved a joint resolution authorizing the President *to decide* whether to use force 'against those nations, organizations, or persons he determines planned, authorized, committed or aided the terrorist attack that occurred on September 11, 2001'. Although the resolution makes a formal reference to the War Powers Resolution of 1973, confirming that only Congress has the power to authorize military action, de facto Congress 'declared [a war] without a specific enemy; that choice [being] left to the president' (Rudalevige 2005: 216).

9/11, thus, gave the presidency ideological justification to claim a renewed primacy within the separated governmental system. Faced with the terrorist threat, the American people needed a President once more, and Bush gave them one. The terrorist attack reaffirmed the need for presidential leadership in the international arena (Schlesinger 2004). After the attack, the USA found its *democratic Prince*, this time supported by Congress as had never happened after World War II (Mann and Ornstein 2006). As the USA had to free itself from all external multilateral constraints, also the President claimed to be free from domestic multi-institutional constraints. As happened during the Cold War, the new war on international terrorism triggered a reordering of domestic institutional practices. Certainly, Congress retained all the institutional tools to downsize the presidential claim to domination, nevertheless it made a political decision not to use them. Till 2006, Congress met all the President's requests, thus allowing Bush to behave as the most executive-oriented President of the post–World War II period. Moreover, the new role of Congress in staunchly backing the President was made possible by the centralized structure Congress had created for combating the President of the previous decade (Polsby 2004).

Under the conditions of a unified party government, and under the shock of 9/11, the procedural and party changes introduced in the post-1994 Congress strongly advantaged the Republican President. In fact, 'the iron discipline of legislative Republicans meant that through his entire [first] term President Bush did not find it necessary to use the veto pen' (Rudalevige 2005: 12). Indeed, as we have seen (Chapter 3), he had to use it only once in the following two years (2005–6). Even in the days of Democratic Party control of Congress and the presidency (such as the Truman period of 1949–52 or the Kennedy–Johnson period of 1961–8), America did not have as close party control of the separated institutions of government as in the 2003–6 period. In fact, in those years (not to mention the unified Democratic government periods of 1977–80 and 1993–4), the governing party (the Democrats) was internally divided between Northern liberals and Southern conservatives. The conservative wing often allied itself with the rival Republican congressional caucuses in the House and Senate to stop or amend undesired party majority proposals. Nothing of the sort happened between 2003 and 2006. The roll call vote in Congress was strictly along party lines. Moreover, this new international emergency called a halt to the decentralizing tendencies of the previous period (Sinclair 2004). However, rather than return power to the states, the new Republican majority has tried to hollow the federal programs out (Hacker and Pierson 2005).

Once again, the dramatic increase of presidential power after 9/11 was made possible by congressional abdication of its own war powers. In the first war against Iraq (1991) as well as in the military intervention in Bosnia and Kosovo, it was Congress which gave discretionary authority to the President (to George H.W. Bush, in the first case, and Bill Clinton, in the second case). After 9/11 broad discretionary powers were recognized not only to the President, but also to the military, the intelligence agencies, and the Attorney General under the rubric of the Patriot Act approved by Congress in November 2001 (Brown 2003). Through the Patriot Act, conditions were created whereby the executive branch of the separated government was able to pursue a domestic security policy without an effective check by Congress (Ackerman 2006). In fact, in both chambers of Congress (and especially in the House of Representatives), the Republican majority has strongly reduced the room for action and influence by the minority party. Contrary to what happened in the past, but in continuity with the experience of the 1990s (especially since 1995), after 9/11 the minority party was not allowed to amend legislation, was not involved in defining the congressional agenda, and was not invited to share institutional responsibilities at the level of congressional committees. In the Senate, the Republican majority has gone so far as threatening the abolition of filibustering (which has represented, since 1806, one of the veto resources at the disposal of the minority, see Chapter 4) through a cloture by a simple majority vote (Caraley 2005; Mann and Ornstein 2006).

The 2003–6 Congress was thus a strict majoritarian institution, where the minority had no powers or influence. This majoritarian transformation of Congress appears even more striking if one considers the narrow majority of seats the Republicans had over the Democrats in both chambers (in the 2005–6 House of Representatives it was 232 to 202 seats, in the Senate 55 to 45 seats). An advantage of seats to which corresponded in the Senate, because of its overrepresentation of small- and medium-sized states largely controlled by Republicans, a minority condition in the general popular vote. Between 2003 and 2006, 'the 49 per cent of the population that did not vote to reelect President Bush, the population represented by the Democrats who hold 47 percent of the seats in the House of Representatives (and) the 50,5 percent of the population represented by Democratic Senators' (Caraley 2005: 401) were de facto disempowered. Moreover, controlling both chambers of Congress and the presidency, the Republican Party was able to ensure its influence would be felt in the Supreme Court for at least a generation, in so far as two justices, one in 2005 and another in 2006 (one of them as Chief Justice), sympathetic to the views of the predominant conservative majority were nominated by the President and confirmed by the Senate, thus strengthening the trend to have 'radicals in robe' in the Court (Sunstein 2005). Although a conventional view (Bickel 1962: 252) has in the past asserted that the Supreme Court has 'the power to construe the Constitution, in matters of greatest moment, against the wishes of a legislative majority', a nonconventional view (Dahl 1957: 247) has long shown that, at the very end, 'the main task of the Court is to confer legitimacy on the fundamental policies of the successful coalition'. Thus, after 9/11, America has centralized power in the presidential office, transforming the executive branch into the dominating institution of the governmental system. On the basis of an 'emergency constitution' (Ackerman 2001), the President has claimed a role incompatible with the 'real constitution'. In particular, in the period 2003–6, America was much more similar to a presidential *system* than to the separated government system with presidential *preeminence* of the past.

However, this strategy came to meet insurmountable obstacles. First, a political obstacle. The electoral success of George W. Bush in 2004 was not an expression of a popular mandate to pursue a clearly defined agenda (Cain 2006). All presidential coalitions are inevitably heterogeneous in the USA, given the multitude of interests the candidate has to aggregate for winning the elections (Dahl 1990). In the Bush case, he certainly benefited in 2004 from the still diffused mood of fear and bewilderment generated by the 9/11 terrorist attack. National security remained at the top of the public's concerns, thus favoring the Republican candidate. It was highly implausible to fire an incumbent President involved in a war. However, as soon as the American intervention in Iraq and Afghanistan was shown to be ineffective and costly (in terms of American soldiers killed and money spent), divisions within the presidential coalition emerged loudly. Divisions which reflected a more general popular criticism of presidential foreign and economic policies. Second, an institutional obstacle. The tight timing of the electoral cycle (every two years there is a federal election) represents a formidable opportunity for popular criticism of presidential choices. Indeed, the mid-term elections of November 2006 gave an opportunity to the Democratic critics of

President Bush's policies to gain control of both the House of Representatives (234 vs. 201 seats) and the Senate (51 vs. 49 seats) and of the majority of states' legislatures and governorships. After all, 'every two-term president since Teddy Roosevelt has suffered losses in his second mid-term election', the only exception being President Clinton who 'in effect suffered his six year election four years early in 1994' (Connelly 2006: 1). In sum, in a Madisonian system, 'there is no such thing as a permanent minority or permanent majority' (Connelly 2006: 4). If the divided government's experience of the previous years is of some help, then one expects that the new Democratic congressional majority will reactivate the checks and balances on presidential power toned down after 9/11. Indeed, congressional investigations on previous presidential choices, congressional hearings of members of the presidency, and congressional monitoring of contemporary presidential policies are formidable tools for putting into reserve the unilateral aspirations of the President and increasing the influence of the new legislative majority. Thus, notwithstanding 9/11, the US President has remained a 'semi-sovereign Prince' (Fabbrini 2005c).

But there is also a third constitutional obstacle that bars the road to any strategy of transforming the separated system into a presidential system. It is the Twenty-Second Amendment of 1951, with its prohibition of the reelection of an incumbent President for more than two mandates. Thanks to this amendment, the President, any President (Hastings 2006), is destined to be a lame duck in (at least) the (second part of his) second mandate. Even if his party has control of Congress, rivalry and competition for selecting the new presidential candidate will call into question the discipline of his congressional supporters.

6.6. Conclusion

In the USA, the post–World War II challenges of international involvement forced central (federal) rulers to look for more centralized institutional practices. Those challenges were met by reinventing the President (Lowi 1988), that is centralizing the decision-making power on foreign and military policies within the presidency. A sort of double decision-making regime came to be practiced within the separation of powers system: one dominated by the President in foreign policy and another more balanced between the Congress and the President in domestic policy. It was a matter of practices rather than of constitutional amendment, because no structural change was introduced in the institutional system. However, practices may change in relation to specific events. In fact, on the foreign policy side, defeat in Vietnam and the resignation of President Nixon following the Watergate scandal triggered a mobilization of interests and institutions opposed to presidential centralization. Congress tried to regain influence in the field of foreign and military policy. Although this attempt was not fully successful, nevertheless it was sufficient for reactivating its powerful constraints on presidential action. Indeed, the institutionalization of a divided government regime (between the last two decades of the Cold War and the first decade of the post–Cold War period) led to a serious weakness of the very institution of the presidency. From the 1970s until 9/11/2001, presidential leadership was continuously challenged, regardless of the party of provenance of the President. At the same time, federal centralization too was successfully halted. Fiscal stress and ideological change in the 1970s and 1980s (with the growth of a neoconservative movement) gave important political resources to those rulers within the states who questioned the expansion of federal power. Thus, a swing took place from the centralization practices of the 1950s and 1960s to the decentralization practices of the following three decades.

9/11 once more changed the institutional equilibrium. Facing a terrorist threat without precedent, the USA has again moved toward a presidential centralization of the national decision-making process. With the federal government no longer divided between 2003 and 2006, a renewed presidential leadership emerged, this time supported by a Congress rigidly controlled by the President's supporters. Indeed, in that period, the USA witnessed an experience of party government without precedent. An extremely cohesive and coherent Republican Party, undoubtedly dominated by the President, was in the condition to control the three branches of government (and also to influence the Supreme Court). The American political experience between 1969 and 2006 shows the plausible double outcome of a separation of powers system operating in conditions of a polarized two-party system. The first outcome is *divided government* and the second is *presidential-dominated government*. If the first shows the paralysis which the system of checks and balances might produce, the second shows the lack of any effective congressional check and balance on the President, when the two chambers of the legislature are controlled by an ideological and centralized 'presidential' party (Blumenthal 2006). This latter experience shows also its difficulty in being institutionalized. Indeed, the electoral and institutional incentives of a separated system have continued to work for hindering the stabilization of a hegemonic coalition and the institutionalization of both a vertical relation between the President and Congress and a unilateral decision-making process by the former. In sum, in the post-World War II era, the US compound republic has continued to alternate between phases of federal and presidential centralization and phases of decentralization and congressional activism, and back again.

7

Structural transformation of European politics: the growth of the supranational European Union

7.1. Introduction

After World War II European politics has changed dramatically. A process of supranational integration has gradually aggregated into a common institutional framework roughly all the nation-states of the European continent.[1] The now called European Union (or EU) is the outcome of such aggregation. It combines confederal and federal, intergovernmental and Community institutional properties.[2] It is a *supranational* polity which combines (in the tradition of 'the lost world of American founding', Hendrickson 2003), inter-states and supra-states properties. The EU is the answer to a centuries-long fight between European nationalisms, a fight which produced two hot wars and a cold war on the European continent in the twentieth century (Haas 1958; Judt 2005). Also the EU, thus, is a 'peace pact', an attempt to create a new political order in Europe, first among the countries of its Western part and then among the latter and the countries of its Eastern and Southern parts. The EU is thus at the same time a new 'states system' and a new 'form of state'. It is, using concepts elaborated in the American Constitutional Convention of 1787, a 'federative system' (Hendrickson 2003) accommodating national and supranational aspirations. It is an international organization with institutional properties of a domestic one. After all, the dramatic experience of the twentieth century showed unequivocally the failure of any project of 'balance of powers' for keeping the peace on the European continent. With the end of World War II, European nation-states' elites needed to look for a more intense cooperation among previous enemies, if they wanted to avoid the repetition of either one of the two exits of European rivalry, anarchy or empire. In this sense, the EU represents the first historical attempt to compound voluntarily the European nation-states within a system of shared sovereignty. This attempt has been extra-ordinarily successful. The EU has definitively healed the fracture within Western Europe and between Western and Eastern Europe, reunifying for the first time in history the continent through peaceful and not military means.

Starting with the Paris Treaty of 1952 which established the European Community on Steel and Coal (ECSC) as an experiment in intergov-ernmental cooperation for the common management of crucial eco-nomic resources, economic regional integration moved gradually forward, notwithstanding the defeat by the French Parliament of a proposal to create a European Defense Community (EDC) in 1954. The ECSC then became the EEC with the Rome Treaty of 1957, subsequently the Euro-pean Community (EC) and finally, with the Maastricht Treaty, the EU. Established in Paris and Rome as a cooperation among six countries in the 1950s, the EU has witnessed several enlargements since (see Chapter 1). It became an organization of nine countries in the 1970s, twelve countries in the 1980s, fifteen countries in the 1990s, twenty-seven countries in the 2000s. In particular the 1990s was a decade of radical transformation for Europe. The unification of Germany in 1990[3] gave a formidable impulse to the process of integration, which reached new heights with the Maas-tricht Treaty of 1992, the Amsterdam Treaty of 1997, and subsequently the 2001 Nice Treaty (which formally laid down the rules which are still governing the functioning of the EU) (Gilbert 2003). After a long period of 'passive consent', the increased competences and the various enlargements of the EU have made the process of integration more con-tested. The decision in 2003 to activate a process of elaboration of a Constitutional Treaty or CT, approved by the heads of the member-states at the intergovernmental conference (IGC) held in Rome in October 2004, represented a further step on the road toward a political Europe. However, the rejection of the CT by the voters in France and the Netherlands in referenda held in May and June 2005 is also indicative of the resistance to the integration process.

From the coordination of common policies in very limited economic sectors, the regional organization now called the EU has dramatically increased the number of policies affected by its decisions. Although in Maastricht three pillars of cooperation were created (the first pillar rep-resenting the policies for the creation of a common market, the second pillar representing foreign and security policies, and the third pillar representing justice and home affairs) corresponding to different forms and logics of cooperation (more Community or federal oriented in the first pillar and more intergovernmental or confederal oriented in the last two), the EU has gradually evolved in the direction of a supranational organization which affects large parts of member-states' politics and policies (Cowles, Caporaso, and Risse 1999; Featherstone and Radaelli 2003; Schmidt 2006). Even monetary sovereignty has been pooled at the Community level, with the adoption by a large group of EU member-states[4] of a common currency (the euro) in 2001 (Martin and Ross 2004). In sum, the EU has become a political system in its own right. Through the process of European integration, the European sovereign states gradually have become EU member-states. As Sbragia (1994: 87) remarked: 'The "sovereign" nation-states that created the Community or joined it after its creation have gradually become transformed into "member-states".'

As the USA at the end of the eighteenth century, also the EU has been motivated by the necessity to aggregate states of asymmetrical size (in terms of demography, economic power, geographical extension, and historical tradition). For this reason, in its half a century process of institutionalization the EU has come to be structured along the lines of a multiple separation of powers both horizontally and vertically. Although not by design as in the USA, the EU institutional system has been structured in an antihierarchical way through the dispersion of decision-making power among different and separated institutions. Especially through the institutional development which took place in the 1990s, it has also become difficult for any EU institution to take unilateral decisions on behalf of the others. Moreover, the progressive waves of enlargement have ended up in hindering the formation of permanent majorities of member-states at the system level, acting as hegemonic coalitions. In sum, the EU has ended up, *by necessity*, organizing itself as a *compound polity*. A polity institutionally different from that of its member-states but not at all dissimilar from the polity which came to be experienced in the USA since the end of the eighteenth century.

7.2. The Growth of European Supranationalism

The interpretation of the EU as an international organization similar to those inter-states associations set up to promote cooperation among sovereign states is still predominant (especially in the field of International Relations) (Moravcsik 1998; Magnette 2005). Indeed, since its very beginning, the EU was more than an intergovernmental body created by its individual member-states in pursuit of specific or precise goals closely supervised by those states. In fact, in order to make intergovernmental cooperation credible, specific supra-states features were included in its institutional framework through the constituting treaties, although such features have required time and opportunities for developing properly. They were the Community features represented by institutions not directly dependent on the constituting states, and thus (exactly for such institutional separation) able to foster cooperation among those constituting states. Through these Community institutions, the costs of inter-states transactions have been reduced, information diffused, and reciprocal trust promoted. Thus, one might even argue that the EU, at least potentially, has been, since its foundation, a supranational polity, combining the institutional features proper of an organization based on intergovernmental agreements and those of a Community project. Without the latter, the preservation of the former features would not have been guaranteed.

Because of the specific institutional structure created for regulating interaction among member-states, the Community institutions grew increasingly independent of their creators (the individual member-states) once this form of cooperation was established (Pierson P. 1996). In the institutionalization process, the EU has gradually developed, combining its intergovernmental configuration with its Community potentials, the features of a supranational organization (Sandholtz and Stone Sweet 1998; Weiler 1999; Fabbrini 2002). The EU is not an international organization, but it will also never become a domestic system. As Mény (2001: 30) wrote: '(t)he stratification of powers since 1957 (EEC, Single European Act or SEA, Maastricht, Amsterdam, utilization of Article 235 to expand the Communities' sphere of action) has transformed an international organization with limited powers into a Union of unique type, with missions and involvements that are almost unlimited'. In this sense, the EU is an institutional experiment in building a supranational political authority while other experiments in regional integration are still limited to economic cooperation.[5] The constitutional foundations of the EU are the treaties signed by its member-states since Rome 1957. The treaties establish the institutional framework of the EU, allocate powers to the various institutions, and periodically redefine these powers in response to changes between the member-states and the Community institutions (see Table 7.1).

Table 7.1 The founding treaties of the EU

Institutional framework	Rome (1957)	SEA (1986)	Maastricht (1992)	Amsterdam (1997)	Nice (2001)
EU Commission	• right of initiative • to draft budget • to act as guardian of treaty • to negotiate international trade agreements	• right of initiative extended • new competences in areas related to the completion of the single market	• powers enhanced in economic and monetary union (EMU) and in foreign policy • further extension of the right of initiative	• president's role strengthened • right of initiative extended	• role of President enhanced • more Commissioners
Council of Ministers	• power to pass legislation • to appoint Commission • control of the budget	• increased use of QMV in areas relating to the single market	• further extension of QMV • right of initiative in justice and foreign affairs together with the Commission	• further extension of QMV and co-decision with the Parliament	• further extension of QMV • re-weighting of votes
European Council	• not mentioned in treaty	• granted legal status	• power of defining the strategic guidelines of the Union	• confirmed role in EMU and strengthened position in the CSFP	• official seat in Brussels
European Parliament	• right to be consulted on legislation • right to dismiss the Commission	• extension of legislative authority through the cooperation procedure	• co-decision powers • greater role in appointing the Commission	• co-decision extended • right to approve appointment of the Commission's President and Commission as a whole	• further extension of co-decision procedure • right to place matters before the Court • legal base for European party funding
European Court of Justice	• guardian of treaties and EC Law	• creation of Court of First Instance	• power to impose fines against MSs (but excluded from second and third pillar)	• increased jurisdiction in third pillar matters	• further sharing of tasks with Court of First Instance • more specialized chambers to improve judicial capacity of the EU • number of judges changed

Source: Re-elaboration from Bomberg and Stubb (2003: 46-7).

Table 7.2 The EU after Maastricht (1992): the three pillars

The European Communities	Common Foreign and Security policy	Cooperation in Justice and Home Affairs
EC	*Foreign policy*	Cooperation between
Customs union and	Cooperation, common	judicial authorities in civil
single market	positions and measures	and criminal law
Agricultural policy	Peacekeeping	Police cooperation
Structural policy	Human rights	Combating racism and
Trade Policy	Democracy	xenophobia
New or amended provisions on:	Aid to non-member	Fighting drugs and the
EU citizenship	countries	arms trade
Education and culture	*Security policy*	Fighting organized crime
Trans-European networks	Drawing on the WEU:	Fighting terrorism
Consumer protection	questions concerning	Criminal acts against
Health	the security of the EU	children, trafficking in
Research and environment	Disarmament	human beings
Social policy	Financial aspects of defense	
Asylum policy	Long term: Europe's	
External borders	security framework	
Immigration policy		
EURATOM		
ECSC		

Source: Re-elaboration from European Union, 2004, *Structure of the European Union*, www.europa.eu.int, Last updated on: 27/4/2004.

The three pillars introduced with the Maastricht Treaty of 1992 (see Table 7.2) institutionalize the two main methods of decision-making adopted by the EU: the Community (or federal) method (regarding the first pillar) and the intergovernmental (or confederal) method (regarding the other two). The supranational character of the EU is more coherently represented by the institutional structure presiding over the decision-making process of the first pillar, where a growing number of decisions were and are being taken through the Community method, whereas the intergovernmental method is proper of the other two pillars (see Chapter 1). Community method means not only that the Council of Ministers (which is the institution representing the governments of the member-states) may recur to a (although a very complex) qualified majority voting (QMV)[6] system for taking decisions. Indeed, even in the first pillar, the logic of consensus is so entrenched that the recourse to QMV is and was rare. Rather, the Community method recognizes a crucial role for the supra-states institutions (such as the European Commission, the EP, and the ECJ). The role, that is, of making possible the cooperation among states, of regulating their behavior, and of adjudicating their disputes. On the contrary, the intergovernmental method is based on voluntary coordination, the decisions are taken only unanimously, and no Community or supra-states institution plays a formal role in coordinating member-states and regulating their disputes.

However, the three pillars are not easily separable in the practical functioning of the EU. The supranational logic of the EU has ended up in influencing also the two intergovernmental pillars. Dramatic events such as the Iraq war initiated in 2003 or the terrorist attacks in European cities in 2004 and 2005 (Madrid and London) have created pressure for more stringent cooperation among the EU member-states also in the second and third pillar. Moreover, the costs of coordination of these latter pillars have so much increased that it has become implausible to assume that the rotating presidency of the EU could by itself meet them.[7] Finally, a decision taken in one pillar has frequently affected the other pillars, thus increasing the need for more efficacious policy harmonization. For instance, it has been increasingly necessary to coordinate trade policy (a crucial field of the first pillar, controlled by the European Commission) and the Common Foreign and Security Policy or CFSP of the second pillar (controlled by the Council of Ministers), because of the evident implications of one policy for the other. This phenomenon has been called 'cross-pillarization' (Table 7.3).

However, although in the practical functioning of the EU system it has become increasingly difficult to keep the three pillars distinct, my analysis here deals primarily with the first pillar. The institutionalization of this pillar epitomizes the transformation of European politics. The need to build a single European market has led to a situation in which an increasing number of traditionally domestic policies are now elaborated, organized, and promoted at the EU level (Fabbrini and Morata 2002; Wallace and Wallace 2003). The Community institutions have acquired competences in a growing number of policy fields as a consequence of the project of building a common *single* market. The legal instruments through which those institutions have exercised their governing role are several: through *directives* (decisions which define the targets but leave the member-states the choice of the means to achieve them), *regulations* (binding decisions directly applicable by the member-states), *administrative acts* (decisions binding only those to whom they are addressed), and *recommendations* (which do not have a binding force). Thus, supranationalism is the outcome of the combination of two methods (the Community and the intergovernmental ones). The EU as a supranational organization has been institutionalized via a complex system of interlocking governmental

Table 7.3 Sharing policies among EU institutions ('cross-pillarization')

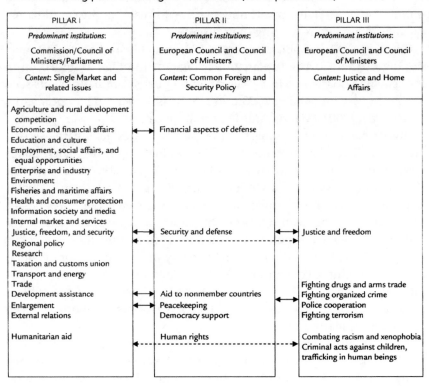

PILLAR I	PILLAR II	PILLAR III
Predominant institutions:	*Predominant institutions:*	*Predominant institutions:*
Commission/Council of Ministers/Parliament	European Council and Council of Ministers	European Council and Council of Ministers
Content: Single Market and related issues	*Content:* Common Foreign and Security Policy	*Content:* Justice and Home Affairs
Agriculture and rural development competition		
Economic and financial affairs	Financial aspects of defense	
Education and culture		
Employment, social affairs, and equal opportunities		
Enterprise and industry		
Environment		
Fisheries and maritime affairs		
Health and consumer protection		
Information society and media		
Internal market and services		
Justice, freedom, and security	Security and defense	Justice and freedom
Regional policy		
Research		
Taxation and customs union		
Transport and energy		
Trade		Fighting drugs and arms trade
Development assistance	Aid to nonmember countries	Fighting organized crime
Enlargement	Peacekeeping	Police cooperation
External relations	Democracy support	Fighting terrorism
Humanitarian aid	Human rights	Combating racism and xenophobia Criminal acts against children, trafficking in human beings

bodies which has proved to be effective in both supporting integration and promoting the consent of member-states (Stone Sweet, Sandholtz, and Fligstein 2001).

7.3. The Institutional Structure of the EU

7.3.1. *The Horizontal Level*

The distribution of powers in the EU can be analyzed considering both the horizontal and the vertical dimension: by the former the relationship between the central Community institutions is meant, and by the latter the relationship between the supranational, national, and subnational institutions. At the horizontal level (Hix 2005), its central institutions are the European Council, the Council of Ministers (or Council of the EU), the EP, and the European Commission. In addition to the ECJ and

Table 7.4 The institutions of the EU (January 1, 2007)

Governmental	Regulatory	Consultative	Judicial
European Council (27 heads of state and government)	European Central Bank (General Council: 27 members)	Committee of the Regions (317 members)	ECJ (27 judges)
Council of Ministers (27 ministers)	European Investment Bank (Governors' Council: 27 members)	Economic and Social Committee (317 members)	Court of Auditors (27 members)
European Parliament (785 members)	Regulatory Agencies		
European Commission (27 Commissioners)			

the Court of Auditors, the EU has also regulatory (such as the European Central Bank) and consultative institutions (such as the Committee of the Regions) which contribute to the complexity of its institutional structure (see Table 7.4).

The European Council (constituted by the heads of governments and states) and the Council of Ministers[8] are intergovernmental bodies representing the executives of the EU member-states, responsible (the former) for delineating the aims of the EU (De Schoutheete and Wallace 2002) and (the latter) for mediating between member-states and EU institutions. This is why some scholars (Burgess 2000: 262) have written about 'the uncertain character of the Council of Ministers'. However, in areas where it decides with QMV it is also the expression of a broader Community interest (Hayes-Renshaw and Wallace 1997). The Council of Ministers has to perform the crucial role of ensuring the coordination of the general economic policies of the member-states. It legislates with the EP in matters connected to the common market and it approves with the EP the EU budget. Legally speaking, the Council is a single entity, but it is in practice divided into several different councils that meet in Brussels, each dealing with a different functional area. Each council is attended by a different type of minister. There are currently nine formations, seven proper of the first pillar and two 'cross-pillarized'.

The formation of the first pillar is: Economic and Financial Affairs (Ecofin), composed of economics and finance ministers of the member-states; Agriculture and Fisheries, one of the oldest configurations, this brings together once a month the ministers for agriculture and fisheries, and the commissioners responsible for agriculture, fisheries, food safety, veterinary questions, and public health matters; Employment, Social Policy, Health, and Consumer Affairs Council (EPSCO), which is composed of employment, social protection, consumer protection, health, and equal opportunities ministers; Competitiveness, created in June 2002, through the merging of three previous configurations (Internal Market, Industry, and Research); Transport, Telecommunications, and Energy, created in June 2002, through the merging of three policies under one configuration, and with a composition also varying according to the specific items on its agenda, meeting once every two months; Environment, which is composed of environment ministers, who meet about four times a year; Education, Youth, and Culture (EYC) which is composed of education, culture, youth, and communications ministers, who meet around three or four times a year. Then, there is the General Affairs and External Relations Council (GAERC) which is composed of ministers for foreign affairs and meets once a month. Since June 2002, it has held separate meetings on general affairs and external relations. The GAERC also coordinates preparation for and follow-up to meetings of the European Council and at its sessions on External Relations, in the context of the second pillar on Common Foreign and Security Policy, the High Representative for Common Foreign and Security Policy also takes part.[9] And finally there is the Justice and Home Affairs Council (JHA), which brings together justice ministers and interior ministers of the member-states, and meets under the rules of the third pillar. However, as seems clear from this description, it is not easy to keep distinct the Council formations dealing with the issues of the first pillar and those of the second and third pillar.

The intergovernmental European Council and the Council of Ministers are checked by more Community-oriented institutions, starting with the European Commission which can be considered the functional equivalent of the executive of the EU. Although its members come from each of the EU member-states, the Commission is required by the founding treaties to represent Community rather than national interests. The Commission monopolizes the power of initiating legislation, in the sense that it (and only it) may submit to the Council of Ministers and the EP legislative proposals on which these institutions will have to legislate (whereas in the areas that fall within the second and third pillar such power is not recognized by the member-states). Moreover, the Commission has to make sure that European laws are properly executed once approved (by the Council of Ministers and the EP). Finally, it is the guardian of the treaties which provide the legal basis of the EU, which means taking responsibility for initiating infringement proceedings at the ECJ against member-states and others who it considers to have breached the EU treaties and other Community laws. The Commission is the only EU institution which negotiates international trade agreements (in the WTO) and other international agreements on behalf of the EU. It closely cooperates in this with the Council of Ministers. The Commission also regulates competition in the EU, vetting all mergers with Community-wide effects and initiating proceedings against companies which violate EU competition laws.

Both the policy proposals the Commission will submit to the Council of Ministers and the EP, and the technical measures it has to adopt to implement legislation already approved by the latter are discussed and negotiated in committees made up of representatives of member-states and Commission's experts. In particular, the Council of Ministers influences the internal working of the Commission through the Committee of Permanent Representatives (or COREPER), and the several committees or groups of experts, chosen by the Council, which oversee the Commission's internal working (Franchino 2000). These committees, which are forums for discussion, are made up of representatives from EU member-states and are chaired by the Commission. They ensure that the Commission is able to establish a dialogue with national governments and administrations before elaborating measures to adopt or before implementing measures eventually adopted. This process is sometimes known by the jargon term of comitology (Ballman, Epstein, and O'Halloran 2002).

Though its members are appointed by the members of the European Council, the Commission has come to enjoy an independent form of legitimacy. In any case, the coordination of common policies proved so complex that the individual member-states have delegated powers to the Community's institutions. The Commission in particular has gradually transformed itself from an agency at the disposal of the Council of Ministers to one that actually structures its internal decision-making process. The Commission helps to draw up the agenda of issues to be discussed by the Council of Ministers, because of its control of information and expertise unavailable to national governments. Recent studies (Christiansen 2002) have confirmed what Lindberg (1963: 71) detected at the very beginning of the Community experience: 'It appears that the EEC institutional system, despite its complexity, actually offers more opportunities for the Commission to take an active role than would otherwise have been the case. . . . the Commission is an active participant at all stages of the process.'

The President of the Commission is appointed by the European Council and approved by the EP. The President of the Commission, together with the European Council, chooses the other commissioners (one for each member-state, starting from 2004)[10] who then have to receive the approval of the EP. The independent legitimacy of the Commission is based first on the fact that its President, although proposed by the European Council, has to receive the approval of the EP to fill the office and, second, on the openness of the Commission to the functional representation of pressure groups. As Dann (2002) notes, the role of the European Council in the appointment of the Commission is one of the main factors that impedes a close fusion of the Commission with the EP. Moreover, the Council of Ministers has two channels to intervene in the application of Community law. First, its members, which represent the governments of the member-states, have executive competences within the jurisdiction of their own state. Second, according to the 1986 SEA, the Council of Ministers can interfere in the Commission implementation powers in those cases specified by the treaty. It has been argued (Hix 2005) that for this reason the EU has a sort of dual executive (as in the semi-presidential system of government), represented by the Council of Ministers on one side and the Commission on the other. However, this interpretation seems to undervalue the sharing-powers logic of the EU, which is not proper of a semi-presidential system (see Chapter 3). In fact, the Council of Ministers shares at the same moment legislative powers with the EP and executive powers with the Commission.

The EP is the popular branch of the EU. It has been elected by popular poll every five years since 1979. Together with the Council of Ministers, it composes the legislative branch of the institutions of the Union. It meets in two locations: Strasbourg and Brussels. It cannot initiate legislation, but it can amend or veto it in many policy areas. In certain other policy areas, it has the right only to be consulted. The EP also supervises the European Commission: it must approve all appointments to it and can dismiss it with a vote of censure. It also has the right to control the EU budget. It represents European instances (Hix and Scully 2003), although these instances are interpreted from the point of view of subnational electoral districts. The EP has been able to increase its influence significantly with the treaties of Maastricht (1992) and Amsterdam (1997). Although endowed with more limited legislative power than national parliaments, the treaties of Maastricht and Amsterdam have finally recognized the EP's power of cooperation and codecision with the Council of Ministers on most legislative issues, whereas the Rome Treaty had only provided for a consultative role. In particular, the codecision procedure has transformed the EP into an effective legislative partner of the Council of Ministers (Pinter 1998) because it has allowed it to play the role of agenda-setter (Tsebelis and Kreppel 1998). Moreover, the Maastricht

Treaty recognized the EP's power to confirm the European Council's choice for the presidency of the Commission (and thus the choice of the members of the Commission negotiated by its President with the leaders of member-states' governments of the European Council). Although this power cannot be confused with the traditional parliamentary power to form a government, nevertheless the EP has established its control on the executive branch of the EU. Its members (MEPs) are organized into confederations of national and regional parties. MEPs are elected on the basis of national constituencies and nation-specific electoral systems.[11] The EP parties are weak organizations, compared with the parliamentary parties of the EU member-states. Political ideology is not the main criterion for aggregating parties and motivating their parliamentary behavior. Frequently, sectional divisions are much more mobilizing than ideological divisions. Indeed, the sectional cleavage crosses each of the main EP parties.[12] Because they are weak, the parliamentary parties do not play any significant role as legislative gatekeepers. Lobbies, business and trade associations, subnational governments, professional associations, epistemic communities, and movements intervene in the legislative process of the EP, without passing through connections with the parliamentary parties (Smismans 2004).

7.3.2. Power-Sharing in Brussels

The legislative and executive powers in the EU are thus diffused among different institutions, and the spheres of action of each institution partially overlap (Crum 2002) (see Figure 7.1). The legislative power is exerted by the Council of Ministers (having deliberation and approval powers) and the EP (having a codecision power in the policy areas indicated by the treaties). The Commission retains the executive power, which implies also the task of monitoring the implementation of EU decisions, flanked by the EU regulatory agencies. However, the exercise of its executive functions is shared with the Council of Ministers which, through the system of comitology, has the power to oversee the acts elaborated and implemented by the Commission. Through the various committees, the Council of Ministers can indicate to the Commission the specific topics and issues that need to be taken into consideration for its proposals, or it can indicate how to implement specific Community decisions. The participation of the committees in the policy process has allowed the Council of Ministers to discuss and negotiate with the Commission on the various issues at stake. Although one might say (Wallace 2001) that the

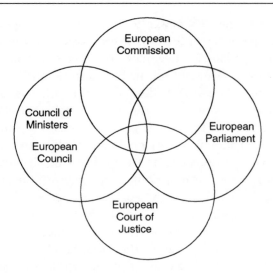

Figure 7.1 Power-sharing between EU institutions

comitology system has strengthened, rather than weakened, the Commission, nevertheless it has pushed the Commission to take into consideration the interests of the Council of Ministers. Finally, the ECJ has come to have a legislative role through the exercise of the 'preliminary rulings' power (on this, later).

Thus in a growing number of policies, each institution needs to find an agreement with other institutions, because each of them has a role in the legislative or executive process. None of them can take unilateral decisions, assuming that it represents the whole of the governmental system. Moreover, the independence of each institution is guaranteed by the different source of their legitimacy, and thus by the different community of interests they represent (Figure 7.2). The Council of Ministers and the EP are elected separately by different constituencies, the former being the expression of (national) electors voting for national offices, and the latter of (national) electors voting for European offices. Thus, while the Council of Ministers is the institutional channel for the expression of national governments in the EU decision-making process, the EP is the institutional channel for giving representation to member-states' electors, organized in subnational electoral districts. Moreover, their elections rarely clash, inasmuch as they follow different time schedules. Thus the Council of Ministers and the EP are accountable to different communities of interest through staggered elections. At the same time, the independence of the Commission resides not only in the treaties, but above all in the balance

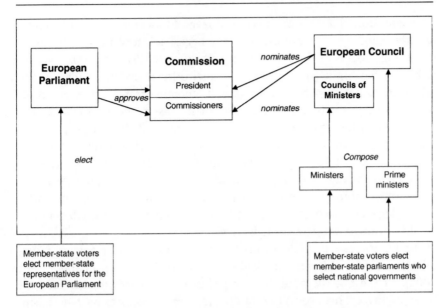

Figure 7.2 Election and appointment of the members of EU institutions

of powers between the European Council (which nominates its President and, with the latter, indicates the commissioners) and the EP (which has the power of 'advice and consent' on those nominees).

In conclusion, the EU is a system of separated governmental institutions sharing powers, radically different from the more familiar system (for Europeans) of fused (parliamentary or semi-presidential) government. The EU is a system in which separated institutions enjoy different sources of legitimacy, operate within different time frames, and nevertheless are required to cooperate in the decision-making process. Although not defined by a formal constitution, the EU governs through a system of separation of powers, functionally preserved by an internal mechanism of checks and balances.

7.3.3. The Vertical Level

On the vertical dimension, power is distributed among the supranational, national, and regional authorities. In order to assess the vertical allocation of power in the EU, referring to both federal and confederal systems is appropriate (Kelemen 2003). In fact, features of both systems can be found in the EU's current territorial structure. The EU has multiple levels of governance and provides member-states and Community interests with representation channels at the central level. Moreover, regional interests are advocated by the Committee of the Regions, intervening in the policymaking process of the EU as a consulting body (Piattoni 2002). Weiler (2000: 2) has argued that 'a set of constitutional norms regulating the relationship between the Union and its member-states...has emerged, which is very much like similar sets of norms in most federal states'. Nevertheless, he also stresses the existence of confederal aspects in the EU. According to Weiler (2000), 'the realities of an intergovernmental Europe are still forcefully in place. Institutionally, Europe is closer to the confederal rather than it is to the federal.' The EU architecture is a unique combination of a confederal institutional arrangement and a federal legal arrangement. Elazar (1998) considers the EU a confederation passing through a process of federalization.

The EU shares with federations the vertical diffusion of power among different territorial levels (Nicolaidis and Howse 2001; Menon and Schain 2006). In the EU, the allocation of policy competences to the different levels of governance seems to recall the features of cooperative federalism. Member-states have kept a supremacy on electorally sensitive domestic issues (such as social policy and industrial relations, but also external relations and defense policy), leaving to the Community institutions the power to define all the policies which are crucial to the functioning of a common market. Interestingly enough, the EU federalization process has Europeanized policies (connected to the functioning of the market) that in traditional federal states have been traditionally controlled by the constituent units, thus leaving to the member-states policies (defense and foreign affairs) that in the traditional federal states have been assigned to the federal center (Sbragia 2005a). Also at the vertical level, powers are segmented and thus shared by reciprocal independent institutions. Cooperation, rather than competition, among the various levels of the polity is promoted, also because the Community level does not benefit from having an autonomous administrative system for implementing its own decisions. Indeed, it needs the cooperation of member-states' structures for honoring even its treaty duties (Figure 7.3).

What is distinctive, therefore, in the EU vertical separation of powers is the coexistence of confederal and federal institutions and processes. If it is true, as Burgess (2000: 262) noted, 'that, in establishing the EEC in 1957, the basic structure of the union resembled more an economic confederation than anything else', it is also true (Burgess 2000) 'that these elements in practice coexisted with distinctly federal features'. The main confederal elements of the EU are represented by the European Council

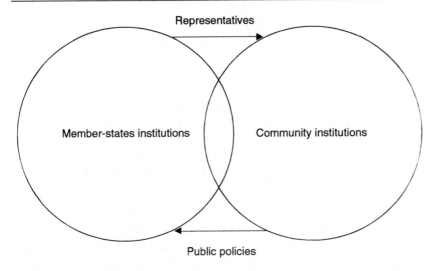

Representatives

Member-states institutions

Community institutions

Public policies

Figure 7.3 Relations between Community and member-states institutions

and its IGC, whereas the federal elements of the EU are the Commission, the EP, and the ECJ, with the Council of Ministers in between. Moreover, regulatory agencies (Majone 2005) such as the European Central Bank in its capacity to control the common European currency are clearly federal institutions. The prolonged although unstable coexistence of these different institutional components brings about a reconsideration of the relationship between confederation and federation. Indeed, although ideologically confederation was interpreted by Hamilton in *Federalist no.15* as a recipe for failure, or in any case a remnant of an institutional past,[13] de facto confederal features were inserted within the new federal structure of the American republic. The US and EU experiences show that the two systems are not incompatible at all, but on the contrary that they have elements (institutions and practices) whose combination is necessary for keeping together state units of different size within a common decision-making framework.

The EU has thus confirmed that the analytical distinction (Watts 1998) between *federation* and *confederation* might not be always applicable, especially when the polity in question aggregates state units previously sovereign (and, again, of different size and powers) (Forsyth 1981). Analytically, a federation has been defined as

a compound polity combining constituent units and a general government, each possessing power delegated to it by the people through a constitution, each empowered to deal directly with the citizens in the exercise of a significant portion of its legislative, administrative, and taxing powers, and each directly elected by its citizens. (Watts 1998: 121)

Whereas in a confederation

the institutions of shared rule are dependent on the constituent governments, being composed of delegates from the constituent governments and therefore having only an indirect electoral and fiscal base. By contrast with federation, in which each government operates directly on the citizens, in confederations the direct relationship lies between the shared institutions and the governments of the member-states. (Watts 1998)

Although this distinction is analytically clear, the empirical reality of building unions of states has challenged it. Indeed, the EU (as the USA before it) had to find ways for accommodating elements of both types of territorial organization, combining them in an original way. Some authors (Hueghlin 2000) have talked of treaty federalism, others (Hooghe and Marks 2001) of a multilevel governance, others (Majone 2005a) of a regulatory state. Caporaso (2000: 141) is right in noticing that 'in political terms, Europe is a multi-level, post-national polity with final authority still located in the constituent states'. However, it is important to notice as well that the member-states exercise their 'final authority' in a supranational institutional framework. With the consequence that each member-state's final authority needs to be mediated with the final authorities of the other member-states.

Moreover, the EU epitomizes a successful experiment not only in supranational integration but also in subnational 'plurification' (Kirsch 1995). The EU has introduced effective incentives to disaggregate the territorial organization of its member-states. Through the development of regional policies, supported by structural funds devoted to the poorer regions for leveling up the conditions of the common market, the EU has recognized the pressure of many regional governments willing to increase their functional independence from their national governments, or even in other cases pushed the latter to create new regional or local authorities for applying for structural Community funds. The processes to create confederal and federal arrangements at both the supranational and national levels appear to reinforce each other. Regional aggregation at the EU level has tended to foster strategies for the subnational decentralization of public authority in its member-states. These processes might be called *federalization*, meaning the ongoing dynamic formation of a polity constituted by territorial units which strive to remain distinct and nevertheless search for a common decision-making framework at both supranational and subnational level (on the concept of *federalization* see Elazar 1987*a*). A federalization process may imply multiple institutional exits, or rather different and changing equilibria among the institutions of *shared-rule* and *self-rule*.

The territorial organization of the EU has inevitably affected the structuring of partisan politics. At the EU level, irrespective of the level of its member-states, partisan politics tends to be structured on sectional rather than on economic, ethnic/cultural, or ideological cleavages. Sectional or geographical cleavages, concerning both the legitimacy of the EU as a decision-making body and the distribution of the resources it controls, have become the sources of the birth and development of new partisan actors and of the structuring of new divisions within the party system. 'Were he alive, Rokkan would certainly acknowledge that the [European parties'] contemporary salience is not what it was during the heroic founding epoch of the late 1800s and early 1900s.... This, I suspect, holds even more for the EU' (Schmitter 2000: 67). As Bartolini (2005) has argued, the decline in the salience of those cleavages increases the relevance of territorial and sectional cleavages (see also Fabbrini 2001).

If one considers both the vertical and horizontal levels of EU institutions, then it seems clear that their complexity cannot be captured only by the concept of federalism. *The EU is more than a federalized polity.* Federalism is not sufficient to capture the defining nature of the EU, because it implies a separation of powers at the vertical level *and not necessarily also at the horizontal level*. Indeed, none of the federal European nation-states of the post–World War II period (Germany, Austria, and Belgium) registered a horizontal separation of powers: they are parliamentary governments, as is the case in the other established non-European federal nation-states (such as Canada, Australia, and India). The only exception is federal Switzerland, which has also a separation of powers at the governmental level, although its executive is a collective body whose presidency has to rotate among its seven members. However, as already argued (Chapter 1), its limited geographic and demographic size makes it an interesting (Zweifel 2002) but unlikely comparative reference for the EU. In sum, the EU is a *compound* system radically different from the noncompound systems of its member-states, but also from a pure international organization.

In conclusion, the Europe which invented the nation-state between the sixteenth and seventeenth centuries has experimented with a supranational organization at the end of the twentieth century. Supranational organization because, as Ruggie (1998: 195) suggests, 'the collectivity of members as a singularity, in addition to the central institutional apparatus of the EU, has become party to the interstate strategic interaction'. Which is to say that the identity of each of its member-states (Ruggie 1998) '... increasingly endogenizes the collectivity they comprise'. This experiment has given rise to a political system whose institutional structure and functional logic have evident dissimilarities to the one that came to be institutionalized in the European nation-states over the previous two centuries. In fact, in the EU, *segmentation and separation of powers concerns both the horizontal and vertical level of the system*. At the same time, both the EU institutional structure and functional logic appear more commonly associated with the US compound polity. Both systems, indeed, had to create a union out of states endowed with asymmetrical powers.

7.4. The Judicial Order of Supranational EU

The judiciary has been crucial in promoting and supporting the institutionalization of a supranational polity in Europe (Stone Sweet and Caporaso 1998). Through a skillful use of the doctrine of the enumerated powers (Weiler 1999), the ECJ, since the 1960s, has effectively constructed a federal legal system, defining the principles and the rules which regulate the division of competences between the Community institutions and the member-state governments. The Court has acted as a truly federal institution, although it has powers and features different from other federal courts, and the US Supreme Court in particular (Johnson 2000). Incrementally, the Court has extended the number of policy areas that require Community action, creating the conditions for growing cooperation between Community and member-state authorities. This positive-sum game between Community and member-state institutions has precluded the oscillation of powers and competences registered in America's competitive federalism experience. At least in the long period of the 'passive consent' to the integration process (i.e. till the Maastricht Treaty), it seemed that the member-state executives had an interest in transferring powers and resources to Community institutions also because that allowed them to be freed from domestic parliamentary control and in the same moment to play the blame avoidance card with their own electorate.

The ECJ is composed of judges supported by *Advocates General* (general attorneys) and it 'presents its decisions as unanimous judgments, no votes are published and dissenting opinions are not permitted' (Stone Sweet

2004: 26). Although there is no formal rule, it is assumed that each member-state has the right to nominate a judge. However, the judges are nominated through common accord by the governments of the member-states for a period of six years. The nomination process is staggered so that every three years half of the judges have to be changed or reconfirmed for another mandate (there are no limits of mandate, but nor is there the life tenure of the US Supreme Court justices). The *Advocates General* are nominated with the same procedure and enjoy the same status as the members of the ECJ. This intergovernmental procedure did not prevent the Court from becoming the most pro-Community institution of the EU. The ECJ is a single supranational institution in the sense that the EU lacks a network of supranational courts because it has no power of appellate review, whereas in the USA judicial decisions may be reviewed by national courts of appeal, especially in cases affecting the supremacy of federal law or the impediment of interstate commerce (Cohen 1996). The ECJ has acquired the crucial power of assessing the coherence between EU and national laws. Because the treaties have assigned the Court the power to guarantee the uniform implementation of Community legislation in order to promote the formation of a common market, the ECJ has ended up interpreting the treaties as quasi-constitutional documents. In this way, the Court has gradually transformed the EU into a supranational constitutionalized regime, or rather it has become 'the supreme inter-preter of EU law' and 'its tasks are to enforce compliance with that law, and to ensure that it is applied in a uniform manner across the EU' (Stone Sweet 2005: 47).

Such a role for the Court was not envisioned by the Rome Treaty (Dehousse 1998). The treaty assigned the Court the power to resolve disputes among states or between states and Community institutions which could not find an acceptable solution at the level of the Council of Ministers or the Commission. However, as happened in the case of the US Supreme Court, ECJ members have come to interpret its role differently due to the challenges and opportunities it has had to face. It is article 177 of the Rome Treaty (article 234 of the Maastricht Treaty) which has allowed the Court to exercise its extensive power. That article requires national courts to ask for a *preliminary ruling* by the ECJ when there is any suspicion of inconsistency between member-state and Community legislation. Although the preliminary ruling of the ECJ is not binding on member-state courts, it has been generally accepted by the latter. Indeed, through the preliminary ruling clause the ECJ has forced member-states to accept the treaties as the supreme law of the land. Step by step, the ECJ rulings have thus created a new supranational legal order (Stone Sweet 2004). Several are the historical decisions taken by the Court, although it is interesting to note (Alter 2001) that the *foundational* decisions came in a period (the 1960s) of stalemate in the integration process (due to the 'empty chair' policy pursued by the President of the French Republic De Gaulle, who opposed the use of QMV in the Council of Ministers, boycotting its meeting). The *Van Gend en Loos* (1963) ruling established the principle of direct effect on individual citizens of the member-states of Community law. The Court, in fact, asserts that 'the Community... constitutes a new legal order of international law for the benefit of which the states have limited their sovereign rights, albeit within limited fields, and the subjects of which comprise not only Member States but also their nationals'. Through the principle of direct effect, the Court has opened the road for a uniform implementation of Community law in all the member-states, empowering the same individual citizens with the right to impose such uniformity on their own governments.

The *Costa* v. *Enel* (1964) and subsequently *Simmenthal* (1977) decisions went a step further, establishing the principle that, in case of conflict between Community and domestic laws, the former has to be considered supreme in relation to the latter. Both decisions severely circumscribed national sovereignty in the policy fields that the treaties consider crucial for the building of a common economic order at the European level. In these fields, the member-state laws which contradict Community laws, even if they were introduced after the approval of the latter, cannot be considered applicable. As the US Supreme Court used the Commerce Clause for fostering the formation of a national market, the ECJ used the above decisions for promoting a process of negative integration (i.e. of the dismantling of national legal barriers), thus allowing Community institutions to legislate on establishing the normative framework for a process of positive integration (Joerges 1997; Fabbrini 2005*b*). In *Simmenthal*, in fact, the Court asserted that

a national court which is called upon, within the limits of its jurisdiction, to apply provisions of Community law [is] under a duty to give effect to those provisions, if necessary refusing its own motion to apply any conflicting provision of national legislation, even if adopted subsequently, and it is not necessary for the court to request or await the prior setting aside of such provisions by legislative or other constitutional means.

With *Cassis de Dijonne* (1978) the Court introduced the principle of mutual recognition between member-state legislations, thus creating the need for a program of harmonization of their legal frameworks. In *Factortame* (1989) the Court made the principle of judicial review of domestic legislation by the national courts even more explicit, asserting that a national court is required to suspend the validity of a domestic law which negatively affects the rights assigned to an individual by Community law, 'notwithstanding any national rule to the contrary preventing' the Court from doing that. Finally, in *Francovich* (1990) the Court asserted that an individual citizen had the right to be compensated for damages sustained when a member-state does not implement a Community law. Of course, such a right has to be claimed in a national court and regulated by national norms.

Certainly, the constitutionalization of the EU by the ECJ was made possible by the support it has received from the national courts (Mancini and Keeling 1994). Article 177 of the Treaty of Rome (or 234 of the Maatricht Treaty) provided the opportunity to create a self-interested alliance between national and Community judicial institutions. That article, indeed, had the effect of strongly empowering national judiciaries, giving them the opportunity to review legislation approved by the national parliaments. A sort of judicial review process has thus developed at the member-state level, a process which has reduced the traditional constitutional review power of the national constitutional courts and has increased the power of the ordinary judiciary institutions. Indeed, constitutional courts have reacted negatively to this invasive role of the national judiciaries backed by the ECJ. A historical transformation in the relations between politics and law has thus gradually developed in Europe, whereas the main institution of politics (the parliament) had to recognize that it was no longer the only depository of national sovereignty. The EU member-states have had to learn to *govern with judges* (Stone Sweet 2000), as has never happened in their long history of national political development.

This historical transformation has taken place through the ECJ and its judicial interpretation of the treaties. If in the first two decades of the integration process (the 1960s and 1970s), the ECJ defined the foundational principles of the Community legal order, in the following decades it has de facto assigned to the national courts the role of guaranteeing the uniform implementation of Community legislation, *even against parliamentary will*. A role that national judiciaries have consciously accepted, not least because the ECJ has traditionally developed a policy of constructive relations (in terms of cooperation and information) with the national judiciaries (every year the Court hosts more than 2,000 national judges, attorneys, and law professors in Luxembourg where it operates). Indeed, the ECJ has been fully aware that 'if national judges chose not to refer cases, the legal system would be stillborn, and the effectiveness of EU law would not have been secured' (Stone Sweet 2005: 48). Moreover, the cooperation between the ECJ and national courts has protected both from member-states' potential political reactions. It is not surprising that national courts have generally accepted and incorporated the preliminary rulings of the ECJ in their judicial decisions, building with the latter cooperative relations; whereas in the USA, because no system of preliminary reference exists and because of the power of the Supreme Court to reverse lower court rulings, the relationship between the Supreme Court and the lower courts has tended to be adversarial (Cohen 1996).

Of course, the role of the ECJ has not gone unchallenged. Not only have national constitutional courts reacted to the expansion of its powers (starting with the German federal constitutional court), but also the governments of the member-states have acted to limit its power, for instance subtracting (with the Maastricht Treaty) crucial policy areas (the second and the third pillars) from the Court's jurisdiction. The Court has been very sensitive to the political pressures of EU member-states, avoiding any overt challenges regarding politically sensitive issues (Conant 2002). Nevertheless, the Court has been very effective in using legal discourse for promoting European integration, especially when member-states' preferences diverged considerably (Caldeira and Gibson 1995). In the end, the Court has managed to establish a new legal order on the European continent and has legitimized itself as the final guardian of that order. As Stone Sweet (2005: 44) argued:

the constitutionalization of the Treaty of Rome not only provoked the gradual emergence of a quasi-federal legal system. It fundamentally altered, within a very wide zone in Western Europe, how individuals, groups, and firms pursue their interests, how judges resolve disputes, and how policy is made at both national and supranational levels.

7.5. Supranational EU as Democratic Polity

If the EU is not just an international organization whose authority derives exclusively from that of the states which constitute it (Schmidt 2004), then it can be considered a political system (or polity) in the proper sense, that is a political system comparable with other domestic political systems (Hix 2005). Using David Easton's terminology (1981), one may argue that the EU is a political system which, on the basis of an autonomous internal logic, is able authoritatively to allocate values to *individuals* (and not only to corporate bodies) within a given territory (the territory of its member-states). Of course, there is no lack of commentators who doubt that the EU can be considered, not just a political system as such, but above all a *democratic* political system. For some scholars, the EU is a mixed system finalized to regulate market relations (Majone 2005*b*) or a neofeudal system of overlapping jurisdictions (Marks 1997; Zielonka 2006). Indeed, the EU is not solely a political system comparable to other domestic political systems, but it is also a democratic one, albeit of particular type. In fact, if a democracy is a political regime in which the decision-makers have been selected by voters, where they are obliged to act within a context of the limitation of powers and are judicially constrained to respect the fundamental rights of citizens, then (as Mény 2005 argued) there is no reason to maintain that the EU is not a democracy. Those who take the decisions in the EU have been selected by citizens in national and European elections; they are compelled to act within a complex system of the separation and the balancing of powers; and they are subject to the control of both national and EU courts (which base their action on the protection of fundamental rights celebrated by both member-states' constitutions and supra-states agreements such as the EU Charter of Fundamental Rights[14] or the European Convention on Human Rights[15]). But if the EU is a democracy, then it is necessary to detect its logic of functioning, its *model*, rather than to debate about it on the basis of a static description of its institutions.

The EU is a *compound* democracy, because it aggregates states and *their* citizens in a supranational institutional framework. These state units, moreover, have a crucial property: they are *asymmetrical in terms of power*. Since the debate in Philadelphia in 1787, democracy is not a property only of small *republics*, nor of *republics* constituted by only one republic. Democracy has been adapted to organize the political process *also* of polities aggregating different and separated states *and their citizens*. Certainly, this type of democracy is different from the one experimented with in the (European) nation-states. But even the latter adopted different types of democracies, if it is true that there are significant differences between (at least) majoritarian and consensus democracies. A compound democracy implies a specific logic of functioning; namely, it has to hinder the formation of permanent hegemonic coalitions (of states, first of all) at the supra-states or supranational level. For this reason, it allocates authoritatively its values to its citizens (i.e. to the citizens of its member-states) through decision-making processes organized around a multiplicity of different public actors and private agents acting within a multiplicity of separated institutions. These separated institutions are connected horizontally, or anyway nonhierarchically, and each of them has some power for affecting the functioning of the others. They share legislative and executive functions in such a way that none of them has the unilateral power to take decisions on behalf of the other institutions. In such a democracy, the formation of majorities has to be systemically hindered. This is why a democracy is compound when it is structured around a multiple separation of powers, both *vertically* and *horizontally*. Compound democracies are mainly structured around cleavages among states or clusters of states (territorial sections) rather than among social classes (as are the competitive democracies) or ethnic–linguistic–religious communities (as are the consensual democracies) (Lijphart 1999; Fabbrini 2005*d*).

If the structurally asymmetrical character of the relations among the state units prevents those relations from being reorganized or synthesized around an institution (the cabinet or government) given or granted ultimate decision-making power, certainly, in the case of the EU, it has not always been so. In the early decades of the undertaking that has produced the EU in its present form, the Council of Ministers functioned as an institution able to monopolize ultimate decision-making power and even to take unilateral decisions (Dinan 2004). Moreover, a group of countries, in particular France and Germany (constituting the so-called Franco-German axis, Hendricks and Morgan 2001), for a long time exerted a hegemonic role within the EU (Hoffmann 1995). But since the 1986 SEA, and the 1992 Treaty of Maastricht the EU (particularly in the first pillar) has progressively structured itself as a system in which several institutions separately but jointly contribute to numerous public policy decisions. Thus, the various waves of enlargement, especially those of 2004 and 2007 which nearly doubled the membership of the EU, have created a context in which it is very difficult for a state, even if large and powerful, or a coalition of states, to exercise a permanent hegemony over the entire structure of the EU decision-making system.

Thus, the originally preeminent institution in the system (the Council of Ministers) has been forced to acknowledge the considerable influence acquired, first, by the Commission. It has then been obliged to recognize the codetermination and codecisional power acquired by the EP since its direct election in 1979, and especially since the SEA and the two fundamental treaties of the 1990s (those of Maastricht 1992 and Amsterdam

1997). However, the growing influence of these Community institutions (representative of supranational interests) has not reduced the influence of the Council of Ministers and therefore of the European Council (representative of the member-states, and therefore of the intergovernmental side of the EU). This institutionalization has gradually strengthened the powers and competences of these various institutions according to a positive-sum game. This has come about because of the system of multiple separation of powers which characterizes the EU. Each institution enjoys an autonomous legitimacy—popularly direct in the case of the EP (since 1979), but also in the cases of the Council of Ministers and the European Council as expressions of electoral majorities in member-states— or derived from a balancing of the latter with the former (the European Commission, whose President and commissioners have been appointed since the 1990s by the European Council on 'advice and consent' by the EP). This institutional system is not just a mixed one, as one could find in predemocratic (or even preliberal) Britain (Majone 2005b). De facto, it is a system of representation and decision-making organized around the democratic principles of separation of powers and checks and balances.

Certainly, if the EU is a democracy, nevertheless it is not a constitutional democracy. The democratic principles of separation of powers and checks and balances are not formalized in a supreme document approved by its citizens. However, the EU is a system which has for some time been constitutionalized, in that it is regulated by a vertically integrated legal system. The principal actor in this constitutionalization process has been the ECJ, which since the 1960s has laid down a set of principles (and in particular the supremacy of Community law over national law, and the direct effect on the member-states' citizens of Community decisions) which have legitimated (and justified) the formation of an integrated legal order (Stone Sweet 2005). It has been thanks to the ECJ that the EU has become a properly constitutionalized system, that is, a system regulated by interstate treaties interpreted as quasi-constitutional documents. The process of constitutionalization has been triggered by increasing levels of transnational activity (exchange and cross-border cooperation) in that their regulation has required increasing intervention by the EU institutions. Transnational activities have given opportunities for action to EU institutions, which have consequently been able to push their own agendas and deepen the integration process (Stone Sweet, Sandholtz, and Fligstein 2001). In particular, the increase in transnational economic activity has exacerbated legal disputes (among economic actors operating in different national legal systems), and this in turn has required the

Community system's judicial organ, the ECJ, to play a more active role. It is interesting that in both the EU and the USA the judicial power has been given the task of creating the normative space for a continental market (Fabbrini 2005*b*).

Thus, the ECJ has used the opportunities afforded it by the treaties to construct a new legal order for a supranational market, doing so by gradually transforming international treaties into documents of quasi-constitutional rank. In other words, it has transformed those treaties into sources of law superior to those of the EU member-states. The EU treaties, which were originally binding only upon the member-states which had negotiated and signed them, have given rise to a legal order which is now also binding on the citizens of those member-states. There has thus arisen a legal order which confers judicially enforceable rights and obligations on all legal persons and parties, public and private, within the territory (of the member-states) of the EU (Weiler 2000). The member-states of the EU had to redefine their sovereignty by sharing it with other states within a broader cooperative aggregate (Weiler 1999). Hence, while it is true that the EU is not based on a formal constitution, it is nevertheless a constitutionalized regime. Of course, and this I would stress in Chapter 9, constitutionalization based on inter-states treaties is different from constitutionalization based on a formal constitution. However, such constitutionalization has made of the EU a proper supranational regime. If it is arguable that democracy in international organizations is highly implausible (Dahl 2005), that argument does not concern the EU which is a supranational and not an international organization (Caporaso 2005).

Thus, after half a century of institutionalization, the EU has acquired the proper features of a supranational democratic polity. A polity can be defined as supranational when it combines inter-states or intergovernmental and supra-states or Community features. In the EU supranational system, intergovernmental negotiation plays an important and sometimes crucial role in the decision-making process. However, the EU institutions possess an independent capacity both to structure that negotiation and to participate in its outcomes. A supranational polity is definable as democratic when its decisions are taken respecting specific criteria and are binding on individuals as well as corporate bodies. As in the case of the supra-states USA, the supranational EU has adopted the features of a compound democracy model. However, while in the USA that model results from a constitutional choice, in the EU it results from a political necessity. But both are original experiments to extend democracy beyond the boundaries of a single *republic*.

7.6. Conclusion

Europe and America witnessed significant structural and political trans-formations in the second half of the twentieth century. In America those transformations were political, in Europe structural. The structural trans-formations in Europe are connected to the process of regional integration. After several hot and cold wars, European nation-states decided to pool their own sovereignty within an organization of supranational coopera-tion finally called the EU. Combining intergovernmental and Community features, the EU has been gradually transformed into a political system functionally and institutionally independent from the member-states which created and supported it. The EU decisions have affected a growing number of policy issues, at both the domestic and continental level. The EU is now a supranational system organized into multiple levels of sepa-ration of powers in order to accommodate the interests of a plurality of states endowed with asymmetrical powers. The EU institutional structure is fragmented and divided vertically and horizontally, and the decision-making power is shared by a multiplicity of institutions and actors. The EU, in its half a century process of institutionalization, has acquired the features of an institutionally pluralistic regime, at odds with the unified and vertically organized institutional regimes of its member-states. Thus, by necessity, the EU has come to be structured like the US compound republic. After centuries of different institutional trajectories, in the post–World War II period, and especially since the 1990s, Europe has moved toward an institutional organization of authority relations characteristic of the American compound republic.

8

Compound democracy in America and Europe: comparing the USA and the EU

8.1. Introduction

Interpretation and analysis of the EU is a growth industry (Keeler 2005). However, most of the literature examines the EU from an EU perspective, that is it assumes that the EU is an exceptional or unique example of a political system. Yet, when the EU is not considered an exceptional case, unsuitable for comparison, it is generally compared to the European nation-states, assumed to be the predominant (if not the natural) type of democratic organization. This approach can explain the heated debate surrounding the EU's democratic deficit. When compared to parliamentary systems, the EU appears to be deficient in democratic terms because its power holders or decision-makers do not enjoy direct popular legitimacy. Its critics seem to assume that the parliamentary model is the only viable solution to the question of the democratization of the EU. Any institutional development is considered positive if it helps the EU to approach the parliamentary model, and negative if it does not.

Notwithstanding the gradual strengthening of the EP in many policy areas and the power acquired by the EP in approving the Commission nominated by the European Council, the institutional development of the EU does not adhere to the fusion of power model. Even though, territorially, the EU has gradually become a multilevel system, sharing many similarities with federal systems, its horizontal structure is separated and not fused. There is no government as such in the EU, as there is in EU member-states. The decision-making process takes place within a panoply of reciprocally separated although functionally connected institutions. In fact, the EU's progress toward vertical federalization combines with a supranational governmental system which is still horizontally separated.

What is analytically distinctive about the EU is the institutional context of multiple separations of power which is foreign to both European parliamentary and federal systems (again, with the single exception of Switzerland). But it is not foreign outside Europe. Indeed, the EU more closely resembles the USA, with its multiple separation of powers system, than its member-states.

The USA and the EU are different species of a common genus of democratic model, the 'compound' one, distinguished by Fabbrini (2005d): the fact that this model embodies both consensual and competitive traits; the (statist) nature of its cleavages; the (separated) structure of its institutions and the (antimajoritarian but not consensual) logic of its functioning. Compound democracies are based on territorial or state cleavages and necessarily function without a government. Such a convergence between the EU and the USA is of great significance, especially considering the institutional differences that have traditionally defined the two sides of the Atlantic, as we have seen in Part I of the book. Here, I proceed to a comparison between the EU and the USA, at the level of both the institutional structure and political process, in order to identify some analytical indications from the US experience useful for conceptualizing the problems that the EU will have to face. Before doing that, however, I will have to free the road from the so-called 'European exceptionalism' argument.

8.2. EU Exceptionalism and Beyond

8.2.1. *Is There a European Exceptionalism?*

The EU is a supranational polity with a necessary degree of institutional ambiguity. This ambiguity has brought some scholars to wonder about its uniqueness[1] and others to assume it is exceptional. Practitioners as well as specialists of the EU ended up considering the EU as a polity without precedent, for the modalities of both its formation and functioning, in the history of the democratic world. Implicitly or explicitly, the idea of an 'EU exceptionalism' is informing scholarly and journalistic accounts of European integration. The traditional theory of American exceptionalism seems to have been exported to Europe, giving rise to a new theory of EU uniqueness (Fabbrini 2005e).

This theory should be disputed. Primarily, in methodological terms. The unique or exceptionalist argument is always theoretically sterile.

In the past, especially in America but also in Europe, the outcome of the exceptionalism approach has been an unfortunate parochialism of political analysis (Shafer 1999; Glaser and Wellenreuther 2002). It was the idea of American exceptionalism that continued to obstruct, in the post–World War II period, systemic comparison between the democratic systems of America and Europe, producing in both of them several generations of scholars knowledgeable only about their own system (Sartori 1990). This reciprocal ignorance nourished a belief in the superiority of American democracy on the one hand and anti-Americanism on the other (Fabbrini 1999*b*). If exceptionalism is interpreted as a combination of specific historical and institutional features, then each and every political system is exceptional. But specificity does not mean uniqueness, since specificity can be recognized as such only through comparison (Sartori 1984). In general, the idiosyncratic approach has produced a great deal of information about specific countries, but no effective understanding of any of them. In the case of the EU, the idiosyncratic approach has produced much valuable information on its policies and institutions, but not an effective understanding of the EU's logic of functioning. It seems implausible to grasp that logic without resorting to a comparative analysis of the EU. Comprehension requires comparison, and comparison is only possible if analytical criteria are available to integrate those specificities into common typological families.

But it is in empirical terms, especially, that the uniqueness argument is anything but convincing. Sure, the EU does indeed have an institutional structure and a functional logic quite different from those of the individual European nation-states (many of which are now EU member-states). But the experience of the European nation-states is not unique in the democratic world, nor can it be considered archetypical. The difference between the EU and its member-states certainly requires systemic comparison, therefore, and some scholars have already begun such inquiry (Schmidt 2006). More particularly, the EU can be fruitfully compared with—especially—federal, noncentralized, or decentralized European nation-states. Such comparison will make it possible to counter the exceptionalist argument by showing, as Sbragia (2005*b*: 173) writes, that 'the EU can draw on a host of national models of democracy with different institutional arrangements'. Indeed, specific institutional aspects of the EU (e.g. the Council of Ministers) represent adaptations to a supranational polity of arrangements already experimented with at the national level (e.g. the German *Bundesrat*). This comparison has its virtues, not only because it contradicts the exceptionalist argument, but also because it makes it possible to understand specific aspects of the EU's logic of functioning, such as the 'joint decision trap', with its conservative bias in the decision-making system (Scharpf 1988, 1999)

However, the EU is more than a federal polity. It can be effectively compared with other federal systems, but the notion of federalism cannot capture the complex nature of the EU, unless we go back to the eighteenth-century notion of 'federative system', which implied more than a territorially decentralized polity (Onuf 1983). If the comparative framework is enlarged to include America as well, it is possible to counter the exceptionalist argument by showing that the EU has evident similarities with the institutional structure and the logic of functioning of the US compound democracy. Within Europe there is only one case, that of Switzerland, which is similar to the EU and the USA in terms of institutional compoundness (indeed the Cantons are proper states) (Blondel 1998; Zweifel 2002). However, as argued in Chapter 1, comparison between a polity of half a billion inhabitants (the EU) and a polity of a few million inhabitants encounters inevitable obstacles, if one wants to understand the tension between the internal and external sides of a compound democracy. Such asymmetry, by contrast, does not impede comparison between the EU and the USA. The latter, in fact, is the only existing democracy whose structural size and political features are comparable with those of the EU.

8.2.2. Beyond Exceptionalism: Which America?

In sum, the exceptionalist argument fails to convince because there is a case which is quite similar to the EU: namely the USA. It is plausible to argue that the USA and the EU are the more similar cases, because both have started from the need to aggregate separated and sovereign states within a supranational or supra-states institutional framework. Both have to accommodate a plurality of national or territorial identities represented by states of asymmetrical sizes. This is why both have come to organize along a principle of multiple separations of powers. Of course, both have a structural size (demographically and territorially) of a continental scope; both have a highly dense and complex economic, technological, and social structure; and both represent long-established democracies. The difference is that the USA, contrary to the EU, has engaged explicitly in the search for a political theory able to keep together separated states or territorial units in a compound democracy. In this sense, although the USA displays significant specific differences vis-à-vis the EU, a comparison with the American democratic model and political theory might be fruitful for an understanding of the EU.

However, no attempt has been made to compare the EU with the USA *in terms of democratic model*. Moreover, when that comparison was attempted, it had a limited scope. The EU was compared either with confederal or with federal America, either with antebellum or postbellum America (Wibbels 2003), but attention was exclusively focused on the territorial organization of power in America in one or other historical period. But, again, the USA is more than a territorial system of decentralized powers. It is a model of democracy which reflects the need to guarantee that, in a union of several sovereign states, decisions are taken without jeopardizing the 'legitimate interests' of the latter. This is why the US democracy functions through multiple separations of powers (vertically, but also horizontally). Its logic is to preclude the formation of majorities at the system level through the formation of different and competitive majorities at the various subsystem levels. Certainly there are differences, in terms of territorial relations, between antebellum and postbellum America. However, in terms of logic, both antebellum and postbellum America are compound democracies, that is systems finalized to prevent the formation of permanent majorities *across the board*. I will discuss just two cases of comparison before moving on to present my own comparison.

Regarding comparison with the confederal USA, Backer (2001) suggests that the EU should learn from the American confederal experience and from Calhoun's theory of state rights. Calhoun's conception starts from the view that, before the Convention of Philadelphia, the country was not a nation but a confederation of nations (Calhoun 1851, now 1995). Calhoun's theory moves toward a more balanced interpretation of the intergovernmental approach, as it is based on the equality of general and constituent governments. According to Backer, the legitimacy of the political system can be obtained from Calhoun's notions of concurrent majorities, of interposition, of weighted suffrage, of multiple checks and balances between and within governments locked together in union. According to this principle, large majorities in the general government and in the collectivity of member-states are required in order to approve any constitutional reform. Such a theory considers the states as the principals whereas supra-state institutions are simply agents of the states' will. Applied to the EU, this theory underlines the necessary intergovernmental nature of the polity, since it stresses the importance of states' rights vis-à-vis the EU's general government, and provides member-states with the rights to limit Community competences. Backer underscores the crucial importance of the states' rights model for the EU and warns against the potential authoritative degeneration of the federal system. Nevertheless, the model advanced by Backer does not fit the EU political system in which strong supra-state features have already been institutionalized. Its principal–agent theory appears more appropriate for the pre-1865 American federal system than for the current EU polity.

Regarding comparison with the federal USA, Habermas (2001) suggests assuming American federalism as a strategic reference system for the EU. He agrees with the project of federalizing the EU in order to create an ever-closer union. Indeed, he values positively an institutional project inspired by the federalism which emerged in the USA after the Civil War and the transformations of the twentieth century. Habermas (2001) is an advocate of the institution of a second chamber of the EP representing the EU member-states. He proposes the institution of a Chamber of Nationalities that would have direct authority over the Commission. Furthermore, the Commission would become responsible to the EP. Finally, he proposes the empowerment of the ECJ, which would gain a similar role to the US Supreme Court. Although Habermas's vision can clearly be defined as supranational, he stresses the need to preserve the national representation system and national implementation styles. Therefore, he advocates an increase in the power of national parliaments and the strengthening of the subsidiarity principle. Boerzel and Risse (2000) also agree with the necessity of federalizing Europe and consider US federalism as one of the main systems to take into consideration for the reform of the EU. They, too, propose the creation of a second chamber of the EP, which has a strong representation of the governments of the member-states. Such a chamber would have the same function of representation as the territorial voices currently held by the Council of Ministers of the EU. Unlike US federalism, though, for the two authors the EU would need a cooperative distribution of competences in order to adjust to the current distribution of powers, which is based on shared sovereignty between the various levels of governance. Furthermore, in order to solve the problem of the lack of a strong party system in the EU, the same authors propose alternative mechanisms of functional legitimacy based on the role of transnational networks of public and private actors.

As stimulating as they are, these approaches not only tend to stress more what the EU *should be* rather than what *it is* but also seem to overlook the very peculiarity of US democracy, which is not exclusively related to the specific relations between the federal center and the federated states. Indeed, the USA is the first democratic country to be organized, *by constitutional choice*, around a multiple separation of powers system finalized to support or promote a specific model of democracy, the *compound democracy model*. Therefore, it is necessary to go beyond not only the idiosyncratic approach, but also the subsystemic comparison which stresses similarities between 'pieces' of the EU and 'pieces' of other states, moving in the direction of a systemic comparison between the EU and the USA as compound democracies. In sum, the EU and the USA are more than confederal or federal systems. They are compound polities characterized by the capacity to govern without having a government. They are inter-states agreement institutionalized within a supra-states framework.

8.3. Comparing the US and the EU Institutional Structure

Keohane (1997) observed that institutions may be considered from either a normative or an instrumental 'optic' (or point of view). Here, I use the latter perspective. By institutional structure, I mean the set of *institutional properties* of a given system, and not just the *juristic features* of the specific institutions constituting it. Institutional properties concern a configuration of incentives and disincentives which exercise their influence on political action. Thus, if it is true that from a legal point of view the specific institutions of the EU and the USA display specific differences, it is also true that from the point of view of the system's logic they have institutional properties which are similar (Fabbrini 2003*b*). The institutional structure which supports the compound democracy model in both the USA and the EU might be conceptualized as constituted by five dimensions (see Table 8.1).[2] First, in both the EU and the USA there is the *institutional separation of the executive* from the legislature. The European Commission and the American President are not selected by the respective legislatures, as happens in EU member-states. In fact, the European commissioners and their President are appointed by the various member-states' government leaders (meeting in the European Council), though they do take into consideration the political or party composition of the EP, and the American President is elected through the Electoral College organized along state lines. Of course, this institutional independence of the executive from the legislature has been differently regulated. The European Commission and its President have to receive the approval of the EP, whereas this procedure is implausible in the American

Table 8.1 Compound vs. noncompound democracies: the institutional structure

Institutional levels	United States European Union	Unitary EU member-states	Federal (or quasi-federal) EU member-state
Executive	institutional separation from the legislature	institutional fusion with the legislature (including semi-presidentialism)	institutional fusion with the legislature
Legislature	dispersed lawmaking process	centralized lawmaking process	semi-centralized lawmaking process
Center/ Periphery	territorial diffusion of power	central control of national territory	territorial diffusion of power
Judiciary	autonomous policymaking role	no autonomous policymaking role	limited autonomous policymaking role
Overall role of the state	regulatory	interventionist/mixed	interventionist/mixed

system of separation of powers. Here, the President's independence is muted somewhat by the complex system of checks and balances. Furthermore, in the EU, the approval procedure should not be confused with parliamentary confidence procedure. The approval procedure is a check on the Commission and a balance of the European Council, and not an act of government formation per se.

Second, both the EU and the USA share a *dispersed lawmaking process*, although they differ in important institutional aspects of their structure of representation. In both cases, there is bicameral representation. The EP, like the House of Representatives, has the function of giving voice to single electors, while the Council of Ministers like the Senate represents the interests of the constituent units of the Union. Of course, the differences are also notable. In the Council of Ministers the executives of the EU member-states are represented, as they are in the German *Bundesrat* where the *Länder* are represented by their own executives, and not state electors as in the American Senate. Moreover, the legislative power of the House of Representatives is incomparably higher than that of the EP. Nevertheless, contrary to the German experience where a division of labor between the two chambers has gradually been defined and where the political tools of internal coordination of that process have always been operative, both in the EU and the USA the lawmaking process is diffused, open to outside influences, and not controlled by centralized political parties. In fact, in the EP, unlike in the German *Bundestag*, political parties are federations of national-level parties with weak ideological or policy-program cohesion, just as the two main parties in the American Congress have traditionally been alliances of state and local organizations and

209

candidates, based on generic ideological connections. In both the USA and EU, the principal policymaking actors are pressure groups, epistemic communities, cross-national lobbies, and, on occasion, social movements. Rules and regulations are elaborated and implemented through networks of private and public actors. The points of access to policymaking are numerous, with the consequence that the EU political parties, like their American counterparts, are unable to act as gatekeepers, as they are able to do in individual EU member-states. However, the American congressional parties, especially the House of Representatives Republican caucus, for long rightly criticized by European observers (Von Beyme 1987) for being the weakest parliamentary parties in established democracies have passed (as we have seen in Chapter 5) through a process of formidable organizational consolidation since the 1990s, and the parties of the EP, although constrained by their internal local and national divisions (such as the divisions between British Conservatives and Continental Christian Democrats in the Popular Party or between Third Way Labour and traditional leftists in the Socialist Party), have also witnessed a process of significant institutionalization (Hix and Scully 2003).

Third, both in the EU and in the USA political power is *territorially diffused between the individual constituent units and the central institutions of the Union*. In both, self-government and shared government combine to produce variable combinations of federal and confederal institutions and principles. The EU has the features of a multilevel polity which parallels the matrix structure of US territorial distribution of powers (Bodnari 2003) and both share a common federal vision (Nicolaidis and Howse 2001). In both the USA and the EU, informal network structures of governance, involving regional and local actors, complement the formal institutions which connect the constituent units with the center. Of course, important institutional differences are present here too. The USA is a formal federal state, or at least it became so after the Civil War of 1861–5, in the sense that (Weiler 2000) (*a*) its constitution has allocated specific powers to federal institutions and (*b*) the exercise of those powers is the supreme law of the land. Thus, federal power, in its own realm, does not need any intermediation to be recognized by the federated states. Of course, the EU is not based on a formal constitution, although it has been a constitutionalized polity through ECJ interpretations of its founding treaties. That means that, in given policy fields, Community institutions have enjoyed legal supremacy vis-à-vis the member-states. Yet there is no corresponding hierarchy of normative authority or rather real power between Community institutions and member-states with regard to this legal supremacy.

As Weiler (2001: 57) pointed out: 'European federalism is constructed with a top-to-bottom hierarchy of norms, but with a bottom-to-top hierarchy of authority and real power', that is (Weiler 2001: 58) 'architecturally, the combination of a "confederal" institutional arrangement and a "federal" legal arrangement seemed for a time to mark Europe's *Sonderweg*—its special way and identity'. However, the federal USA too has preserved confederal elements. The principle of subsidiarity used for regulating the relations between the various territorial levels of government in the EU seems to be the functional equivalent of the principle of enumerated powers used for regulating the relations between the federal center and the federated states in America.

Fourth, in both the EU and the USA the judiciary plays *a policymaking role*. The ECJ (like the American Supreme Court) has acquired institutional autonomy from the other legislative and executive powers, exercising control over the 'constitutional' legitimacy of EU and national laws. Moreover, by imposing the supremacy of Community law vis-à-vis domestic law, the ECJ has created the legal conditions for favoring, within the scope of the treaties, a process of judicial review in EU member-states. Through the referral procedure, domestic courts can refer to the ECJ whenever a piece of domestic legislation appears to conflict with Community laws, bypassing the domestic constitutional court. Of course, it is the domestic judiciaries which subsequently have to adopt and implement ECJ rulings. This referral procedure has thus allowed domestic courts, allied with the ECJ, to erode the principle of domestic parliamentary sovereignty. And with it the judicial structure built around that principle. In sum, the ECJ, with the backing of the national judiciaries, has promoted a process of judicialization of politics previously unknown to Europeans. Although this practice concerns domestic legislation, but not Community legislation, it is plausible to assert that the EU has weakened the Kelsenian model (Kelsen 1928) of centralized constitutional review introduced after World War II in all the European countries, and favored a sort of Madison model of diffused judicial review.

By gradually dismantling many of the national barriers which obstructed the free movement of goods, capital, workers, and services across the EU member-states, the [ECJ has been instrumental in promoting a supranational legal order for a European common market. Thus, not unlike the American experience of market-building, also in the supranational Europe of the second half of the twentieth century it was the Community judiciary which neutralized state barriers, thus creating the need to fill the void with new rules of integration by the

EU institutions. 'In dealing with the discriminatory effects of regulatory barriers to trade, the [ECJ] has played an active role in *negative* integration. [At the same time] the Court has provided the window of opportunity for the Community to foster *positive* integration through the creation of a new regulatory regime' (Egan 2001: 108). In a comparative study of member-states' resistance to Union authority, Goldstein (2001) showed how, in half a century, the member-states of the nonfederal EU surprisingly offered much less resistance to ECJ rulings than the antebellum federated states of the federal USA to Supreme Court ones. In explaining why, Goldstein (2001: 157) remarks: 'there appears to be an optimum level of confederalness in institutional arrangements for avoiding state resistance to union authority', and this level was better approximated by the EU than by antebellum USA. That is (Goldstein 2001: 156), 'Euro-American comparison...attributes causal force to European institutional feature for the difference in degree of member-state resistance between the two unions'. The EU has been governed by judges as the USA continues to be. What is true for the USA, that is that 'scarcely any political question arises in the United States that is not resolved, sooner or later, into a judicial-thinker' (Graber 2004), is equally true for the EU.

Fifth, both the EU and the USA have *the features of a regulatory state*. Not unlike the US experience, the positive integration of EU member-state economies was carried out through regulation (Majone 2005a), and not by direct intervention European style (i.e. public control of economic sectors). Constrained by its institutional fragmentation of powers, lacking its own fiscal capacities (the Community budget cannot exceed 1.3% of the collective GDPs of the member-states), surrounded by a general mistrust for the idea of a European state, the EU has gradually become a regulatory state. After all, regulative policies may be designed and pursued by inadequately staffed public structures of regulators (as the EU's are), leaving to the groups regulated the cost of implementing them. If the Commission has had a very important role in promoting the Community regulatory pattern (regulatory policies, indeed, increase its power vis-à-vis the other Community institutions), nevertheless this pattern has been forcefully supported by multinational corporations interested in operating in a market with homogeneous rules. As a consequence, the EU intervenes in several sectors connected to the functioning of the market, promoting uniformity, predictability, certainty in economic interactions. The EU has gradually identified as public goods deserving a regulatory intervention items such as environmental protection, consumer information, social health, and, of course, market competition. The EU, like the USA, has gone through social regulation, identifying noncommodity values worthy of public protection. The EU, like the USA, has thus refrained from pursuing strategies which demarketize aspects of social and working life, as continues to happen, on the contrary, in the EU member-states.

Of course, also in this regard there are institutional differences between European and American regulation. Because of the EU's institutional features, regulations emerged through the direct involvement of affected interest groups, whereas in the US regulation was imposed on them. Thus, the EU's problem has not been to prevent the capture of the regulators by the regulated (as has happened in the USA), but rather to make a coordinated system of governance out of the multiplicity of regulations elaborated in specific networks of private and public actors. Moreover, also the EU's independent agencies have many of the limitations to be found in US agencies. The EU regulatory regime has the same problems of coordination and lack of accountability detected in the American experience. Agencies' competences frequently overlap and their rules are frequently contradictory. The complexity of Community politics, due also to the open-ended process of integration, implies a weak political control on the regulatory agencies. Inevitably, the regulatory action of the EU has met resistance at the level of its member-states. The conflict between the EU's and the member-states' views on regulation has been partially settled by the ECJ with the *Cassis de Dijon* decision of 1978. On the basis of this decision, the Commission started to promote, at the turn of the 1980s, a new regulatory approach (Ferrera 2005), based on three assumptions: (*a*) Community regulation has to be substituted, whenever possible, by the reciprocal recognition of the legislation and standards of each of the member-states; (*b*) Community harmonization of standards has to concern itself with the basic requisites of health and security; and (*c*) the definition of these requisites has to be decided by Community and national agencies through a process of so-called mutual deferral.

In short, in the EU,

a new strategy of delegating regulatory responsibility to private standards bodies was designed to shift the burden of market integration away from the politicking of Community institutions. The idea underpinning regulatory reform was to shift the issue of market-building from intergovernmental bargaining to include a host of other public and private players to set the rules. This symbiotic relationship enables public sector officials to use private sector resources to achieve their goals of fostering common rules for the common market. (Egan 2001: 108)

EU member-states also started to adopt regulatory strategies in the second half of the 1990s. The wind of neoliberalism, with its call for privatization and liberalization of traditionally public-controlled sectors, has created both opportunities and the need to regulate them. Nevertheless, in most EU member-states, public authorities continue to have a direct responsibility in managing (or in influencing the choice of the managers of) crucial firms and corporations (e.g. in the fields of telecommunications and media). One might say that, at the domestic level, the state has mixed features, that is it is interventionist *and* regulatory.

Thus, Europe, which registered for more than two centuries a differential development of institutional structures of its nation-states vis-à-vis America, at the end of the twentieth century, through the formation of the EU, is converging toward the former's experience. Regardless of the many specific differences, the EU has more similarities with the USA along *all five dimensions* than with the single EU member-states, semi-presidential and federal states included. Of course, the differences between the EU and the USA both culturally and constitutionally continue to be many and significant, the main one being in the fact that the USA is based on a formal constitution, although cyclically reinterpreted through the twenty-six amendments approved between 1789 and 1971 and the decisions of the Supreme Courts (Ackerman 1998), whereas the EU is without one, although a process of constitutionalization has been activated by the ECJ since the 1960s.

8.4. The Political Process in Compound and Noncompound Democracies

Thus, in the EU, as in the USA, *there is no government as such*. The government is the interactive sum of separated institutions which all contribute to the structuring of the decision-making process. These institutions are nested within a larger governance network, composed of formal and informal institutions, within which operate public and private actors, where none of those institutions has the final decision-making authority *in all the dimensions of the policymaking process*, nor the possibility to act unilaterally. A governance pattern of decision-making is characterized by an informal political process, an inconstant constellation of involved actors and horizontal relations among them (Kooiman 2003). The implications for the *political process* of this logic of governance are quite significant if compared with the implications for the political process of the governmental logic proper to noncompound democracies (see Table 8.2).

Table 8.2 Compound vs. noncompound democracies: the political process

Features	Compound democracies	Noncompound democracies
Function of elections	To form governors	To form a government
Political representation	Multiple, differentiated	Party dominated
Interest intermediation	Pluralist	Neo-corporatist
Political cleavages	Sectional, geographic	Social, ideological
Level of political responsibility	Subsystemic	Systemic
Scope of political issues	Specific	General
Nature of political process	Open, segmented	Closed, controlled
Decision-making logic	Deliberative	Nondeliberative

Where the power is fragmented and dispersed, the function of elections is not to form a government, as it is in noncompound democracies, but to select single governors in order to fill specific elected public offices (Coultrap 1999). The members of the various institutions are elected in different ways, on the basis of different time schedules, and by different constituencies. This is why, in compound democracies, parties tend to be weak electoral organizations, identified by their name rather than by their ideologies, when they operate at the supranational or supra-state level. Although in the course of time they might increase their institutional leverage in one or in the other institution, nevertheless their electoral weakness has constrained their political representation capacities. After all, parties are necessarily weak, as organizations, when they operate in political systems whose decision-making power is segmented and located at different institutional levels. In these systems, political representation is inevitably multiple and differentiated, precisely because a decision-making process with multiple accesses opens up opportunities for the participation of several other actors rather than just political parties. They may be state governments or special interest groups, regional executives or single individuals, epistemic communities or national parliaments, that is, actors expressing a plurality of communities of interest that the parties are not able to aggregate. This is a significantly different situation from that of the EU member-states, where the electoral process is generally dominated by political parties which, although cyclically challenged by other political actors (Cain, Dalton, and Scarrow 2003), continue to control the system of political representation (Mair, Muller, and Plasser 2004).

Compound democracies prize interest-group pressure more than electoral mobilization. Interest intermediation does not rely on parties but on group networks and resources. Certainly, functional interest groups also have a role in noncompound democracies, but this role is subordinated to that played by the parties (Ware 1998). This is why these democracies tend to have a structured, corporatist-type organization of interest representation, whereas compound democracies have an unstructured, pluralist approach to the intermediation of interests, which has been traditionally proper to the USA. Within the EU 'policy outcomes become less predictable; majorities become more difficult to mobilize. The power of public coercion is blunted, but so is the capacity of the state to overcome private exploitation. The most accurate *appellation* for this system in interest intermediation is *pluralism*' (Schmitter 2000: 36, italics in the text). In addition to the inevitable differences, 'while pluralism idealizes important elements of the American experience with democracy, the EU manifests some of the very same characteristics that make the US the archetypical pluralist system' (Coultrap 1999: 127). Also in the EU, as happens in the USA, interest groups move, as Cain (2005) argues, from one shop to another, looking for the best offer.

Moreover, in Europe, as an effect of both the structural transformation of economies and cultures, and the institutional displacement of decision-making resources from the national to the continental arena, traditional class and religious cleavages have tended to wane as the driving forces of the structure of the party system (Bartolini 2005). Whereas, on the contrary, sectional or geographical cleavages, concerning both the legitimacy of the EU as a decision-making body and the distribution of the resources it controls, are becoming the source of the birth and development of new partisan actors and of the structuring of new divisions within the party system (Delwit, Kulahci, and Van de Walle 2004). As one well-informed observer has put it: 'Brussels is getting closer to Washington than to Bonn, Paris or London' (see Schmitter 2000: 35). In the EP, as in the US Congress, sectional cleavage is a significant mobilizing source of partisan competition and conflict.

Because compound democracies are based on subsystems of policymaking, it is difficult to have *governmental responsibility* across the board. Not only do single elected officials tend to be accountable to their specific constituencies, but it is implausible that a common 'governmental program' might come to be shared by officials operating in different institutions, representing different interests, and constrained by different electoral deadlines. Of course, that could happen, as has generally happened in the USA since the 1930s, as an answer to dramatic historical challenges. On those occasions, the electorate seemed to share a common view which helped to elect politicians sensitive to the current mood in the various separated institutions. However, electoral realignment, when and if it happened (Mayhew 2002), was not able to guarantee a continuity of partisan coherence in the policymaking process, because the separation of powers sooner or later started to exercise its dividing effects (Polsby 2004). In the USA, the rule has been a confusion of responsibility which has frequently produced institutional combat and stalemate. In compound democracies it is hard to identify who is responsible for what, thus making the accountability of the decision-makers a difficult endeavor. That accountability has continued to have an individual tone, and not a collective one like that found in the European nation-states (Dunn 1990; Lucas 1993), because of the nature of the representational systems (Sartori 1968).

It is the MEP, or the minister in the Council, or the head of state in the European Council who is *individually accountable* to specific constituencies, and although the EP has imposed a collegial responsibility of the Commission, this cannot be confused with *governmental responsibility* as such. As Jones (1994) remarked, in the USA there might be a *government of parties* but rarely a *party government* (as happened between 2003 and 2006). This is why in compound democracies the level of political responsibility is subsystemic, while it is certainly systemic in the noncompound democracies of EU member-states, and the scope of the political issues is specific and not general, as in the noncompound democracies of the EU member-states. Each election has its own scope or significance and the elector rarely has the opportunity to give a general assessment of the system's performance. Certainly in the USA, the presidential elections (in the era of the modern presidency) have come to represent the occasion for a national dialogue on the direction the country should take. However, that seems to have been more an effect of environmental conditions, rather than of the institutional nature of the presidential elections per se. In fact, when facing complex issues at home and abroad, since the 1930s the USA has reinvented the institution of the President in order to deal with these new challenges. However, the presidential election has kept its fragmented nature thanks to the Electoral College which splits that election into as many states as there are in the union. The President continues to be indirectly elected by ad hoc state Great Electors elected in turn by their respective state electors, although the mass media and party competition have tended to transform the indirect election into a popular election. The constraints of the Electoral College nevertheless remain, as shown by the presidential election of 2000 when the winner of the presidential election was eventually determined by a Supreme Court decision. Indeed, much of the US political process continues to be driven by local, regional, and state interests. Of course, localism and sectionalism are also part of the political process in noncompound democracies, but here subsystemic issues by necessity have to find harmonization with the systemic need of the government of the day to win the next elections.

Contrary to noncompound democracies, in compound democracies *political responsibility* is thus diffused, precisely because they are based on separated institutions sharing decision-making power. This diffusion has been made even more arcane by the governance structure within which the governmental institutions are nested. This institutional complexity has an evident *defensive* role. Compound democracies can function properly if they are protected from internal and external pressures or challenges, or rather, if they can maintain a high degree of *elite control* on the decision-making process. Internally, they cannot withstand a high mobilization of voters, because that would jeopardize the fragile equilibrium between highly and lowly populated states. Decision-makers have to take into consideration other criteria than 'one man-one woman/one vote'. In their choices, they have to ponder territorial as well as individual interests, technical considerations as well as political ones, minority interests such as those of the stronger and more powerful groups. In a compound democracy, the decision-making process does not depend on the outcome of the last election, because there are as many 'last elections' as there are institutions involved in that process. In a compound democracy the will of the electors is dispersed, as is popular sovereignty. Electoral strength is not the only (or main) resource to utilize in the decision-making process (Bessette 1994). Contrary to noncompound democracies, electoral strength is one of the criteria for defining power relations among political actors, but not the only or exclusive one. Indeed, if the electoral process generates different (and competitive) majorities in different (and separated) institutions, how is it possible to recur to the popular will for establishing a hierarchy of roles in the decision-making process? This is why compound democracies need to deliberate on the basis of several, and not only electoral, considerations. Their functioning is based on arguments and not only votes, on persuasion and negotiation, and not only force. Indeed, the use of force might challenge the very stability of the asymmetrical relations between the constituent states.[3] On the contrary, noncompound democracies base their decision-making process on power relations between political actors defined in the electoral arena, although this feature has been differently regulated, either by means of an electoral majoritarian dynamic in competitive democracies or by means of PR in consensual ones.

Externally, compound democracies are not at ease with the challenges ensuing from playing a global role, because that role implies a centralization of the decision-making process which is at odds with its systemic logic. Indeed, the integration of post–World War II Western Europe was made possible by a sort of European isolationism from global responsibilities, its security being guaranteed by US military forces within NATO. As we know, the same institutionalization and development of the US compound republic in the course of the nineteenth century was made possible by its isolationism from European affairs, isolationism protected by the British navy. Separated by the curtain of the Cold War, Western European countries were able to gradually build their systems of sharing-rules and self-rules: the formidable external threat represented by the USSR was an indisputable pressure for promoting supranational integration. Started as an answer to previous wars, the EU came to be justified by the need to avoid subsequent ones. The very existence of the USSR was instrumental for neutralizing resistances to the supranational project, both within the European nation-states but also from the US political elites and public opinion. A united Western Europe was considered an indispensable condition for 'keeping the Russians out', not only 'the Germans down and the Americans in' (Ikenberry 2000: ch. 6). Supranational integration helped to root a liberal democratic culture even in countries (such as West Germany and Italy) who got rid of it between the two world wars. In its turn, the sharing of a common democratic culture contributed to the institutionalization of the Community system, because it favored the formation of a mood of mutual trust among EU member-states' elites. However, with the end of the Cold War and the recomposition of the European continent, the EU can no longer justify its security-consumer status. Moreover, its huge geographical size, demographic dimension, and economic power will increase the pressure for a growth in its international involvement. That will create inevitable tensions, as it did in the USA. Indeed, the changes brought by 9/11 on the international system have had an unprecedented impact also on the EU (Jabko and Parsons 2005).

In short, compound democracies are fragile political enterprises. They have to be antihierarchical orders to satisfy their anti-hegemonic need. However, an anti-hegemonic order is weak on decision-making and accountability capacity because of the antihierarchical structure which supports it. In an antihierarchical structure, decision-making power is diffused among different institutions and each of them enjoys some power of veto to obstruct undesired decision-making outcomes and to preclude unilateral decisions. It is this distribution of vetoes which contributes to the low effectiveness (if not ineffectiveness in given conditions) of the decision-making process in a compound democracy. In compound democracies, it is always better not to decide than to decide unwisely. However, even compound democracies have to take decisions if they want to promote or protect their own interests and values (especially when they organize continental size economies). Here lies the paradox compound democracies have to face: their low decision-making capacity represents a challenge to their stability but that stability might be jeopardized also by a high decision-making capacity. Compound democracies have to transform that paradox into a puzzle to be resolved, if they want to keep their compound nature and at the same time affect the internal and external contexts which condition them.

8.5. Compoundness and Foreign Policy in the USA and the EU

The difficulty of identifying clear responsibility and accountability lines in compound democracies emerges particularly in foreign policymaking. Compound democracies being unions of states are inevitably sensitive to the exercise of their power in the international arena. Certainly, foreign policy tends to strengthen the supra-states or supranational features of those democracies. In the USA, in fact, in the era of the modern presidency, the President has been allowed to play a preeminent role in foreign policymaking. After all, as Hamilton (now in Beard 1964: 297) argued in *Federalist no. 70*, 'decision, activity, secrecy, and dispatch will generally characterize the proceedings of one man in a much more eminent degree than the proceedings of any greater number; and, in proportion as the number is increased, these qualities will be diminished'. Being the constitutional Commander-in-Chief, the President has tried to maximize his executive position. It is sufficient to recall that, because the constitution assigns the Congress the power to declare war, the President has waged many wars without declaring them.[4] However, presidential preeminence in foreign policy has continued to be constitutionally wrapped within a complex system of checks and balances (Shapiro, Kumar, and Jacobs 2000). The Congress has retained its formal powers, even if it did not decide to use them (Fisher 2005). The Senate has continued to play a quite vigilant role in the international engagement of the country, ratifying only half of the treaties brought before it (Wayne 2000). At the same time, the various presidents have tried to escape from these constraints, for example by signing executive agreements with foreign nations rather than international treaties, because the latter are subject to Senate ratification by a two-thirds majority, while the former are not.

Moreover, as we know, the post-Vietnam era has dramatically multiplied the number of private actors involved in foreign policymaking. Interest groups have engaged in a continuous pressure on members of Congress in support of the more diverse causes (defense and promotion of specific economic sectors, but also of specific cultural or moral views), an investigatory media has affected the definition of the public agenda, think tanks and policy entrepreneurs have advanced their ideological or technical proposals. Even during the Cold War, US foreign policy registered incongruousness and incoherence behind the strategic framework of containment of Soviet communism. The difficulty of detecting the US national interest in the international arena simply hardened after the end of the Cold War. In the divided government of the 1990s, the House has used its budgetary powers to impose the interests or values of important constituencies on the foreign policy agenda. The Senate has used its constitutional prerogatives to strike down presidential proposals, frequently on the basis of the interests of powerful electoral groups in one or the other state. Divided government, combined with the disappearance of the Soviet Union, made it possible that various foreign policy sectors came to be controlled or conditioned by specific private groups. US foreign policy was *privatized*. 'To take an extreme case, American policy towards Cuba has been "captured" by the émigrés in Florida in a way that is very familiar to students of American regulatory policies' (Jervis 1999: 217). Private groups and ideological lobbyists were able to impose their priorities on the congressional committees, thanks to the resources at their disposal and the votes they could mobilize. Even foreign governments may influence US foreign policy, either directly through an official relation with the President or members of Congress or indirectly through the electoral mobilization of conationals' immigrant associations which can make the difference in many congressional districts (Ikenberry 2000: ch. 6). In sum,

foreign governments may also try to manipulate the U.S. domestic political system directly, by *penetrating* the American body politic and giving individual politicians strong incentives to favor closer ties.... (T)he Israel lobby...is far and away the most successful example of a country using the U.S. political system to gain influence over U.S. foreign policy. [But the success] of Indian and Armenian lobbies...show that the Israeli example is far from unique. (Walt 2005: 25, italics in the original)

In many cases, these foreign interests have special relations with specific geographical areas of the USA. In fact, geography has continued to play a crucial role in rendering foreign policymaking complex, because the main states or regional areas of the country have different interests in different parts of the world due to their location and the type of immigrant communities developed within them (Trubowitz 1999).

Thus, US foreign policy from the end of World War II has been punctuated by peaks of congressional–presidential conflicts followed by longer phases of reciprocal appeasement, as the 1950s and the first half of the 1960s (Ikenberry 1999: Part Four and Five), and of course between 2001 and 2006. The War Powers Resolution of 1973 formalized the end of the 'imperial presidency', but it could not reverse the presidential ascendancy in foreign policy. The institutionalization of a divided government between 1968 and 2000 reduced the incentives for appeasement and cooperation between the two branches. Finally, the global role of the country has increased the complexity of presidential foreign policies, with inevitable consequences of rivalry and conflict within the same executive branch, in particular between the State and Defense Departments. With the growing militarization of US foreign policy, the Defense Department has come to play such an influential role as to challenge the constitutionally recognized authority of the State Department in foreign policy (as happened in a clamorous way with the decision to invade Iraq in 2003, a decision imposed by the Secretary of Defense against the doubts of the Secretary of State, see Woodward 2004). Thus, a new competition for the privilege to control foreign policy has emerged in the post–World War II era within the same presidency, pitting the NSC against the departmental presidency and, within the latter, the State against the Defense Department. Each contrast has brought with it a tension within the intelligence community, with the different agencies regularly located on different sides of the contingent division (Staar 2003).

Certainly, especially after 9/11, the President has tried again to impose its will and agenda in the foreign policymaking process. For doing that he needed to praise the virtue of national sovereignty over the various multilateral institutions of the world system. Thus, the USA, which traditionally regarded the concept of national sovereignty with suspicion and used its institutional structure to impede the rise of any such potential Leviathan, seemed to embrace the concept as a beacon for its own international politics. US post–World War II multilateralism (which was congenial to its idea of an internal multilateral system of separation of powers) has seemingly given way to a renewed appreciation for the preeminence of the nation-state, and in particular of the US one. 'US First' is the latest incarnation of the Westphalian state, while the EU, pooling the national sovereignties of its member-states in a supra-states framework, is moving in a post-Westphalian direction. As Keohane (2002: 744) remarked, the tension between the EU and the USA in the 2000s has also to do with this opposite movement: 'as the EU has moved away from classical conception of external sovereignty, the United States has continued to embrace it, contributing to divergence in their policies, and to increasing discord in their relationship'.

However, notwithstanding this attempt at 'Westphalization' of the USA (Spiro 2000), its institutional structure continues to display compound features. As it emerged after the mid-term elections of November 2006, even in foreign policy the USA continues to be characterized by fragmented structures of political authority, which make it difficult to detect a univocal and permanent position. In spite of the presidential claim to predominance in foreign policy, even the most executive-oriented President George W. Bush had to learn that it is impossible to run foreign policy against the will of the Congress. In the USA, it continues to be difficult to define something akin to a *national interest*, which is presumed to be the engine of international relations. As Nye (2002: 112) remarked:

American foreign policy-making is a messy process for reasons deeply rooted in our political culture and institutions. The Constitution is based on the eighteenth-century liberal view that power is best controlled by fragmentation and countervailing checks and balances. In foreign policy, the Constitution has always invited the president and Congress to struggle for control. That struggle is complicated when the Congress and presidency are controlled by different political parties.

Although more rationalized than the EU foreign policymaking, the USA one still exhibits a quite significant degree of compoundness (see Figure 8.1).

If it is true that compound democracies have difficulty in answering the question: 'who decides what?', this is more true for the EU than the USA, because the former is much less institutionalized than the latter and encounters more limited pressures from the international environment to rationalize its internal decision-making process. In the EU case, the Common Foreign and Security Policy (CFSP) represents the most intergovernmental pillar of the Community structure that emerged from the Maastricht Treaty of 1992 (Hill 1996). As we have seen, this pillar is intergovernmental because its decisions are formally monopolized by the Council of Ministers. A High Representative for the CFSP (see Chapter 7),

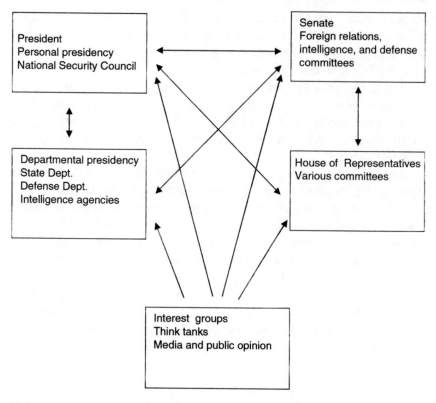

Figure 8.1 US foreign policymaking structure

who is also Secretary-General of the Council, presides over foreign policy-making, supported by a Secretariat of the Council and a Policy Planning and Early Warning Unit. However, the Commission also has its own for-eign policy structure, headed by a Commissioner for External Relations, and supported by a Common External Service organized along specific units in charge of important foreign policy issues. Thus, the Commission, also because of its exclusive competence in foreign trade policy, plays a very important (although undervalued) role in the EU foreign policymak-ing process. A strong cooperation exists between the Secretariat of the Council and the Common External Service of the Commission (Howorth and Keeler 2000) (see Figure 8.2).

Moreover, the Commission, and only the Commission, represents the EU in international economic fora such as the WTO (Griller and Weidel 2005). Because foreign economic policy is of great importance to the EU, it is inevitable that the Commission tends to transfer its influence,

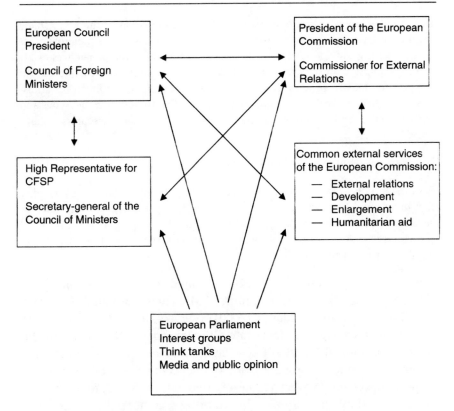

Figure 8.2 EU foreign policymaking structure

information, and relations from the economic to the political foreign policy. This is why the relation between the High Representative for the CFSP and the Commissioner for External Relations has oscillated between cooperation and competition. Formally, the EP should have no role in the foreign policymaking process. However, its institutionalization has brought about an increase of its weight in the European foreign policy debate, especially in relation to issues with domestic constituencies such as human rights and environmental protection. In fact, the EP was instrumental in pressuring the Council of Ministers and the Commission to support the creation of the International Criminal Court or ICC or to sign the Kyoto Protocol. As Stetter (2004: 724) remarked, in the EU

actors and institutions operate within a functionally structured space which consists, firstly, of the general 'policy space' provided for by the political system of the EU and, secondly, of the specific functional features of EU foreign policies. It is this functional context of EU foreign policies that allows not only the Council and member states, but also actors such as the Commission or the EP to shape seemingly 'intergovernmental' bargains across the pillars. Thus, the cross-pillar politics setting provides a stable framework within which the preferences of EU actors—alongside those of national governments—are constantly channeled into the decision-making process. This does not imply that, for example, the Commission or Parliament is able to dominate policy-making. Indeed, member states and the Council continue to hold the most powerful institutional resources in both areas

But it means that (Stetter 2004: 725)

EU foreign policy covers the whole spectrum of policies in both areas including first pillar provisions, whereas CFSP is not a distinct policy area but the label for several specific decision-making rules for parts of EU foreign policies... The legal principles developed for the first pillar can, under certain conditions, be equally applied to the second pillar.

Thus, EU foreign policy cannot be delimited to only the second pillar (intergovernmental) structure (Smith 2001). There is a significant 'cross-pillarization'. As Von Bogdandy (2000) observed, the EU is a single polity, because its pillars do not demarcate different organizations but only different capacities with partially specific legal instruments and procedures. For instance, in discussing the action of the EU in conflict prevention and crisis management, Novack (2006: 11) argued that the EU, for pursuing a coherent and integrated policy, has to bring together policy areas which 'fall under the separate pillars'. This appears to be so also with regard to the third intergovernmental pillar on Justice and Home Affairs (JHA), which has promoted a growing role for the Community institutions (and the Commission in particular) in the coordination and harmonization of member-states' policies, especially after the Madrid and London terrorist attacks of 2004 and 2005. The divisions among the EU member-states on the military intervention in Iraq in 2003 have regrouped, but not rena-tionalized, Community foreign policy (Hill 2004). Thus, the EP and the Commission, but also media organizations, research institutes, and interest groups have come to play a role in EU foreign policymaking (Caporaso 2000: ch. 4). Certainly, it has been difficult to Europeanize also defense policy, because this policy seems to represent the last bastion of the national sovereignty of the EU's (larger) member-states (but also because it is monopolized by an international organization such as NATO).

Moreover, the EU member-states have different military capabilities, different historical legacies in the various parts of the world, different national political cultures (some member-states traditionally being neutral countries, whereas others were heavily involved in colonial domination), and different perceptions of the international threats in relation to their geographical collocation. However, even this policy has been subjected to the same Community influence registered by the policies of the first pillar. Within the constraints of its compoundness, the EU has started to grow its teeth (Howorth and Keeler 2005: 40–1). In sum, if in the EU it was historically the Council of Foreign Ministers and the European Council (since its inception at the end of the 1970s) which claimed preeminence in foreign policy, of course within the constraints of the member-states' preferences, however, with the institutionalization of the EU, foreign policy responsibilities came to be shared also by the Commission, with the High Representative playing the role of the functional link between the Commission and the two Councils. Moreover, all of them had to take into consideration the EP's requests, because they reflected streams of influential public opinion in the various member-states. Finally, with the various enlargements, the Council of Foreign Ministers has become a multilateral institution per se, where none of the member-states (even the larger or the founding members) is able to impose its unilateral will on the others. Preferences have to be accommodated, mediated, and negotiated, as happens in properly multilateral institutions.

Certainly, the USA and the EU play a different role in the international arena. The USA is a hyper-power, with a global *military* reach, while the EU is a regional power, with a global *economic* reach. In the USA, the preeminence of the President in foreign policy has been recognized, at least since the 1930s, both by Congress and the Supreme Court (with the *United States* v. *Curtiss-Wright Corporation* of 1936), whereas the EU lacks any such institution. However, both polities have a haphazard decision-making structure in foreign policy which generates contradictory outcomes. Because of their compoundness, both the USA and the EU have difficulties identifying an unequivocal and permanent general interest. This is also true for the USA, notwithstanding the international role it has played since the end of World War II. This has made the missionary zeal with which the USA has cyclically presented and pursued its foreign policy aims particularly strident. 'The political culture of American exceptionalism complicates matters by making our foreign policy uniquely moralistic' (Nye 2002: 112). Although, in the USA, either a formidable military challenge (as Soviet communism) or dramatic unconventional threats (as Islamic terrorism) have pressured the separated institutional actors to coalesce around the President in his constitutional quality of

Commander-in-Chief, this support of the President has not canceled the many divergences emerging within the separated institutions. Of course, nothing of this sort has happened in the case of the EU, first because it does not play an international role comparable to the USA, and second because its internal institutional relations are much more fluid.

8.6. Political Stability and Political Institutions: What Lessons from America?

Because compound democracies have weak decision-making systems, they are always in danger of failure or imploding. Nevertheless, the US compound democracy has been a successful experiment in terms of political stability. Why has this happened? To answer this question might be useful not only for understanding US political development, but also for deriving important analytical clues on the difficulties of the EU political development. A political system is stable when its citizens display a general sense of belonging to the 'political community', when there is continuity in its structure of government ('regime'), and when there is an orderly changeover in its governing elites ('authority') (Easton 1990; Shapiro and Hardin 1996). If one considers that the contemporary theory of political development (Orren and Skowroneck 2004) has demonstrated the link between stability and institutions (these latter being the principal factor in political stability if they are strong, March and Olsen 1995), and given that the founders of the new American republic on the contrary entrusted political stability to a weak system of government, the inevitable question is how has it been possible in the USA for weak institutions to foster stability in the political system (Mezey 1989), when in developing countries weak institutions have produced precisely the opposite outcome (Chantornvong 1988; Fukuyama 2004).

Generally speaking, the point is that the theory of political development which ties political instability to the inability of governments to meet the demands of citizens presupposes the existence of a politically active citizenry. But a citizenry of this kind did not exist in the USA when its government institutions were in their infancy. At the end of the eighteenth century, only a minority of the population was politically active, precisely because only a small proportion of the electorate (whites, males, and property owners) had the right to vote (Morone 1990). Moreover, not only did government institutions precede the formation of the political institutions of popular mobilization (mass parties and interest groups), but they recognized the preeminence of the legislature when that mobilization finally developed during the nineteenth century. Furthermore, the theory of political development presupposes not only an extensive and politically active citizenry, but also a citizenry which regards the state (the government) as responsible for the nation's welfare. In the USA of the eighteenth and the early years of the nineteenth centuries, this notion had yet to come into being and expectations therefore still did not have an economic basis. The availability of land and resources in the West also acted as a safety valve for potential social tensions. Conditions were radically different in post–World War II Europe. Not only did European citizenries regard the state as responsible for their welfare (Kaase and Newton 1995; Klingemann and Fuchs 1995), but they lacked similar safety valves with which to dispel conflict over resources and their distribution.

Therefore, when in the USA suffrage was extended and the frontier of the West was barred, the governmental institutions were already sufficiently consolidated (despite the tremendous shock of the Civil War) to the point that they were perceived as relatively efficient and therefore generally legitimated. In the USA political conflicts created difficulties for the system of government, but these conflicts were absorbed by an institutionalization of the government structure which had already taken place. Certainly, conflicts tended to erupt between executive and legislature, with the effect of engendering policy incoherence. However, such conflicts and incoherence did not breed political instability, neither in the consolidation phase of the republic, because of the features assumed by the institutionalization process (the preeminence of the legislature), nor in the subsequent phase of the development of a presidential government, thanks to the features assumed by the political process.

Presidential government came to organize itself at a national level around a loosely structured party system and around nonparty agencies of mobilization (movements, interest groups, functional associations, lobbies) which permitted the democratic participation of citizens without this entailing the regimentation of their party loyalties. Of course, this flexibility of the party system was enhanced by particularly favorable economic and cultural conditions. The continent-wide scale of the social and economic system ensured the constant and relatively widespread mobility of positions of status and income; a mobility which reduced the likelihood that social and political conflicts would crystallize (Lipset 1963). Moreover, associated with this mobility was a dominant political culture which encouraged the individualistic perception of social advantages and disadvantages. This explains why, although class conflict has not been lacking in the USA, it has not generated a party system like those in European nation-states. Moreover, a markedly federal system contributed to the diffusion of demands that elsewhere were directed at the two central components of government (Lipset 1996).

One might ask why the flexibility of the party system is important for a separated system. It is because the principal constitutional weakness of the latter is that it does not have a democratic principle with which to resolve potential conflicts between executive and legislature (Linz 1990). Neither of the two components of government can pass a motion of no-confidence on the other, and then entrust the electorate with the task of resolving the political conflict between them. Nor is the impeachment of the President an easy option because it is an instrument which cannot be legitimately used on the grounds of political divergences, but is only available in cases of the President's constitutional disloyalty. Certainly, the three cases of congressional recourse to impeachment of the President (and especially the third)[5] show how uncertain the boundary between 'political divergence' and 'constitutional disloyalty' might be. However, at least till the 1990s, America was able to avoid the dangers of the constitutional delegitimation of the executive by relying on its flexible party system (Dodd and Jillson 1994). The fluidity of the party alignments in Congress has enabled the President (in the period of presidential government) to overcome situations of stalemate by forming cross-party coalitions, according to a dynamic which, in the case of crucial legislation, tended to set progressives against conservatives rather than Democrats against Republicans.

Thus, in a separated governmental system, in the event of an open conflict between executive and legislature, a strongly structured and polarized two-party system may create more problems than it is able to solve, as happened in the periods of divided government especially that in the 1990s. Under these conditions, the strengthening of the congressional parties exacerbated, rather than reduced, the conflict between the two branches of government. But also when there is no conflict between executive and legislature, a strongly structured and polarized two-party system may create more problems than it is able to resolve, if the partisanship of Congress prevents it from placing a check on presidential action, as happened between 2001 and 2006. This is one of the systemic paradoxes of US separation of powers. A paradox which substantiates itself in the fact that, with strong parties, it may neutralize the paralyzing postulates of separation of powers while simultaneously amplifying their effects (Schram and Wilson 1993). In Europe, on the contrary, the context is quite different. If the party alignments are still fluid at the EU level, in the EU member-states they are instead the expression of deeply rooted socioeconomic cleavages. If the intense partisan politics of the EU member-states moves on to the Community institutions, then the latter would certainly have to face a serious challenge to their stability.

The American experience shows that central governmental institutions generally experienced difficulty in managing distributive (or redistributive) policies, with their highly conflictual implications, in particular when they were not yet sufficiently institutionalized and legitimized. Indeed, during the congressional government era these policies were pursued by the states and the social conflict implied by them remained at the state level. Even during the nationalization period of the presidential government era, the federal state has refrained from promoting universal distributive policies, focusing rather on supporting specific social groups. These policies soon backfired, reopening a process of policy transfer to the states. Thus, political stability in America was guaranteed by the channeling of social conflict into the states' political system in the nineteenth century and by the paucity of the federal state's distributive intervention in the twentieth century. These conditions help explain why stability was achieved in America despite its relatively weak institutions. Moreover, when that conflict emerged during the nationalization period, it was absorbed by a fully constitutionalized political system. This implies yet another paradox for the EU. If the EU wants to increase its legitimacy, it needs to politicize its decision-making and political processes, transposing the social and political conflict from the member-states to the Community institutions. However, this very displacement could jeopardize the stability of those institutions because, first, they are not structured to deal with the political implications of distributive conflicts and, second, because they are not legitimized by a formal constitutional pact among its constituent parts. Will the EU manage to approve a functional equivalent of a formal constitution? This is the topic of Chapter 9.

8.7. Conclusion

The EU is not an exceptional polity. It is a supranational system which functions according to the logic of a compound democracy. Although the institutional structure and the political process of the EU are quite different from those of its member-states, they are not so different from the institutional structure and political process of the USA. Both the

EU and the USA have institutional and functional properties proper to polities which need to take decisions but nevertheless lack a centralized decision-making process. This absence affects also their foreign policy-making process, which is a crucial policy area in polities as large and powerful as the USA and the EU are. Both have a pluralistic decision-making structure which inevitably generates incongruent and contradictory outcomes. Indeed, the strength of compound polities, as the US experience of political development shows, is in the weakness of their institutions, although that weakness increases their problems, when those polities have to face internal and external challenges. Especially when this decision-making process has to answer to the demands raised by a turbulent international system and a politically mobilized domestic society (see Chapter 10). Indeed, in Europe, that fragility appears to be much more challenging than in the USA, also because the EU institutional compound polity does not enjoy the legitimacy coming from an accepted constitution. The USA and the EU challenge the basic distinction between competitive versus consensual democracies. Their experiences seem to ask for a revision of our comparative framework, based on a dualistic typology which contrasts democracies (mainly) functioning around the principle of majority (majoritarian or competitive democracy) and democracies (mainly) functioning around the principle of unanimity (consensual or consociational democracy). The EU and the USA do not fit in either of them. The EU and the USA represent two different species of the genus of the compound democracy. Their differences, although they are significant, keep them apart from the other established democratic regimes.

9

The constitutionalization of the US and the EU compound democracies

9.1. Introduction

At the Laeken European Council of December 2001, government and state leaders of the EU member-states decided to promote a 'Convention on the Future of Europe' to draft a project of a Constitutional Treaty or CT for the EU (Norman 2003). The convention met in Brussels from February 2002 to June 2003. A draft constitutional treaty was delivered to the presidents and prime ministers gathered in Salonicco, Greece, for the meeting of the European Council on June 20, 2003. It was then discussed, amended, but not approved by the European Council meeting on October 15, 2003 in Rome. Finally, it was approved in a revised version by a European Council meeting in Ireland in June 2004 and subsequently formally signed by the heads of states and governments in an IGC organized in Rome in October 2004. Here, I will refer to this final version of the CT for my analysis. As of January 1, 2007, the CT was approved by eighteen member-states, generally through a parliamentary vote, and in Spain and Luxembourg through a popular referendum. The CT was then rejected by French and Dutch voters in a national referendum held in May and June 2005 respectively, and it is still waiting to be submitted for approval in the other seven countries.

In this chapter, I deal with the question of the constitutionalization of the EU. I will do so after having defined the nature of the constitution-making process activated in Europe by the Laeken decision. The nature of the EU constitution-making process will be defined in the context of a systematic comparison with the constitution-making process of the USA. In fact, also in this regard, the two experiences have much more in common than is generally accepted. To date, very few attempts (Bellamy 1996;

Fabbrini 2004c; Sbragia 2005b, 2007; see also the still useful Friedrich 1967) have directly compared the constitutional experience of the EU with that of the USA. Certainly, while the EU does not have a constitution, the American political experience started precisely from a formal constitution. Or rather from two constitutions (Wood 1969; Banning 1986), as the Articles of the Confederation were approved definitively in 1781 and then the federal Constitution elaborated in Philadelphia in 1787, which replaced the previous constitution definitively in 1789 (when it was approved by the majority, 9 of 13, of the states). However, as we have seen, although the EU does not have a formal constitution, it has been characterized, since its very inception, by a process of constitutionalization (Weiler 1999). Of course the comparison is justified by the fact that the institutional outcome of the process of constitutionalization of the EU has striking similarities with the institutional structure of the USA.

Here, by *constitutionalization* (Pennock and Chapman 1979), I refer to a set of procedures and principles utilized, in a given society and at a given historical period, (*a*) to define the nature of the supreme law of the land (*which constitution?*); (*b*) to promote the strategy of limitation of public powers *(for which polity?)*; and (*c*) to select the actors of the constitutional plan (*which constitution-making process?*). It is my aim to show, first, similarities and dissimilarities between the constitutionalism of the EU and that of the USA, along the three levels of analysis (Fabbrini 2004c). Second, I discuss more in detail the features of the CT signed in Rome in October 2004, stressing its coherence with the compound nature of the EU. Finally, I deal with the contested process of its ratification.

9.2. US Constitutionalism from a Comparative Perspective

9.2.1. *The Constitution as a Frame of Government*

Despite the American standard of the written document, democratic constitutions can be written or unwritten. Even where there is a written constitution, as in the USA, constitutional conventions have been introduced in order to regulate systemic challenges unknown at the time of drafting. There are other democratic countries that do not follow the American example and rely exclusively on constitutional conventions (such as Britain). Through the preamble to its written constitution, the USA also introduced a novel conception of republican government: the constitution as the expression of a covenant among people organized in distinct territorial communities. As Elazar (1988: 91) stressed:

a covenant differs from a compact in that its morally binding dimension takes precedence over its legal dimension.... Normally, a covenant precedes a constitution and creates the people or civil society that then proceeds to adopt a constitution of government for itself. Thus a constitution involves implementing a prior covenant—effectuating or translating a prior covenant into an actual frame of government.

It is the people's will which creates, through the constitution, the specific system of government to which the same people thus delegate the responsibility to solve their individual and collective problems. The distinction between citizens and governors is clear: the latter have to operate within the institutional constraints defined by the former, through their constitution. This is why the American constitution is *dualistic*, because it precludes any possibility of collapsing the constitutional will of the people into the last political majority of the governors, as happens in European nation-states with a *monistic constitution* (see Chapter 3). In European nation-states, the contingent qualified majority of the parliament may change or amend the constitution, whereas in the USA the amendment process requires the involvement of states' legislatures or conventions, and not only of the congressional chambers.

Using the American experience of 1787, here I refer to the constitution as a *written document*, distinct from other legal texts, by these three criteria (Elster 1997): (a) it is regarded as the supreme text of the legal order; (b) it regulates matters that are more fundamental than others; and (c) it may be changed only through very stringent amendment procedures. Not all democratic constitutions respect these three criteria: New Zealand has a constitution according to (a) and (b), but not (c); Israel according to (b) and (c), but not (a); the amendment procedure requires an absolute majority in France, but a qualified majority of two-thirds of the members of the legislature in Hungary; some constitutions regulate electoral laws in a very detailed way; others in a very general sense (Poland, Czech Republic); others not at all (France, Italy, Hungary). Which is to say that 'all constitutions regulate fundamental matters, although not only such matters nor all such matters' (Elster 1997: 125).Therefore in the USA, through the constitution, a hierarchy of norms was set up (to which, however, an across-the-board hierarchy of institutions and organized powers did not correspond). In the American case, the definition of a hierarchy of norms was not a simple endeavor. In fact, the difficulty in identifying that correlation had much to answer for the failure of the first American constitution, the so-called Articles of Confederation of 1781 and in the crisis of the second in the period 1861–5. In Philadelphia, the delegates arrived with 'a broad agreement on the desirability—indeed, the political necessity . . .—of offering a government in the republican form' (Jillson 1988: 23). As Madison reported in his *Records* of the convention (Jillson 1988: 23), 'in general the members seem to accord in viewing our situation as peculiarly critical'. However large the consensus on the idea of a supreme text was, it was more limited with regard to regulating fundamental matters.

The fundamental matters concerned the power relations between the center and the associated territorial units (the states). The Union had to be a pact among states, but the terms of the pact were inevitably open to intense negotiation. Eventually, those relations had a *federal solution*, but probably none at that time understood what it meant. Indeed, as we know, many confederal features were included in the federal solution. In any case, the various cleavages which divided the Philadelphia Con- stitutional Convention (even the one on slavery) were subdued by the sectional divisions. In sum, even the slavery question was subdued within the more general question of how to distribute competences between the center and the states. The new American republic was the outcome of a *process of aggregation* of previously sovereign territorial units of govern- ment, which tried to retain as much power as possible once they decided to pool together their sovereignty. The Philadelphia framers assumed as a crucial question the solution to the distribution of powers, primarily vertically (among the federal center and the federated states) and then horizontally (among the federal governmental institutions). Once the constraints on the governmental capacity for arbitrary behavior were introduced, there was no need to specify other matters which deserved special protection, such as individual rights. Free from any centralized governmental control, the citizens could pursue their own interests or their own happiness as they deemed appropriate. This is why the Philadel- phia constitution defines the basic structures, institutions, and procedures of the polity, *but not the rights to be protected*. In Philadelphia, rights were considered implicit, or rather they were considered (by Madison in particular, see Matthews 1995: ch. 6) constitutive of civil society, and not of the political realm per se.

It was the persuasive action exercised by Thomas Jefferson on the framers (and Madison in particular), and above all the need to appease the opposition of the anti-federalists to the new federal constitution, which put pressure on laying down a battery of individual rights to add to the constitution as the first ten amendments (*Bill of Rights*). Written by Madison, approved by the two chambers of Congress in 1789, the ten amendments were finally approved by the states in 1791. Since then, there have been only twenty-six amendments (Bernstein 1995: especially Part II), as the procedure to amend the constitution is quite rigorous. Some of the amendments significantly altered both the institutional structure of the republic and the interpretation of the fundamental rights, both implicit and explicit, to be protected (Levinson 1995). Yet other important constitutional changes (especially since the New Deal of the 1930s) were brought about through alternative channels, such as judicial sentences of the Supreme Court, once the amendment procedure became inaccessible because of the resistance that powerful and privileged social and territorial minorities could raise in Congress or in the state legislatures. Supreme Court decisions soon became an integral part of American constitutionalism (Ackerman 1998: Part Three).

Thus the American constitution is first a *frame of government* and then a protector of rights (Elazar 1985). A frame of government and not a state constitution, because in Philadelphia (and even much later) there was no sense of the state as a 'reified entity which continues to exist regardless of how it is constitutionalized (or not constitutionalized) at any particular moment' (Elazar 1985: 234). It was the constitution which established the political pact on whose basis the body politic took its life (Toinet 1988). Although this constitutional model was later adopted outside Europe by Canada, Australia, New Zealand, and South Africa, most European nation-states in the twentieth century (and especially after World War II) followed a rather different constitutional model. In (Western) Europe, the constitution had the features of a *state code*, which was the expression of a *declared democratic ideology*, on whose basis society had to be organized (Elazar 1985). In fact, European nation-states' constitutions start with a definition of fundamental (individual, but much more social and economic) rights and end with a specification of powers and procedures to preserve them. It is a code because of its highly specific and detailed character. It can be amended, of course, but it is quite rigid by virtue of its structured nature. Examples of quite rigid constitutions are those of Austria (which formally preserved its constitution of the 1920s), Italy (1948), the Federal Republic of Germany (1949), and Spain (1978). The Fourth Republic of France (1946) is another example: in fact, it took a dramatic political crisis in 1958 (the civil war in the French colony

Algeria) to substitute it with a new one (the constitution of the Fifth Republic).

9.2.2. The Institutional Implications of US Compoundness

As we know, the Philadelphia constitutional convention created a system of multiple separation of powers. That system is the Madisonian answer to the fear that factionalism could disrupt the new republican polity. Its 'complex system of checks: national representation, bicameralism, indirect election, distribution of powers, and the federal–state relationship would operate in concert to counteract the effects of faction despite the inevitability of the factional spirit' (Sunstein 1993: 186). On the contrary, the European nation-states neither came to have a system of multiple separation of powers nor have they pursued, in the past, a constitutional strategy of creating a compound polity. As we know, in Europe only Switzerland pursued the road of the *multiple separation*, largely imitating, since the adoption of its 1848 constitution, the American one.

What then are the institutional implications of the American compound republic? The empirical experience suggests three basic features. First, *the federal structure favors the overrepresentation of smaller territorial units*. The 'Connecticut compromise' accepted at the Philadelphia Constitutional Convention implies that the smaller states have much more representative power than the larger states in all matters regarding states' affairs (Dahl 2001: 18). Thus each state, regardless of its population, received the same allocation of two senators in the federal Senate. A decision which has significantly altered the principle of democratic representation. In the senatorial elections of November 2000 'the ratio of overrepresentation of the least populated state, Wyoming, to the most populous state, California, [was] just under 70 to 1. By comparison, among the advanced democracies the ratio runs from 1.5:1 in Austria to 40:1 in Switzerland. In fact, the US disproportion is exceeded only in Brazil, Argentina, and Russia' (Dahl 2001: 50). This was a decision of significant importance, given that the Senate has special powers in crucial fields of national policy (see Chapters 2 and 6). Thus, through the election of the senators, states' electorates can influence crucial policies constitutionally allocated at the center, such as judicial and foreign policies. Moreover, this overrepresentation of smaller states' electorates exercises its effects in presidential elections. The Electoral College (see Chapter 2) allows smaller states to have a disproportionate influence over the choice of the chief executive of the country. This overrepresentation was and continues to be the price to be paid in order to keep the compound republic together. Nevertheless, in America, the price in terms of unequal representation has been significantly high. As Dahl (2001: 49) stressed, 'some degree of unequal representation also exists in the other federal system. Yet the degree of unequal representation in the US Senate is by far the most extreme.'

Second, *the governmental system favors the competition (if not the combat) between the legislature and the President.* Contrary to parliamentary systems where the government may operate only on the basis of the direct or indirect legislature's confidence, in systems with separation of powers the President does not represent legislative majorities. He is elected independently of the legislature, by a community of electors different from that electing the members of the legislature and its mandate has a time span different from the mandates of the two chambers of the legislature. In order to make these institutions work, the principle of separation of powers has been constitutionally tamed by the principle of checks and balances. Each institution enjoys some of the powers proper to the other institutions, powers which have to be used in order to motivate reciprocal cooperation. The President has a veto on congressional legislation which puts pressure on Congress to consider its views on specific bills, the Senate has the power to advise and grant its consent on several matters, which urges the President to take into account its preferences. The structure of separation and the incentives to cooperate are constitutionally combined in order to generate reciprocal institutional control. In the USA, the institutional competition between the President and Congress is a functional equivalent of the political competition between the government and the opposition in European parliamentary and semi-presidential systems. Unless there is a dramatic crisis to face (in this case, in the short run, the political actors of the various institutions will gather around the President's leadership), the incentives of the system work for pushing one institution against the other, because of the lack of any confidence relations between them. In conditions of divided government, such competition might take the form of a proper institutional combat. Yet competition among institutions has a different nature from competition among political parties or coalitions. The independent President and Congress *have* to cooperate in order to generate legislation, whereas in European nation-states this is not necessarily true for government and opposition (if the former has a sufficiently workable majority in parliament, as it is in competitive parliamentarianism). Where there are severely divided political majorities emerging from temporarily differentiated presidential and congressional elections, the institutional competition has frequently become an institutional struggle, with negative implications in terms of lawmaking capacity. Moreover, this combination of separation and cooperation has introduced a formidable hurdle to the detection of 'who is responsible for what?'. Responsibility in decision-making is shared and widespread. Elections do not create a government, as they do in parliamentary and semi-presidential systems, but they are procedures to fill institutional positions at different levels of a separated governmental system.

Third, *the constitutional system of multiple separation of powers puts pressures on the judiciary to play a policymaking role.* Of course the judiciary can play this role thanks to the power of judicial review. In the USA, the power of judicial review is diffused at all levels of the judicial system, whereas in European nation-states the power to check the constitutionality of a law is monopolized by the constitutional court. In the USA, the Supreme Court, the highest judicial level endowed with the power of judicial review, is the highest level of the judicial system, whereas in the European nation-states the constitutional court is neither a judicial nor a political body. The American Supreme Court plays the positive role of protector of constitutional interests within the lawmaking process, through its legal interpretation of the political acts of Congress and President. This has been possible thanks to the system of separation of powers which makes the constitution the only locus of sovereignty (Ackerman 1991; Holmes 1995: 167; Bellamy 1996). In the face of the constitution, or beneath it, all federal institutions have the same legitimacy, because all of them derive their powers from the same source. The US constitutional system is thus a horizontal (or antihierarchical) system, contrary to the vertical European nation-states' constitutional systems, because based on the supremacy of the parliament. In European nation-states, on the contrary, parliament is the depository of popular will, and without its consent the government cannot operate. This is why in European nation-states, contrary to America, the judiciary is interpreted by legislators as an organ, rather than a power, of the state (Shapiro and Stone Sweet 1994, 2002).

9.2.3. *The Ambiguous Mandate of the Philadelphia Constitutional Convention*

The US constitution-making process took place through an indirectly elected assembly, called a constitutional convention. Upon the suggestion of the Continental Congress, the legislatures of the thirteen previous colonies and now sovereign states agreed to send their own delegates to a convention to be held in Philadelphia to discuss plausible solutions for ameliorating the functioning of the existing constitution (the Articles of Confederation), in particular regarding its capacity to guarantee a reasonably effective central government in meeting the challenges to internal and external peace. The mandate was so ambiguous, that the outcome of the convention was not an amelioration of the confederal constitution of 1781 but its substitution with a new federal constitution. In other words, the framers convened in Philadelphia in 1787 went much beyond the vague mandate they had received from both the Continental Congress and the legislatures of their states (Wood 1969), although the new constitution was logically connected to the old one (Hendrickson 2003).

The US constitution-making model of the indirectly elected convention was then adopted in very few other cases. In Europe, it was adopted only in Bonn in 1949, where the delegates were nominated by the elected *Länder* legislatures, which were the first representative institutions set up after the war. The reason is clear: indirect elections increase the distance between constitutional framers and people. In fact, with the successive extension of suffrage, the Philadelphia constitution-making model became increasingly unacceptable. Subsequently, constitution-making by directly elected assemblies has been the most frequent mode of constitution-making in the twentieth century (Elster 1997: 130). Constitutions were elaborated by constituent assemblies elected through universal suffrage for the sole task of writing a new constitution. Only in this regard the Philadelphia Convention of 1787 served as a model. The popular election of the constitutional assembly was in itself a crucial arena for defining the broad constitutional options to be elaborated in the following debate. Directly elected constitutional conventions tended to be less deliberative than indirectly elected ones, in the sense that the very process of election set sufficient guidelines to constrain (either in a positive or in a negative way) the ensuing process of constitutional elaboration: hard times for constitutional ambiguity.

It is said that constitutions are chains imposed by Peter when sober on Peter when drunk (Holmes 1995: ch. 5). Through a constitution, 'people in a newly formed nation...commit themselves, in advance, to a certain course of action' (Sunstein 2001: 97). But constitutions are typically written at a time of crisis—a time when it is not so obvious that the framers will be particularly sober (see the example of post-1989 Bulgaria where the constitution-making assembly wrote an extremely illiberal article against the Turkish minority, Elster 1997). Although the Philadelphia Convention was not held as a consequence of an erupted crisis, nevertheless the diffused fear of a confederacy's implosion played an important role in motivating the search for a new institutional design. There was a shared perception, among the elites of the new states, that the Articles of Confederation were not sufficient for dealing with the challenges of an internal or external war. One cannot be trapped by the myth surrounding US constitution-making (Black 1988), as if the convention were an academic seminar and not the political answer to a political fear. Indeed, the convention debate was not a purely rational exercise as might appear reading the rationalization of its internal contrasts offered *post hoc* by *The Federalist*, but rather a political battle between states' representatives expressing different, if not opposing, interpretations of the unionist paradigm (i.e. of the relation between integration and independence).

If in modern constitution-making processes the political parties were the actors who tended to promote those arrangements more favorable to themselves (Elster 1997), in Philadelphia it was the states' interests which tended to favor arrangements congenial to their holding power (although some of the more influential, among them the Virginian group, promoted also an explicit national or supra-states view). The Philadelphia convention was able to keep the contrasts among states at a low level of intensity (thus promoting a series of compromises) thanks also to the high margin of action the elite could enjoy from popular scrutiny (in fact, late-eighteenth-century America was a society of limited communication and elite-controlled information). There was certainly passion in the post-Philadelphia debate for the approval of the new constitution (Wood 1992), but it was weaker than that generated by the constitutional debates in contemporary politically mobilized societies. In modern media societies, this approach to constitution-making appears implausible. Constitution-making in the twentieth century contained fewer elements of secrecy (committee discussion) and more of publicity (plenary assembly discussion). To strike a balance between the two was not easy. Finally, if the Philadelphia Constitutional Convention lasted little less than four months (from the opening on May 25 to the final adjournment on September 17, 1787), since then constitutional assemblies have had to work within a time limit so that no group could use delaying tactics to get its own way.

In short, the Philadelphia model of constitution-making (based on an indirectly elected assembly with an ambiguous mandate, characterized by the predominance of state interests and working in a secretive manner) found no equivalent in twentieth-century Europe.

9.3. Constitutionalism in the EU: Toward a Supranational Constitution

9.3.1. *Constitutionalization without a Constitution*

Differently from the USA, the EU did not start from a constitution. The EU is the outcome of interstate treaties aimed at fostering the formation of a common market on a continental scale. These treaties were imposed by historical events and by wise politicians and public officials (Parsons 2003). Their aim was to officially conclude the century-long European civil war, *through* a transnational cooperation on a growing number of economic matters among the European nation-states (Lindberg 1963). In fact, fixing the building of a common market as the Community target implied a very broad perspective for Community action (Haas 1958). It was the promotion of that perspective which triggered the process of institutionalization of the European Community which finally become the EU with the Maastricht Treaty of 1992 (Pierson 1996). This process of integration was, at times, incremental and, at other times, characterized by breakthroughs (Caporaso 2005). The incrementality of much of the process was punctuated by critical junctures which made it possible to introduce significant innovations in the structure of the treaties, 'especially when the right actor was in the right place' (Ross 1995).

In particular, the process of institutionalization of the EU supranational polity was triggered by three factors (Fligstein and Stone Sweet 2001): (*a*) the increase in transnational economic activity which demanded new supranational rules (positive integration) and not only the abolition of old domestic ones (negative integration). Here the main actors were firms and entrepreneurs; (*b*) the increase in transnational economic activity which brought an increase in legal litigation which demanded a more active role of the judicial organ of the Community system, the ECJ. Here the main actors were economic actors and judicial elites; and (*c*) the increase of legal litigation provided EU institutions with an incentive to define new rules and to introduce new laws. The ECJ was at the center of this threefold pressure. In fact, the ECJ used the opportunities provided by the treaties to promote a new legal order for a supranational market. This was made possible because 'individuals in real cases and controversies (usually against public authorities) became the principal "guardians" of the legal integrity of Community law within Europe similar to the way that individuals in the United States have been the principal actors in ensuring the vindication of the Bill of Rights and other federal law' (Weiler 1999: 20).

The ECJ has thus transformed intergovernmental treaties into quasi-constitutional documents. Its creative legal reasoning was recognized as legitimate thanks to the organic character of the founding treaties. As was remarked some time ago in a pioneering piece of research, if 'the . . . three international conventions: the Treaty of Paris and the Treaties of Rome do not constitute a federal charter [they nevertheless] . . . have an organic character' (Elazar and Greilsammer 1985: 93). Constitutionalization of the treaty system means the transformation of the EU into a multi-tiered quasi-federal polity founded on higher law constitutionalism. As Weiler (1999: 29) put it, 'there can be no argument that the Community legal order as it emerged from the foundational period appeared in its operation much closer to a working constitutional order' than to a traditional international regime. The EU treaties have gradually evolved from a set of legal arrangements binding on sovereign states, into a vertically integrated legal order that confers judicially enforceable rights and obligations on all legal persons and parties, public and private, within the EU territory. In this regard, the preliminary reference procedure was crucial. As a mode of constitutional adjudication, the preliminary reference procedure functions much like the concrete review found in national constitutional systems. Thus, if it is true that the EU is not based on a formal constitution, nor is it true that the EU is not a constitutional regime. If the USA started from a constitution and then witnessed a contradictory process of constitutionalization, at least until the Civil War of 1861–5, in the EU the process of constitutionalization has proceeded without the support of a formal constitution. In both cases, it was the judiciary which promoted a supra-state (in the USA) or a supranational (in the EU) legal order aimed at guaranteeing the development of a common continental market (Egan 2001; Goldstein 2001).

9.3.2. The Institutional Implications of EU Compoundness

A supranational regime entails the existence of an internal structure of institutions and procedures comparable to that found in domestic political systems. The internal structure of the first pillar of the EU features a multiple separation of powers. The distribution of decision-making power is aimed at spreading power, not at concentrating it as happens within EU member-states. The EU institutional structure has gradually evolved into a system of separated institutions sharing governmental power. The governmental and territorial institutions enjoy distinct and separated sources of legitimacy, but they have incentives to cooperate in the lawmaking procedure, especially after the codetermination procedure established in Maastricht.

What then are the specific institutional implications of the EU compound polity? The analysis suggests three basic features. First, *the multi-level territorial organization of the EU overrepresents the smaller states*. As in the US federal system, the smaller states' interests in the EU have been overrepresented since the Rome treaties of 1957; a fact which became sensitive with the approval of the SEA in 1986 that increased the number of policy issues decided on the basis of a QMV within the Council of Ministers. The arcane system chosen at the Nice IGC of 2000 to recalculate both the weight of the votes within the Council of Ministers and the distribution of seats within the EP was an attempt to balance the (over-)representation of smaller states' interests with an increase in that of the larger states' interests. Nevertheless, it is not yet clear if this rebalancing can distance the EU from the situation in the USA of overrepresentation of smaller states' interests. In an EU of twenty-seven member-states, this overrepresentation is not sufficient, per se, for generating policy advantages. In fact, in the EU, power relations among states and regions tend to change according to their capacity to build successful coalitions. In the EU formal institutions and procedures count, but they do so within a larger decision-making context shaped by a plurality of actors and networks. As in the USA, organization is the crucial resource of the territorial power game. Of course organization is dependent on institutional factors, but the latter do not generate unequivocal effects (Boerzel 2001). Efficient and unitary states (such as France and Britain) may be more effective in the bargaining process taking place in the Council of Ministers, but federal or regional states (as Germany and Spain) may display a larger number of institutional actors (*Länder, Comunitad Autonomas* apart from national governments) able to maximize the distributive gains of the EU in more than one institution. When the governments of federal states are able to pursue a coordinated policy with the executives of the regions or states at the EU level, they have proved much more effective in influencing specific EU policies than powerful unitary states. In short, in an increasingly expanding polity, coalition capacity appears to be the preeminent resource that each territorial unit has to acquire.

Second, *the complex governmental system promotes cooperation among actors which diminishes inter-states conflict.* Cooperation is inevitable in sharing-powers systems. Moreover, within the EU, decision-making is regulated by several procedures according to the policy in question. The shifting, with the SEA of 1986, from unanimity to QMV in the Council of Ministers entailed a very detailed definition of the issues to which one procedure applies rather than another. The EP's power of codetermination, introduced six years later, further enlarged the classification of issues to which the procedure could be applied. The various procedures were cumulative, without taking into account incoherence or overlap among them. Consequently, 'the combination of possible variations in Council voting procedures with different legislative paths incorporating a greater or lesser role for the European Parliament has produced no fewer than 25 different legislative procedures' (Mény and Knapp 1998: 445). The interesting point is that this confusion of powers has helped to strengthen the EU, rather than weaken it. To a certain extent, confusion of power appears to have been the price paid by the Community to keep the level of internal conflicts low, especially between the pro-integration member-states and the so-called euro-skeptics. Thus, if the US separation of powers at the governmental level has produced institutional combat between the President and Congress, the EU's confused separation of powers has helped to generate a reverse effect. In both cases, we do not have a government in which to entrust policy responsibility. Governmental responsibility is shared by so many institutional and private actors that it is impossible to detect 'who did what?'.

Third, *the process of constitutionalization has magnified the policymaking role of the ECJ.* European legal integration has transformed the nature of European governance. It has altered the way individuals and companies pursue their interests, how judges resolve their disputes, how policy is made. By binding together the EU and the national legal orders in complex and structured ways, the constitutionalization of the treaty system has served to enhance the policymaking role of both the ECJ and ordinary judges. The process of constitutionalization was engendered by a growing partnership between the ECJ and national judges. National judges become agents of Community order, whenever they resolve disputes governed by EU law. But this process depended on the willingness of national judges to use article 177 of the Rome Treaty (or 234 of the Maastricht Treaty) and to faithfully implement ECJ interpretations of EU law. This willingness was granted because in so doing national judges enhanced their control of other political institutions (the national executive and parliament). As Weiler (1999: 27) notes: 'the national court and the European Court are thus integrated into a unitary system of judicial review'. Within the EU member-states, that system has favored low-level judges—more than constitutional court judges. In fact, 'national constitutional courts have been the least willing to accept constitutionalization without reservation' of the EU, because they do not adjudicate on matters of EU law (Stone Sweet 2000: 166). Nevertheless they have to adapt to a constitutional legal order that increasingly subsumes the national constitutional order into the Community legal order. The consequences might be disturbing for the European tradition of parliamentary sovereignty. In today's multi-tiered European polity, the sovereignty of the legislature appears to be largely reduced.

9.3.3. *The Detailed Mandate of the Brussels Constitutional Convention*

In Laeken, not only for the first time was the term *constitution* adopted in an official EU document, but a peculiar type of *constitution-making* model was pursued (Devuyst 2003). What are its main characteristics? First, as with the Philadelphia Convention, the Brussels Convention was an indirectly elected assembly. Its composition differed from all the previous experiences of indirectly elected assemblies. Its 105 members (plus 13 observers from the candidate states, the 12 which entered the EU in 2004 and 2007, plus Turkey) represented both the member-states and the Community institutions, as is inevitable in a supranational polity. Contrary to what happened in Philadelphia, where only the representatives of the states participated.

Moreover, the member-states' representatives were drawn not only from the governments, but also from the parliaments (the same is true for the observers) (Crum 2004). The Community representatives were equally drawn from the Commission as well as from the Parliament; and some of the convention members operated in their personal capacity, and not on behalf of specific institutions. Nevertheless, the balance seemed to favor the EU institutions' interests. A Presidium of a limited number of constitution-makers, with the power of setting the agenda of the constitutional debate, was established at the apex of the Convention. This core of the Convention was dominated by representatives of the EU institutions: ten of its twelve members were designated by EU institutions. However, although no national governments' representatives have been co-opted to this leadership group, the latter (especially those representing the intergovernmental perspective on the EU) had other chances to make their opinions heard by the Presidium's members. The same Convention Secretariat included staff detached from the Commission and the EP. In short, although not directly elected, in the Brussels Convention all the institutions of the multilevel polity were (although not fairly) represented (Philippart 2002).

Second, unlike the Philadelphia Constitutional Convention, the Brussels Convention got a very detailed mandate (Hoffman and Vergés-Bausili 2003). The Convention did not have carte blanche, nor was it organized in order to discuss generic options for 'an ever closer Union' (a purpose more limited, in any case, than the one of the American framers that strove to build 'a more perfect Union'). The Laeken Council laid down fifty-six substantive questions, divided into four themes: (*a*) the division and definition of competences between Community and member-states' institutions; (*b*) the simplification of EU instruments; (*c*) the enhancing of democracy, transparency, and efficiency within the Community institutions; and (*d*) the reorganization of the treaties. Through the selection of these substantive questions and the hierarchical definition of the importance of the issues, the European Council attempted to shape the constitution-making process within the convention. This was no guarantee that the Convention would work within the received parameters, although it was very difficult for its members to change the agenda completely, as had happened in Philadelphia, given the public scrutiny of their work. Moreover, the very large and heterogeneous composition of the Convention was conceived as a strategy of reciprocal checks in order to prevent any unwanted outcome (for the European Council). In any case, the mandate was to draft a *frame of government constitution* of the American type, and not the *constitution as a code* of the European nation-states' type. The Charter of Rights, recognized by the IGC of Nice but not included in the 2001 Treaty (De Burca 2001), has thus received due constitutional recognition, but will have the characteristics of a bill of rights added to the governmental frame, rather than those of a moral statement which justifies the constitution itself, as happened in many European nation-states.

Third, unlike the Philadelphia Convention, the Brussels Convention has been organized in a quite open, loose, inclusive, and transparent way (Closa 2004). The mandate transferred to the Convention required the latter to promote a Forum of organizations of civil society, whose opinions were regularly investigated (Lombardo 2003). All the Convention's materials were available on the web and the media had easy access to the various contributions offered in the debate. This openness was considered necessary to lend the constitution-making process its legitimacy, but it was also the outcome of a constitution-making process taking place at a time of a highly developed media system. Probably, the secrecy of Philadelphia is gone for ever. In short, the Brussels Convention had a different legal and political status from the one held in Philadelphia. Legally, the latter was constituted by state legislature representatives, whereas in the former member-state representatives had to deal with influential supranational actors. Politically, the Brussels Convention had to work within established consensual constraints, whereas the Philadelphia Constitutional Convention could consider its outcome legitimate with the approval of just nine of the thirteen states constituting the union. Nevertheless, both were attempts to answer to a mood of emergency, however different the nature of the latter. Both were finalized to create a pact among states, which could threaten each other (in the American case) or already did that (in the European case). Indeed, the Brussels Convention represented an attempt to extend the virtues of the pact to Eastern Europe, thus ending definitively the Cold War, like the previous treaties of Paris and Rome ended the hot wars.

9.4. Has the Brussels Convention Challenged the EU Compound Nature?

The constitutional road pursued by the EU manifests some interesting similarities with that pursued in the USA. The IGC of the European Council in Rome signed a *frame of government* constitution, whose aim is to preserve the EU *compound nature*, drafted by an indirectly elected constitutional convention. In the three dimensions considered, EU constitutionalism is much closer to US constitutionalism than to the constitutional experience of the EU member-states. In particular, the CT seems to have recognized the need to institutionalize the antihierarchical structure that the EU has acquired in its half a century of development. Needless to say the EU and the USA will continue to manifest many differences in crucial aspects of their institutional and cultural patterns. While constrained by their respective historical paths, the constitutional evolution of the USA and the EU is making the Atlantic Ocean less wide than it used to be. Certainly, the CT signed in Rome in October 2004 reflects a compromise between different interests and cultures (Amato 2003; Magnette 2004). However, this compromise does not challenge the compound nature of the EU (Ziller 2003). Let me argue why.

9.4.1. *The Horizontal Dimension*

Here, the main reforms regard the empowerment of the Council of Ministers and the EP, the accountability of the Commission to the EP, the institution of a permanent President of the European Council (for 2.5 years, renewable for a second mandate) and of a Minister for Foreign Affairs. Clearly, the CT tries to rationalize the organization of the Council of Ministers and to strengthen its decision-making efficiency. After a prolonged battle between advocates of Community interests (the President of the Commission foremost) and advocates of the intergovernmental vision (the representative of the British government foremost), it was agreed to extend the number of policies which can be decided by QMV, although the sectors of foreign (articles I-40 and III-196) and fiscal policies (article III-59) remain subject to the unanimity rule. Thus, article I-22 states that 'except where the Constitution provides otherwise, decisions of the Council shall be taken by qualified majority'. The Council is also organized into three Councils: the General Affairs Council, responsible for ensuring consistency in the work of the Council of Ministers; the Legislative Council, which is in charge of enacting, jointly with the EP, European laws and European framework laws; and the Foreign Affairs Council, which 'shall, on the basis of strategic guidelines laid down by the European Council, flesh out the Union's External policies, and ensure that its actions are consistent' (article I-23).

Moreover, the CT includes provisions aiming to strengthen the EP. The latter is considered a co-legislator with the Council: in fact, according to article I-19, 'the European Parliament shall, jointly with the Council, enact legislation and exercise the budgetary function, as well as functions of political control and consultation'. Thus, the CT provides for the approval (through majority voting) of the President of the Commission by the EP. However, it is the European Council which, by qualified majority, has the power to propose to the EP a candidate for the Presidency of the Commission, taking into account the outcome of the elections of the EP (article I-26). 'The Commission President shall be responsible to the European Parliament for the activities of the Commissioners' (article I-25). The approval of the President of the Commission by the EP provides a check on the European Council power to nominate him or her.

Regarding the Commission, the CT requires a new organization. The College is composed of thirteen commissioners, the President, and the Minister of Foreign Affairs, who is also the Vice President of the Commission (article I-25). Furthermore, the Commission President shall appoint nonvoting commissioners. The number of commissioners has been reduced, causing the disappointment of the small member-states, which were pushing for twenty-five commissioners (one commissioner for each member-state). It was presumed that this would grant an equal position to each member-state in the Commission (Ansa, 16/05/2003). In order to enhance the Commission's accountability, article I-25 defines also the relationship between the Commission and the EP, stating that 'The Commission, as a college, shall be responsible to the European Parliament.... The European Parliament may pass a censure motion on the Commission. If such a motion is passed, the European Commission and Commissioners must all resign'.

But it was the institution of the (semipermanent and no longer rotating each semester) President of the European Council which seems to represent the most innovative reform. According to article I-21, the President of the European Council must be elected by the European Council and will keep his or her position for a term of two and a half years. Such a position is renewable once. The powers of the President of the European Council are limited to directing and chairing the works of the Council itself, ensuring proper preparation and continuity and endeavoring to facilitate cohesion and consensus within it. In order to avoid interinstitutional competition, article I-21 provides that these tasks have to be fulfilled 'in cooperation with the President of the Commission, and on the basis of the works of the General Affairs Council'. Finally, the Constitution establishes the role of Minister for Foreign Affairs (article I-27). This minister is responsible both to the Commission and to the Council of Ministers. She or he is appointed by the European Council, which provides him or her with a mandate to contribute to elaborating the EU common external, security, and defense policies. At the same time, she or he is one of the vice-presidents of the European Commission, and within this institution is responsible for handling external relations and coordinating other aspects of external action.

In short, although the innovations introduced by the CT are significant, it does not seem that they will generate a centralization of the EU's governmental system along the traditional parliamentary lines. Instead, they seem to rationalize the existing system of separation of powers and checks and balances. Indeed, the more important of those innovations, such as the (semi)permanent presidency of the European Council and the role of Minister for Foreign Affairs, confirm the structure of sharing powers between the Council of Ministers, the Commission, and the EP. They continue to be separated institutions sharing governmental powers.

9.4.2. *The Vertical Dimension*

The CT provides institutional incentives to balance the relationship between supranational, national, and subnational interests. In this respect, the main provisions regard the definition of the method according to which the EU institutions exert their powers, the distribution of policy competences, the relationship between Community law and member-states law, the implementation of the principle of subsidiarity, and the role of national parliaments.

The preliminary draft of the CT made public by the Convention on October 28, 2002 introduced the term 'federal' among the definitions and objectives of the Union. It stated, in fact, that the purpose of the CT was to create 'a Union of European States, which, while retaining their national identities, closely coordinate their policies at the European level, and administer certain common competences on a federal basis' (The European Convention, The Secretariat, CONV369/02, article 1). However, the term 'federal' disappeared in the final text of the CT, to be substituted with the term 'Community'. Now, the CT states that 'the Union shall coordinate the policies by which the Member States aim to achieve these objectives and shall exercise in the community way the competences they confer on it' (article I-1). No further specification is given with respect to the meaning of the term 'community way'. Although the term 'federal' does not appear in the CT, the territorial system devised by the latter has de facto similarities to a federal system with strong confederal elements. The rationalization of the organization of the Council and the empowerment of the EP formalizes a bicameral representation system of a federal type, where the EP is the chamber representing individual electors and the Council of Ministers represents member-state interests. However, the articulation of the Council of Ministers in three Councils (and especially the persistence of the Foreign Affairs Council) introduces a powerful confederal feature within the federal structure of bicameral representation. Although this role assigned to member-states' governments is checked by the recognition that the Commission continues to be the only institution with legislative initiative power.[1]

Concerning the allocation of policy competences, the CT openly recognizes the multilevel governance nature of the EU, formalizing a distinction between exclusive (article I-12) and shared competences (article I-13),

Table 9.1 Allocation of competences along territorial lines: CT proposal

Exclusive EU competences	Shared EU and member-state competences
Monetary policy for the member-states who have adopted the euro	Internal market
	Area of freedom, security, and justice
Custom union	Agriculture and fisheries, excluding the
Common commercial policy	conservation of marine biological resources
Conservation of marine biological resources under the common fisheries policy	Transport and trans-European networks
	Energy
Competition policy	Social policy[1]
	Economic and social cohesion
	Environment
	Common safety concerns in public health matters
	Consumer protection

[1] For the aspects defined in part III of the Constitution.

according to the model of cooperative federalism (see Table 9.1). However, as in the US federalism, the CT circumscribes the powers of the center (the EU), leaving to the member-states the remaining ones. According to article I-9, 'under the principle of conferral, the Union shall act within the limits of the competences conferred upon it by the Member States in the Constitution to attain the objectives set out in the Constitution. Competences not conferred upon the Union in the Constitution remain with the Member States'.

In order to avoid decision-making stalemate in policy areas where intergovernmental contrasts might emerge, the mechanism of enhanced cooperation is enclosed in article I-43, which states that 'Member States who wish to establish enhanced cooperation between themselves within the framework of the Union's non-exclusive competences may make use of its institutions and exercise those competences by applying the relevant provisions of the Constitution'. This provision sets the basis for the creation of a core Europe, composed of states willing to reach a deeper integration. To this antihierarchical territorial system corresponds, as in other federal systems, a clear hierarchy of legal norms. According to article I-10 of the CT, 'the Constitution and law adopted by the Union's institutions in exercising competences conferred on it, shall have primacy over the law of the Member States'. This article recognizes formally the principle of primacy which was established by the ECJ since 1963. Such a provision strengthens the federal feature of the EU and makes the role of the ECJ formally comparable to that of a federal court.

Furthermore, the CT strengthens the role of national parliaments in the Community decision-making process, for reducing the legitimacy deficit of EU institutions, through the formalization of the principle of subsidiarity. As requested by the working group on national parliaments, the 'Draft Protocol on the role of National Parliaments in the European Union', annexed to the CT, recognizes the need for the involvement of national parliaments in the activity of the EU and proposes to ensure their supervision of the governments' action within the Council. The CT underlines the importance of the principle of subsidiarity, which preserves the multilevel governance structure of the EU. According to the 'Protocol on the application of the principles of subsidiarity and proportionality', annexed to the CT, the Commission has to justify its legislative proposals always with reference to the principle of subsidiarity. Moreover, 'any national parliaments or any chamber of a national Parliament of a Member State may, within six weeks from the date of transmission of the Commission's legislative proposal, send to the Presidents of the EP, of the Council and of the Commission a reasoned opinion stating why it considers that the proposal in question does not comply with the principle of subsidiarity'. This protocol was the result of the action of both a working group on subsidiarity and the Commission (Barnier and Vitorino 2002).

Also at the vertical level, the CT has introduced significant innovations, which, nevertheless, have rationalized, but not altered, the previous territorial distribution of power. Dehousse (2003) has critically argued that 'as regards its content, the draft constitution is dominated by states' fears to see their influence diluted in the European system. Large states were concerned to avoid the emergence of strong European institutions, while smaller countries were afraid by the prospect of a domination by "large" member states.' De facto, the hybrid nature of the EU (De Witte 2003), which integrates Community and intergovernmental features, with full recognition of the important role played by the subnational or regional levels of government, has been preserved. Indeed, as Dehousse (2003) again remarked: 'the so-called "European constitution" displays more elements of continuity than elements of rupture with the past'. Separated institutions representing different territorial levels of governance continue to share powers and policy competences. In sum, the CT seems to have confirmed the ongoing structure of multiple separation and sharing of powers both at the horizontal and vertical levels.

9.5. Constitutionalization as a Contested Process

9.5.1. *The Case of the EU*

The outcomes of the French and Dutch referenda, held respectively in May and June 2005, and more generally the process of approving the Treaty on Europe's constitutional future, furnish a good occasion to reflect on constitutionalization as a contested concept. Various cleavages have opened up in the debate on the CT's approval. The first is the traditional one between the countries of (Western) continental Europe and the countries of (Northern) insular Europe. This cleavage has for years accompanied the process of European integration, in particular since 1973 when Britain, Denmark, and Ireland entered the EU (Gilbert 2003). One may even argue that it is a historical cleavage which reflects the differing historical experiences of the 'islands' and the 'continent' in formation of the nation-state and its international extensions. Britain continues to head a coalition of EU member-states which view integration as principally an economic process. At issue for these member-states is the constitutionalization of a market, not of a polity. Indeed, they regard the deepening of the integration process as a threat to national sovereignty to be countered by pressing for further enlargement (Geddes 2004).

It is evident from the point of view of public policies that the national sovereignty of the member-states, including the 'islands' of Europe, has for some time been curtailed. Of course, this has not impeded these member-states from defending their founding myths: also because, in the case of these countries, the defense of sovereignty springs from the distinct historical phenomenon of democratic nationalism: it is nationalism which has enabled them (especially Britain) to preserve democracy. Very different, of course, has been the historical experience of the continental countries of Europe: indeed, in their case, nationalism has erased democracy, owing to a set of cultural and ecological factors. We know that the development of the democratic state has encountered much more unfavorable conditions in the 'land-bound' European countries than it has in the 'sea-bound' ones. In the former, nationalism has been antidemocratic, bending to (or sustaining) the centralist ambitions of dominant authoritarian groups. Inevitably, for the EU member-states heir to this historical experience and memory, integration has represented the antidote to the virus of authoritarian nationalism, while those that have inherited the 'island' experience view integration as a threat to their democratic identity. For this reason, the countries of continental Europe interpret constitutionalization as a political rather than economic phenomenon, and are suspicious of any enlargement not preceded by further deepening (Hendricks and Morgan 2001). If the integration of Europe is a response to the evil of nationalism, then these countries believe that it must have the decision-making instruments with which to balance the national interests of its member-states. Although, in the case of France (Guyomarch, Machin, and Ritchie 1998), sectors of the political elites seem to interpret European integration also (or mainly) as an occasion for increasing the international influence of the country (assuming that France is the hegemonic 'power' in the EU and thus the EU is 'France at large'). Thus, France too has a strong nationalistic component.

Since 2004, this long-standing geographical cleavage has been over-lapped by a second one: that between the old member-states of Western Europe and the new ones of Eastern Europe. Although also this cleavage has a territorial basis, it is manifest in distinctive cultural forms. The new member-states of the EU believe that they have regained their national sovereignty after almost half a century (and in some cases, like the Baltic states, much longer) of enforced dependence on the USSR superpower. We know, of course, that independence and sovereignty do not coincide, given that the latter is a legal condition and the former a material capability. And the countries in question know this as well. De facto, the new member-states of the EU have scant independence, in that they do not possess the basic resources (technological, economic, demographic, administrative, political) that can guarantee their independence. They view the EU as a customs union, an open market in which they can remedy their economic and institutional laggardness without the constraints of the Community regulations (which fix standards of environmental protection, migratory flows, or industrial relations, which the new member-states consider penalizing). For this reason, their view should not be confused with that of the Northern 'islands', given that their material and institutional backwardness induces them to challenge market regulation itself, or economic constitutionalization as such. Hence, while the Northern 'islands' tend anyway to adopt a regulatory stance on the European market, the member-states of Eastern Europe seem to distrust it. While the confederalism of the former recognizes the importance of the Community institutions and rules, the confederalism of the latter is more than skeptical of them. In short, for the new member-states, the EU is above all an opportunity for trade and flows (also migratory), rather than being a system to regulate and harmonize economic transactions across the continent. Indeed, the spread of these rules is sometimes perceived as an imperial policy pursued by the West toward the European East (Zielonka 2006).

Of course, these geographical cleavages are only rough indicators of the constitutional divisions existing within the EU. As such, they do not reflect the divisions within the EU countries. In the Northern 'islands' as well as in the Eastern member-states there are positions in favor of greater political or federal integration, just as in the member-states of Western Continental Europe there are powerful coalitions pushing for economic or confederal integration. Indeed, the French and Dutch referenda show that in Continental Europe there is growing a fear of further political integration. These geographical cleavages are overlapped by crosscutting territorial cleavages of a political kind. In particular there has arisen (as evidenced by the French and Dutch referenda) a cleavage between those who believe that the EU is a political regime with a *democratic deficit* and those who maintain instead that the EU has gone too far in its democratization process (Taggart 2006). While the latter position has come to overlap with the confederal one (propounded in the Northern 'islands' in Europe, as well as in many of its Eastern member-states) it does not coincide with that view. It has been motivated by criticism of the Brussels technocracy, although this criticism is not necessarily made in the name of homeland democracy (see Moravcsik 1992 for a critique of this criticism). The former position stems in its turn from a criticism leveled for some time against the EU by the more radical sections of public opinion (Marquand 1979). Its proponents seemingly regard the EU with the eyes of the national democracies, in particular those with fusion of powers systems, and therefore with the supremacy (if not the centrality) of parliament. For these critics, the EU takes too many decisions, without the decision-makers being accountable for their outcomes. Only the members of the EP, the critics point out, have been elected democratically, while this is not the case of the members of the Commission or of the government representatives in the Council of Ministers. Above all, the EU does not have a political decision-making body (like the cabinet in parliamentary systems) which voters can judge politically (Hix, Noury, and Roland 2004). Here, the legitimacy of a political system depends on the direct accountability of its decision-makers, and this presupposes an electoral relation between the latter and the electorate. Nothing of the kind exists in the EU. In the EU it is impossible to establish 'who is responsible for what', given the sharing-power system that structures the decision-making process. 'The fact is'—writes Nicolaidis (2004: 98)—'that Europeans cannot hold their politicians accountable for what the EU does'.

The debate on the democratic deficit has had a major impact on European public opinion. Part of the latter has declared itself in favor of the greater parliamentarization of the EU, while another significant section continues to maintain that if any parliaments are to be strengthened they should be the national ones, certainly not the supranational EU parliament. This constitutional cleavage has generated much controversy because it has raised (like the territorial cleavage) the issue of the EU's democratic legitimacy. Should the legitimacy of the EU's decisions reside in its parliament or should it continue to reside in the national parliaments? In both cases, however, the EU has continued to be regarded as an extension of national democracy. As such, therefore, it must necessarily be based on a single source of legitimacy (no matter if this lies at the 'center' or in the member-states). This vision of a single (though differentiated) source of legitimacy has been vigorously opposed by other actors (regional and local governments, interest groups, citizens' movements) which interpret the EU as a multilevel system (Hooghe and Marks 2001) and stress its multiple sources of legitimacy (also because it is in their interest to do so). At least until the SEA, the EU was based exclusively on the (indirect) legitimacy deriving from its member-states. Finally, it is of interest to notice that these various cleavages have not found (nor could they) party-based representation across the left/right spectrum. Indeed, they have de-structured the political parties, creating convergences (among member-state parties belonging to different EU groupings) and divergences (within these various groupings) which cannot be related to the divisions within national party systems.

9.5.2. The Case of the USA

If one bears the implications of the EU's compound nature in mind, it is only apparently paradoxical that its constitutionalization process has followed a route very similar to that of the USA. There too, in fact, much opposition has been raised against constitutionalization. And in the USA too there has been primarily a geographical cleavage, one which indeed still influences the divisions within Congress and the presidential electoral process (Bensel 1987). Not only did this cleavage once engender a dramatic Civil War but it embodied economic and social divisions which elsewhere (in Western Europe) led to the birth of the modern party systems (Bartolini 2005). That is to say, this geographical cleavage has economically and socially structured the US territorial areas or *regional sections*. In the USA, economic conflict among social classes has taken the form of economic competition among geographical areas, so that the latter have come to comprise specific and distinct production systems, mercantile sectors, and domestic and international market strategies (Sbragia 1996). However, although conflict among the states has been prompted by economic or ideological factors, it has always had to be justified by reference to the constitution. It was conflicting interpretations of the 1787 Constitution that led to the civil war between the Northern and Southern states in 1861–5, and it was differing interpretations of the states' prerogatives that led, a century after the Civil War, to the conflict on civil rights between the states who had preserved racial segregation and those that deemed it unconstitutional (Ostrom V. 1991).

However, the conflict between the federalist and confederalist views has always been highly *mobile*. Confederalism justified the more democratic positions in the initial phase of the new republic, and then the more anti-democratic ones of the Civil War. And for federalism conversely, in that it indubitably matched the interests of the dominant economic groups in the initial phase of the new republic, but then gave form and principles to antislavery interests during the 1860s Civil War, or to antisegregationist ones during the 1960s civil rights period. Yet, no matter how mobile this conflict may have been relative to its actors, it has always been expressed in constitutional language. In the USA, territorial conflict came to express a cleavage concerning the democratic nature of the political system. While for a large part of the nineteenth century some defenders of the states' powers (and critics of the federal center's power) had argued that the latter, unlike the former, for obvious geographical reasons, could not ensure participation by citizens in its decisions, at the end of that century and the beginning of the twentieth, criticism of the federal center's democratic deficit assumed very different features. Having been forced to acknowledge the process of nationalization that had traversed US politics (increasingly more decisions were taken in Washington, DC, Lunch 1987), the critics of the democratic deficit set out to democratize the federal institutions. The Progressives and the Populists thus advocated reform of both the national and local systems (Kazin 1995). These reforms led, among other things, to the introduction of the primaries for the selection of presidential candidates, the transformation of the presidential elections into majoritarian contests (with the introduction of the winner-takes-all system in the electoral colleges of many states), and the direct election of senators with the Seventeenth Amendment.

Other attempts at reform have been thwarted by the resistance of certain states. Consider the opposition raised by the small- and medium-sized states against abolition of the Electoral College for election of the President: a College in which (like the Senate) the small states have always been overrepresented compared with the large ones. Still today, and notwithstanding events in Florida during the presidential elections of 2000, the abolition of the Electoral College is impracticable. And in any case, both its defenders and critics continue to argue their respective positions on the basis of the constitution, which for the former has institutionalized a confederal balance between the small and large states (so that the indirect election of the President should be preserved), and for the latter has instead introduced a federal sovereignty superior to that of the federated states (whence the possibility of introducing the direct election of the President by a national college). Thus, in the USA, conflicts have always been couched in terms of a 'constitutional discourse'. The constitution has continued to furnish the linguistic and conceptual materials for its own criticism, as well as for its interpretation. Constitutional disputation has been the constant feature of the conflict, defining it (with the exception of the Civil War) through construction of a shared discourse. This does not mean that the conflict has been subdued: quite the opposite, in fact. Since the years of the Philadelphia Constitutional Convention, the USA has gone through periodic crises of constitutionalization. So it was in the 1830s regarding the role and independence of financial power; so it was in the 1860s regarding the sovereignty of the states in imposing slavery; so it was in the 1930s regarding the role of the federal institutions; so it was in the 1960s regarding civil rights; and so it is in the 2000s regarding the powers of the federal government to restrict the rights of citizens.

All these conflicts have been waged through the constitution, or in other words, through the mobilization of some or other interpretation of the constitution in regard to issues of the moment (Agel and Bernstein 1993). As Sbragia (2007: 2) remarked, Americans 'have learned to live with that tension, but (they) have never fully resolved it'. The constitution's language has delimited and defined what has to be considered legitimate political discourse. Through constitutional debate, Americans have defined their differences, but also have learned to appreciate their similarities. They have become a single nation of citizens still belonging to different (territorial, ethnic, linguistic) communities. The constitutional debate has made possible the formation of a constitutional people. America has been constructed politically, or better constitutionally, although the premises of such construction have been reputed fragile by many, who have thus invoked the need of a cultural definition of the national identity. One may consequently argue that Americans have been united not so much by a common interpretation of the constitution as by their efforts to justify their divergent interests through one or another interpretation of the constitution. Constitutionalization became a contested concept much earlier in the USA than it did in the EU. And it still continues to be so because the reforms introduced have not altered (nor could they) the nature of the country's separated government (which is the structural origin of the constitutional dispute). As a consequence, the growth of the country's international power has strengthened the President, but this has not detracted from the powers of Congress. It has strengthened the federal center, but this has not reduced the powers of the federated states. The institutions have grown according to the positive-sum logic distinctive of systems with a multiple separation of powers (i.e. with distinct and competing legitimacies).

9.6. Constitutionalization as Democratization

Compound democracies, therefore, are based on structures which 'disperse' sovereignty: fragmenting and separating it, thereby preventing those who possess a portion of such sovereignty from claiming to represent the whole. This fragmentation of public authority has been the guarantor of the stability of compound democracies, but it may prove to be (and has done so) a source of uncertainty for them. It has been a source of their stability because fragmentation gives all actors the resources and powers with which to assert their preferences, or with which to obstruct those of others if these neutralize their own. Systems based on structural asymmetry in their constitutive components cannot organize themselves on the basis of fusion of powers models of government which permit the formation of relatively stable (though periodically replaceable) hegemonies. It is true that the fusion of powers system has been adopted by countries (most notably Germany) which have also given a federal structure to their states. Nevertheless, and especially in post–World War II Germany, the federal separation of territorial powers has served to establish an equilibrium (economic, demographic, cultural) among those separated territorial powers (Jefferey and Savigner 1991), the purpose being to prevent any recurrence of the Prussian situation where one territorial unit hegemonized the others and imposed its centralist model (Ziblatt 2006). In short, the differences in Germany among the *Länder* have nothing in common with either those in the EU (between member-states with more than 80 million inhabitants and others with not even 500,000) or those that still persist in the USA (where the rate of disproportionality in representation of the states in the Senate is one of the highest among the federal systems) (Dahl 2001). For this reason, neither the USA nor the EU can adopt parliamentary systems, since this would cure the illness by killing the patient. With a parliamentary system, in fact, there would be states able to exercise permanent control over the legislature, while the other states would be permanently in the minority—unless one assumes that inter-states cleavages could be replaced by cross-states ones, through the formation of coalitions among the electorates of various member-states. This eventuality is highly unlikely, however, because in compound democracies it is partisan cleavages that are absorbed by interstate ones, not vice versa. For what reason, therefore, would the smaller member-states wish to remain in a system where they would be in the permanent minority?

However, the compound nature of these democracies is also the source of their uncertainty. The conflicts within them never have (relatively) definitive outcomes. This is because there could never be a definitive solution to the conflicts of interests and views between their member-states: between large and small member-states, between member-states oriented to the international market and member-states oriented to the domestic one, between member-states with a post-state or post-national culture and those instead proud of their state or national traditions, between member-states with solid democratic traditions and those whose traditions are tinged with authoritarianism (political or racial). Nor, further, could there be a definitive solution to the conflicts among the various conceptions of democratic legitimacy. The democratic deficit can never be resolved in the compound democracies, and this induces a constant contest to reformulate and redefine the notion of political legitimacy. In compound democracies, *political legitimacy* is a process, rather than being a relation (between governors and governed). In these democracies there are no bottleneck structures in which the relation between these latter can crystallize (as in the parliamentary elections of noncompound democracies). For this reason, constitutionalization is an open process in compound democracies. And it starts to be so in the noncompound democracies as well, now that they have begun to de-structure themselves both territorially and insti-tutionally (in the former case by encouraging the institutionalization of regional and municipal differences; in the latter by granting more than merely functional autonomy to powers like the judiciary). Accord-ingly, the existence of the democratic deficit is an opportunity to foster public debate on democracy which may even engender disputes on the places and principles that should promote it. The US and EU experi-ences show that the effect (not always intended) of discussion on the democratic deficit has been an accentuation of *democratization*, sometimes at the federal level (in the USA) or Community level (in the EU), and sometimes at the level of the member-states and their local administra-tions (the regions in the EU and the municipalities in the USA) (Sbragia 2005*b*).

Compound democracies have managed to consolidate themselves when they have been able to transform the constitutionalization contest into a drive for democratization. But this outcome cannot be taken for granted, because if discord in an open system is not *self-disciplined*, it may paralyze that system (as happened in the USA in the period 1861–5). In light of the experience on the other side of the Atlantic, one may say that it is not opposition to constitutionalization that should be a cause of concern, but rather the inability of the contenders to develop a public discourse inclusive of their differences. Permanent dialogue on interpretation of the supra-states or supranational pact should be conducted with concepts and in a language which by their nature allow 'creative disagreement' (Lord and Magnette 2004). If the constitution is viewed as an open process, this creative disagreement may draw on the diverse traditions and visions reflecting the legal pluralism of such democracies for creating a common constitutional patriotism (Delmas-Marty 2002). Both the USA and the EU are constitutionally op-ed polities which can be held together by a *method* to handle disagreement, rather than by a *model* for its resolution. And it could not be otherwise if it is true that both are informed by a principle of multiple legitimacy. Multiple legitimacies generate competition and conflict (and not only cohabitation and coexistence) (Kohler-Koch 2000; Fossum 2003). Indeed, compound democracies cannot rely on previously established (cultural) identities for settling their differences. Their people or *demos* is created through contestation on rules and norms, if that con-testation is expressed through a shared language and accepted procedures. This is why, as it has been in the USA, in compound democracies the supranational identity has a political nature. It is instrumental and not primordial, it is *post hoc* and not *ex ante*. Unions of states cannot rely on a pre-constituted common identity for resolving conflicts between states and between citizens. That identity is the outcome and not the premise of their functioning. A supranational identity that will not substitute, but complement, the specific national identities of the states constituting the compound democracy.

In sum, in compound democracies, the process counts more than the ends pursued, pluralism more than uniformity, deliberation more than decision (Checkel 2001). In compound democracies, constitutional differences are systemic and not contingent. Of course, also noncompound democracies with governmental fusion of powers (such as Canada, Schultze 2000) have internal differences in interpretation of their constitutions. But these differences may be resolved by the winning political and electoral majority (although it might be advisable not to do so). There are no majorities, either political or electoral, in compound democracies. The USA has ruled them out by choice, the EU by necessity. Of course, the history of the USA has not always complied with the theory. However, two centuries later, the USA still works as a compound democracy, despite enormous challenges it has had to face. The EU is a compound democracy by necessity because it still cannot rely on an adequate and shared justification of its existence. The debate that has finally begun at the European level on the CT has provided an extraordinary opportunity to discuss the reasons for integration with the only inclusive language available, that is, constitutional language. The outcome of the debate is less important than the debate itself. What really matters for the future of Europe is that this debate should construct a discourse able to frame a dialogue on the reasons for the differences among Europeans. As the Americans, also 'Europeans' can be constructed through a constitutional process, although the weight of their historical identities will certainly make this construction much more difficult than the construction of Americans (Citrin and Sides 2003). But in order to develop this discourse, Europeans must refer to an accepted common document which delimits the powers of the institutions and defines the rights and duties of citizens. No matter whether this base document is called a 'constitution' or a 'constitutional treaty' or a 'basic treaty'. What is important is that it should be able to structure European conflictual conversation on the constitutional order best suited to a union of twenty-seven or more member-states and almost half a billion citizens. A union of such magnitude cannot be held together by a common constitutional identity (or, for that matter, by a single sovereignty, Aalberts 2004). What is required is a shared willingness to discuss that identity.

Only dialogue couched in a common language can unite what divides Europeans. Certainly, that dialogue is possible if all the member-states and all important social groups (regardless of their size, history, interests, and culture) see it as advantageous to belong to a larger aggregate able to guarantee internal peace and external security, indispensable conditions for promoting economic growth and democratic values in all of them.

9.7. Conclusion

The Brussels Convention and the Convention which elaborated the Charter of Rights presented at the Nice IGC on December 2000 represent the first attempts to deal with the question of the constitutional legitimacy of the EU. Although the EU is a constitutionalized political regime, the CT elaborated by the Brussels Convention and revised by the European Council has tried to move the EU from a *material* to a *formal* constitutional order. The CT has fundamentally tried to give a formal recognition to the quasi-constitutional nature of the EU (Mény 2003). The CT, incorporating the Charter of Rights and rationalizing the existent structure of multiple separation of powers, has defined the boundaries of the European constitutional pluralism. Certainly, its Preamble, institutional structure, recognition of fundamental rights, and definition of sources of European law, are proper of a pact among states and their citizens, and not of the pact among individuals proper of the EU member-states' constitutional documents. Through the CT the EU has substituted a material constitution with a formal one. But it is a formal constitution for a union of states. And in a union of states the concept itself of constitutionalism is open to discussion; indeed it is, or may be, a matter of intense dispute. In a compound democracy the constitution is a *process* more than it is a *document*. Precisely because of its compound nature, the EU is subject to a process of contested constitutionalization: a process, that is, in which opposing views on the constitution are bound periodically to enter into a conflict which is never definitively resolved. As it happened and continues to happen in the USA. Hence, in compound democracies the constitution is not solely a project; it is above all a process—indeed, it is an endless process. The process for the approval of the CT has transformed the EU from a *constitutional project* (Walker 2004) to a *constitutional process* (Shaw 2005)— a process comprising conflict among diverse arguments, principles, and visions concerning the organization that European compound democracy should assume, the strategies that should be pursued to restrict the power of the Community actors participating in authoritative decisions, and the guarantees that should be introduced to promote individual rights and to protect social ones.

This experience is assimilating the EU to the USA. The USA has based its own development on the theory of an *anti-hierarchical and anti-hegemonic polity* where no specific interest (supra-states, state, sectional, economic, social, political) should have the chance to transform itself into *the* general interest. Thus limiting the concentration of powers through their dispersion and fragmentation has been functional to the need to guarantee a dynamic equilibrium among a multitude of 'ambitions' or institutional interests. By contrast, the EU is a compound polity which needs to construct its own theory for being a fully coherent compound democracy (Friese and Wagner 2002). 'Without a robust theory and practice of division and separation, it is difficult to construct fuller unions that are not hierarchical' (Deudney 1995: 226). The EU has to elaborate a theory of separation and sharing of powers for guaranteeing a 'dynamic equilibrium' among asymmetrical member-states and their citizens. Such equilibrium implies the systemic preclusion of the formation of stable majorities able to control the polity across the board. To keep together distinct (national, ethnic, cultural, linguistic, historical) communities it is necessary to guarantee each of them that their interests will be taken into consideration. At the same moment, such equilibrium has to be based on a dynamic confrontation between different views of the polity. Such confrontation is a condition for creating a shared identity, if conducted with the same language. In this endeavor, it is not the USA which should be a model for the EU; rather, it is the Madisonian approach (Fabbrini and Sicurelli 2004) to the compound of separated and sovereign states and their citizens which might be helpful to achieve a better understanding of the dilemmas facing the European integration process. As Ostrom (1987: 9) remarked:

[for Europeans] (t)o find [the American, *ndr*] theory useful for thinking about problems does *not* mean that Europe should copy the American model. That would show intellectual poverty—of doing no more than imitating the American example. The task, rather, is to use conceptions and the associated theoretical apparatus as intellectual tools to think through problems and make an independent assessment of appropriate ways for addressing the problem of contemporary Europe.

10

Conclusion: The puzzle of compound democracy: a comparative perspective

10.1. Introduction

Compound democracies, like the USA and the EU, are unions of asymmetrical states and their citizens. Because of that, they need to function with weak decision-making systems (i.e. systems which make it difficult to take decisions). Such a weakness is a guarantee that none of the states or interests involved in the polity will ever be in the condition to impose its will on the others. Thus, decision-making power is separated and shared by a plurality of actors operating within a multitude of reciprocally independent institutions. Such dispersion of power implies also a dispersion of responsibility. Compound democracies are democracies *without a government as a single institution,* and yet they have to take authoritative decisions. Certainly, in specific historical periods and in specific policy realms, both in the USA and the EU one or another of the separated institutions sharing powers had the possibility of playing a preeminent role vis-à-vis the other institutions. In the USA, it was the Congress which played this role in the nineteenth century, and the President in the following one. But, with the congressional reaction to presidential abuses of power at the end of the 1960s, the executive's preeminence has been continuously questioned by the legislature and the vast coalition of interest and institutions supporting it. In the EU, in the early decades of the integration process, the Council of Ministers functioned as an institution able to monopolize ultimate decision-making power (Dinan 2005). But since the 1986 SEA, and thereafter the 1992 Treaty of Maastricht which organized it into three pillars, the EU (particularly in the first pillar) has progressively structured itself as a system in which several institutions (the Council of Ministers, the Commission, the EP, and the

European Council) separately but jointly contribute to numerous public policy decisions. Moreover, the several waves of enlargement have progressively transformed the same Council of Ministers into a multilateral institution, where none of the member-states' governments is any longer in the condition to exercise a hegemonic role or to impose its unilateral decision on the others. However, decision-making structures which diffuse power also diffuse responsibility. In compound democracies, it is systemically difficult to detect 'who is responsible for what'. Indeed, the USA and the EU have been regularly exposed to the accusation of being characterized by a democratic deficit, although of a different degree. This is the puzzle compound democracies have to manage. They need weak decision-making and unclear accountability systems for preserving internal compoundness. However, decision-making weakness obstructs their operative capacity and unclear accountability alienates their citizens.

By contrast, noncompound democratic systems are organized around a government, regardless of whether this is formed by competitive or consensual means (Fabbrini 2005*d*). The political experience of noncompound European nation-states is based on the fusion of governmental powers, with the executive expressing a legislative majority and thus authorized to have the monopoly of decision-making power. This legislative majority may be the outcome of different electoral and party processes. In consensual democracies, the legislative majority results from a long-drawn-out process of consultation and bargaining between party elites after the election, resulting generally in an oversized coalition government. In competitive democracies, the legislative majority results from bipolar or two-party electoral competition, resulting generally in one-party or limited coalition government. In both cases, decision-making power is concentrated in the cabinet or executive, which brings together government and parliament. The concentration of this power makes it also possible to identify who is in charge of it, 'who is responsible for what'. To be sure, many European nation-states have become territorially noncentralized in that they aggregate territorial units to which they grant powers and competences distinct from those of the center (according to a federal model in Germany, Belgium, Austria, and of course in Switzerland; or according to a quasi-federal model in Spain and the Netherlands; or according to a regional model in Italy, France, and Britain). Yet none of these noncentralized democracies (apart from Switzerland) combines a vertical separation of powers with a horizontal one (among governmental institutions). Thus, even those European democracies which introduced separation of powers at the territorial or vertical level have never challenged the fusion of power at the governmental or horizontal level. They are generally parliamentary democracies, that is, democracies with a fusion of powers. And this also applies to semi-presidential systems (like that of France of the Fifth Republic) whose sovereignty resides in a legislative assembly. In short, noncompound democracies are democracies of undivided sovereignty (MacCormick 1999), which means of concentrated decision-making and clear accountability patterns.

In this concluding chapter, I try to better conceptualize the puzzle of compound democracy, through a comparison of the decision-making and accountability patterns of the USA and EU with those proper of noncompound European nation-states. Because the USA is much more institutionalized than the EU as compound democracy, it is inevitable that it will be the main focus of comparison with noncompound democracies. However, if the EU is moving in the direction of the compound USA, then similar trends may be expected to emerge in both of them. Of course, this is an analytical exercise which stresses predominant trends rather than reconstructing detailed processes. For that, I will consider Europe separately, as both compound EU and noncompound European nation-states, although the two are more and more integrated as EU member-states. This distinction is however necessary for better understanding the change which has taken place between a Europe of nation-states and a Europe of EU member-states.

10.2. Decision-making Patterns in Compound and Noncompound Democracies

10.2.1. *Compound Democracies: The USA and the EU*

A decision-making process can be analyzed in relation to three levels: (*a*) the institutional nature of its structure; (*b*) the locus where ultimate decisions are taken; and (*c*) the number of actors involved (see Table 10.1). Regarding the first level, compound democracies are structured around separated powers. The American decision-making structure has become even more separated as it shifted from the congressional to presidential government. Whereas during the congressional government period, the Congress was the main arena of decision-making, in the subsequent presidential government period the decision-making process became more segmented and diffused. In fact, whereas in the former period separation

Table 10.1 Patterns of decision-making in compound and noncompound democracies

Levels of analysis	Structure of decision-making	Locus of the decision-making	Actors of the decision-making
Compound democracies	*Separated*	*Dispersed*	*Many*
Compound USA (congressional government)	Within Congress and between Congress and the states	Congressional committees, parties' caucuses, institutional leadership offices, state legislatures	Party and congressional leaders, state party leaders
Compound USA (presidential government)	Within Congress and between Congress and the President	Presidency, congressional Speakerships, congressional committees	President, House and Senate institutional leaders, interest groups' representatives, lobbyists
Compound EU (post-1992 Maastricht)	Within Community institutions and between them and member-states	Within and between Council, Commission, EP, Community comitology	Member-states' government leaders, member-states' ministers, Commission President and commissioners, MEPs, experts and interest groups' representatives
Noncompound democracies	*Fused*	*Centralized*	*Few*
Noncompound Europe (competitive parliamentarianism)	Parliamentary majority-Cabinet	Cabinet	Prime Minister (*primus super pares*)
Noncompound Europe (consensual parliamentarianism)	Parliamentary groups-Cabinet-party headquarters network	Cabinet and party headquarters	Prime Minister (*primus inter pares*), ministers and party leaders
Noncompound Europe (consonant semi-presidentialism)	Parliament-Cabinet-Presidency of Republic	Executive (Presidency of the Republic)	President of the Republic (*primus sine pares*)
Noncompound Europe (dissonant semi-presidentialism)	Parliament-Cabinet-Presidency of the Republic	Executive (Cabinet)	Prime Minister (*primus super pares*)

of powers was mainly separation within Congress and between Congress and states' legislatures, in the latter period the growth of the presidential role has further multiplied the arenas involved in the decision-making process. This, of course, complicated the role of creating bridges and links between the various institutions. In the congressional government period, the decision-making link within the legislature and between the latter and the states passed through the state and congressional parties and leaderships, especially the majority party leadership. Whereas in the presidential government period, the link passed more through both the congressional and presidential parties. Even more internally separated is the decision-making structure of the EU. Especially after the 1992 Maastricht Treaty, a growing number of policies are discussed and decided through the involvement of the Council of Ministers, the Commission, the EP, and member-states' institutions (such as their parliaments, subnational governments, and judiciaries).

A separated decision-making structure inevitably implies a dispersion of the locus where decisions are taken. In compound USA, during the congressional government period, the main loci of decision-making were the congressional committee structure and institutional leadership offices, plus state legislatures which retained important powers; whereas in the presidential government period the loci included the presidency (especially on foreign policy issues) and the main offices of congressional power (especially on issues of domestic politics, such as the House Speakership, committee chairpersons, the Senate leaders). Even here, the EU seems to exacerbate the dispersion of the decision-making process. The loci where decisions are taken are a multitude, with each institution multiplying at its turn the locus within itself. At the same time, in compound democracies many are the actors involved in the decision-making process. If in the congressional government era, the states' party and legislative leaders were the main actors, many more actors came to play a role in the presidential government era. The President first of all, but also the House and Senate institutional leaders, the chairmen of the most influential committees (such as Appropriations, Ways and Means, and Budget Committees in the House or Appropriations, Foreign Relations, and Judiciary Committees in the Senate), and the leaders of the congressional caucuses, and a multitude of private actors. In sum, 'in America the separation of legislative and executive institutions ensures that...there is no central point for decision-making. Responsibility is diffused. If senior officials are to be politically neutral, who in Washington is the government and who the opposition?' (Heclo 1986: 104). Again, the number of actors contributing to the decision-making process is even larger in the EU, also because there is no such convention, as in the USA, to recognize the preeminence of certain actors (such as the President) in certain policy fields (such as foreign and military policy). Certainly, in the modern presidency era, the American system of government has enhanced the President's role (also through the personalization of his office). But this has not strengthened his decision-making capacities. Because the President must operate in a separation of powers system, the personalization of his role has paradoxically reduced his governmental resources by weakening the party and institutional connections between himself and the Congress. Only the onset of a serious international threat (as happened after 9/11/2001) introduced pressure to discipline the relations between branches of government, to locate the decision-making power in the presidential office, and to authorize the President to behave as Commander-in-Chief. Nevertheless, those pressures soon met with insurmountable constraints. Even in the presidential era, no actor is able to control for long the decision-making process monopolistically.

10.2.2. Noncompound Democracies: The Case of European Nation-States

In the European fusion of power systems, decision-making has taken a quite different form. Let us start with the case of competitive parliamentarianism, whose systemic imperative is the reaching and implementing of governmental decisions (Lijphart 1999). By voting for a party, or for a coalition of a few parties, the electors indirectly appoint a government; that is, they elect a clear parliamentary majority (which does not necessarily correspond to an electoral majority where elections are based on plurality uninominal electoral systems) which enables the winning party or coalition thus appointed to govern. 'British voters are presented with programs, frequently clearly defined, which the victorious party, by virtue of its theoretical "mandate", considers itself committed to implementing' (Mény and Knapp 1998: 225). And it can govern, because the decision-making structure which supports its action is fused. The cabinet is an expression of the parliamentary majority, it is its executive branch. However, because of its electoral legitimacy and superior technical capacity, reverse relations between the two came soon to develop. It is the cabinet now which leads its own parliamentary majority, imposing its will on the various policies in question. The fused structure of the decision-making allows the government to take decisions, on whose basis policy results are achieved, which are then submitted to the electors for their approval or condemnation in the following election.

The bipolar or two-party nature of political competition, and the government–opposition dynamic which drives parliamentary activity, has tended even in this case to personalize the electoral battle and thus governmental action. The leaders of the two major parties, with their personal characteristics, significantly influence the public representation of the political conflict. This electoral personalization, once the government has been formed, has made the Prime Minister the main actor of the decision-making process (allowing him or her to act as *primus super pares* of the other ministers). It has led, that is, to the 'presidentialization' of the premiership. However, the 'presidentialization' of the premiership, and therefore of the cabinet, has encountered the major obstacle constituted by the principle of collective (party) responsibility on which parliamentarianism is institutionally based. While in the 1980s, Doring (1987: 123) wrote that 'it is the dependence of the chief executive on election by his party that effectively militates against whatever presidential features there may be in the [British] Prime Minister's powers', recent studies have shown that modern parliamentary democracies 'provide ample evidence of the extent of structurally induced presidentialization' (Poguntke and Webb 2005*b*: 21). Nevertheless, although many parliamentary democracies evince the 'erosion of more collective partified forms of politics... we do not suggest that [presidentialized forms of politics have] entirely supplanted them' (Webb and Poguntke 2005: 336). Thus, in competitive parliamentary Europe as well, the political link between the executive and the legislature continues to be the majority party; the locus of decision-making continues to be an executive made up of party politicians (i.e. the cabinet); and the main actor continues to be the Prime Minister, because of her or his role as party leader, although constrained by the collegial nature of the cabinet system.

The crucial role of the parties in the decision-making process has grown even more pronounced in consensual parliamentarianism. Here, the government's composition is the outcome of postelectoral negotiations among the main parties in the political system, each of them representing a cultural, ethnic, religious, linguistic, or territorial constituency that must be included (consociated) in the government formation. In consensual parliamentary Europe, therefore, the decision-making structure is still fused, being constituted by an executive nested in the parliament. However, that fusion has implied not only institutions (legislature, and its parliamentary groups, and executive), but also extra-parliamentary organizations. However, the locus of decision-making has still remained the cabinet, although many decisions are taken through an informal involvement of the extra-parliamentary party headquarters, connected to the executive through their ministers in the coalitional executive. Thus, the main decision-making actors have been generally a group of politicians, not all of them necessarily with a formal role in the government. In coalition governments, the Prime Minister has acted as the mediator, or referee, among the various party factions represented within the executive, and she or he has performed more the role of its chairman than of its leader. In sum, she or he has been largely a *primus inter pares* because she or he has been prevented from imposing his or her will on the other members of the executive (see Table 10.1). Because consensual parliamentarianism is significantly less centralized than competitive parliamentarianism, it continues to provide an extraordinarily favorable environment for party action.

European semi-presidential systems, and specifically the semi-presidentialism of France of the Fifth Republic, display a pattern of decision-making different from that of parliamentary systems, although it should not be confounded with the pattern of compound democracies. Because of its indivisible sovereignty, also France of the Fifth Republic has a fused structure of decision-making, although the direct and separated (from the parliament) election of the President of the Republic makes the integration between legislative and executive powers more complex. However, the parliament is the only institution representing popular sovereignty. As such, its support or confidence is necessary to the executive for explicating its institutional role. Although elected separately from the parliament, the President of the Republic does not enjoy an independent executive power, for example he cannot veto laws approved by the parliament. He has been asssigned a *domain reservée* in military policy, he has a role in nominating high public civil servants, he can claim exceptional powers in emergency contexts as envisaged by article 16 of the constitution, but he is not a separated power in itself. Indeed, he is one of the two heads of the executive, with the Prime Minister being the other. The decision-making structure is thus fused around the network parliament–cabinet–presidency of the Republic, where the latter two represent properly the executive power, the main locus of the decision-making process.

In France, because of the direct and separated election of the head of state and because the parliament is organized on the basis of a majoritarian (uninominal runoff) electoral formula, it has been possible to introduce serious disincentives against fragmentation of the party system (Elgie 1997). Unlike other semi-presidential systems based on PR (such as Finland's and pre-1982 Portugal's), the French one has thus induced the party system to aggregate around two poles since its marked fragmentation under the Fourth Republic. Indeed, French politics during the Fifth Republic were structured around a *quadrille bipolaire* (which became, in the 2000s, a two-party competition) which efficaciously implemented a political logic based on government versus opposition. However, as we know, the distinct election of the President and the parliament has had major consequences on decision-making by the Janus-faced executive, producing situations of *political consonance* or *political dissonance* between the presidential and parliamentary majorities. When the presidential and parliamentary majorities resulting from the election have coincided (political consonance), the President has been the effective leader of the government (and the leadership of the government was more individual than collective). In this case, the President usually appointed a Prime Minister of his choice, although the candidate has had to enjoy the confidence (even if indirect) of the parliament (and of the parties in the majority). The President certainly had to take account of his party's wishes (and those of the other parties in the coalition), but his predominance has been generally accepted by his supporters. Thus, the President's dominant role as the individual leader of the decision-making process has not been questioned. The legitimacy deriving from his direct popular election has transformed him into a *primus sine pares* within the executive. However, when the presidential and parliamentary majorities did not coincide (political dissonance), the decision-making process has displayed a different pattern from the previous one. The Prime Minister has been able to prevail over the President and consequently strengthened the role of the parties in the parliament (Elgie 1993), although she or he has had to take account of the President's views, especially in military and foreign relations. Thus, in dissonant semi-presidential France as in competitive parliamentary Europe, the decision-making link has been formed by the parties in the majority coalition; the locus of decision-making has been the cabinet; and the main actor has been the Prime Minister acting as a *primus super pares* among his ministers, although not toward the President of the Republic (see Table 10.1). It remains to be seen whether the 2000 constitutional reform (see Chapter 3) will reduce the chances of political dissonance.

10.3. Crisis Management in the USA and European Nation-States

Have these different decision-making patterns had repercussions on the crisis management capacities of the American and European governmental systems? I will not consider here the case of the EU, because of its limited experience of crisis management. One might argue (Polsby 1984) that crisis management is the system's capacity to react to/anticipate a breakdown in the political or institutional equilibrium. One might further argue that a crisis is whatever someone in power officially declares it to be, even though this declaration must then be sufficiently realistic to elicit sufficient consensus among the other actors in the system. If so, then how a crisis is defined may have differing implications for domestic and foreign policy. Whereas an international crisis produces an across-the-board identification with the leader of the government (in European nation-states), or of the executive (in the USA), who makes it official and therefore creates support for the policies that she or he adopts to deal with it, a domestic crisis may not lead to either identification or support, because different interests and groups may perceive the crisis in different ways (some may suffer while others may profit from it). In sum, if war is an equalizer, unemployment may be a divider. That said, it can be argued that compound US and noncompound European democracies have differed in crisis management as well (Fabbrini 1995).

In American history, responsibility for crisis management has been assigned to the President, and not only in foreign policy. After all, the institution of a monocratic executive has been an antenna sensitive to the malaise of public opinion, but also an operational instrument with which to respond to 'sudden attacks' or to deal with emergency situations. As Shklar (1991: 74) has pointed out, in periods of change ever since the Jacksonian period of the 1830s, the President has been required to be the representative 'of the people as a whole ... Only the President can act as the tribune of the people and protect them against the predatory assaults of the money-power' or against the threats of a foreign power. Thus, even during the long century of congressional government, the President was expected to act as the people's representative in emergency situations, although not all the presidents fulfilled that expectation. But of course it was in the subsequent period of presidential government that the President came to play the main or exclusive decision-making role in emergency situations. Yet the President's crisis management capacity has manifested a basic weakness: it can only be effective in the short run.

In order to understand the reasons for this weakness, one must look at the presidential role in the context of the American electoral cycle.

In a classic study devoted to understanding the features of the (then) 'new' presidential era, Rossiter (1956) pointed out that the American President has come to concentrate into his person approximately ten constitutional and political roles: among constitutional roles, those of head of state, head of government, head of the diplomatic service, head of the armed forces, and principal initiator of legislation; among political ones, those of party leader, leader of public opinion, manager of economic prosperity, leader of the Western alliance, and chief administrator of the executive. If one excludes those political roles (such as leader of the Western alliance, and manager of economic prosperity) that stemmed from the importance assumed by the USA during the Cold War, and those constitutional roles resulting from the country's specific institutional dynamics, then as regards his remaining roles, at least formally, there is no significant difference between the President (of the presidential era) on the one hand, and the Prime Minister in a European parliamentary system and the President of the Republic in the French semi-presidential system, on the other. Both the former and the latter have played a role in legislation; they have usually been the leaders of the parties; they have presided over the administrative apparatus of the executive; and they have tended to focus the attention of public opinion. However, if one moves from the formal level to that of political behavior, clear and major differences emerge.

Unlike a Prime Minister, who cannot operate against the parliamentary majority, and unlike a semi-presidential President, who needs at least the passive support of a parliamentary majority, the American President can operate without the confidence of the Congress, which is not institutionally constrained by any form of co-responsibility toward the executive. Indeed, both the American President and Congress represent electoral constituencies which differ from each other. Thus, the President is certainly more independent than a Prime Minister or a semi-presidential President, but also more lacking of political support than the latter. As a consequence, the President has been forced to rely more and more on public opinion, appealing to it for support in his dealings with the separated Congress. The President has 'gone public', as we know (Kernell 1992). Of course, the European prime ministers, too, have gone increasingly public, especially in crisis situations. But, unlike the American President, they do not have to appeal to public opinion in order to neutralize the legislature. By definition, European prime ministers enjoy the active support of the parliamentary majority or (in the case of minority governments) the nonactive opposition of the majority of parliamentary members, whereas this is not the institutional condition of the American President. One might say that in the case of the American President, the support of public opinion has frequently replaced support by the party, whereas for a European Prime Minister, it has complemented it.

Indeed, in the second half of the twentieth century (with the significant exception of the period 2003–6), the American President had to build a legislative majority coalition for each of his proposals, crossing party lines and personal idiosyncrasies (Rockman 1985). Nothing similar has been required of the European governmental leaders in the post–World War II period. In both competitive and consensual parliamentary systems, the Prime Minister has been the point of arrival of a legislative majority, whereas the American President has frequently been its point of departure (Kernell 2005). The difference with respect to the semi-presidential President has been equally clear-cut: whereas the French President can govern only if he has a parliamentary majority which supports him, the power of the American President does not depend on the legislature's confidence. However, while the role of the American President is institutionally undisputed, it might nevertheless be politically constrained. Given that the system of government is unable to foster, on a systemic basis, the growth of stable and recognizable party majorities around the President except in extraordinary periods of threat, the President is forced to inject increasing doses of public opinion appeal (popular leadership) into his governmental leadership.

How has the complexity of the presidential roles impinged on the presidential capacity to manage crisis situations? In the USA, the President has enjoyed the evident advantage, compared with the Prime Minister of a parliamentary system, of being able to initiate, with resoluteness and decisiveness, a new course of action designed to deal with a crisis situation. This advantage has been obvious since the beginnings of presidential government. However, the President may fully exercise his power only if the crisis is brief and explosive. If, instead, the crisis is prolonged, and therefore of lesser impact, and because the President needs the support of Congress to handle the crisis, the system of the separation of powers has activated powerful conditioning mechanisms. Major foreign policy crises, such as the Vietnam War of the 1960s or the Iraq War of the 2000s, have revealed this temporally constrained pattern of crisis management. The President has certainly used such crises to increase his role vis-à-vis the Congress, but at the same time he has been obliged to deal with them within the short time constraint of the congressional electoral cycle. This has been a 'short' time constraint because, in the USA, the electoral cycle starts anew every two years with the election of all the members of the House and one-third of the members of the Senate. This permanent electoral campaign (King 1997) has conditioned the members of Congress in their support for presidential initiatives, especially in foreign policy. A war is rarely popular, especially when it has no clear deadline, because it exacts more lives and taxes than voters are willing to accept.

Certainly the President may temporally neutralize this short-term constraint, especially the midterm election one, for example (as Lyndon B. Johnson did in 1966 or George W. Bush in 2002) promoting or supporting congressional candidates sympathetic with his need to run a war in a longer perspective. Indeed, in both cases, the two presidents were able to get more time from the Congress for pursuing their military strategies in a foreign country (Vietnam and Iraq). However, in both cases, the lack of any significant immediate success on the field led to electoral upheaval and discontent that Congress, in the end, had to represent. This is why it is said that US intervention in Vietnam was firstly defeated in Washington, DC (and this probably will be said also of the intervention in Iraq). Thus, it is not only for cultural but also for institutional reasons that the USA has always found it difficult to transform itself into an imperial country engaged in occupying and administering a foreign country on a prolonged basis. The electoral logic of its governmental system does not favor prolonged crisis management by the President, even if the crisis requires it. Every modern American President has been aware that he must operate within the constraints of an electoral cycle which does not permit long-term planning of the management of a crisis (see Table 10.2). However, those constraints also offer an opportunity for checking presidential initiatives. If they do not help in supporting coherent good policies, nevertheless they hinder the continuation of coherent bad policies.

The experience of competitive parliamentary Europe has been quite different (King 2002). Here the Prime Minister cannot take the

Table 10.2 Crisis management in America and Europe

	short term	long term
Individual leadership	Separated America (presidential government) Semi-presidential Europe (France V—political dissonance)	Semi-presidential Europe (France V—political consonance)
Collective leadership	Consensual parliamentary Europe	Competitive parliamentary Europe

decision-making initiative but must first convince the cabinet (a difficult task in the case of a coalition government) and also her or his party (or the parties in the coalition). But if the crisis is prolonged, and if the Prime Minister's work of twofold persuasion has been successful, then she or he may implement his or her policies with determination. Institutional support from the executive and from (the majority of) the legislature has followed suit. The four to five years' cycle of parliamentary election leaves him or her sufficient room of maneuver in managing the foreign policy crisis. Certainly, when prime ministers have refrained from seeking this double support, adopting instead a presidential style of governing, they have usually run into trouble. In Britain, for example, Margaret Thatcher's (Prime Minister in the period 1979–90) and Tony Blair's (Prime Minister in the period 1997–2007) presidential prerogatives have been periodically contested by other ministers or party members in the parliamentary majority. In Thatcher's case, indeed, the party parliamentary leaders and the cabinet's most prominent members finally reminded her of the government's collective responsibility and, in 1990, dumped her with a simple majority vote by her party's parliamentary caucus. And in Blair's case, in reaction to his controversial decision to invade Iraq in the spring of 2003 in isolated alliance with the USA, a vociferous opposition group within the party has constantly reminded him that his decision did not enjoy its full support (or that of public opinion in the country). Nevertheless, because of the lack of institutional constraints, once the British Prime Minister has got the support of the government and the parliamentary majority, she or he is allowed to pursue a course of action with coherence, although such coherence may be utilized for a bad decision. Indeed, in noncompound (competitive) Europe vis-à-vis compound America, it is easier to pursue good decisions, but it is also much more difficult to interrupt a bad decision.

The historical evidence thus shows that also in parliamentary competitive Europe the Prime Minister plays a crucial role in managing a crisis, on the condition, however, that she or he is able to get the collective support of the cabinet (and the parliamentary majority). Systems with a fusion of powers do not have short time electoral cycle constraints (national elections for parliament are held every four to five years and there are no midterm elections in between, apart from regional or European ones which have no effect on national government); nor do they have an incentive structure which induces the legislature to maintain its distance from the executive. The electoral fate of the members of the parliamentary majority is the same as that of the members of the executive, for the two groups of politicians will stand together in the next elections: it is therefore not in their interest to criticize each other. Nor does the parliamentary majority have incentives to weaken the government's capacity to manage an international crisis. The crisis management capacity of European nation-states with consensual parliamentary systems has been different, though. Large coalition governments are generally fragile political enterprises. In consensual parliamentary Europe, more so than in the previous parliamentary system, it is the executive that has responsibility for dealing with crises, but it has been unable to rely on stable support from its partisan components. Indeed, in these systems, loyalty among the parties in the coalition is generally thin, and this has worked against cohesiveness in the executive when difficulties in crisis management arise. Thus, in consensual parliamentary Europe, the impetus for short-term solutions to crises has come from a coalition logic rather than from an electoral cycle (Table 10.2).

In the case of the French semi-presidential system—and assuming that the crisis is not of a magnitude to justify recourse by the President of the Republic to the exceptional powers envisaged by article 16 of the Fifth Republic constitution—crisis management has assumed different features in periods of political consonance or dissonance, although the preeminence of the President vis-à-vis the Prime Minister in dealing with an international crisis has been undisputed. Under conditions of political consonance, the President has fully utilized his direct legitimacy to undertake personal initiatives, although even the most personal of these initiatives subsequently has had to be submitted to the approval of the government and the parliamentary majority. Conversely, under conditions of political dissonance, the President of the Republic has necessarily had to seek the support of his adversary Prime Minister and the parliamentary majority backing him or her, with inevitable constraints on the time perspective of his handling of the crisis. Thus, whereas in the former case individual leadership has operated in a long-term horizon, in the latter the same individual leadership has been obliged to find a short-term solution lest it fall prisoner to an adverse parliamentary majority. Nor has the electoral cycle played a short-term constraining role on the President's management of an international crisis, in this system. The electoral fate of the President of the Republic has been the same as that of his parliamentary majority, because each of them has depended on the other for re-election (although the staggered election of the parliament and the President before the 2000 constitutional reform introduced some time constraints on the latter's choices). In conditions of political dissonance, divergences between the President and the parliament have inevitably pushed for short-time solutions.

Hence, although a system of government cannot deputize for the quality of a leader and his or her capacity to take appropriate decisions in conditions of crisis, the institutional features of that system may nevertheless contribute to that capacity if it exists in personal form (Reynolds 2002). The US system of government has induced the President to give priority to short-term solutions. He must apply rapid solutions to even complex situations which would probably require more prudent and gradual action, and he must seek to achieve immediate success to forestall institutional opposition. Obviously, however, the squeezing of every crisis into the short period has in certain circumstances had dramatic consequences both externally and domestically. Indeed, serious international crises imply a long-term approach in order to be solved or tamed, a possibility that the USA cannot guarantee its President (Chubb and Peterson 1989). By contrast, both parliamentary and semi-presidential Europe have institutional mechanisms which, given certain political conditions, ensure that a crisis can be addressed within a longer time frame. However, the American individual management of crises has enabled more reactive intervention in crisis situations than has the collective leadership of European nation-states.

10.4. Accountability Patterns in Compound and Noncompound Democracies

Accountability is an elusive concept in democratic theory (Przeworski, Stokes, and Manin 1999). The concept has a strongly subjective connotation, one peculiar to political cultures of a markedly individualistic stamp (generally speaking, the Anglo-Saxon cultures),[1] which emphasize the individual tie between representative and represented (Sartori 1968). In fact, being accountable and being responsible are not necessarily the same thing. Political responsibility in a democracy may express a program-based linkage—not simply one of personal trust—between the representatives and the represented; provided, of course, that one believes that its character should reflect a confrontation between opposing political coalitions or parties, not just between rival individual leaders or candidates. With these specifications, I now compare patterns of accountability in compound and noncompound democracies, on the assumption that accountability is a process which can be analyzed at three levels: *who* is the main actor subject to governmental accountability, to *which* institution does she or he have to give account between elections, and to *whom* does she or he have to give account at elections (see Table 10.3).

In compound democracies, where many actors contribute to the decision-making process, those required to account are many. In the US case, it is useful to distinguish between the congressional and the presidential periods. During the congressional government period, the main actors in the accountability process were the party elites of the House and Senate, in particular those controlling the majority in the two chambers, and their counterparts in the states. Between elections these were kept under control by the minority party in the Congress, or better the leadership of one chamber used its institutional resources for checking the leadership of the other chamber. Moreover, state legislatures and parties played an important role in controlling federal elites. At elections their behavior was evaluated by state voters mobilized by powerful state party machines. In the presidential government period, the accountability process has grown much more complex. If the nationalization process has reduced the role of state legislatures and party leaders, nevertheless it has also increased the number of federal actors involved in the decision-making process. Thus, not only the President but also each single congressman or congresswoman have to give account individually, to each other (and to public opinion), between elections and then to separated electorates during the election. Accountability is thus diffused in the American system of government, because so too is decision-making power. No elected official (not even the President) may represent the government as such: each of them must answer individually for his or her actions, although the parties have certainly played a coordinating role. Such dispersion of accountability is even more pronounced in the EU. Several are the individual actors involved in the process, several are the institutions to which they have to account between elections, several are the electorates to whom they have to respond. Also in the EU electoral accountability is fragmented and disaggregated.

Quite different is the accountability pattern of noncompound democracies. Here, the accountability is primarily a collective relation. It concerns collective actors (political parties) who account for their collective actions in the government. Whereas the US President has had limited, if not negligible, obligations as regards institutional accountability to both his party and cabinet, the extent of a European Prime Minister's accountability to both bodies has been considerable. The Prime Minister is appointed to office in competitive systems because she or he is (has

Table 10.3 Patterns of accountability in compound and noncompound democracies

Levels of analysis	Whose	To which (between elections)	To whom (at the elections)
Compound democracies	*Individual actors*	*Multiple institutions*	*Separated electorates*
Compound US (congressional government)	Congressional and party elites	Each chamber of Congress; state legislatures and parties	State and infra-state (district) voters
Compound US (presidential government)	President, House Speaker and Senate leaders, congressional committees' chairmen	Separated institutions (President, Senate, House, congressional committees)	Supra-state, state, and infra-state voters
Compound EU (post-1992 Maastricht)	Members of Council of Ministers and European Council, President and members of the Commission, EP representatives	Separated institutions (European Council, Council of Ministers, Commission, EP)	Electors voting for national and electors voting for EU offices
Noncompound democracies	*Collective actors*	*Single institution*	*Unified electorate*
Noncompound Europe (competitive parliamentarianism)	Cabinet	Parliamentary opposition	National electorate
Noncompound Europe (consensual parliamentarianism)	Cabinet-party elites	Network of party elites	National electorate
Noncompound Europe (consonant semi-presidentialism)	Executive (President of the Republic *and* Cabinet)	Parliamentary opposition	National electorate
Noncompound Europe (dissonant semi-presidentialism)	Executive (Prime Minister *plus* Cabinet)	Parliamentary opposition	National electorate

been or is considered to be) the leader of the majority party or of the major party of the coalition; and in consensual systems with coalition governments because she or he enjoys the trust of the parliamentary majority as a whole, and of the party leaders of its various components. This is why, in competitive parliamentary Europe, the cabinet is the main actor to give account, and as a collegial entity it is checked by another collective actor—the parliamentary opposition—between elections; it is then to the national electorate that the government will give account at the next elections. In consensual parliamentary Europe, by contrast, the various elites of the parties composing the government, more than the executive as such, are the main actors in the accountability process. However, they act as representatives of collective actors, if not of collective identities. The party elites take the most important decisions, whether or not they are comprised within the formal structure of the executive. Here, the fusion among the Prime Minister, the cabinet, and the parliamentary majority is politically guaranteed by permanent negotiations between the party leaders constituting the latter (Blondel and Muller-Rommel 1993). In large coalition governments, the elites of each party check the elites of the other parties. There is no formal role for the opposition. At elections, each party appeals to its historical section of the electorate for reconfirmation as its representative, regardless of what that party has accomplished in government. It is a 'prospective' accountability. The case of competitive parliamentary Europe is different. In a bipolar or two-party political system, the national electorate can pass 'retrospective' judgment on the government's actions (and those of its parliamentary majority). Finally, in consensual parliamentary Europe, the role of public opinion is less important than it is in competitive parliamentary Europe as long as the electorate is segmented into different communities of identity which identify with one or another party.

Semi-presidential France, again, has displayed different patterns of accountability, according to whether consonance or dissonance has obtained between the presidential and parliamentary majorities (Elgie 2003). Also here, the actors involved in the accountability relations are mainly collective, although the personal election of the President of the Republic has added an individual element to that collective relation. At times of political dissonance the Prime Minister has exerted effective control over the government and its activities thanks to the support of his or her party, so that she or he and his or her executive (i.e. the majority party or coalition) have been the principal actor in the accountability process. At times of political consonance, by contrast, the President has been the main actor required to account for the decisions taken, although he has frequently eluded such accountability by shifting blame to the Prime Minister (Suleiman 1994). Not infrequently, the Prime Minister has acted as a 'lightning rod' for the President, thereby obscuring his accountability.[2] It should be noted, however, that the blame-avoiding game has also taken place in conditions of political dissonance, with the Prime Minister using the excuse of presidential constraints on his or her action to justify poor performance. Between elections, in conditions of consonance, the President and his executive have had to answer not only to the parliamentary opposition but to public opinion as well, given the popular role of the President of the Republic. By contrast, in conditions of dissonance, once the Prime Minister has gained the support of his or her party and cabinet, she or he has had to answer mainly to the parliamentary opposition, which has been able to confront the executive in parliament. Here, the pattern has been very similar to that of competitive parliamentary Europe. In the cases of both consonance and dissonance, the final stage in the accountability process has been controlled by the national electorate, which has been able to pass retrospective judgment on the government and its leaders.

Thus, from the point of view of accountability as well, the compound pattern has been significantly different from the noncompound one. In the USA, the presidential transformation of the separated government since the 1930s has required the legislature to be the main check over the executive. Although, in the post–World War II period, the Congress pursued different strategies to deal with presidential preeminence (cooperation, conflict, subordination; Dodd 2004), it was nevertheless the most powerful restraint on the President, especially during periods of divided government. Indeed, when the legislature chose not to exercise its constitutional control on the President, as it did in 1965–8 and especially in 2003–6, the outcome was the 'imperial presidency' (Schlesinger 1973, 2004; Rudalevige 2005). In the EU, the post-Maastricht institutionalization of a separated system has strengthened the checks and balances between institutions, favoring the formation of a system of interlocking bodies. One might argue that, in compound democracies, in-between-elections accountability is institutionally guaranteed. Congress is the main check on the President (Polsby 1997*b*); the EP and the Commission are the main checks on the Council of Ministers. In noncompound democracies, in contrast, it is politically guaranteed. The government is controlled by the parliamentary opposition in both competitive parliamentary and semi-presidential Europe, or by its internal party elites in consensual parliamentary Europe. Thus, in noncompound democracies, the mechanism of in-between-elections accountability has been activated by political parties (either in the form of parliamentary opposition or in that of reciprocal control between party elites), whereas in compound democracies it has been activated by institutions. Of course, this has been made possible in noncompound democracies by the existence of a single institutional arena (the legislative assembly) and in compound democracies of many institutional arenas where decisions are taken.

Moreover, in compound democracies there is no such entity as a national electorate. The various decision-makers have to account to distinct and separated electorates, at the infra-state, state, and supra-state level. Without a national electorate, there is no electoral mandate the elected have to respect. When power is segmented, also accountability is fractured. In sum, if in noncompound democracies there is a government, at the top of the decision-making structure, which take decisions for the polity (*erga omnes*) and thus accounts for them as a collective actor, in compound democracies such a pattern is implausible. In compound democracies, decisions are taken by individual actors, operating within separated institutions and on behalf of separated electorates. No collective entity (a majority party or coalition operating through a centralized executive) may emerge. Although the USA is a much more rationalized compound democracy than the EU, in both cases it is evidently difficult to answer the question: 'who is responsible for what?'

10.5. Conclusion

Instead of evaluating the EU and the USA on the basis of the democratic criteria elaborated on the basis of the European nation-states' experiences, it is better to understand why they function so differently from the latter. The USA and the EU are primarily unions of asymmetrical states which had to resort to different criteria for making their democratic life possible. There is no universal standard of democratic organization. Indeed, the USA and the EU represent, in their own way, an original attempt to extend democracy beyond the borders of a *single republic*. For this reason, they have had to organize themselves in such a way as to prevent the formation of a majority able to control the entire system, without giving up the requirement to legitimize their structure of authority through popular will. Thus, with the development of the EU, the difference between America and Europe in their decision-making and accountability patterns has significantly diminished. The EU, as the USA, is a multiple separation of powers system where the loci of decision-making are dispersed and many are the actors involved in the final decision. In the EU, as in the USA, in-between-elections accountability has been guaranteed by institutional checks and balances rather than by party opposition. Thus, both the USA and the EU govern through separated and concurrent majorities. In compound democracies there is no unified legislative majority, able to govern through a centralized institution (a cabinet or a government) and thus required to account collectively for its behavior. Certainly, the USA is a much more structured compound democracy than the EU. In the USA, the definition of the roles of the various federal institutions is generally clear and recognized. In the EU, such definition is frequently open to question (Shelcher 2005). Indeed, Community institutions govern through steering, in the sense, as Sbragia (2000: 236) remarked, that they are 'structurally designed to keep certain substantive questions off the table while insisting that others be kept on the table'. Nevertheless, the USA (Committee on the Constitutional System 1987; Jones 1997) and the EU have much more difficulty in taking decisions and in making accountable those who took them than noncompound democracies. These patterns appear particularly hindering when compound democracies have to deal with global responsibilities and mobilized societies.

Certainly, noncompound democracies, as those of the European nation-states, have more coherent decision-making and more transparent accountability patterns. However, such patterns have two limits. First, they have their costs: coherence does not mean necessarily soundness (from the electors' point of view) and transparency can arrive too late (for the electors to make a change). For example, regarding the prosecution of the Iraq War, it was easier for US voters to send a message against the war to the President (in the 2006 mid-term elections) than it was for British voters to do the same with their own Prime Minister (they had to wait the longer timetable of the national elections). Second, these patterns are not suitable to compound democracies. They fit the condition of unified sovereignty systems, but not of those characteristic of unions of many sovereignties. Moreover, just as the formation of a system of sovereign states was not a viable option in the American continent, to go back to the system of sovereign states is also an undesirable option in the European continent. The EU is the outcome of a peace pact among European nation-states imposed by a sequence of dramatic hot and cold wars. No other option, but supranational integration, has been available for promoting peace in the European continent. NATO has been a necessary condition for *keeping the peace* (Howorth and Keeler 2003), but it is not a sufficient condition for *building it*. For doing that, it has been required to integrate markets and citizenships in a larger supranational institutional framework. Moreover, in a globalized world, the integration process has added new meanings to the old ones. Through supranational integration, the new EU member-states have been able to promote internal economic growth, to consolidate their democratic systems, to modernize their own societies, and to promote the international role of Europe. The single nation-states of Europe are no longer able, as such, to achieve those aims by themselves. Indeed, the integration of the American continent has had equivalent consequences on the USA (and its federated states). Because neither the options of going back to the old system of states (Morgan 2005) nor the option of building a new continental state (Mancini 1998) are available (and desirable), it seems much more advisable, for Europeans, to deal with the constraints of their compound democracy. As the USA already experienced, the internal enlargement and the international projection of the EU have increased the domestic and global challenges it has to face. These challenges cannot be dealt with by weak decision-making and unclear accountability patterns, nor can they be governed by introducing patterns of decision-making and accountability centralization.

The EU is thus experiencing what the USA already experienced: compoundness is a condition for its survival and consolidation, but the internal and external environment generates permanent challenges to that compoundness. Something can be done for rationalizing compoundness, although such rationalization implies the sharing of a method for doing that. If that method will be constitutional and if it will generate in its application a constitutional identity among citizens, then it will be less difficult to look for those institutional devices necessary for consolidating the EU compound democracy. Here the puzzle of compound democracy. A puzzle is a problem which challenges human creativity. Will Europeans have sufficient political creativity to keep their compoundness while improving its democratic performance at the same time? And will Americans be able to preserve creatively their compound democracy, notwithstanding the internal and external pressures for neutralizing it?

Notes

Chapter 1

1. I shall frequently use the term 'America' for the sake of brevity, and in homage to Tocqueville, although it would be more respectful to the multinational nature of the American continent to keep the term 'United States of America' or 'USA', as I shall do in direct comparisons with the European Union or EU.

2. For economy of discourse, I will use the name of 'European Union' or EU throughout the book, although integrated Europe has had different 'names' during its historical development: it started as the European Coal and Steel Community after the Paris Treaty of 1951, it became the European Economic Community after the Rome Treaty of 1957, subsequently the European Union with the Maastricht Treaty of 1992. Moreover, in Maastricht the European Union came to include three pillars, the first concerning the policies of the common market (called also European Community), the second the Common Foreign and Security Policy, and the third concerning the cooperation on Justice and Home Affairs. Although it is the first pillar which manifests the institutional features that are the object of my analysis, I will use the name of EU (and not European Community) for stressing a logic which has not remained confined only within this pillar.

3. 'Watergate' is a general term used to describe a complex web of political scandals between 1972 and 1974. The word specifically refers to the Watergate Hotel in Washington, DC. It was here that the Watergate Burglars, on President Nixon's authorization, broke into the Democratic Party's National Committee offices on June 17, 1972. Although re-elected for a second term in the elections of the following November, by early 1974, the nation was consumed by Watergate. After the House of Representatives authorized the Judiciary Committee to consider impeachment proceedings against Nixon, on the evening of August 8, 1974, Nixon delivered a nationally televised resignation speech.

4. The Paris (1951) and Rome (1957) treaties were signed by six countries (Belgium, France, Italy, Germany, Luxembourg, and the Netherlands). The founding members were subsequently joined by: Denmark, Ireland, and Britain (1973); Greece (1981); Spain and Portugal (1986); Austria, Finland, and Sweden (1995);

Cyprus, the Czech Republic, Estonia, Hungary, Latvia, Lithuania, Malta, Poland, Slovakia, and Slovenia (2004); and finally Bulgaria and Romania (2007).

Chapter 2

1. The rebellion in 1787 in Massachusetts by debt-ridden farmers, who took up arms when the legislature refused to issue more paper money to help them avoid foreclosures, gave the signal that only strong federal institutions could preserve the internal order of society.

Chapter 3

1. The system by which the members of the Electoral College are elected is established by the ordinary law of the respective state legislature (although the constitution stipulates that persons already holding public office may not be elected members of the Electoral College). Today, forty-eight states use the so-called 'winner-takes-all' method whereby the presidential candidate who gains most votes in a particular state has the right to obtain, with the delegates who have run in his name, all the seats in the Electoral College that pertain to that state. Maine and Nebraska, on the contrary, elect a Great Elector for each congressional district in the state, and two Great Electors at the state level on a plurality basis. The consequence is that, within the five Great Electors of Nebraska and the four of Maine, there may be support for different presidential candidates. The law of 1934 stipulated that this election must be held on 'the first Tuesday after the first Monday of November', at four-yearly intervals, although the Electoral College of each state meets to formalize the victor (again on the basis of the 1934 law) on 'the first Monday after the second Wednesday of December following the November election'. Each Electoral College meets in the capital of its state, and therefore separately from the other state electoral colleges. The results are sent to the President of the Senate (who is the Vice President of the USA), who authenticates them in the presence of the Senate and the House of Representatives. Finally, on the basis of the Twentieth Constitutional Amendment of 1933, the candidate elected President takes (presidential) office at the stroke of 'midday on the 20th of January' following the November election and the December formalization of its result. For this reason, the presidential elections (i.e. the election of the electoral colleges which then elect the President) are held in even years but the presidential term begins in odd ones. Finally, the Twenty-Second Constitutional Amendment of 1951 establishes that 'no person shall be elected to the office of the President more than twice'.

2. As in Austria, Denmark, France, Luxembourg, the Netherlands, Portugal, even against the opinion of the government. On government's proposal in Finland, Greece, Britain, Spain, and Ireland. In Belgium and Germany only when the parliament is stalled. Only in Sweden the power of parliament's dissolution is assigned exclusively to the government and not to the head of state.

3. The constitution grants the President ten days to review a measure passed by the Congress. If the President has not signed the bill after ten days, it becomes law without his signature. However, if Congress adjourns during the ten-day period, the bill does not become law. The presidential decision of postponing the signing of a law when the Congress is expecting to adjourn is called a 'pocket veto'.

4. Fifth Republic France is not the only case of a semi-presidential system. However, in the other Western democracies with similar institutional features (Austria, Finland, Iceland, Ireland, and Portugal), the President of the Republic has such scant governmental powers (vis-à-vis the Prime Minister) that they can be considered parliamentary systems, although this interpretation has been contested (see Elgie 1999). Finland and Portugal (this latter before the reform which increased the power of the parliament of 1982) more closely resemble(d) the French model.

5. In 1986–8, when the President of the Republic was the Socialist François Mitterrand and the Prime Minister was the Gaullist Jacques Chirac; in 1993–5, when the President of the Republic was the Socialist François Mitterrand and the Prime Minister was the Gaullist Edouard Balladur; and in 1997–2002, when the President of the Republic was the Gaullist Jacques Chirac and the Prime Minister was the Socialist Lionel Jospin.

6. Although, in critical elections, as in Germany in 2005, the two alternative coalitions may be stuck in a stalemated electoral outcome, which can only be resolved through the formation of a grand coalition between the two main parties.

Chapter 4

1. The term comes from the early seventeenth century, where buccaneers were known in England as filibusters. This term had evolved from the Spanish *filibustero* which had come from the French word *flibustier*, which itself evolved from the Dutch *vrijbuiter* (freebooter).

2. The threat consisted in a proposal to increase the Supreme Court justices by a number equivalent to those aged over 70, which would have greatly altered its internal composition.

3. The neoconservative surge began in the South during the 1960s, strengthened in the 1980s with the two Reagan presidencies, and then exploded in the 1990s with, first, the Republican conquest of the House of Representatives in

the midterm elections of 1994 and, then, George W. Bush's success in the two presidential elections of 2000 and 2004.

Chapter 5

1. 'Prior to enactment of the Bipartisan Campaign Reform Act of 2002 (BCRA), money for election related activities that was generally raised and spent outside federal regulation was known as "soft money" or non-federal funds. . . . The intent of BCRA, which amends the previous Federal Election Campaign Act (FECA), is to restrict the raising and spending of soft money. . . . The term "hard money," has typically been used to refer to funds raised and spent in accordance with the limitations, prohibitions, and reporting requirements of the FECA. Unlike soft money, hard money may be used in connection with a federal election. Under the FECA, hard money restrictions apply to contributions and expenditures from any "person," as defined to include, "an individual, partnership, committee, association, corporation, labour organization, or any other organization or group of persons, but does not include the Federal Government or any authority of the Federal Government".' (Whitaker 2004: 4–5)

Chapter 6

1. Especially in Part II of the book, in order to make the comparison with the EU more focused, I will use alternatively the terms of USA and America. Indeed, ' "Europe" increasingly means the European Community in much the same way that "America" means the United States' (Weiler 1999: 12).
2. The drafters of the US constitution somehow distinguished between 'republic' and 'democracy', considering the latter (because based on a 'small number of citizens, who assemble and administer the government in person', as Madison wrote in *Federalist no. 10*, now in Beard 1964: 72) a less evolved form of popular government than the former (because based on representation). However, 'Madison's famous distinction between the terms democracy and republic was somewhat arbitrary and a-historical. Even some of his contemporaries, like James Wilson, referred to the new representative system as democracy. The term democracy soon came into general usage' (Dahl 2006: 156–7).
3. Indeed, in the *Afterword* to his expanded edition (2006) of *A Preface to Democratic Theory*, first published in 1956, Robert A. Dahl seemed to revise his previous interpretation of Madisonian democracy. He writes (Dahl 2006: 164): 'Madison's experience from 1790 onward led him, I believe, to develop somewhat greater trust in majorities . . . and a greater distrust of minorities that, in his view, threatened the interests of the majority'.

4. As reported in Chapter 2, every four years for the President, every six for the Senate although one-third of the senators are elected in coincidence with the election for the House which takes place every two years.

5. State (instituted in 1789), Treasury (1789), Interior (1849), Agriculture (1862), Justice (1870), Commerce (1903), Labor (1913), Defense (1947), Housing and Urban Development (1965), Transportation (1966), Energy (1977), Education (1979), Health and Human Services (1979), Veteran Affairs (1988), and Homeland Security (2002).

6. In the period 1947–8, the House and the Senate had a Republican majority while the President was the Democratic Harry Truman. In the period 1955–60, both chambers of Congress were controlled by the Democrats, while the President (Dwight Eisenhower) was a Republican. In both cases, however, there were no significant policy differences between the two majorities.

7. The exceptions being, in this case, the unified party government of the periods 1977–80 and 1993–4, when the Democrats had a majority in both chambers of the Congress and controlled the presidency.

8. The impeachment procedure is carefully regulated by article II, section IV, of the constitution, although the standard for impeachment is highly ambiguous, being 'treason, bribery, or other high crimes and misdemeanours'. In fact, although treason and bribery are obvious, the constitution is silent on what constitutes a 'high crime or misdemeanor'. Several commentators have suggested that Congress may decide for itself what constitutes an impeachable offense. In 1970, then-Representative Gerald R. Ford defined the criteria as he saw it: 'An impeachable offense is whatever a majority of the House of Representatives considers it to be at a given moment in history.' Four years later, Ford would assume the presidency, following a vote to approve impeachment proceedings against Richard Nixon. The impeachment procedure is in two steps. The House of Representatives must first pass 'articles of impeachment' by a simple majority. The articles of impeachment constitute the formal allegations. Upon their passage, the defendant has been 'impeached'. Next, the Senate tries the accused. In order to convict the accused, a two-thirds majority of the senators present is required. Conviction automatically removes the defendant from office. In the case of the impeachment of a President, the Chief Justice of the USA presides over the proceedings. On this, see Gerhardt (2000).

9. The *Iran–Contra Affair* was one of the largest political scandals in the USA during the 1985–8 period. It involved several members of the Reagan personal presidency who in 1986 helped sell arms to Iran, an avowed enemy, and used the proceeds to fund the Contras, an anticommunist guerrilla organization in Nicaragua, thus infringing a decision of Congress not to support them. On the basis of congressional investigations and hearings, several members of the Reagan presidency were obliged to resign. A presidential commission, instituted at the end of 1986 and chaired by Senator John Tower delivered, in

February 1987, a Report recognizing the responsibility of the National Security Council and the Vice-President, but not of the President, in the scandal. Indeed, two top officials of the National Security Council were indicted on multiple charges in March 1988.

10. The special prosecutor (later renamed 'independent counsel' by the Ethics Act 1978) is an interim member of the presidency. She or he is appointed by the Secretary of Justice and then confirmed by one of the federal courts. She or he should enjoy a certain amount of independence in investigating allegations of wrongdoing by members of the presidency, if not (as in Nixon's case between 1973 and 1974 or in the Clinton case between 1993 and 1999) by the President himself. In reality, his or her independence from the Secretary of Justice (or even from the President himself) continues to be a matter of fierce constitutional conflict between Congress, the presidency, and the Supreme Court. However, the special prosecutor's powers are investigative (i.e. she or he is empowered to bring a member of the presidency before a court). The judicial consequences of unlawful behavior by a member of the presidency can only be derived from the appropriate judicial instances. On this, see Fisher (1997: 25, 77–8).

11. These activities are favored by congressional hearings so that they come to interact with the interests of the media and the dispositions of the courts of justice. Ginsberg and Shefter (1995) argue that, between 1974 and 1992, a sort of alliance (against the Republican control of the presidency) formed among the Democratic Congress, a number of leading Democratic newspapers and television stations, and liberal sectors of the investigative judiciary.

Chapter 7

1. As of January 1, 2007 the population of the EU's 27 member-states is about 493 million people. Outside the EU, there are the European Free Trade Agreement (EFTA) states of Norway, Iceland, and Liechtenstein. They are members of the European Economic Area (EEA) which allows them to participate in most aspects of the EU's single market without acceding to the EU. Switzerland, the fourth EFTA state, rejected EEA membership in a referendum; however, it has established close ties to the EU by means of various bilateral treaties. Turkey started preliminary negotiations for entering the EU in 2005. Of the Balkan states, Croatia is an official candidate country and started accession negotiations in October 2005; Macedonia has been given official candidate status as of 2005; Albania, Bosnia-Hercegovina, Montenegro, and Serbia are officially recognized as potential candidates. Ukraine, Georgia, Moldova, Armenia, Azerbaijan, and Kazakhstan have also expressed membership aspirations,

though none have submitted formal applications and none are expected to do so in the short term. Morocco officially applied to join the EU in 1987 but was rejected on the grounds that it was not in Europe.

2. To adapt to the EU language, I will use the term 'intergovernmental' instead of 'inter-states' or confederal features and the term 'Community' instead of 'supra-states' or federal features (see Chapter 1).

3. German reunification (*Deutsche Wiedervereinigung*) took place on October 3, 1990, when the area of the former German Democratic Republic (GDR, commonly called East Germany), reorganized in the form of five *Länder*, was incorporated into the Federal Republic of Germany (FRG, commonly called West Germany), already constituted by eleven *Länder*. Negotiations between the GDR and FRG, held after the GDR parliamentary elections of March 18, 1990, culminated in a Unification Treaty. The reunified Germany remained a member of the European Community (thus the European Union) and NATO. There is still debate as to whether the events of 1990 should be properly referred to as a 'reunification' or a 'unification'. In general, the term 'reunification' was carefully avoided by the political elites who did the negotiations. The official term in German is *Deutsche Einheit* or 'German unity'.

4. The euro is the currency (as January 1, 2007) of thirteen European Union countries, stretching from the Mediterranean to the Arctic Circle (namely Belgium, Germany, Greece, Spain, France, Ireland, Italy, Luxembourg, the Netherlands, Austria, Portugal, Finland, and Slovenia). Euro banknotes and coins have been in circulation since January 1, 2002 and are now a part of daily life for 315 million Europeans living in the euro area. The euro currency is managed by the European Central Bank.

5. As the Association of Southeast Asian Nations (ASEAN subsequently AFTA) inaugurated in 1967 by Indonesia, Malaysia, Philippines, Singapore, Thailand, later joined by Brunei, Vietnam, Laos, Myanmar, and Cambodia; or the Asian Pacific Economic Cooperation (APEC) inaugurated in 1989 by Indonesia, Singapore, Brunei, Malaysia, Philippines, Thailand, this joined by Australia, Japan, New Zealand, South Korea, USA, Canada, China, Hong Kong, Taiwan, Mexico, Papua New Guinea, Chile, Peru, Russia, Vietnam; or Mercado Comun de Sur (MERCOSUR), inaugurated in 1991 by Brazil, Argentina, Paraguay, Uruguay, later joined by Chile and Bolivia; or the North American Free Trade Agreement (NAFTA) inaugurated in 1994 by Mexico, USA, and Canada.

6. Qualified Majority Voting is a voting procedure employed in the Council of Ministers (or Council of the European Union). According to the procedure, each member-state has a fixed number of votes. The number allocated to each country is roughly determined by its population, but progressively weighted in favor of smaller countries. The 2001 Nice Treaty established that, to pass a vote by QMV, all three of the following conditions must apply: (*a*) the proposal

must be supported by 255 votes out of a total of 345—about 74% of the votes; (b) the proposal must be backed by a majority of member-states; and (c) the countries supporting the proposal must represent at least 62% of the total EU population.

7. In the EU each member-state has to preside over the organization for a period of six months, in accordance with a preestablished schedule. The presidency of the EU coincides with the presidency by one member-state of the Council of Ministers of all the member-states. The presidency has as its primary responsibility to organize and chair all meetings of the Council. However, working out compromises capable of resolving difficulties is in practice also a primary responsibility. The post as President of the Council of Ministers is for each separate meeting held by the responsible government minister of the member-state holding the presidency. Separate from the Council of Ministers there is the European Council, which meets at European summits about four times per year. The task as President of the assembled European Council is similarly performed by the head of government or head of state of the member-state holding the presidency. The President is primarily responsible for preparing and chairing Council meetings, and has no executive powers.

8. In the common EU language, the term Council of Ministers is generally preferred to that of Council of the European Union.

9. The High Representative for the CFSP is the main coordinator of the EU foreign policy (and also of the European Security and Defense Policy—or ESDP—which has become a crucial part of the CFSP since the Cologne European Council of 1999). She or he is also the Secretary-General of the Council of Ministers, the Secretary-General of the Western European Union, and the President of the European Defense Agency. As Secretary-General of the Council of Ministers, the High Representative examines and prepares most decisions before they are presented for decision.

10. Prior to this date, there were twenty commissioners. In the months after the 2004 enlargement, the size of the Commission was temporarily increased to thirty members—consisting of the twenty commissioners already in post, plus one from each of the ten acceding new member-states. The number was reduced to twenty-five, with one commissioner from each member-state, when the new commission took office in November 2004. With the accession of Bulgaria and Romania as member-states in 2007, the Commission further enlarged to twenty-seven commissioners.

11. Elections for the EP occur once in every five years, on the basis of course of universal adult suffrage. There is no uniform voting system for the election of MEPs; rather, each member-state is free to choose its own system subject to three restrictions: (a) the system must be a form of proportional representation, under either the party list or Single Transferable Vote system; (b) the electoral area may be subdivided if this will not generally affect the proportional nature of the voting system; and (c) any election threshold on the national

level must not exceed 5%. The allocation of seats to each member-state is based on the principle of digressive proportionality, so that, while the size of the population of each country is taken into account, smaller states elect more MEPs than would be strictly justified by their populations alone. As the number of MEPs granted to each country has arisen from treaty negotiations, there is no precise formula for the apportionment of seats among member-states. No change in this configuration can occur without the unanimous consent of all governments.

12. That is (if we consider those groupings with more than forty MEPs as of January 1, 2007): European People's Party—European Democrats; Group of the Party of European Socialists; Alliance of Liberals and Democrats for Europe; Union for Europe of the Nations; European Greens—European Free Alliance; European United Left—Nordic Green Left.

13. He wrote: 'The great and radical vice in the construction of the existing Confederation is in the principle of legislation for state or governments ... as contradistinguished from the individuals of whom they consist'. Hamilton's opinion has been so widely shared that the *Federalist* published in the American classics series, edited by Charles A. Beard (1964) omitted to publish the articles (Numbers 15–22) on the defects of the Articles of Confederation. Beard (1964: 90) comments: 'Inasmuch as the Articles of Confederation were discarded by the adoption of the Constitution, [this part of the *Federalist*] is now mainly of historic interest'.

14. The Charter is a document containing human rights provisions, solemnly proclaimed by the European Parliament, the Council of the European Union, and the European Commission in December 2000.

15. All the member-states of the EU have subscribed to the Convention for the Protection of Human Rights and Fundamental Freedoms, also known as the European Convention on Human Rights (ECHR), adopted under the auspices of the Council of Europe in 1950 to protect human rights and fundamental freedoms. The Council of Europe is an international organization constituted by forty-six nation-states of the European region. The Convention established the European Court of Human Rights. Any person who feels their rights have been violated under the Convention by a state party can take a case to the Court; the decisions of the Court are legally binding, and the Court has the power to award damages. The establishment of a Court to protect individuals from human rights violations is an extremely innovative feature for an international convention on human rights, as it gives the individual an active role on the international arena (traditionally, only states are considered actors in international law). The European Convention is still the only international human rights agreement providing such a high degree of individual protection. State parties can also take cases against other state parties to the Court, although this power is rarely used.

Chapter 8

1. On this, see the very interesting debate between Jim Caporaso, Gary Marks, Andrew Moravcsik, and Mark Pollack hosted by the ECSA Review (vol. X, n. 3, fall 1997, 1–5), titled *Does the European Union Represent an n of 1?* (also at http://www.ecsa.org/N1debate.htm). See also mine (Fabbrini 2005*d*).
2. Here and in the following paragraph, I use the category of 'noncompound democracies' to include both the unitary and federal EU member-states; for a partially different approach, see Schmidt (2006).
3. On the only historical experience (the Civil War of 1861–5) in which force was used to resolve a mortal conflict and on its effects of purging the political culture of the country from giving legitimacy to the use of force, see Greenstone (1993).
4. Congress has formally declared war only five times in the history of the country (the Anglo-American War in 1812, the Mexican War in 1846, the Spanish–American War in 1898, World War I in 1917, and World War II in 1941), while the list of undeclared wars of the USA includes: Naval War with France of the period 1789–1800; the First Barbary War of the period 1801–5; the Second Barbary War of 1815; the Korean War of the period 1950–3; the Vietnam War of the period 1964–73; the Grenada intervention of the period 1979–84; the War in Lebanon of 1983; the Panama intervention of 1989; the Persian Gulf War of 1991; the Somalia intervention of 1992; the intervention in the former Yugoslavia of 1999; the Afghanistan War of 2001; the Iraq War of 2003. However, in the post–World War II period, the Congress has specifically authorized the use of force (*but not voted a declaration of war*) in the following cases: in Vietnam, Lebanon, the (first) Gulf War, Afghanistan, and Iraq (Cook 2002; Grimmett 2002).
5. In 1867 the President, after a deep conflict with Congress for the right to dismiss the Secretary of the War Department General Stanton without the advice and consent of the Senate, was subjected to an impeachment procedure (and, finally, he was saved by only one vote, but Stanton was reinstated). In 1974, President Nixon resigned, once he realized that he would have been subjected to an impeachment procedure for the Watergate affair. In 1999, the impeachment of President Clinton failed in the Senate by a narrow margin of votes.

Chapter 9

1. According to article 1–46, citizens also have initiative power: 'A significant number of citizens, no less than one million, coming from a significant number of Member States, may invite the Commission to submit any appropriate proposal on matters where citizens consider that a legal act of the Union is required for the purpose of implementing this Constitution'.

Chapter 10

1. Not coincidentally, the Anglo-Saxon countries have been those that have experimented most widely with first-past-the-post electoral systems; precisely those systems, that is, which emphasize the personal vote. More in general, see the still useful Early and Knight (1981).
2. Consider the cases of Jacques Chirac in 1976, Pierre Mauroy in 1984, and Jean-Pierre Raffarin in 2005, who were sacrificed after a presidential defeat.

Bibliography

Aalberts, T. E. (2004). 'The Future of Sovereignty in Multilevel Governance Europe: a Constructivist Reading', *Journal of Common Market Studies*, 42/1: 23–46.

Abramson, P. R. (2007). *Change and Continuity in the 2004 and 2006 Elections.* Washington, DC: C.Q. Press.

Ackerman, B. (1991). *We the People: Foundations.* Cambridge, MA: Harvard University Press.

____ (1998). *We the People: Transformations.* Cambridge, MA: Harvard University Press.

____ (1999). *The Case Against Lameduck Impeachment.* New York, NY: Seven Stories Press.

____ (2000). 'The New Separation of Powers', *Harvard Law Review*, 113/3: 633–726.

____ (2001). 'The Emergency Constitution', *Yale Law Journal*, 113/5: 1029–91.

____ (2006). *Before the Next Attack: Preserving Civil Liberties in an Age of Terrorism.* New Haven, CT: Yale University Press.

Agel, J. and Bernstein, R. B. (1993). *Amending America: if We Love the Constitution So Much, Why Do We Keep Trying to Change It?* Lawrence, KS: University Press of Kansas.

Aldrich, J. H. (1995). *Why Parties? The Origin and Transformation of Political Parties in America.* Chicago, IL: The University of Chicago Press.

____ and Niemi, R. G. (1996). 'The Sixth American Party System: Electoral Change 1952–1992', in S.C. Craig (ed.), *Broken Contract? Changing Relationships between Americans and their Government.* Boulder, CO: Westview Press, pp. 87–109.

Alesina, A. and Glaser, E. L. (2005). *Un Mondo di Differenze: Combattere la Povertà negli Stati Uniti e in Europa.* Rome-Bari: Laterza.

Alter, K. (2001). *Establishing the Supremacy of European Law: The Making of an International Rule of Law in Europe.* Oxford: Oxford University Press.

Amato, G. (2003). 'The European Convention: First Achievements and Open Dilemmas', *International Journal of Constitutional Law*, 1/2: 355–63.

Anderson, P. (2002). 'Force and Consent', *New Left Review*, September–October, 1–18.

Ansell, C. K. (2004). 'Restructuring Authority and Territoriality', in C.K. Ansell and G. Di Palma (eds.), *Restructuring Territoriality: Europe and the United States Compared.* Cambridge: Cambridge University Press, pp. 3–18.

Ansell, C. K. and Di Palma, G. (2004) (eds.). *Restructuring Territoriality: Europe and the United States Compared.* Cambridge: Cambridge University Press.

APSA (2004). *American Democracy in an Age of Rising Inequality,* Report of the American Political Science Association, Task Force on Inequality and American Democracy, Washington DC.

Backer, L. C. (2001). 'The Extra-National State: American Confederate Federalism and the European Union', *Columbia Journal of European Law,* 2: 173–240.

Ball, T. and Pocock, J. G. A. (1988) (eds.). *Conceptual Change and the Constitution.* Lawrence, KS: University Press of Kansas.

Ballman, A., Epstein, D., and O'Halloran, S. (2002). 'Delegation, Comitology and the Separation of Powers in the European Union', *International Organization,* 56/3: 551–74.

Banning, L. (1986). 'From Confederation to Constitution: The Revolutionary Context of the Great Convention', in APSA/AHA, *This Constitution. Our Enduring legacy.* Washington, DC: C.Q. Press, pp. 23–35.

Bardach, E. and Kagan, R. (1982) (eds.). *Social Regulation: Strategies for Reform.* San Francisco, CA: Institute for Contemporary Studies.

Barnier, M. and Vitorino, A. (2002). *The Commission's Right of Initiative,* The European Convention, CONV 230/02, 9 March.

Bartels, L. M. (2002). 'The Impact of Candidates Traits in American Presidential Elections', in A. King (ed.), *Leader's Personalities and the Outcome of Democratic Elections.* Oxford: Oxford University Press, pp. 44–69.

Bartolini, S. (2000). *The Class Cleavage: The Political Mobilization of the European Left, 1860–1980.* Cambridge: Cambridge University Press.

—— (2005). *Restructuring Europe: Centre Formation, System Building, and Political Structuring Between the Nation State and the European Union.* Oxford: Oxford University Press.

—— and Mair, P. (1990). *Identity, Competition and Electoral Availability: The Stabilisation of European Electorate 1885–1985.* Cambridge: Cambridge University Press.

Baum, L. (1992). 'Supreme Court Activism and the Constitution', in P. F. Nardulli (ed.), *The Constitution and American Political Development: an Institutional Perspective.* Urbana, IL: University of Illinois Press, pp. 151–76.

Beard, C. A. (ed.) (1964). *The Enduring Federalist.* New York, NY: Ungar.

—— (ed.) (1986). *An Economic Interpretation of the Constitution of the United States.* New York: Macmillan.

Bednar, J. (2003). 'The Madisonian Scheme to Control National Government', in S. Kernell (ed.), *James Madison: The Theory and Practice of Republican Government.* Stanford, CA: Stanford University Press, pp. 217–42.

Beer, S. H. (1993). *To Make a Nation: The Rediscovery of American Federalism.* Cambridge, MA: Harvard University Press.

—— (1995). 'Federalism and the Nation State: What Can Be Learned from the American Experience?', in K. Knop et al. (eds.), *Rethinking Federalism:*

Citizens, Markets, and Governments in a Changing World. Vancouver: UCB Press, pp. 224–49.

Bell, D. (1991). 'The *Hegelian Secret*: Civil Society and American Exceptionalism', in B. E. Shafer (ed.), *Is America Different? A New Look at American Exceptionalism*. Oxford: Clarendon Press, pp. 46–70.

Bellamy, R. (1996) (ed.). *Constitutionalism, Democracy and Sovereignty: American and European Perspective*. Aldershot, UK: Aveburry.

Bensel, R. F. (1987). *Sectionalism and American Political Development: 1880–1980*. Madison, WI: The University of Wisconsin Press.

Bernstein, R. B. (1995). *Amending America: if We Love the Constitution So Much, Why Do We Keep Trying to Change It?* Lawrence, KS: University Press of Kansas.

Bessette, J. M. (1994). *The Mild Voice of Reason: Deliberative Democracy and American National Government*. Chicago, IL: The University of Chicago Press.

Bickel, A. M. (1962). *The Least Dangerous Branch: The Supreme Court as the Bar of Politics*. New York, NY: Simon and Schuster.

Biskupic, J. and Witt, E. (1997). *Guide to the Supreme Court*. Washington, DC: Congressional Quarterly Press.

Black, E. (1988). *Our Constitution: The Myth that Binds Us*. Boulder, CO: Westview Press.

Blond, J. R. and Fleisher, R. (1990). *The President in the Legislative Arena*. Chicago, IL: The University of Chicago Press.

Blondel, J. (1992). *Introduction to Comparative Government*. London: Longman.

—— (1998). 'Il Modello Svizzero: un Futuro per l'Europa', *Rivista italiana di scienza politica*, 28/2: 203–27.

—— and Muller-Rommel, F. (eds.) (1993). *Governing Together: Extent and Limits of Joint-Decision-Making in Western European Cabinets*. London: Macmillan.

Blumenthal, S. (2006). *How Bush Rules: Chronicle of a Radical Regime*. Princeton, NJ: Princeton University Press.

Bodnari, F. (2003). 'What Can the EU Learn from the American Dual Federalism?', paper presented at the *Annual Meeting of the American Political Science Association*, 28–31 August.

Boerzel, T. (2001). 'Europeanization and Territorial Institutional Change: Toward Cooperative Regionalism?', in M. G. Colwes, J. Caporaso, and T. Risse (eds.), *Europeanization and Domestic Change: Transforming Europe*. Ithaca, NY: Cornell University Press, pp. 137–58.

—— and Risse, T. (2000). 'Who is Afraid of a European Federation? How to Constitutionalize a Multi-Level Governance System', in C. Joerges, Y. Mény, and J. H. H. Weiler (eds.), *What Kind of Constitution for What Kind of Polity? Responses to Joschka Fischer*. Florence, EUI, Robert Schuman Centre for Advanced Studies, pp. 45–59.

Bomberg, E. and Stubb, A. (2003). *The European Union: How Does It Work?* Oxford: Oxford University Press.

Boorstin, D. J. (1965). *The Americans: The National Experience*. New York, NY: Vintage Books.

Brodkin, K. (2002). *How Jews Became White Folks and What That Says About Race in America*, 4th edn. Brunswick, NJ: Rutgers University Press.

Brown, C. (ed.) (2003). *Lost Liberties: Ashcroft and the Assault on Personal Freedom*. New York, NY: New York Books.

Brubaker, R. (1992). *Citizenship and Nationhood in France and Germany*. Cambridge, MA: Harvard University Press.

—— (1999). *Nationalism Reframed: Nationhood and the National Question in the New Europe*, 2nd edn. Cambridge: Cambridge University Press.

Bryce, J. (1888). *The American Commonwealth*. London: The Macmillan Company.

Budge, I. and Keman, H. (1993). *Parties and Democracy: Coalition Formation and Government Functioning in Twenty States*, 2nd edn. Oxford: Oxford University Press.

Burgess, M. (2000). *Federalism and European Union: The Building Of Europe, 1950–2000*. London: Routledge.

Bush, G. W. (2002). The National Security Strategy of the United States of America, Washington DC, 20 September.

Bzdera, A. (1993). 'Comparative Analysis of Federal High Courts: A Political Theory of Judicial Review', *Canadian Journal of Political Science*, 26: 3–29.

Cain, B. E. (2002). 'The United States in Evolution: Majoritarian Reforms in a Madisonian System', in G. Peele, C. J. Bailey, B. Cain, and B. G. Peters (eds.), *Developments in American Politics*. New York, NY: Palgrave, pp. 300–16.

—— (2005). 'Citizens in American Federalism: Locating Accountability in a Dispersed System', in S. Fabbrini (ed.), *Democracy and Federalism in the European Union and the United States: Exploring Post-National Governance*. London: Routledge, pp. 104–16.

—— (2006). 'America After the 2004 Elections: Bold Policies and Political Quicksand', in S. Fabbrini (ed.), *The United States Contested: American Unilateralism and European Discontent*. London: Routledge, pp. 161–76.

—— and Jones, W. T. (1989). 'Madison's Theory of Representation', in B. Grofman and D. Wittman (eds.), *The Federalist Papers and the New Institutionalism*. New York: Agathon Press, pp. 11–30.

—— Dalton, R. J., and Scarrow, S. E. (eds.) (2003). *Democracy Transformed? Expanding Political Opportunities in Advanced Industrial Democracies*. Oxford: Oxford University Press.

Caldeira, G. A. and Gibson, J. L. (1995). 'The Legitimacy of the Court of Justice in the European Union: Models of Institutional Support', *The American Political Science Review*, 89: 356–76.

Calhoun, J. (1851). *A Disquisition on Government*. New York, NY: C. Gordon Post.

Calleo, D. P. (2000). 'The US Post-Imperial Presidency and Transatlantic Relations', *The International Spectator*, 35/3: 69–79.

—— (2001). *Rethinking Europe's Future*. Princeton, NJ: Princeton University Press.

Campbell, C. (1998). *The U.S. Presidency in Crisis: A Comparative Perspective*. Oxford: Oxford University Press.

—— and Rockman, B. (1991) (eds.). *The Bush Presidency: First Appraisals*. Chatham, MA: Chatham House.

Caporaso, J. (1996). 'The European Community and Forms of State: Westphalian, Regulatory or Post-Modern', *Journal of Common Market Studies*, 34: 29–52.

—— (2000). *The European Union: Dilemmas of Regional Integration*. Boulder, CO: Westview Press.

—— (2005). 'The Emergence of the EU Supranational Polity and Its Implications for Democracy', in S. Fabbrini (ed.), *Democracy and Federalism in the European Union and the United States: Exploring Post-national Governance*. London: Routledge, pp. 57–75.

Cappelletti, M., Seccombe, M., and Weiler, J. (1986). 'Integration through Law: Europe and the American Federal Experience: A General Introduction', in M. Cappelletti, M. Seccombe, and J. Weiler (eds.), *Integration through Law: Europe and the American Federal Experience*, 1, 1. Berlin: De Gruyter, pp. 3–68.

Caraley, D. J. (2005), 'Complications of American Democracy: Elections Are Not Enough', *Political Science Quarterly*, 120/3: 379–405.

Cassese, S. (2001). *La Nuova Costituzione Economica*. Rome-Bari: Laterza.

Chambers, W. N. and Burnham, W. D. (eds.) (1975). *The American Party Systems: Stages of Political Development*, 2nd edn. New York: Oxford University Press.

Chantornvong, S. (1988). 'Tocqueville's *Democracy in America* and the Third World', in V. Ostrom, D. Feeny, and H. Pitcht (eds.), *Rethinking Institutional Analysis and Development*. San Francisco, CA: Institute for Contemporary Studies.

Checkel, J. T. (2001). 'Taking Deliberation Seriously', ARENA Working Paper, Oslo, 1/14, http://www.arena.uio.no/publications/wp01_14.htm

Christiansen, T. (2002). 'La Commissione Europea', in S. Fabbrini (ed.), *L'Unione Europea: le Istituzioni e gli Attori di un Sistema Sopranazionale*. Rome-Bari: Laterza, pp. 126–50.

Chubb, J. E. (1992). 'The Constitution, Institutionalization, and the Evolution of Federalism', in P. F. Nardulli (ed.), *The Constitution and American Political Development: An Institutional Perspective*. Chicago, IL: University of Chicago Press, pp. 262–89.

—— and Peterson, E. (1989). 'American Political Institutions and the Problem of Governance', in J. E. Chubb and E. Peterson (eds.), *Can the Government Govern?* Washington, DC: The Brookings Institution.

Citrin, J. and Sides, J. (2003). 'Can There Be Europe Without Europeans? Problems of Identity in Multinational Communities', in R. Herman, M. Brewer, and T. Risse (eds.), *Institutions and Identities in the New Europe*. Cambridge: Cambridge University Press, pp. 161–85.

Closa, C. (2004). 'The Convention Method and the Transformation of EU Constitutional Politics', in E. O. Eriksen, J. E. Fossum, and A. J. Menéndez (eds.), *Developing a Constitution for Europe*. London: Routledge, pp. 183–206.

Cohen, J. C. (1996). 'The European Preliminary Reference and the US Supreme Court Review of State Court Judgments: A Study in Comparative Judicial Federalism', *The American Journal of Comparative Law*, 44: 421–61.

Committee on the Constitutional System (1987). A Bicentennial Analysis of the American Political Structure: Report and Recommendations. Washington, D.C.

Conant, L. (2002). *Justice Contained: Law and Politics in the European Union*. Ithaca, NY: Cornell University Press.

Conlan, T. (1998). *From New Federalism to Devolution: Twenty-Five Years of Intergovernmental Reform*. Washington, DC: Brookings Institution Press.

Conley, R. S. (2002). *The Presidency, Congress and Divided Government: A Postwar Assessment*. College Station, TX: A&M University Press.

Connelly, W. F. Jr (2006). 'Wall vs. Wave?', *The Berkeley Electronic Press*, 4/3: 11.

Cook, G. P. (2002). *Recognizing War in the United States via the Interagency Process*, paper prepared for the Course on Interagency Process, National Defense University, National War College.

Corwin, E. S. (1957). *The President: Office and Powers*. New York, NY: New York University Press.

Coultrap, J. (1999). 'From Parliamentarism to Pluralism: Models of Democracy and the European Union's Democratic Deficit', *Journal of Theoretical Politics*, 11/1: 107–35.

Cowles, M. G., Caporaso, J., and Risse, T. (eds.) (1999). *Transforming Europe: Europeanization and Domestic Change*. Ithaca, NY: Cornell University Press.

Cox, G. W. and McCubbins, M. D. (1993). *Legislative Leviathan: Party Government in the House*. Berkeley, CA: University of California Press.

Crotty, W. J. (1980). *Political Reform and the American Experiment*. New York, NY: Thomas Y. Crowell.

—— (1982). *Party Reform*. London: Longman.

Crum, B. (2002). 'Legislative-Executive Relations in the EU', *Centre for European Policy Studies*. Brussels: Mimeo.

—— (2004). 'Politics and Power in the European Convention', *Politics*, 24/1: 1–11.

Daalder, H. (1995). 'Paths Toward State Formation in Europe: Democratization, Bureaucratization, and Politicization', in H. E. Chehabi and A. Stepan (eds.), *Politics, Society and Democracy*. Boulder, CO: Westview Press, pp. 113–130.

—— and Lindsay, J. M. (2003). *America Unbound: The Bush Revolution in Foreign Policy*. Washington, DC: Brookings Institution Press.

Dahl, R. A. (1957). 'The Supreme Court as a National Policy-Maker', *Journal of Public Law*, 4: 236–49.

—— (1976). *Democracy in the United States: Promise and Performance*, 3rd edn. Chicago, IL: Rand McNally.

—— (1990). 'Myth of Presidential Mandate', *Political Science Quarterly*, 105/3: 335–72.

—— (1994). *The New American Political Disorder*. Berkeley, CA: Institute of Governmental Studies Press.

____ (2001). *How Democratic Is the American Constitution?* New Haven, CT: Yale University Press.

____ (2005). 'Is International Democracy Possible? A Critical View', in S. Fabbrini (ed.), *Democracy and Federalism in the European Union and the United States: Exploring Post-national Governance*. London: Routledge, pp. 194–204.

____ (2006). *A Preface to Democratic Theory: Expanded Edition*. Chicago, IL: University of Chicago Press.

____ and Tufte, E. (1973). *Size and Democracy*. Stanford, CA: Stanford University Press.

Dalton, R. and Wattenberg, M. (eds.) (2000). *Parties Without Partisans: Political Change in Advanced Industrial Democracies*. Oxford: Oxford University Press.

Dann, P. (2002). 'Looking through the Federal Lens: The Semi-Parliamentary Democracy of the EU', Jean Monnet Working Paper, 5, http://ideas.repec.org/p/erp/jeanmo/p0005.html

Davidson, R., Webb Hammond, S., and Smock, R. (1998). *Masters of the House: Congressional Leadership Over Two Centuries*. Boulder, CO: Westview Press.

Davis, J. W. (1997). *Presidential Primaries and the Caucus-Convention System: A Source-Book*. New York, NY: Greenwood Press.

Davis, S. R. (1978). *The Federal Principle: A Journey through Time in Quest of a Meaning*. Berkeley, CA: University of California Press.

De Burca, G. (2001). 'The Drafting of the European Union Charter of Fundamental Rights', *European Law Review*, 26: 126–38.

De Schoutheete, P. and Wallace, H. (2002). 'The European Council', *Notre Europe*, Research and European Issues, 19.

De Tocqueville, A. (1969). *Democracy in America*. Garden City, NY: Anchor Books.

De Witte, B. (2003) (ed.). *Ten Reflections on the Constitutional Treaty for Europe*. Florence: EUI, Robert Schuman Centre for Advanced Studies and Academy of European Law.

Dehousse, R. (1998). *The European Court of Justice and the Politics of Judicial Integration*. New York, NY: Palgrave.

____ (2003). 'We the States: Why the Anti-Federalists Have Won', *European Studies Association Review*, 16/4: 105–21.

Della Sala, V. (2005). 'European Polity-Building: Searching for Legitimacy between Economic and Social Europe', in S. Fabbrini (ed.), *Democracy and Federalism in the European Union and the United States: Exploring Post-National Governance*. London: Routledge, pp. 133–47.

Delmas-Marty, M. (2002). *Towards a Truly Common Law: Europe as a Laboratory of Legal Pluralism*. Cambridge: Cambridge University Press.

Delwit, P., Kulahci, E., and Van de Walle, C. (eds.) (2004). *The Euro-Parties: Organization and Influence*. Brussels: Free University of Brussels.

Dershowitz, A. M. (2001). *Supreme Injustice: How the High Court Hijacked Election 2000*. Oxford: Oxford University Press.

Derthick, M. (2001). *Keeping the Compound Republic: Essays on American Federalism*. Washington, DC: The Brookings Institution Press.

Deudney, D. H. (1995). 'The Philadelphia System: Sovereignty, Arms Control, and Balance of Power in the American States-Union, circa 1787–1861', *International Organization*, 49/2: 191–228.

Deutsch, K. (1953). *Nationalism and Social Communication*. Cambridge, MA: Harvard University Press.

Devuyst, Y. (2003). *The European Union at the Crossroads. The EU's Institutional Evolution from the Schuman Plan to the European Convention*, 2nd edn. Brussels: P.I.E.-Peter Lang.

Di Palma, G. (2004). 'Postscript: What Inefficient History and Malleable Practices Say About Nation-States and Supranational Democracy When Territoriality Is No Longer Exclusive', in C. K. Ansell and G. Di Palma (eds.), *Restructuring Territoriality: Europe and the United States Compared*. Cambridge: Cambridge University Press, pp. 246–69.

Dinan, D. (2004). 'Reconstituting Europe', in M. G. Cowles and D. Dinan (eds.), *Developments in the European Union*. New York, NY: Palgrave Macmillan, pp. 26–46.

—— (2005). *Ever Closer Union. An Introduction to European Integration*. New York, NY: Palgrave Macmillan.

Dodd, L. C. (ed.) (2004). *Congress Reconsidered*. Washington, DC: C.Q. Press.

—— and Jillson, C. (eds.) (1994). *The Dynamics of American Politics: Approaches and Interpretations*. Boulder, CO: Westview Press.

Donnelly, D., Fine, J., and Miller, E. S. (2001). *Are Elections For Sale?* Boston, MA: Beacon Press.

Doring, H. (1987). 'Party Government in Britain: Recent Conspicuous Constraints', in R. S. Katz (ed.), *Contemporary Party Governments: European and American Experiences*. Berlin: de Gruyter, pp. 118–54.

Draper, T. (1997). 'Is the CIA Necessary?', *The New York Review of Books*, 64/13: 18–22.

Dubinsky, P. R. (1994). 'The Essential Function of Federal Courts: The European Union and the United States Compared', *The American Journal of Comparative Law*, 42: 295–364.

Dunn, J. (1990). *Interpreting Political Responsibility*. Princeton, NJ: Princeton University Press.

Duverger, M. (1951). *Les Partis Politiques*. Paris: Armand Collin.

—— (1986) (ed.). *Les Régimes Semi-présidentiels*. Paris: PUF.

Dye, T. R. (1990). *American Federalism: Competition among Governments*. Lexington, MA: Lexington Books).

Early, S. T. Jr and Knight, B. B. (1981). *Responsible Government: American and British*. Chicago, IL: Nelson Hall.

Easton, D. (1981). *Political System*. Chicago, IL: University of Chicago Press.

—— (1990). *The Analysis of Political Structure*. London: Routledge.

Egan, M. (2001). *Constructing a European Market*. Oxford: Oxford University Press.

Einaudi, M. (1950). *The Roosevelt Revolution* (New York, NY: Greenwood Press).

Eisner, M. A. (2000). *Regulatory Politics in Transition*, 2nd edn. Baltimore, MD: The Johns Hopkins University Press.

Elazar, D. J. (1985). 'Constitution-Making: The Pre-eminently Political Act', in K. G. Banting and R. Simon (eds.), *Redesigning the State: The Politics of Constitutional Change in Industrial Nations*. Toronto: University of Toronto Press, pp. 232–48.

—— (1987*a*). *Exploring Federalism*. Tuscaloosa, AL: University of Alabama Press.

—— (1987*b*). 'Foreword', in V. Olstrom (ed.), *The Political Theory of a Compound Republic*. Lincoln, NE: University of Nebraska Press.

—— (1988). *The American Constitutional Tradition*. Lincoln, NE: University of Nebraska Press.

—— (1994). *The American Mosaic: The Impact of Space, Time, and Culture on American Politics*. Boulder, CO: Westview Press.

—— (1998). *Constitutionalizing Globalization: The Postmodern Revival of Confederal Arrangements*. New York, NY: Rowman and Littlefield Publishers.

—— (2001). 'The United States and the European Union: Models of their Epochs', in K. Nicolaidis and R. Howse (eds.), *The Federal Vision and Levels of Governance in the US and in the EU*. Oxford: Oxford University Press, pp. 31–53.

—— and Greilsammer, I. (1985). 'Federal Democracy: The USA and Europe Compared: a Political Science Perspective', in M. Cappelletti, M. Seccombe, and J. Weiler (eds.), *Integration through Law*, 1, 1, *A Political, Legal and Economic Overview*. Berlin: De Gruyter, pp. 71–149.

Eldersveld, S. J. and Walton, H. (2000). *Political Parties in American Society*, 2nd edn. New York, NY: Palgrave Macmillan.

Elgie, R. (1993). *The Role of the Prime Minister in France, 1981–1991*. London: Macmillan.

—— (1997). 'Two-Ballot Majority Electoral Systems', *Representation*, 34/2: 89–94.

—— (1999) (ed.). *Semi-Presidentialism in Europe*. Oxford: Oxford University Press.

—— (2001). 'Cohabitation: Divided Government French Style', in R. Elgie (ed), *Divided Government in Comparative Perspective*. Oxford: Oxford University Press, pp. 106–26.

—— (2003). *Political Institutions in Contemporary France*. Oxford: Oxford University Press.

—— (2004). 'Semi-Presidentialism: Concepts, Consequences and Contesting Explanations', *Political Studies Review*, 2/3: 314–30.

Elkin, S. L. (1996). 'Madison and After: The American Model of Political Constitution', *Political Studies*, 64/3: 592–604.

Elster, J. (1997). 'Ways of Constitution-Making' in A. Hadenius (ed.), *Democracy's Victory and Crisis*. Cambridge: Cambridge University Press, 123–42.

Emmot, B. (2002). 'Present at the Creation: Our Law, Your Law', *The Economist*, June 29.

Epstein, L. (1986). *Political Parties in the American Mold*. Madison, WI: The University of Wisconsin Press.

Ertman, T. (1997). *Birth of the Leviathan: Building States and Regimes in Medieval and Early Modern Europe*. Cambridge: Cambridge University Press.

Esping-Andersen, J. (1990). *The Three Worlds of Welfare Capitalism*. Princeton, NJ: Princeton University Press.

—— (1992). *Politics Against Market*, 2nd edn. Princeton, NJ: Princeton University Press.

Fabbrini, S. (1993). *Il Presidenzialismo degli Stati Uniti*. Rome-Bari: Laterza.

—— (1995). 'Between Parliamentarism and Presidentialism: a Comparative Perspective on Governmental Systems', *Journal of Behavioral and Social Sciences*, 2: 109–29.

—— (1998). *Quale Democrazia: l'Italia e gli Altri*, 3rd edn. Roma-Bari: Laterza.

—— (1999a). 'The American System of Separated Government: An Historical-Institutional Interpretation', *International Political Science Review*, 20/1: 95–116.

—— (1999b). 'American Democracy from a European Perspective', *Annual Review of Political Science*, 2: 465–91.

—— (2002) (ed.). *L'Unione Europea: le Istituzioni e gli Attori di un Sistema Sopranazionale*. Rome-Bari: Laterza.

—— (2003a). 'Bringing Robert A. Dahl's Theory of Democracy to Europe', *Annual Review of Political Science*, 6: 119–37.

—— (2003b). 'A Single Western State Model? Differential Development and Constrained Convergence of Public Authority Organization in Europe and America', *Comparative Political Studies*, 36/6: 653–78.

—— (2004a). 'America and Europe in the Post-Cold War Era', in R. Janssens and R. Kroes (eds.), *Post-Cold War Europe, Post-Cold War America*. Amsterdam: VU University Press, pp. 87–100.

—— (2004b). 'The European Union in American Perspective: The Transformation of Territorial Sovereignty in Europe and the United States', in C. K. Ansell and G. Di Palma (eds.), *Restructuring Territoriality. Europe and the United States Compared*. Cambridge: Cambridge University Press, pp. 163–87.

—— (2004c). 'Transatlantic Constitutionalism: Comparing the United States and the European Union', *European Journal of Political Research*, 43/4: 547–69.

—— (2005a) (ed.). *Democracy and Federalism in the European Union and the United States: Exploring Post-national Governance*. London: Routledge.

—— (2005b). 'To Build a Market Without a State: The EU in American Perspective', in S. Fabbrini (ed.), *Democracy and Federalism in the European Union and the United States: Exploring Post-national Governance*. London: Routledge, pp. 119–32.

—— (2005c). 'The Semi-Sovereign American Prince: The Dilemma of an Independent President in a Presidential Government', in T. Poguntke and P. Webb (eds.), *The Presidentialization of Politics: A Comparative Study of Modern Democracies*. Oxford: Oxford University Press, pp. 313–35.

310

_____ (2005d). 'Madison in Brussels: The EU and the US as Compound Democracies', _European Political Science_, 4/2: 188–98.

_____ (2005e). 'Is the EU Exceptional? The EU and the US in Comparative Perspective', in S. Fabbrini (ed.), _Democracy and Federalism in the European Union and the United States: Exploring Post-National Governance_. London: Routledge, pp. 3–24.

_____ (2006). 'US Unilateralism and American Conservative Nationalism', in S. Fabbrini (ed.), _The United States Contested: American Unilateralism and European Discontent_. London: Routledge, pp. 3–29.

_____ and Morata, F. (eds.) (2002). _L'Unione Europea: le Politiche Pubbliche_. Rome-Bari: Laterza.

_____ and Sicurelli, D. (2004). 'The Federalisation of the EU in the Light of the Compound Republic Theory', _Regional and Federal Studies_, 14/2: 232–54.

Farrand, M. (1966). _The Records of the Federal Convention of 1787_. New Haven, CT: Yale University Press.

Featherstone, K. and Radaelli, C. (2003) (eds.). _The Politics of Europeanization_. Oxford: Oxford University Press.

Feldman, N. (2005). _Divided by God: America's Church-State Problem and What We Should Do About It_. New York, NY: Farrar, Straus and Giroux.

Ferguson, N. (2005). 'The Widening Atlantic', _The Atlantic Monthly_, January–February, now in http://www.theatlantic.com/doc/prem/200501/ferguson

Ferrera, M. (2005). _The Boundaries of Welfare: European Integration and the New Spatial Politics of Social Protection_. Oxford: Oxford University Press.

_____ and Rhodes, M. (eds.) (2000). _Recasting European Welfare States_. London: Frank Cass.

Filippov, M., Ordeshook, P., and Shvetsova, O. (2004). _Designing Federalism: A Theory of Self-Sustainable Federal Institutions_. Cambridge: Cambridge University Press.

Finer, S. E. (1969–1970). 'Almond's Concept of the Political System: A Textual Critique', _Government and Opposition_, 5/1: 3–21.

Fiorina, M. (1992). _Divided Government_. London: Macmillan.

_____ (2005). _Culture Wars? The Myth of Polarized America_. New York, NY: Pearson Morgan.

Fisher, L. (1997). _Constitutional Conflicts Between Congress and the President_, 4th edn. Lawrence, KS: University Press of Kansas.

_____ (2004). _Presidential War Power_, 2nd edn. Lawrence, KS: University Press of Kansas.

_____ (2005). 'Deciding on War Against Iraq: Institutional Failures', in R. Y. Shapiro (ed.), _The Meaning of American Democracy_. New York, NY: The Academy of Political Science, pp. 115–36.

Fligstein, N. (2001). _Architecture of Markets: An Economic Sociology of Twenty-First Century Capitalist Societies_. Princeton, NJ: Princeton University Press.

_____ and Stone Sweet, A. (2001). 'Institutionalizing the Treaty of Rome', in A. Stone Sweet, W. Sandholtz, and N. Fligstein (eds.), _The Institutionalization of Europe_. Oxford: Oxford University Press, pp. 29–55.

Flora, P. (1999). 'Introduction and Interpretation', in S. Rokkan, *State Formation, Nation-Building and Mass Politics in Europe: The Theory of Stein Rokkan*. Oxford: Oxford University Press, pp. 1–91.

Foner E. (1997). 'Blacks and the US Constitution: 1789–1989', in A. Ware (ed.), *The United States*, 1. Aldershot: Dartmouth, 63–74.

Forsyth, M. (1981). *Unions of States: The Theory and Practice of Confederation*. New York, NY: Holmes & Meier Publishers.

Fossum, J. E. (2003). 'The European Union in Search of an Identity', *European Journal of Political Theory*, 2/3: 319–40.

Franchino, F. (2000). 'Control of the Commission's Executive Function', *European Union Politics*, 1/1: 63–92.

Friedrich, C. J. (1967). *The Impact of American Constitutionalism Abroad*. Boston, MA: Boston University Press.

Friese, H. and Wagner, P. (2002). 'The Nascent Political Philosophy of the European Polity', *The Journal of Political Philosophy*, 10/3: 342–64.

Fukuyama, F. (2004). *State-Building: Governance and World Order in the 21st Century*. Ithaca, NY: Cornell University Press.

Gaddis, J. L. (1991). 'Toward the Post-Cold War World', *Foreign Affairs*, 70/1: 1–19.

Gallagher, M., Mair, P., and Laver, M. (2005). *Representative Government in Modern Europe*. New York, NY: McGraw-Hill.

Garton Ash, T. (2004). *Free World: America, Europe, and the Surprising Future of the West*. New York, NY: Random House.

Geddes, A. (2004). *The European Union and British Politics*. New York, NY: Palgrave Macmillan.

Gergen, D. (1991/1992). 'America's Missed Opportunities', *Foreign Affairs*, 71/1: 1–19.

Gerhardt, M. (2000). *The Federal Impeachment Process: a Constitutional and Historical Analysis*. Chicago, IL: University of Chicago Press.

Gilbert, M. (2003). *Surpassing Realism: The Politics of European Integration since 1954*. Lanham: Rowman and Littlefield.

Ginsberg, B. E. and Shefter, M. (1991). *Politics by Other Means: The Declining Significance of Elections in America*. New York, NY: Basic Books.

—— —— (1995). 'Ethics Probes as Political Weapons', *Journal of Law and Politics*, 11/3: 497–511.

Glaser, E. and Wellenreuther, H. (2002) (eds.). *Bridging the Atlantic: The Question of American Exceptionalism in Perspective*. Cambridge: Cambridge University Press.

Glazer, N. (1997). *We Are All Multiculturalist Now*. Cambridge, MA: Harvard University Press.

Goldstein, L. F. (2001). *Constituting Federal Sovereignty: The European Union in Comparative Context*. Baltimore, MD: The Johns Hopkins University Press.

Goldwin, R. A. (ed.) (1961). *A Nation of States: Essays on the American Federal System*. Chicago, IL: University of Chicago Press.

Graber, M. A. (2004). 'Resolving Political Questions into Judicial Questions: Tocqueville's Thesis Revisited', *Constitutional Commentary*, 21/2: 485–545.

Greenfeld, L. (1992). *Nationalism: Five Roads to Modernity*. Cambridge, MA: Harvard University Press.

Greenstein, F. I. (2000). *The Presidential Difference: Leadership Style from FDR to Clinton*. Princeton, NJ: Princeton University Press.

Greenstone, J. D. (1993). *The Lincoln Persuasion: Remaking American Liberalism*. Princeton, NJ: Princeton University Press.

Greven, M. T. and Pauly, L. W. (2000) (eds.). *Democracy Beyond the State: The European Dilemma and the Emerging Global Order*. Lanham, MD: Rowman and Littlefield.

Griller, R. and Weidel, B. (2005) (eds.). *External Economic Relations and Foreign Policy in the European Union*. Wien: Springer.

Grimm, D. (1985). 'The Modern State: Continental Tradition', in F. X. Kaufman, G. D. Majone, and V. Ostrom (eds.), *Guidance, Control and Evaluation in the Public Sector*. Berlin: de Gruyter, pp. 89–109.

—— (1997). 'Does Europe Need a Constitution?', in P. Gown and P. Anderson (eds.), *The Question of Europe*. London: Verso, pp. 239–64.

Grimmett, R. F. (2002). 'Instances of Use of United States Armed Forces Abroad, 1789–2001', CRS Reports and Issue Bries for Congress (Washington, DC).

Grofman, B. and Wittman, D. (1989) (eds.). *The Federalist Papers and the New Institutionalism*. New York, NY: Agathon Press.

Gunlicks, A. (2003). *The Laender and German Federalism*. Manchester, UK: Manchester University Press.

Guyomarch, A., Machin, H., and Ritchie, E. (1998). *France in the European Union*. New York, NY: Palgrave Macmillan.

Haas, E. B. (1958). *The Uniting of Europe: Political, Social and Economic Forces, 1950–1957*. London: Stevens and Sons.

—— (1997). *Nationalism, Liberalism and Progress: The Rise and Decline of Nationalism*. Ithaca, NY: Cornell University Press.

Habermas, J. (2001). 'So, Why does Europe need a Constitution?', *Policy Papers on Constitutional Reform of the EU*. Florence: EUI, Robert Schumann Centre, http://www.iue.it/RSCAS/e-texts/CR200102UK.pdf

Hacker, J. S. and Pierson, P. (2005). *Off Center: The Republican Revolution and the Erosion of American Democracy*. New Haven, CT: Yale University Press.

Hall, J. A. and Ikenberry, G. J. (1989). *The State*. Minneapolis, MN: University of Minnesota Press.

Hall, P. (1986). *Governing the Economy: The Politics of State Intervention in Britain and France*. Oxford: Oxford University Press.

Hallin, D. C. and Mancini, P. (2004) (eds.). *Comparing Media Systems: Three Models of Media and Politics*. Cambridge: Cambridge University Press.

Hart, J. (1995). *The Presidential Branch: From Washington to Clinton*, 2nd edn. Chatham, MA: Chatham House.

Hartz, L. B. (1955). *The Liberal Tradition in America*. New York, NY: Harcourt Brace Jovanovich.

Hastings, D. D. (2006). 'Quacking Like a Duck? Bush II and Presidential Power in the Second Term', *International Affairs*, 80/4: 665–80.

Hayes-Renshaw, F. and Wallace, H. (1997). *The Council of Ministers of the European Union*. London: Macmillan.

Heclo, H. (1986). 'Whitehall and Washington Revisited: An Essay on Constitutional Lore', in R. Hodder-Williams and J. Ceaser (eds.), *Politics in Britain and the United States: Comparative Perspective*. Durham, UK: Duke University Press, pp. 88–118.

—— (1989). 'The Emerging Regime', in R. A. Harris and S. M. Milkis (eds.), *Remaking American Politics*. Boulder, CO: Westview Press, pp. 290–320.

Helms, L. (2005). *Presidents, Prime Ministers and Chancellors: Executive Leadership in Western Democracies*. New York, NY: Palgrave Macmillan.

Hendricks, G. and Morgan, A. (2001). *The Franco-German Axis in European Integration*. Cheltenham, UK: Edward Elgar.

Hendrickson, D. C. (2003). *Peace Pact: The Lost World of the American Founding*. Lawrence, KS: University Press of Kansas.

—— (2006). 'Of Power and Providence', *Policy Review*, 135, http://www.hoover.org/publications/policyreview/2913746.html

Hernson, P. S., Shaiko, R. G., and Wilcox, C. (2004) (eds.). *The Interest Group Connection: Electioneering, Lobbying and Policy-making in Washington*. Washington, DC: C.Q. Press.

Higgs, R. (1987). *Crisis and Leviathan: Critical Episodes in the Growth of American Government*. Oxford: Oxford University Press.

Hill, C. (1996) (ed.). *The Actors in European Foreign Policy*. London: Routledge.

—— (2004). 'Renationalising or Regrouping? EU Foreign Policy since 11 September 2001', *Journal of Common Market Studies*, 42/1: 143–63.

Hinckley, B. (1990). *The Symbolic Presidency: How Presidents Portray Themselves*. London: Routledge.

Hirschman, A. O. (1970). *Exit, Voice and Loyalty*. Cambridge, MA: Harvard University Press.

Hix, S. (2005). *The Political System of the European Union*, 2nd edn. New York, NY: Palgrave Macmillan.

—— and Scully, R. (2003). 'European Parliament at Fifty', *Journal of Common Market Studies*, Special Issue, 41/2: 353–73.

—— Noury, A., and Roland, G. (2004). 'How To Choose the European Executive: A Counterfactual Analysis, 1979–1999', in C. B. Blankart and D.C. Mueller (eds.), *A Constitution for European Union*. Boston, MA: MIT Press, 169–201.

Hodder-Williams R. (1992). 'Six Notions of *Political* and the United States Supreme Court', *The British Journal of Political Science*, 22/1: 1–20.

Hoffman, L. and Vergés-Bausili, A. (2003). 'The Reform of Treaty Revision Procedures: The European Convention on the Future of Europe', in T. A. Borzel and R. A. Cichowski (eds.), *The State of European Union: Law, Politics and Society*, vol. 6. Oxford: Oxford University Press, pp. 127–46.

Hoffmann, S. (1995). *The European Sisyphus: Essays on Europe, 1964–1994*. Boulder, CO: Westview.

Holmes, S. (1995). *Passions and Constraints: On the Theory of Liberal Democracy*. Chicago, IL: University of Chicago Press.

Hooghe, L. and Marks, G. (2001). *Multilevel Governance and European Integration*. New York, NY: Rowman and Littlefield Publishers.

Hopkin, J. (2001). 'Bringing the Members Back In? Democratizing Candidate Selection in Britain and Spain', *Party Politics*, 7/3: 346–61.

Horton, C. A. (2005). *Race and the Making of American Liberalism*. Oxford: Oxford University Press.

Howorth, J. and Keeler, J. (2000). *European Integration and Defense: The Ultimate Challenge?*, *Chaillot Paper*, WEU-ISS, 43.

____ ____ (2003) (eds.). *Defending Europe: The EU, NATO, and the Quest for European Autonomy*. New York, NY: Palgrave.

____ ____ (2005). 'A European Union with Teeth?', in N. Jabko and C. Parsons (eds.), *The State of the European Union: With US or Against US? European Trends in American Perspective*, 7. Oxford: Oxford University Press, 31–52.

Hudson, W. E. (1996). *American Democracy in Peril: Seven Challenges to America's Future*. Chatham, MA: Chatham House Publisher.

Hueghlin, T. O. (2000). 'From Constitutional to Treaty Federalism: A Comparative Perspective', *Publius*, 30/4: 137–53.

Huntington, S. P. (1968). *Political Order in Changing Societies*. New Haven, CT: Yale University Press.

____ (1981). *American Politics: The Promise of Disharmony?* Cambridge, MA: Harvard University Press.

____ (2004). *Who Are We? America's Great Debate*. New York, NY: Simon and Schuster.

Ignatiev, N. (1995). *How the Irish Became White*. London: Routledge.

Ikenberry, J. G. (1999) (ed.). *American Foreign Policy: Theoretical Essays*. New York, NY: Longman.

____ (2000). *After Victory: Institutions, Strategic Restraint and the Rebuilding of the Order after Major Wars*. Princeton, NJ: Princeton University Press.

____ (2002). 'America's Imperial Ambition', *Foreign Affairs*, 81/5: 44–60.

Jabko, N. and Parsons, C. (2005) (eds.). *The State of the European Union: With US or Against US? European Trends in American Perspective*, 7. Oxford: Oxford University Press.

Jacobs, L. R. and Shapiro, R. Y. (2000). 'Conclusion: Presidential Power, Institutions and Democracy', in R. Y. Shapiro, M. J. Kumar, and L. R. Jacobs (eds.), *Presidential*

Power: Forging the Presidency for the Twenty-First Century. New York, NY: Columbia University Press, pp. 489–508.

Jacobs, M., Novak, W. J., and Zelizer, J. E. (2003) (eds.). *Democratic Experiment: New Directions in American Political History.* Princeton, NJ: Princeton University Press.

Jacobson, G. C. (1990). *The Electoral Origins of Divided Government.* Boulder, CO: Westview Press.

James, S. (1999). *British Cabinet Government.* London: Routledge.

Jefferey, C. and Savigner, P. (1991) (eds.). *German Federalism Today.* Leicester: Leicester University Press.

Jervis, R. (1999). 'Mission Impossible: Creating a Grand Strategy', in D. J. Caraley (ed.), *The New American Interventionism: Lessons from Successes and Failures.* New York, NY: Columbia University Press, pp. 205–18.

Jillson, C. C. (1988). *Constitution Making: Conflict and Consensus in the Federal Convention of 1787.* New York, NY: Agathon Press.

Joerges, C. (1997). 'The Market Without the State? The "Economic Constitution" of the European Community and the Rebirth of Regulatory Politics', *European Integration online papers* (EIoP), 1/19, http://ideas.repec.org/a/erp/eiopxx/p0020.html

Johnson, H. A. (2000). 'Judicial Institutions in Emerging Federal Systems: The Marshal Court and the European Court of Justice', *John Marshall Law Journal*, 33: 1063–72.

Jones, C. O. (1994). *The Presidency in a Separated System.* Washington, DC: The Brookings Institution.

—— (1997). 'Separating to Govern: The American Way', in B. E. Shafer (ed.), *Present Discontents: American Politics in the Very Late Twentieth Century.* Chatham, MA: Chatham House Publishers, pp. 47–72.

—— (1999). *Separate but Equal Branches: Congress and the Presidency*, 2nd edn. Chatham, MA: Chatham House Publishers.

Judt, T. (2005). *Postwar: A History of Europe Since 1945.* New York, NY: William Heineman.

Kaase, M. and Newton, K. (1995). *Beliefs in Government.* Oxford: Oxford University Press.

Katz, R. S. and Crotty, W. J. (2006) (eds.). *Handbook of Party Politics.* Thousands Oaks, CA: Sage.

—— and Kolodny, R. (1994). 'Party Organization as an Empty Vessel: Parties in American Politics', in R. S. Katz and P. Mair (eds.), *How Parties Organize.* London: Sage, pp. 23–50.

—— and Mair, P. (1992). *Party Organization: a Data Handbook of Party Organizations in Western Democracies.* London: Sage.

Katznelson, I. K. (1985). 'Working-Class Formation in the State: Nineteenth Century England in American Perspective', in P. B. Evans, D. Rueschemeyer, and T. Skocpol (eds.), *Bringing the State Back In.* Cambridge: Cambridge University Press, pp. 257–84.

_____ and Shefter, M. (2002) (eds.). *Shaped by War and Trade. International Influences on American Political Development*. Princeton, NJ: Princeton University Press.

_____ and Zolberg, A. (eds.) (1986). *Working Class Formation. Nineteenth Century Patterns in Western Europe and the United States*. Princeton, NJ: Princeton University Press.

_____ Geiger, K., and Kryder, D. (1993). 'Limiting Liberalism: The Southern Veto 1933–1950', *Political Science Quarterly*, 108/2: 283–306.

Kazin, M. (1995). *The Populist Persuasion: an American History*. New York, NY: Basic Books.

Keating, M. (1999). 'Asymmetrical Government: Multinational States in an Integrated Europe', *Publius*, 29/1: 71–86.

Kelemen, R. D. (2003). 'The Structure and Dynamics of EU Federalism', *Comparative Political Studies*, 36/1–2: 184–200.

Keeler, J. T. S. (2005). 'Mapping EU Studies: The Evolution from Boutique to Boom Field 1960–2001', *Journal of Common Market Studies*, 43/3: 551–82.

Kelsen, H. (1928). 'La Garantie Jurisdictionnelle de la Constitution', *Revue de Droit Publique*, 44: 197–257.

Keohane, R. O. (1997). 'International Relations and International Law: Two Optics', *Harvard International Law Journal*, 38/3: 487–502.

_____ (2002) (ed.). *Power and Governance in a Partially Globalized World*. London: Routledge.

Kernell, S. (1992). *Going Public: New Strategies of Presidential Leadership*, 2nd edn. Washington, DC: Congressional Quarterly Press.

_____ (2003) (ed.). *James Madison: The Theory and Practice of Republican Government*. Stanford, CA: Stanford University Press.

_____ (2005). *The Logic of American Politics*. Washington, DC: C.Q. Press.

Key, V. O. Jr (1964). *Politics, Parties, and Pressure Groups*. New York, NY: Thomas Y. Crowell.

King, A. (1997). *Running Scared: Why America's Politicians Campaign Too Much and Govern Too Little*. New York, NY: The Free Press.

_____ (2002) (ed.). *Leaders' Personalities and the Outcome of Democratic Elections*. Oxford: Oxford University Press.

King, D. (1997). 'The Segregated State? Black Americans and the Federal Government', in A. Ware (ed.), *The United States*, 1. Aldershot: Dartmouth, pp. 123–46.

_____ (2000). *Making Americans: Immigration, Race, and the Origins of the Diverse Democracy*. Cambridge, MA: Harvard University Press.

_____ (2005). *The Liberty of Strangers: Making the American Nation*. Oxford: Oxford University Press.

Kirsch, G. (1995). 'The New Pluralism: Regionalism, Ethnicity, and Language in Western Europe?', in K. Knop et al. (eds.), *Rethinking Federalism: Citizens, Markets, and Governments in a Changing World*. Vancouver: UCB Press, pp. 59–74.

317

Klingemann, H.-D. and Fuchs, D. (1995) (eds.). *Citizens and the State*. Oxford: Oxford University Press.

Koch, A. and Peden, W. (1944). *The Life and Selected Writings of Thomas Jefferson*. New York, NY: Random House.

Kohler-Koch, B. (2000). 'Framing: The Bottleneck of Constructing Legitimate Institutions', *Journal of European Public Policy*, 7/4: 513–31.

Konig, D. T. and Matson, C. D. (1990). *A Union of Interests: Political and Economic Thought in Revolutionary America*. Lawrence, KS: University Press of Kansas.

Kooiman, J. (2003). *Governing as Governance*. London: Sage.

Krasner, S. D. (1999). *Sovereignty: Organized Hypocrisy*. Princeton, NJ: Princeton University Press.

Kratochwil, F. (1986). 'Of Systems, Boundaries and Territoriality: An Inquiry into the Formation of the State System', *World Politics*, 39/1: 27–52.

Krauthamer, C. (2001). 'The New Unilateralists', *The Washington Post*, June 8.

Le Duc, L., Niemi, R. G., and Norris P. (1996). 'The Present and Future of Democratic Elections', in L. Le Duc, R. G. Niemi, and P. Norris (eds.), *Comparing Democracies: Elections and Voting in Global Perspective*. London: Sage, 1–12.

Levinson, S. (1995) (ed.). *Responding to Imperfection: The Theory and Practice of Constitutional Amendment*. Princeton, NJ: Princeton University Press.

Lieven, A. (2004). *America Right or Wrong: An Anatomy of American Nationalism*. Oxford: Oxford University Press.

Lijphart, A. (1999). *Patterns of Democracy*. New Haven, CT: Yale University Press.

Lind, M. (2006). *The American Way of Strategy: U.S. Foreign Policy and the American Way of Life*. Oxford: Oxford University Press.

Lindberg, L. N. (1963). *The Political Dynamics of European Economic Integration*. Stanford, CA: Stanford University Press.

Linz, J. (1990). 'The Perils of Presidentialism', *Journal of Democracy*, 1/1: 51–69.

—— (1994). 'Presidential or Parliamentary Democracy: Does It Make a Difference?', in J. J. Linz and A. Valenzuela (eds.), *The Failure of Presidential Democracy*. 1. Baltimore, MD: The Johns Hopkins University Press, pp. 3–87.

Lipset, S. M. (1963). *Political Man: The Social Bases of Politics*. Baltimore, MD: Johns Hopkins University Press.

—— (1979). *The First Nation: The United States in Historical and Comparative Perspective*, 2nd edn. New York, NY: W.W. Norton.

—— (1996). *American Exceptionalism: A Double-Edge Sword*. New York, NY: W.W. Norton.

—— and Marks, G. (2000). *It Didn't Happen Here: Why Socialism Failed in the United States*. New York, NY: W.W. Norton.

—— and Rokkan, S. (1967). 'Cleavage Structures, Party Systems and Voter Alignments: An Introduction', in S. M. Lipset and S. Rokkan (eds.), *Party Systems and Voter Alignments*. New York, NY: The Free Press, 1–64.

Lombardo, E. (2003). 'The Participation of Civil Society in the Debate on the Future of Europe: Rhetorical or Action Frames in the Discourse of the Convention?',

Universidad de Saragoza, *Working Paper*, http://unizar.es/union_europea/files/workpapers3_UE.pdf

Lord, C. and Magnette, P. (2004). 'E Pluribus Unum? Creative Disagreement about Legitimacy in the EU', *Journal of Common Market Studies*, 42/1: 183–202.

Lowi, T. J. (1978). 'Europeanization of America? From United States to United State', in T. Lowi and A. Stone (eds.), *Nationalizing Government: Public Policies in America*. Beverly Hills, CA: Sage, 15–29.

—— (1985). *The Personal President: Power Invested Promise Unfulfilled*. Ithaca, NY: Cornell University Press.

—— (1988). 'American Democratic Experiences in Perspective', in F. Krinsky (ed.), *Crisis and Innovation: Constitutional Democracy in America*. New York, NY: Basil Blackwell, pp. 31–46.

—— (1992). 'The State in Political Science: How We Become What We Study', *American Political Science Review*, 86/1: 1–6.

—— (1997). 'Party Government and the Constitution in the U.S. President and Congress in a New and Dysfunctional Separation of Powers', paper presented at the Conference on *Comparing Presidentialisms*, Rome University La Sapienza, Italy, April.

—— and Ginsberg, B. (1990). *American Government: Freedom and Power*. New York, NY: W.W. Norton.

Lucas, J. R. (1993). *Responsibility*. Oxford: Oxford University Press.

Lunch, W. M. (1987). *The Nationalization of American Politics*. Berkeley, CA: The University of California Press.

MacCormick, N. D. (1999). *Questioning Sovereignty: Law, State and Nation in the European Commonwealth*. Oxford: Oxford University Press.

Magnette, P. (2004). 'Deliberation or Bargaining? Coping with Constitutional Conflicts in the Convention on the Future of Europe', in E. O. Eriksen, J. E. Fossum, and A. J. Menéndez (eds.), *Developing a Constitution for Europe*. London: Routledge, 207–25.

—— (2005). *What Is the European Union: Nature and Prospects*. New York, NY: Palgrave Macmillan.

Mair, P., Muller, W. C., and Plasser, F. (2004) (eds.). *Political Parties and Electoral Change: Party Responses to Electoral Markets*. London: Sage.

Maisel, S. (2002). *The Parties Respond: Changes in American Parties and Campaigns*. Boulder, CO: Westview Press.

Majone, G. D. (1992) (ed.). *Deregulation and Re-regulation? Regulatory Reform in Europe and the United States*. Chicago, IL: Thomson Learning.

—— (2005a) (ed.). *Regulating Europe*, 2nd edn. London: Routledge.

—— (2005b). *Dilemmas of European Integration: The Ambiguities and Pitfalls of Integration by Stealth*. Oxford: Oxford University Press.

—— and La Spina, A. (1991). 'Lo Stato Regolatore', *Rivista Trimestrale di Scienza dell'Amministrazione*, 3: 3–61.

319

Malbin, M. J. (2003). *Life After Reform: When the Bipartisan Campaign Reform Act Meets Politics*. New York, NY: Rowman and Littlefield.

Mancini, G. F. (1998). 'Europe: The Case for Statehood', *European Law Journal*, 4/1: 29–43.

—— and Keeling, D. T. (1994). 'Democracy and the European Court of Justice', *The Modern Law Review*. 57: 175–90.

Mann, M. (1993*a*). 'Nation-States in Europe and Other Continents: Diversifying, Developing, Not Dying', *Daedalus*, 122/3: 115–40.

—— (1993*b*). *The Sources of Social Power. Volume II. The Rise of Classes and Nation-States, 1760–1914*. Cambridge: Cambridge University Press.

—— (2003). *Incoherent Empire*. London: Verso.

Mann, T. E. and Ornstein, N. J. (2006). *The Broken Branch: How Congress Is Failing America and How to Get Back on Track*. Oxford: Oxford University Press.

Marbach, J., Katz, E., and Smith, T. (2006) (eds.). *Federalism in America*. Two Volumes. New York, NY: Greenwood Press.

March, J. G. and Olsen, J. P. (1995). *Democratic Governance*. New York, NY: The Free Press.

Marks, G. (1997). 'An Initial Attempt to Explain Reallocation of Authority among Regimes, with Particular Reference to Diffusion of Authority in European Integration and the Disintegration of the Carolingian Empire', paper presented at the annual meeting of the American Political Science Association, Washington, DC.

Marquand, D. (1979). *A Parliament for Europe*. London: Jonathan Cape.

Marshall, T. H. (1950). *Citizenship and Social Class and Other Essays*. Cambridge: Cambridge University Press.

Martin, A. and Ross, G. (2004) (eds.). *Euros and Europeans: Monetary Integration and the European Model of Society*. Cambridge: Cambridge University Press.

Matthews, R. K. (1995). *If Men Were Angels: James Madison and the Heartless Empire of Reason*. Lawrence, KS: University Press of Kansas.

Mayhew, D. (1991). *Divided We Govern: Party Control, Law Making and Investigations, 1946–1990*. New Haven, CT: Yale University Press.

—— (2002). *Electoral Realignments: A Critique of an American Genre*. New Haven, CT: Yale University Press.

McCarthy, N., Poole, K. T., and Rosenthal, H. (2006). *Polarized America: The Dance of Ideology and Unequal Riches*. Boston, MA: MIT Press.

McCormick, J. M. (2000). 'Clinton and Foreign Policy: Some Legacies for a New Century', in S. S. Schier (ed.), *The Postmodern Presidency: Bill Clinton's Legacy in U.S. Politics*. Pittsburgh, PA: University of Pittsburgh Press, pp. 60–83.

McCormick, R. L. (1986). 'Walter Dean Burnham and the *System of 1896*', *Social Science History*, 10/3: 245–62.

McDonald, F. (2000). *States' Rights and the Union: Imperium in Imperio*. Lawrence, KS: University Press of Kansas.

McDonald, J. T. (1990). 'Building the Impossible State: Towards an Institutional Analysis of State Building in America', in J. E. Jackson (ed.), *Institutions in*

American Society: Essays on Market, Political and Social Organizations. Ann Arbour, MI: University of Michigan Press, pp. 217–39.

McKay, D. (2001). *Designing Europe: Comparative Lessons from the Federal Experience*. Oxford: Oxford University Press.

Mejer, K. J. (1999). *Politics and Bureaucracy: Policy-Making in the Fourth Branch of Government*. Chicago, IL: Thomson Learning.

Menon, A. and Schain, M. A. (eds.) (2006). *Comparative Federalism: The European Union and the United States in Comparative Perspective*. Oxford: Oxford University Press.

Mény, Y. (2000). *Tra Utopia e Realtà: una Costituzione per l'Europa*. Florence: Passigli.

____ (2001). 'National Squares and European Circle: The Challenge of Adjustment', in A. Menon and V. Wright (eds.), *From the Nation State to Europe?* Oxford: Oxford University Press, pp. 29–45.

____ (2003). 'The Achievements of the Convention', *Journal of Democracy*, 14/4: 57–70.

____ (2005). 'The EU and the Challenge of a Post-National Constitution', in S. Fabbrini (ed.), *Democracy and Federalism in the European Union and the United States: Exploring Post-National Governance*. London: Routledge, pp. 183–93.

____ and Knapp, A. (1998). *Government and Politics in Western Europe*, 3rd edn. Oxford: Oxford University Press.

Merriam, C (1908). *Primary Elections*. Chicago, IL: University of Chicago Press.

Mervin, D. (1987). 'The President and Congress', in M. Shaw (ed.), *The Modern Presidency: From Roosevelt to Reagan*. New York, NY: Harper and Row, pp. 83–118.

Mezey, M. L. (1989). *Congress, the President and Public Policy*. Boulder, CO: Westview Press.

Milkis, S. M. (1993). *The President and the Parties: The Transformation of the American Party System Since the New Deal*. Oxford: Oxford University Press.

Mitterrand, F. (1964). *Le Coup d'Etat Permanent: les Débats de Notre temps*. Paris: Plon.

Moe, T. (1989). 'The Politics of Bureaucratic Structure', in J. E. Chubb and P. E. Peterson (eds.), *Can the Government Govern?* Washington, DC: Brookings Institution Press, pp. 267–330.

Moravcsik, A. (1992). 'In Defense of Democratic Deficit: Reassessing Legitimacy in the European Union', *Journal of Common Market Studies*, 40/4: 603–24.

____ (1998). *The Choice for Europe: Social Purpose and State Power from Messina to Maastricht*. Ithaca, NY: Cornell University Press.

Morgan, G. (2005). 'Realism and European Political Integration: The Lessons of the United States', *Journal of European Political Science*, 4/2: 199–208.

Morgenthau, H. J. (1948). *Politics among Nations: The Struggle for Power and Peace*. New York, NY: McGraw-Hill.

Morone, J. A. (1990). *The Democratic Wish: Popular Participation and the Limits of American Government*. New York, NY: Basic Books.

321

Mullins, K. and Wildavsky, A. (1991). 'The Procedural Presidency of George Bush', *Society*, 28/2: 49–59.

Nagel, R. F. (2001). *The Implosion of American Federalism*. Oxford: Oxford University Press.

Natham, J. A. and Oliver, J. K. (1994). *Foreign Policy Making and the American Political System*. Baltimore, MD: The Johns Hopkins University Press.

Nettle, J. P. (1968). 'The State as a Conceptual Variable', *World Politics*, 20/4: 559–92.

Neustadt, R. E. (1990). *Presidential Power and the Modern Presidents: The Politics of Leadership from Roosevelt to Reagan*. 3rd edn. New York, NY: The Free Press.

—— (2001). 'The Weakening White House', *British Journal of Political Science*, 31/1: 1–12.

Nicolaidis, K. (2004). 'We the Peoples of Europe. . .', *Foreign Affairs*, 83/6: 97–110.

—— and Howse, R. (2001) (eds.). *The Federal Vision and Levels of Governance in the US and in the EU*. Oxford: Oxford University Press.

Norman, P. (2003). *The Accidental Constitution: The Story of the European Convention*. Brussels: Eurocomment.

Novack, A. (2006). 'Civilian Crisis Management: The EU way', *Chaillot Paper*, 90. Paris: EU Institute for Security Studies, http://www.iss-eu.org/chaillot/chai90.pdf

Nye, J. S. Jr (2002). *The Paradox of American Power: Why the World's Only Superpower Can't Go It Alone*. Oxford: Oxford University Press.

OECD (2005). 'Net Social Expenditure', *OECD Social, Employment and Migration Working Paper*, 29, http://www.oecd.org/dataoecd/56/2/35632106.pdf

Offe, C. and Preuss, U. K. (1991). 'Democratic Institutions and Moral Resources', in D. Held (ed.), *Political Theory Today*. Stanford, CA: Stanford University Press, pp. 143–71.

Onuf, P. (1983). *The Origins of the Federal Republic: Jurisdictional Controversies in the United States, 1775–1787*. Philadelphia, PA: University of Pennsylvania Press.

—— and Onuf, N. (1994). *Federal Union, Modern World: The Law of Nation in an Age of Revolution, 1776–1814*. Madison, WI: Madison House Publishers.

Orren, K. and Skowroneck, S. (1996). 'Institutions and Intercurrence: Theory Building in the Fullness of Time', in I. Shapiro and R. Hardin (eds.), *Political Order*, Nomos, 38. New York, NY: New York University Press, pp. 11–146.

—— —— (2004). *The Search for American Political Development*. Cambridge: Cambridge University Press.

Ostrom, E. (1991). 'Rational Choice Theory and Institutional Analysis: Toward Complementarity', *American Political Science Review*, 85/1: 237–43.

Ostrom, V. (1987). *The Political Theory of a Compound Republic: Designing the American Experiment*, 2nd revised edn. Lincoln, NE: University of Nebraska Press.

—— (1991). *American Federalism: Constituting a Self-Governing Society*. San Francisco, CA: ICS Press.

—— (1997). *The Meaning of Democracy and the Vulnerability of Democracies*. Ann Arbour, MI: The University of Michigan Press.

Page, E. C. (1995). 'Patterns and Diversity in European State Development', in J. Hayward and E. C. Page (eds.), *Governing the New Europe*. Durham: Duke University Press, pp. 9–43.

Panebianco, A. (1988). *Political Parties: Organization and Power*. Cambridge: Cambridge University Press.

Parsons, C. (2003). *A Certain Idea of Europe*. Ithaca, NY: Cornell University Press.

Pennock, J. R. and Chapman, J. W. (1979) (eds.). *Constitutionalism*, Nomos, 20. New York, NY: New York University Press.

Peters, R. M. Jr (1997). *The American Speakership: The Office in Historical Perspective*, 2nd edn. Baltimore, MD: The Johns Hopkins University Press.

Pharr, S. J. and Putnam, R. D. (2000) (eds.). *Disaffected Democracies: What's Troubling the Trilateral Countries*. Princeton, NJ: Princeton University Press.

Philippart, E. (2002). 'The European Convention: Anatomy of the New Approach to Constitution-Making in the EU', *EUSA Review*, 15: 5–7.

Phillips, K. (2002). *Wealth and Democracy*. New York, NY: Broadway Books.

Piattoni, S. (2002). 'Il Comitato delle Regioni', in S. Fabbrini (ed.), *L'Unione Europea: le Istituzioni e gli Attori di un Sistema Sopranazionale*. Rome-Bari: Laterza, pp. 227–48.

Pierson, C. (1996). *The Modern State*. London: Routledge.

Pierson P. (1996). 'The Path to European Integration: A Historical Institutional Analysis', *Comparative Political Studies*, 29/2: 123–63.

Pinter, J. (1998). 'From Closed Doors to European Democracy: Beyond the Intergovernmental Conferences', in M. Westlake (ed.), *The European Union beyond Amsterdam: New Concepts of European Integration*. London: Routledge, pp. 47–60.

Pious, R. (1996). *The Presidency*. Boston, MA: Allyn and Bacon.

Poggi, G. (1991). *The State: Its Nature, Developments and Prospects*. Stanford, CA: Stanford University Press.

Poguntke, T. and Webb, P. (2005*a*) (eds.). *The Presidentialization of Politics: A Comparative Study of Modern Democracies*. Oxford: Oxford University Press.

———— (2005*b*). 'The Presidentialization of Politics in Democratic Societies: A Framework for Analysis', in T. Poguntke and P. Webb (eds.), *The Presidentialization of Politics: A Comparative Study of Modern Democracies*. Oxford: Oxford University Press, pp. 1–25.

Polanyi, K. (1944). *The Great Transformation*. New York, NY: Beacon Press.

Pollack, M. A. (2003). *The Engines of European Integration: Delegation, Agency and Agenda Setting in the European Union*. Oxford: Oxford University Press.

Polsby, N. W. (1968). 'The Institutionalization of the U.S. House of Representatives', *American Political Science Review*, 62/1: 144–68.

—— (1983*a*). 'Some Landmarks in Modern Presidential-Congressional Relations', in A. King (ed.), *The Presidency, the Executive Branch, and Congress in the 1980s*. Washington, DC: AEI Press, pp. 1–25.

—— (1983*b*). *Consequences of Party Reform*. New York, NY: Oxford University Press.

Polsby, N. W. (1984). *Political Innovation in America: The Politics of Policy Initiation*. New Haven, CT: Yale University Press.

—— (1986). *Congress and the Presidency*, 4th edn. Englewood Cliffs, NY: Prentice-Hall.

—— (1997*a*). *On the Distinctiveness of the American Political System*, in A. Brinkley, N. W. Polsby, and A. Sullivan, *New Federalist Papers*. New York, NY: W.W. Norton, pp. 29–34.

—— (1997*b*). 'Political Opposition in the United States', *Government and Opposition*, 32/4: 511–21.

—— (2004). *How Congress Evolves: Social Basis of Institutional Change*. Oxford: Oxford University Press.

Posner, P. L. (1998). *The Politics of Unfunded Mandate: Wither Federalism?* Washington, DC: Georgetown University Press.

Poulard, J. V. (1990). 'The French Double Executive and the Experience of Cohabitation', *Political Science Quarterly*, 105/2: 243–67.

Powell, G. B. Jr (2000). *Elections as Instruments of Democracy*. New Haven, CT: Yale University Press.

Prechel, H. N. (2000). *Big Business and the State: Historical Transitions and Corporate Transformations, 1880s–1990s*. New York, NY: SUNY Press.

Preston, T. (2001). *The President and His Inner Circle: Leadership Styles and the Advisory Process in Foreign Affairs*. New York, NY: Columbia University Press.

Preuss, U. K. (1995). *Constitutional Revolution: The Link Between Constitutionalism and Progress*. New York, NY: Humanities Press.

—— (1996). 'The Political Meanings of Constitutionalism', in R. Bellamy (ed.), *Constitutionalism, Democracy and Sovereignty: American and European Perspectives*. Aldershot, UK: Avebury, pp. 11–27.

Przeworski, A. (2003). *States and Markets: A Primer in Political Economy*. Cambridge: Cambridge University Press.

—— Stokes, S., and Manin, B. (1999) (eds.). *Democracy, Accountability and Representation*. Cambridge: Cambridge University Press.

Ranney, A. (1975). *Curing the Mischiefs of Faction. Party Reform in America*. Berkeley, CA: University of California Press.

—— (1990). *Governing: an Introduction to Political Science*. Englewood Cliffs, NJ: Prentice Hall.

—— Wolfinger, R. E., and Polsby, N. W. (1999) (eds.). *On Parties: Essays Honouring Austin Ranney*. Berkeley, CA: IGS Press.

Renshon, S. A. (2001) (ed.). *One America?: Political Leadership, National Identity and the Dilemmas of Diversity*. Washington, DC: Georgetown University Press.

Reynolds, A. (2002) (ed.). *The Architecture of Democracy: Constitutional Design, Conflict Management and Democracy*. Oxford: Oxford University Press.

Rhodes, R. A. W. (1994). 'State-Building Without a Bureaucracy: The Case of the United Kingdom', in I. Budge and D. McKay (eds.), *Developing Democracy*. London: Sage, pp. 165–88.

Richley, J. A. Jr (1992). *The Life of the Parties: History of American Political Parties.* New York, NY: The Free Press.

Riggs, F. W. (1988). 'The Survival of Presidentialism in America: Para-Constitutional Practices', *International Political Science Review*, 9/4: 247–78.

Riker, W. H. (1964). *Federalism: Origin, Operation, Significance.* Boston, MA: Little Brown.

Rimmerman, C. A. (1993). *Presidency by Plebiscite: The Reagan-Bush Era in Institutional Perspective.* Boulder, CO: Westview Press.

Roberts, R. N. and Doss, M. T. (1997). *From Watergate to Whitewater: The Public Integrity War.* New York, NY: Greenwood Press.

Rockman, B. A. (1985). The Leadership Question: The Presidency and the American System. New York, NY: Praeger.

____ (1988). 'The Style and Organization of the Reagan Presidency', in C. O. Jones (ed.), *The Reagan Legacy: Promise and Performance.* Chatham, MA: Chatham House, pp. 3–29.

Roediger, D. R. (1999). *The Wages of Whiteness: Race and the Making of the American Working Class.* London: Verso.

Rohr, J. A. (1995). *Founding Republics in France and America: A Study in Constitutional Governance.* Lawrence, KS: University Press of Kansas.

Rokkan, S. (1968) (ed.). *Comparative Research across Cultures and Nations.* Paris: Mouton.

____ (1970). *Citizens, Elections, Parties: Approaches to the Comparative Study of the Processes of Development.* Oslo: Universitetsforlaget.

____ (1973*a*). 'Centre-Formation, Nation-Building and Cultural Diversity: Report on a Unesco Programme', in S. N. Eisenstadt and S. Rokkan (eds.), *Building States and Nations: Models and Data Resources*, 1. Beverly Hills, CA: Sage, pp. 13–38.

____ (1973*b*). 'Cities, States, and Nations: A Dimensional Model for the Study of Contrasts in the Development', in S. N. Eisenstadt and S. Rokkan (eds.), *Building States and Nations: Models and Data Resources*, 1. Beverly Hills, CA: Sage, pp. 73–97.

____ (1999). *State Formation, Nation-Building and Mass Politics in Europe: The Theory of Stein Rokkan*, edited by P. Flora, S. Kuhnle, and D. Urwin. Oxford: Oxford University Press.

____ and Meritt, R. (1966) (eds.). *Comparing Nations: The Use of Quantitative Data in Cross-National Research.* New Haven, CT: Yale University Press.

Rose, R. (1996). *What is Europe? A Dynamic Perspective.* New York, NY: HarperCollins.

Rose-Ackerman, S. (1993). *Rethinking the Progressive Agenda: The Reform of the American Regulatory State*, 2nd edn. New York, NY: The Free Press.

Ross, G. (1995). *Jacques Delors and European Integration.* Cambridge: Polity Press.

Rossiter, C. B. (1948). *Constitutional Dictatorship: Crisis Government in the Modern Democracies.* Princeton, NJ: Princeton University Press.

____ (1956). *The American Presidency.* New York, NY: Harcourt, Brace and World.

Rozzel, M. J. and Pederson, W. D. (1997) (eds.). *FDR and the Modern Presidency: Leadership and Legacy*. Westport, CT: Praeger.

Rudalevige, A. (2005). *The New Imperial Presidency: Renewing Presidential Power After Watergate*. Ann Arbour, MI: The University of Michigan Press.

Ruggie, J. G. (1998). *Constructing the World Polity: Essays on International Institutionalization*. London: Routledge.

Sabato, L. and Larson, B. (2001). *The Party's Just Begun: Shaping Political Parties for American Future*. New York, NY: Longman.

Salisbury, R. H. (2000). *Interest Groups Politics*. New York, NY: Harper Collins.

Samples, J. (2006). *The Fallacy of Campaign Finance Reform*. Chicago, IL: University of Chicago Press.

Sandholtz, W. and Stone Sweet, A. (eds.) (1998). *European Integration and Supranational Governance*. Oxford: Oxford University Press.

Sands, P. (2005). *Lawless World: America and the Making and Breaking of Global Rules from FDR's Atlantic Charter to George W. Bush's Illegal War*. London: Penguin Press.

Sartori, G. (1968). 'Representational Systems', in *International Encyclopedia of the Social Sciences*, 13. New York, NY: Macmillan and Free Press, pp. 465–74.

—— (1984). 'Guidelines for Concept Analysis', in G. Sartori (ed.), *Social Science Concepts: A Systematic Analysis*. London: Sage, pp. 15–85.

—— (1990). 'Comparazione e Metodo Comparativo', *Rivista Italiana di Scienza Politica*, 20/3: 397–416.

—— (1996). *Comparative Constitutional Engineering: An Inquiry into Structures, Incentives, and Outcomes*, 2nd edn. New York, NY: Palgrave Macmillan.

Sassoon, D. (1996). *One Hundred Years of Socialism: The West European Left in the Twentieth Century*. New York, NY: The New Press.

Sbragia, A. M. (1992). 'Thinking About the European Future: The Uses of Comparison', in A. M. Sbragia (ed.), *Euro-Politics: Institutions and Policy-Making in the new 'European' Community*. Washington, DC: Brookings Institution Press, pp. 257–91.

—— (1994). 'From *Nation-State* to *Member State*: The Evolution of the European Community', in P. M. Lutzeler (ed.), *Europe after Maastricht: American and European Perspectives*. Oxford: Berghahn Books, pp. 69–87.

—— (1996). *Debt Wish: Entrepreneurial Cities, U.S. Federalism, and Economic Development*. Pittsburgh, PA: University of Pittsburgh Press.

—— (2000). 'The European Union as Coxswain: Governance by Steering', in J. Pierre (ed.), *Debating Governance: Authority, Steering and Democracy*. Oxford: Oxford University Press, pp. 219–240.

—— (2002). 'The Dilemma of Governance with Government', *Jean Monnet Working Papers*, 3, New York University School of Law, http://ideas.repec.org/p/erp/jeanmo/p0003.html

—— (2005a). 'Seeing the European Union through American Eyes: The EU as Reflection of the American Experience', *European Political Science*, 4/2: 179–87.

____ (2005b). 'Post-National Democracy as Post-National Democratization', in S. Fabbrini (ed.), *Democracy and Federalism in the European Union and the United States: Exploring Post-National Governance*. London: Routledge, pp. 167–82.

____ (2007). 'An American Perspective on EU Constitutional Treaty', *Politics*, 27/1: 2–7.

Scharpf, F. W. (1988). 'The Joint-Decision Trap: Lessons from German Federalism and European Integration', *Public Administration*, 66/3: 239–78.

____ (1997). *Games Real Actors Play: Actor-Centered Institutionalism in Policy Research*. Boulder, CO: Westview Press.

____ (1999). *Governing in Europe: Effective and Democratic?* Oxford: Oxford University Press.

Schickler, E. (2002). 'Congress', in G. Peele, C. J. Bailey, B. Cain, and G. Peters (eds.), *Developments in American Politics*. New York, NY: Palgrave, pp. 97–114.

Schlesinger, A. M. Jr (1973). *The Imperial Presidency*. New York, NY: Houghton Mifflin.

____ (2004). *War and the American Presidency*. New York, NY: W.W. Norton.

Schmidt, V. A. (2004). 'The European Union: Democratic Legitimacy in a Regional State', *Journal of Common Market Studies*, 42/5: 975–97.

____ (2006). *Democracy in Europe: The EU and National Polities*. Oxford: Oxford University Press.

Schmitter, P. C. (2000). *How to Democratize the European Union and . . . Why Bother?* Lanham, MD: Rowman and Littlefield.

Schramm, P. W. and Wilson, B. P. (1993) (eds.). *American Political Parties and Constitutional Politics*. Lanham, MD: Rowman and Littlefield.

Schulze, H. (1994). *Staat und Nation in der Europäischen Geshichte*. Munich: Beck.

Schultze, R. O. (2000). 'Constitutional Reform as a Process', in R. O. Schultze and R. Sturm (eds.), *The Politics of Constitutional Reform in North America: Coping with New Challenges*. Opladen: Leske und Budrich.

Schwartz, M. A. (1974). *Politics and Territory*. Montreal: McGill-Queen's University Press.

Selznick, P. (1985). 'Focusing Organizational Research on Regulation', in R. C. Noll (ed.), *Regulatory Policy and the Social Sciences*. Berkeley, CA: University of California Press.

Shafer, B. E. (1999). 'American Exceptionalism', *Annual Review of Political Science*, 2: 445–63.

Shapiro, I. and Hardin, R. (1996) (eds.). *Political Order*. New York, NY: The New York University Press.

Shapiro, M. (2002). 'The Success of Judicial Review and Democracy', in M. Shapiro and A. Stone Sweet, *On Law, Politics and Judicialization*. Oxford: Oxford University Press, pp. 149–83.

____ and Stone Sweet, A. (1994). 'The New Constitutional Politics of Europe', *Comparative Political Studies*, 26/4: 397–420.

Shapiro, M. and Stone Sweet, A. (2002). *On Law, Politics and Judicialization*. Oxford: Oxford University Press.

Shapiro, R. Y., Kumar, M. J., and Jacobs, L. R. (2000) (eds.). *Presidential Power: Forging the Presidency for the Twenty-first Century*. New York, NY: Columbia University Press.

Shaw, J. (2005). 'What Happens If the Constitutional Treaty Is Not Ratified?', in I. Pernice and J. Zemaneck (eds.), *The Treaty On a Constitution for Europe: Perspective After the IGC*. Baden-Baden: Nomos.

Shaw, M. (1987). 'Introduction', in M. Shaw (ed.), *The Modern Presidency: From Roosevelt to Reagan*. New York, NY: Harper and Row, pp. 1–10.

Shelcher, C. (2005). 'Jurisdictional Integrity, Polycentrism, and the Design of Democratic Governance', *Governance*, 18/1: 89–111.

Shklar, J. N. (1991). *American Citizenship: The Quest for Inclusion*. Cambridge, MA: Harvard University Press.

Silverstein, G. (1996). *Imbalance of Powers: Constitutional Interpretation and the Making of American Foreign Policy*. Oxford: Oxford University Press.

Sinclair, B. (2004). 'Context, Strategy and Choice: George W. Bush and the 107th Congress', in C. Campbell and B. A. Rockman (eds.), *The George W. Bush Presidency: Appraisals and Prospects*. Washington DC: C.Q. Press, pp. 105–32.

Skocpol, T. (1992*a*). *Protecting Soldiers and Mothers: The Political Origins of Social Policy in the United States*. Cambridge, MA: Harvard University Press.

—— (1992*b*). 'State Formation and Social Policy in the United States', *American Behavioral Scientist*, 35/4–5: 559–84.

—— (1997). *Boomerang: Health Care Reform and the Turn Against Government*. New York, NY: W.W. Norton.

Skowroneck, S. (1987). *Building a New American State: The Expansion of National Administrative Capacities 1877–1920*, 3rd edn. Cambridge, MA: Cambridge University Press.

—— (1997). *The Politics Presidents Make: Leadership from John Adams to Bill Clinton*, 2nd edn. Cambridge, MA: Harvard University Press.

Slomp, H. (2000). *European Politics into the Twenty-First Century: Integration and Division*. Westport, CT: Praege.

Smismans, S. (2004). *Law, Legitimacy, and European Governance: Functional Participation in Social Regulation*. Oxford: Oxford University Press.

Smith, A. D. (1991). *National Identity*. Reno, NV: University of Nevada Press.

—— (1995). 'The Nations of Europe after the Cold War', in J. Hayward and E. C. Page (eds.), *Governing the New Europe*. Durham: Duke University Press, pp. 44–66.

Smith, M. E. (1993). 'Beyond Tocqueville, Myrdal and Hartz: The Multiple Traditions in America', *The American Political Science Review*, 87: 549–66.

—— (1997). Civic Ideals: Conflicting Visions of Citizenship in U.S. History (New Haven, CT: Yale University Press).

—— (2001). 'European Foreign and Security Policy', in S. Bromley (ed.), *Governing Europe: Governing the European Union*. London: Sage, pp. 255–86.

Sorauf, F. J. (1992). *Inside Campaign Finance: Myths and Realities*. New Haven, CT: Yale University Press.

Spiro, P. (2000). 'The New Sovereigntists', *Foreign Affairs*, 79/6: 9–15.

Spitzer, R. J. (1988). *The Presidential Veto: Touchstone of the American Presidency*. Albany: State University of New York Press.

Spruyt, H. (1994). *The Sovereign State and Its Competitors*. Princeton, NJ: Princeton University Press.

Spybey, T. (1996). *Globalization and World Society*. Cambridge: Polity Press.

Staar, R. F. (2003). 'The US Intelligence Community', *The Review of Policy Research*, 20/4: 713–26.

Stanley, H. W. and Niemi, R. G. (2003). *Vital Statistics on American Politics, 2003–2004*. Washington, DC: C.Q. Press.

Sterling, J. Y. (1966). *The Washington Community, 1800–1828*. New York, NY: Harcourt, Brace and the World.

Stetter, S. (2004). 'Cross-pillar Politics: Functional Unity and Institutional Fragmentation of EU Foreign Policies', *Journal of European Public Policy*, 11/4: 720–39.

Stoker, G. (1998). 'Governance as Theory: Five Propositions', *International Social Science Journal*, 50/155: 17–28.

Stone Sweet, A. (2000). *Governing with Judges: Constitutional Politics in Europe*. Oxford: Oxford University Press.

—— (2004). *The Judicial Construction of Europe*. Oxford: Oxford University Press.

—— (2005). 'The Constitutionalization of the EU: Steps towards a Supranational Polity', in S. Fabbrini (ed.), *Democracy and Federalism in the European Union and the United States: Exploring Post-National Governance*. London: Routledge, pp. 44–56.

—— and Caporaso, J. (1998). 'From Free Trade to Supranational Polity: The European Court and Integration', in W. Sandholtz and A. Stone Sweet (eds.), *European Integration and Supranational Governance*. Oxford: Oxford University Press, pp. 92–133.

—— Sandholtz, W., and Fligstein, N. (2001) (eds.). *The Institutionalization of Europe*. Oxford: Oxford University Press.

Suleiman, E. N. (1994). 'Presidentialism and Political Stability in France', in J. J. Linz and A. Valenzuela (eds.), *The Failure of Presidential Democracy: Comparative Perspective*, 1. Baltimore, MD: The Johns Hopkins University Press, pp. 137–62.

—— (2003). *Dismantling Democratic States*. Princeton, NJ: Princeton University Press.

Sunstein C. R. (1993). 'The Enduring Legacy of Republicanism', in S. L. Elkin and K. E. Soltan (eds.), *A New Constitutionalism: Designing Political Institutions for a Good Society*. Chicago, IL: The University of Chicago Press, pp. 174–206.

—— (2001). *Designing Democracy: What Constitutions Do*. Oxford: Oxford University Press.

—— (2005). *Radicals in Robe: Why Extreme Right-Wing Courts Are Wrong for America*. New York, NY: Basic Books.

Taggart, P. (2006). 'The Domestic Politics of the 2005 French and Dutch Referendums and Their Challenge for the Study of European Integration', *Journal of Common Market Studies*, 44, Annual Review: 7–25.

Taylor, A. J. (2005). *Elephant's Edge: The Republican as a Ruling Party.* Westport, CT: Praeger Publishers.

The Economist (2001). 'Working Out the World', March 31.

Tilly, C. (1975) (ed.). *The Formation of National States in Western Europe.* Princeton, NJ: Princeton University Press.

—— (1985). 'War Making and State Making as Organized Crime', in P. Evans, D. Rueschemeyer, and T. Skocpol (eds.), *Bringing the State Back In.* Cambridge: Cambridge University Press, pp. 169–91.

—— (1990a). *Coercion, Capital and the European States, AD 990–1990.* Cambridge: Basil Blackwell.

—— (1990b). 'State and Counterrevolution in France', in F. Fehér (ed.), *The French Revolution and the Birth of Modernity.* Berkeley, CA: University of California Press, pp. 49–68.

Toinet, M.-F. (1988). 'Introduction', in M.-F. Toinet (ed.), *Et la Constitution Crea l'Amerique.* Nancy: Presses Universitaires de Nancy, pp. 5–11.

Torstendahl, R. (1992) (ed.). *State Theory and State History.* London: Sage.

Trubowitz, P. (1999). 'Political Conflict and Foreign Policy in the United States: A Geographical Interpretation', in G. J. Ikenberry (ed.), *American Foreign Policy: Theoretical Essays.* New York, NY: Longman, pp. 393–409.

Tsebelis, G. and Kreppel, A. (1998). 'The History of Conditional Agenda-Setting in European Institutions', *European Journal of Political Research*, 33/1: 41–71.

—— and Money, J. (1997). *Bicameralism.* Cambridge: Cambridge University Press.

Tucker, R. W. and Hendrickson, D. C. (1990). 'Thomas Jefferson and American Foreign Policy', *Foreign Affairs*, 69/2: 135–56.

Tulis, J. K. (1987). *The Rhetorical Presidency.* Princeton, NJ: Princeton University Press.

Turner, F. J. (1932). *Sections in American History.* New York, NY: Henry Holt.

Tushnet, M. (2003). *The New Constitutional Order.* Princeton, NJ: Princeton University Press.

Vile, M. J. C. (1967). *Constitutionalism and Separation of Powers.* Oxford: Clarendon Press.

Vogel, D. (1996). *Kindred Strangers: The Uneasy Relationship between Politics and Business in America.* Princeton, NJ: Princeton University Press.

Von Beyme, K. (1987). *America as a Model: The Impact of American Democracy in the World.* Aldershot, UK: Gower.

Von Bogdandy, A. (2000). 'The European Union as a Supranational Federation. A Conceptual Attempt in the light of the Amsterdam Treaty', *Columbia Journal Of European Law*, 6: 27–54.

Walker, N. (2004). 'The EU as a Constitutional Project', *The Federal Trust*, Online paper, 19, http://www.fedtrust.co.uk/uploads/constitution/19_04.pdf

Wallace, H. (2001) (ed.). *Interlocking Dimensions of the European Union*. New York, NY: Palgrave.

____ and Wallace, W. (2003) (eds.). *Policy-Making in the European Union*, 5th edn. Oxford: Oxford University Press.

Walt, S. M. (2005). *Taming American Power: The Global Response to U.S. Primacy*. New York, NY: W.W. Norton.

Waltz, K. N. (1999). 'Globalisation and Governance: The James Madison Lecture', *PS: Political Science and Politics*, 32/4: 693–700.

Walzer, M. (1996). *What It Means To Be An American: Essays on the American Experience*. New York, NY: Marsilio.

____ (1997). *On Toleration*. New Haven, CT: Yale University Press.

Ware, A. (1995). *Political Parties and Party Systems*. Oxford: Oxford University Press.

____ (1998). *Citizens, Parties and the State: A Reappraisal*. Cambridge: Polity Press.

____ (2002). 'Divided Government in the United States', in R. Elgie (ed.), *Divided Government in Comparative Perspective*. Oxford: Oxford University Press, pp. 21–39.

Warshaw, S. A. (1996). *Power-sharing: White House-Cabinet Relations in the Modern Presidency*. New York, NY: State of New York Press.

Wattenberg, M. P. (1991). *The Rise of Candidate-Centered Politics. Presidential Election in the 1980s*. Cambridge, MA: Harvard University Press.

Watts, R. L. (1987). 'The American Constitution in Comparative Perspective: A Comparison of Federalism in the United States and Canada', *Journal of American History*, 174: 769–91.

____ (1998). 'Federalism, Federal Political Systems, and Federation', *Annual Review of Political Science*, 1: 117–37.

Wayne, S. J. (2000). 'The Multiple Influences on US Foreign Policy-Making', *US Foreign Policy Agenda*, http:/usinfo.state.gov/journals/itps/03000/ijpe/pj51wayn.htm

Webb, P. and Poguntke, T. (2005). 'The Presidentialization of Contemporary Democratic Politics: Evidences, Causes, and Consequences', in T. Poguntke. and P. Webb (eds.), *The Presidentialization of Politics: A Comparative Study of Modern Democracies*. Oxford: Oxford University Press, pp. 336–56.

Weiler, J. H. H. (1999). *The Constitution of Europe: 'Do the new Clothes have an Emperor?' and other Essays on European Integration*. Cambridge: Cambridge University Press.

____ (2000). 'Federalism and Constitutionalism: Europe's Sonderweg', Harvard Law School, *Jean Monnet Chair Working Papers*, http://ideas.repec.org/p/erp/jeanmo/p0075.html.

____ (2001). 'Federalism Without Constitutionalism: Europe's Sonderweg', in K. Nicolaidis and R. Howse (eds.), *The Federal Vision: Legitimacy and Levels of Government in the United States and the European Union*. Oxford: Oxford University Press, pp. 54–70.

Whitaker, L. P. (2004). 'Campaign Finance: Constitutional and Legal Issues of Soft Money', *CRS Reports and Issue Briefs for Congress*. Washington, DC.

Wibbels, E. (2003). 'Bailouts, Budget Constraints, and Leviathans: Comparative Federalism and Lessons from Early United States', *Comparative Political Studies*, 36/5: 475–508.

Wiebe, R. H. (1995). *Self Rule: A Cultural History of American Democracy*. Chicago, IL: The University of Chicago Press.

Wildavsky, A. (1988). *The New Politics of the Budgetary Process*, 2nd edn. Glenview, IL: Scott, Foresman and Company.

Wilenski, H. (2002). *Rich Democracies: Political Economy, Public Policy and Performance*. Berkeley, CA: University of California Press.

Wilentz, S. (2005). *The Rise of American Democracy: Jefferson to Lincoln*. New York, NY: W.W. Norton.

Wills, G. (1978). *Inventing America: Jefferson Declaration of Independence*. New York, NY: Vintage Books.

—— (1999). *A Necessary Evil: A History of American Distrust of Government*. New York, NY: Simon and Schuster.

—— (2001). *Explaining America: The Federalist*, 2nd edn. London: The Penguin Group.

Wilson, G. K. (1994). 'The Westminster Model in Comparative Perspective', in I. Budge and D. McKay (eds.), *Developing Democracy*. London: Sage, pp. 189–201.

—— (1998). *Only in America? The Politics of the United States in Comparative Perspective*. Chatham, MA: Chatham House.

Wilson, W. (1908). *Constitutional Government in the United States*. New York, NY: Columbia University Press.

—— (1956) *Congressional Government: A Study in American Politics*. Baltimore, MD: Johns Hopkins University Press.

Wood, G. (1969). *The Creation of the American Republic, 1776–1787*. Chapel Hill: University of North Carolina Press.

—— (1992). *The Radicalism of the American Revolution*. New York, NY: Alfred A. Knopf.

Woodward, B. (2004). *Plan of Attack*. New York, NY: Simon and Schuster.

Young, J. S. (1966). *The Washington Community 1800–1828*. New York, NY: Harcourt, Brace and World.

Ziblatt, D. (2006). *Structuring the State: The Formation of Italy and Germany and the Puzzle of Federalism*. Princeton, NJ: Princeton University Press.

Zielonka, J. (2006). *Europe as Empire: The Nature of Enlarged European Union*. Oxford: Oxford University Press.

Ziller, J. (2003). *La Nuova Costituzione Europea*. Bologna: Il Mulino.

Zolberg, A. R. (2006). *A Nation by Design: Immigration Policy in the Fashioning of America*. Cambridge, MA: Harvard University Press.

Zweifel, T. D. (2002). *Democratic Deficit? Institutions and Regulation in the European Union, Switzerland and the United States*. Lanham, MA: Lexington Books.

Index

Index

House of Representatives (United States)
(*cont.*)
separation of powers 62–3
Speaker 62–3, 121–2

immigration
immigration communities, interests
of 221–2
quotas 43–5
tribes, territorial dispersion of 32–3
impeachment 157–8, 161–2, 230
industrial relations 101
industrial revolution 110, 111–12
institutions *see also* institutions (European
Union); institutions (United States)
compound democracy model 3–4
decision-making 204
democracy-building 2–3
elections 215
fusion of powers 74–7
nation state 21–2
policy-making 214
political process 214–17, 252
institutions (European Union) *see also*
Council of Ministers (European
Union); European Commission,
European Council; European Court of
Justice; European Parliament
accountability 286, 288
authority 21
checks and balances 209
Committee of the Regions 187–8
committees 183
confederal systems 187–90, 211–12
Constitutional Treaty of the EU 247,
249–51, 256–7, 264
constitutionalization of European
Union 244–7
COREPER 183
decision-making 3–8, 202–3, 231–2,
244–6, 267, 271–2
election and appointment of
members 183–7
European exceptionalism 204–7
executive 181, 184–5, 208
federal systems 187–91, 202–3, 210–11
foreign policy 223–7
government power 4
horizontal level 180–5, 191, 202–3
legislature 182–6, 208–9
list of institutions 180–1
member state institutions, relations
with 189
qualified majority voting (QMV) 245

partisan politics 191
political parties 185, 191, 209–10
power-sharing 185–7
regions 187–8, 190
regulatory agencies 189, 213
sectionalism 191
separation of powers 188–92, 201, 208,
271
horizontal 191
multiple 7, 11–14, 198–9, 203
vertical 188–91
shared-rule and self-rule 190
structure of institutions 180–92
supremacy of EC law 210–11
territorial diffusion 210
territorial organization of EU 188–91
transnational activities 199
United States, compared with 208–14
vertical level 187–92, 202–3
institutions (United States) *see also* Congress
(United States); House of
Representatives (United States);
President (United States); Senate
(United States); Supreme Court
(United States) 13–14, 267
ambitions, checks on 8
antihierarchical institutional order,
compound democracy as 145–9, 219
centralization 9–10
checks and balances 8, 146, 150, 152
constituencies, election by
different 147–8
constitutionalization 238–40
decentralization 10
design of 145–7, 152
dispersed lawmaking process 209
divided government era, presidential
system in 171–2
European Union, comparison
with 208–14
federalism 82–3, 210
foreign policy 223, 232
independence 59–60, 65–6, 82–3
number of 271–2
partisan politics 112
political parties 115–22, 129, 135–6,
210
political stability 228–31
power-sharing 149–52
regulation 213
separation of powers 4, 55, 59–71, 208–9
structure, formation of 3
territorial diffusion 210
times, election at different 147–8

342